TURNING LEFT AROUND
THE WORLD

Machu Picchu, Peru

David and Helene shared the adventure, the sights,
the laughs… and even the tears

Front cover illustration by Tim Bulmer

Mirador Publishing,
10 Greenbrook Terrace
Taunton
Somerset
UK
TA1 1UT

TURNING LEFT AROUND THE WORLD

By

DAVID C MOORE

REVIEWS FOR '*TURNING LEFT AROUND THE WORLD*'

"The book is well written and very easy to read. The travels were enlightened by sometimes very humorous interaction between David and his wife Helene, his tongue in cheek wit and Helene's comebacks often had me laughing out loud." – *Jane Wright, Amazon Reviewer*

"I enjoyed Turning Left Around the World and David's style of writing is just right for a memoir of this kind—funny, self-deprecating at times, and humorous, while also being instructive about the local cultures and traditions that they encountered and experienced." – *Gisela Dixon, Readers' Favourite*

"A book well worth reading, without being staid or preaching it has geography, history, adventure laughs and pathos, a truly enjoyable read." – *E.M.Parker, Amazon Reviewer*

"This book was a delight. A travelogue of great detail and a terrific balance of historical facts, sociological observations and nature descriptions. It helped that the narrator, yes that very British man, David, was…well, so very British. The sort of man that says goodness…a lot. But he's also funny and observant. David is obviously someone who shows genuine interest in and pays respect to local cultures. And again…funny, funny guy. And for those who do travel and have the money to do it in style, this can probably serve as a tour guide. Really enjoyable read. What a trip." – *Mia D (NetGalley Reviewer)*

"I'm pleased to have been able to enjoy reading about David and Helene's adventure, reading about the people that they met along the way. But far more I enjoyed reading about all the places David and Helene visited." – *Bookread2day*

"This inspirational 'grey-gap-year' tale will make you laugh and cry" – *Andrew Morris, Editor of the Silver Travel Adviser*

"David writes with a warmth and humour that charms the reader from tears to laughter and back again with a turn of the page. An easy to read guide of their travels with an often tongue in cheek view of the countries visited. A truly entertaining and informative read with a good dose of humour - highly recommend. – *Emma Jane, Book Reviewer*

"An entertaining must-read for any discerning traveller" – *Audley Traveller magazine*

To my wife, Helene.

Thank you for pushing me way out of my comfort zone. Thank you for being head of operations and logistics. But most of all, thank you for being there. What an adventure.

ACKNOWLEDGEMENTS

Many thanks to the wonderful team at Audley Travel who patiently listened to our likes, dislikes and often unusual requests and who worked so hard to make our dream adventure a reality. Particular thanks to Natalie, the concierge team and country specialists who added so much during our visits to the countries they love and we now know so well.

Thanks also to all the guides who kept us away from the crowds, did our queuing for us when the occasional need arose and answered every one of our hundreds of questions. Particularly, Saiber who introduced me to the wonderful world of Pachacutec in Peru and Grace for her infectious enthusiasm on the Galápagos Islands.

Thanks to Sarah Luddington the Mirador editor and publisher for the faith she showed in me and the encouragement to "keep writing and enjoy it" throughout the adventure.

Thanks to Tim Bulmer for the front cover illustration, letting me get the brief wrong a few times and the wonderful interpretation of Helene and I, "with the tighter chin."

Thanks of course to Helene, Charlotte and Elliot who keep my feet on the ground and my foot out of my mouth when I get carried away with it all.

Finally, thank you for reading my book, I hope it inspires you to plan your own adventure.

"Twenty years from now you will be more disappointed by the things you didn't do, than by the ones you did do.
So, throw off the bowlines, sail away from the safe harbour.
Catch the trade winds in your sails.
Explore. Dream. Discover."

H. Jackson Brown, Jr.

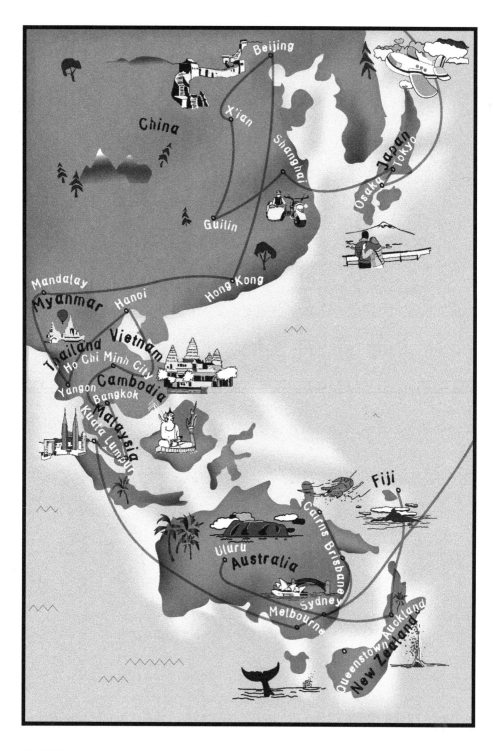

ROUTE MAP by OKAYdesign Studio

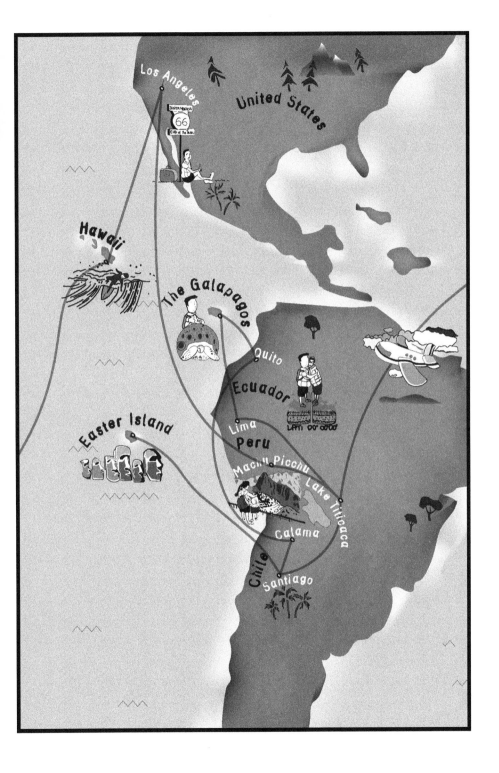

CONTENTS:

	Prologue	13
1.	**Day 1 – 5: CHILE.**	**17**
	Santiago – *On the Wagon*	
2.	**Day 6 – 10: CHILE.**	**24**
	Easter Island – *"I am Rapa Nui"*	
3.	**Day 11 – 14: CHILE.**	**31**
	The Atacama Desert – *The Sweetest Death*	
4.	**Day 15 – 17: CHILE.**	**38**
	The Casablanca Valley – *Hello Luchito*	
5.	**Day 18 – 22: ECUADOR.**	**42**
	Quito and Mashpi Lodge – *Hugging, Howling and Humming*	
6.	**Day 23 – 27: ECUADOR.**	**51**
	Hacienda Zuleta – *That Condor Moment*	
7.	**Day 28 – 34: ECUADOR.**	**58**
	The Galápagos Islands – *Lonesome George and other New Friends*	
8.	**Day 35 – 42: PERU.**	**70**
	Lima, Arequipa and Colca Canyon – *Dancing in the Streets*	
9.	**Day 43 – 50: PERU.**	**81**
	Lake Titicaca, Cusco and the Sacred Valley – *The Incredible Mr. Pachacutec*	
10.	**Day 51 – 55: PERU.**	**97**
	Machu Picchu – *There's a Hidden Castle in the Sky where the Kings Live*	
11.	**Day 56 – 60: PERU.**	**108**
	The Amazon Jungle – *Intrepid Explorers*	
12.	**Day 61 – 78: USA.**	**126**
	Hawaii – *ALOHA!*	

13. **Day 79 – 87: FIJI.**   139
Tokoriki – *Paradise Found*

14. **Day 88 – 99: FIJI.**   146
Fiji Island Cruise – *Who puts the Ah! In Relaxation?*

15. **Day 100 – 112: NEW ZEALAND.**   155
North Island – *Rolling Back the Years*

16. **Day 113 – 127: NEW ZEALAND.**   171
South Island – *Wails, Whales, Wales*

17. **Day 128 – 140: AUSTRALIA.**   189
Cairns and the Great Barrier Reef –
Friends shaking hands, 'How do you do?'

18. **Day 141 – 155: AUSTRALIA.**   200
The Sunshine Coast – *In the Rain*

19. **Day 156 – 172: AUSTRALIA.**   210
Ayers Rock – *A Black Bridge, a Red Rock and a Blue Mountain*

20. **Day 173 – 185: AUSTRALIA.**   225
Sydney and Melbourne – *A Wonderful Christmas Time*

21. **Day 186 – 192: MALAYSIA.**   236
Kuala Lumpur and Singapore – *Entry to the Orient*

22. **Day 193 – 211: THAILAND.**   246
Bangkok and Ko Phra Thong – *Remember us?*

23. **Day 212 – 233: CAMBODIA.**   262
Otres and Phnom Penh – *A Remarkable Encounter*

24. **Day 234 – 240: CAMBODIA.**   277
Siem Reap – *A Look Back in Anger*

25. **Day 241 – 244: VIETNAM.**   287
Hanoi and Ho Chi Minh City – *A Long, Long Legacy*

26. **Day 245 – 263: VIETNAM.**   296
Hoi An, Da Nang and Hue – *Good Morning Glory*

27. **Day 264 – 273: MYANMAR.**   311
Yangon, Mandalay and Bagan – *Where China meets India*

28. **Day 274 – 281: CHINA.**   334
Hong Kong and Beijing – *"We're gonna build a wall"*

29. **Day 282 – 291: CHINA.**   341
X'ian, Guilin and Shanghai – *The Emperor of Two Miracles*

30. **Day 292 – 306: JAPAN.**   353
Tokyo, Kanazawa and Kyoto – *A Final Hurrah*

PROLOGUE:

'What on earth is this?' I asked my wife Helene, as she presented me with a large tube accompanied by two boxes of pins, one blue the other pink. 'It's not more DIY is it? You know I don't like DIY.'

'No, and you're not very good at it either. This is about us, now you're planning to retire.'

I had briefly mentioned that the wheels of industry may continue to turn if I was to put myself out to pasture in my sixtieth year. Never one to procrastinate about these things Helene had been planning how best to ease her occasionally stubborn and stuffy husband into engaging with a project we had often discussed but never progressed.

I should have known from previous experience. When Helene moved in some 15 years ago her packing boxes were marked up as expected: bathroom, bedroom, dining room etc. But they also included some a little more unexpected.

'Where do these go, Guv?' asked one of the removal men.

'What does it say on the boxes? They're all clearly marked.'

'Spanish kitchen, Guv.'

'Spanish kitchen? We don't have a Spanish kitchen.'

We do now.

I pulled out the contents of the tube and unfurled a huge colourful map of the world, well over a metre and a half across.

'It's a map of the world,' I said, stating the obvious and hoping for a bit more of a clue here. 'And pins.'

'Yes, the blue ones are for you and the pink for me,' said Helene, taking back the pink box I was holding. 'All you have to do is put the map up and start sticking pins in the places you've always wanted to go.'

'Why?' I wasn't quite sure where this was headed yet, but felt as if I had taken the first step on an escalator that would inevitably take me to a predetermined destination, predetermined by Helene, perhaps many of them

'It'll be fun,' she said.

'Why?'

'Come on, you can go first, darling,' she said, clutching my hand and leading me to the wine cellar where the map was apparently destined to be sited.

And so, the plan was hatched. I somehow agreed to a strategy that was not to include any locations we had previously visited, which immediately excluded most of Europe, Scandinavia and some of the US, and our research began. I have to say it was a lot of fun. Helene revisiting the 10 years of Conde Nast's Traveller magazine back issues she had accumulated and me working out where and when the Rugby Sevens, Ashes and British Lions' tours may be.

A few weeks later we stood together examining our work, the map of the world was littered with the colourful pins, surprisingly most were in pairs of blue and pink.

'We have our route,' announced Helene, 'let's follow the sun and go west.'

Examining the map, it appeared we were to start in South America. Not the obvious Brazil and Argentina but the more challenging Peru, Ecuador and Chile. I cheated slightly with two pins on the Galápagos – I'm a sucker for Attenborough's nature programmes and have always wanted to go – there was also a pink pin virtually obscuring an island way out in the Pacific that on closer inspection turned out to be Easter Island.

The route would take us via the cluster of islands that is Hawaii and on to Fiji, we had both been recommended to visit. New Zealand north and south islands were a unanimous selection and Australia was covered in pink pins around Sydney and a blue one right in the centre where I guessed Ayers Rock may be. Sydney was now the home of Helene's "bestest friend" from school and the invitation had been outstanding for 10 years or more. This apparently was not up for debate; fair enough.

South East Asia had a variety of pins in countries that would have been impossible to visit only 30 years ago. Cambodia, Vietnam and Burma, to my surprise now called Myanmar, alongside Singapore, Malaysia and Thailand.

Hong Kong, China and Japan were all sitting comfortably with two coloured pins in each. But there were some that didn't make the cut: Egypt, Moscow, India and the Maasai Mara, but as Helene explained, 'We can do those on a normal holiday.'

'Normal holiday?' I said. 'Well what's this we're planning?'

'This, David, is a once-in-a-lifetime adventure,' she replied.

I'm not quite sure when I came up with the idea of a 10 month around the world adventure, but as we surveyed our course around the globe it seemed like a great plan nevertheless.

We had our route just about identified, what remained seemed like the Rubik's cube of holiday planning, and even with Helene's 2 metre tower of Traveller magazines we would struggle to solve the flights, accommodation and "must-sees" conundrum. We needed to search for a specialist who understood our purpose, our dream and us. We found Audley Travel – *tailor-made journeys for the discerning traveller.*

What a splendid approach they take. Before any discussion around the route and destinations began they spent time getting to know our likes and dislikes before tailoring an itinerary specifically for us. Lots of adventure, but no bungee jumping, plenty of access to the culture of the indigenous people, time in the deserts, rainforest and jungle, with big cities in-between, opportunities to meet the wildlife and importantly discover the foods and wines of each country we visit. We were beginning to get very excited.

Audley took over the tour logistics supported by Helene, so all we had to do now was work out the timing, the finance, what to do with the house and its contents, and our cars, arrange insurances, inoculations and visas, select what clothes to pack and a thousand other incidentals, perhaps the most important of which was how to tell our friends and family.

Telling the kids – okay, 27 and 30 year-old son and daughter – that we were spending nearly a year mostly on the other side of the world, was going to be the most difficult; apparently not.

'You're going around the world, not being posted to Afghanistan,' said Charlotte, always the voice of reason. 'Everyone does it now, and we'll keep in touch by WhatsApp and Instagram.'

'What's what and Insta who?' It appeared I was about to enter the digital world of social media, or vice versa.

There was then the broader family and friends to consider, so we decided to throw a party.

'Let's have a "drink us dry" party,' suggested Helene, 'then we won't need to put all your wine into storage.' On the face of it this seemed like a good idea, wine storage is expensive, and I could hide the good stuff, so a few people over for drinks and some nibbles to say cheerio, perfect.

It turned out to be "a hundred of our closest friends" as Helene put it. I didn't think we knew a hundred people let alone invite them to the house for a drink and nibbles. A band was booked, apparently a must for a real party, the marquee ordered – "what happens if it rains?" asked Helene and we were nibbling on a gluten free 75lb pig roast; obviously crisps and nuts just won't do.

The problem with parties is that everyone brings a bottle or two of fizz or something equally celebratory, usually more than they could possibly drink. So, the upshot was that the "drink us dry" party had the opposite effect by adding to the bottle volume I had to put into storage.

After months of planning, budgeting, organising and drafting more lists and spreadsheets than we could possibly pin on the fridge, we were at last about to embark on our 10 month adventure around the world. We were unsure of what awaited us as we prepared to leave our comfort-zone in leafy Berkshire.

How we were supposed to pack 10 months of clothes for climates that would vary from below freezing to well over 30 degrees, all in a maximum of 23 kilos, was beyond me, but not Helene. Little and large zippy-uppy travel bags arrived to make it all easier by segregating our clothes into single packs: shirts in one, shorts in another and a small one for smalls – brilliant. All packed into a large case and a cabin bag each; well packed Helene.

It's one of the three questions most people asked when we were quizzed over the adventure; "How on Earth do you pack for 10 months?" usually from female friends. "How did you plan it?" asked by the men and the slightly more worrying from both, "Do you think you'll still be talking to each other at the end of it?"

Thanks to friends and family we would not see until May the next year, they delivered us to Heathrow with a generous but acceptable 3 hours to spare. With two First Class seats still available we took the opportunity to upgrade from Business and start our adventure the way we meant to go on, turning left around the world. So, it was the Concorde Lounge for Helene and a great night's sleep on the 14 hour flight to Santiago for me.

CHAPTER 1

DAY 1 to 5: CHILE
Santiago

On the Wagon

A nd so, the adventure begins...
As we exited the Comodoro Arturo Merino Benitez International, big name for a small airport, but the longest non-stop destination for BA, there was the unmistakably irritating sound of vuvuzelas.

'What's all this?' I said. 'I know this is South America but we're not in Mexico.'

'Maybe that's just the way they welcome foreigners here,' suggested Helene.

Perhaps.

We arrived in Santiago the capital of Chile early Sunday on a cold and misty morning, with light rain. Our guide, Eva met us with driver Erik.

'Sorry for the weather,' said Eva, 'it's a bit miserable for you, but you're probably used to it, coming from London.'

'That's okay,' we chorused.

'We'll do a bit of shopping,' suggested Helene.

'Well, there won't be much open on a Sunday,' said Eva.

'Okay, we'll check in, unpack and go for an early, long lazy lunch,' I offered. Always a good alternative to shopping.

'Probably not,' Eva said uncomfortably, 'it's election day so all the bars are closed, and I'm afraid the restaurants can't serve alcohol either.'

'What,' I said, 'they can't be trusted to cast their vote accurately if they have a drink?'

'Sightseeing?' prompted Helene.

'Oh, I wouldn't,' Eva warned, 'because of the match. The fans can be a bit boisterous, even when they're sober.' That would be the vuvuzelas at the airport then.

It turned out that Chile had reached the final of the Confederations Cup, some dodgy FIFA moneymaking enterprise held every 4 years comprising eight international teams from six confederations, usually won by Brazil. It was to be played later that day with the support of the whole city. I guess Chile don't make too many finals.

The first day of our adventure was not shaping up the way I had expected. It just happened to be the day of Chile's elections, odd day for elections but that's okay. So, Sunday 2nd July, voting day, was declared a "dry state day". No alcohol to be served in any bar, restaurant or hotel until 2 hours after voting closed at 11:00 PM so that everyone could vote sober. Great!

So, Santiago was occupied by thousands of very sober football supporters wearing the red, white and blue of Chile in some extraordinary head gear from punk wigs to bowler hats – how odd. As with most football matches in South America this one also came with its fair share of armed Carabineros, a variety of armoured vehicles and mounted police seemingly prepared for a pitched battle. We also had a warning from hotel security not to venture out after sun down at 6:15. What was the point, no bars open anyway.

Our hotel was the Luciano K Hotel – *a cultural jewel in the heart of the gastronomic Lastarria neighbourhood* and certainly well placed overlooking the Parque Forestral where 30,000 had gathered for the Pride March the day before we arrived, resulting in almost as many council cleaners desperately tidying their equivalent of Hyde Park. Designed by the architect Luciano

Kulczewski in the 1920's it once boasted to be the highest building in Chile, all seven floors of it. It also had the first lift in the country and the first central heating.

Another first was that it was on this rooftop terrace bar and restaurant with its spectacular views over the snow covered Andes that the Moores took their first ever selfie, all part of our digital revolution, thanks to daughter Charlotte's wonderful friends and their thoughtful departure gift.

The Andes or Andean Mountains to give them their full title is the longest continental mountain range in the world. They form a continuous ridge along the western edge of South America about 2,700 km long with an average height of over 6,000 metres, the highest outside Asia.

They also happen to be sitting on three tectonic plates which means earthquakes are extremely common. But, few are serious enough to cause the sort of devastation Santiago experienced at 03:34 on 27th February 2010 when an 8.8 magnitude earthquake hit killing seven hundred people and razing buildings to the ground, some of which are still being rebuilt today. However, this was not as bad as the 1960 quake which measured a massive 9.5 and triggered tidal waves and volcanic eruptions that made over two million homeless.

The Chilean Earthquake Tracker, yes it has its own website, showed the city had eleven earthquakes during the week we arrived , the strongest of which measured 5.2, and 53 in the last month, most of which were around 4.0 – didn't feel a thing.

The architecture of Santiago reflects both the geological problems they have to deal with and the country's varied commercial influences from the Spanish Conquistadors and Inca Empire through to its early independence led by the wonderfully named Bernardo O'Higgins.

The Italians, Germans, French and British all attempted to get their hands on the mineral rich land so as earthquakes flattened buildings whoever was the current wealthy incumbents at the time would rebuild huge family homes in their own style. The result is a cornucopia of architectural styles; French chateaux only a road or so from Spanish villas, and British colonial piles brick to brick with Italian palaces, none of which remain in their original format. They are now mostly converted to student university accommodation; lucky them. It makes for a unique city incomparable with any single European counterpart.

Unsurprisingly, this cosmopolitan influence extends to the wide and diverse food available, from Tapas and great ensaladas, to fish stews, huge steaks and fish or meat ceviche, all washed down with lashings of Pisco Sour, a sort of wine brandy. Helene's favourite was Alto del Carmen mixed with lemon juice, and of course excellent local Chilean wines. The best local beers I found and believe me after the alcohol ban was lifted I did some searching, were Cerveza Austrel from Patagonia and the draft Pilsner Kross, not dissimilar to Amstel.

We often try and find the non-touristy restaurants full of old gnarled locals and tiptoe our way around the menu in search of gluten free offerings for Helene. There are two most definitely worth mentioning. Firstly, *Como Agua Para Chocolate* apparently translates to "like water for chocolate" based on a famous Mexican novel about a steamy woman who likens "getting to the boil" to when hot water is added to chocolate. Not sure I fully understand, but think *Fifty Shades* and we're probably in the right direction.

It is run by a fiery blonde lady; it is loud, frenetic and colourful with a fountain full of flowers and a bed for six. Literally, a beautiful large brass bed complete with pillows where three guests are seated either side to enjoy a full a la carte meal with silver service on silk and lace bed linen. I quite enjoyed the theme going on there.

The other is *Bocanariz*, a great concept where they've flipped the menus. You choose the wine first from the best 369 Chile has to offer, either by the glass, a wine flight or by the bottle. Interestingly, the wines are presented not by region but by grape and drinking style, so we selected the Signature wine flight and a bottle of the best Chilean Sauvignon – the wine flight was only three small glasses for 6,600 Pesos, about £7.75.

Despite the fact that all coins are in hundreds and all notes in thousands, usually tens of thousands, which would suggest massive inflation, the Chilean economy is doing pretty well, with unemployment under 5% and inflation well under control. Its main industry is still mining but has moved on from nitrate to copper which sounds far safer and accounts for nearly half of its exports.

I digress, back to the wines. Having selected your wines for the evening you then turn your attention to the menu which is categorised by style of food to match your wine selection: steaks for Malbec, chicken or pastas with Pinot Noir, salads and lightly spiced dishes for Sauvignon; you get the picture. A fascinating way to approach an evening, we thoroughly enjoyed it, although the couple on the next table found the task too intimidating and complicated so got up and walked out. Each to their own I guess.

The following morning was still grey and misty when Eva and Erik collected us at the Luciano K for a guided sightseeing tour of Santiago, well what we could see of it.

'It's the smog this time,' announced Eva cheerily, as we set off in the gloom, and in scarves, gloves and colourful bobble hats. Erik, the driver who we believed didn't have any English, seemed to think our attire was highly amusing.

'Let's going to the mountain to see the viewing later,' he suggested through his giggles. I guess we were half right.

'Seems like a good idea,' I agreed, 'what do you thinking, Helene?' A warning nudge.

'Yes, perhaps the markets first?' she suggested.

La Vega Central is the largest food market in the city where everything seems to come in huge volumes. Barrows loaded with broccoli, carts full of cauliflower, huge fish I didn't recognise being hacked into saleable and portable chunks alongside buckets full of clams and a small truck filled with hanging pigs. You can't beat the sights, sounds and smells of a local market, it excites all the senses, so we moved on to the Central Mercado which we could find with our eyes shut, it's all about fish so we just followed our noses.

'This would be good for lunch, yes?' suggested Eva.

'You must be joking, I can hardly breathe,' said Helene, 'in fact I feel a bit queasy, can we go?'

'But it's fish, Helene, you love fish,' I said, pointing out some of the selection from menu photographs above dozens of food stalls.

'You could have ceviche, there's plenty of raw fish here,' I laughed. We left.

As compensation for the assault on our nostrils Eva led us out of the frenetic fish market to the peace of the flower market, perhaps too peaceful.

'I'll leave you here to look around,' said Eva, motioning us into a hushed and serene warehouse with small stalls side by side around its perimeter, each manned by quiet elderly couples concentrating hard on their floral creations.

'This is better,' sighed Helene.

'This is odd,' I replied, as we walked into the empty middle of the warehouse. No one tried to sell us anything or beckon us over to assess their merchandise, very odd indeed.

'I think this might be…' I started.

'Oh yes, this is much better,' interrupted Helene, as she led us over to one of the hushed stalls.

'I think this might be a specialist floral supplier,' I tried to explain as the stall owner offered a sympathetic smile and Helene began to examine the red and white roses, white lilies and pink carnations.

'There's not many people here,' she said, looking around at the few elderly visitors dressed in black and shuffling between the stalls, all of which seemed to be selling the same limited selection of stems and similar floral decorations.

In amongst the loose flowers were a selection of tied arrangements, mainly wreaths and white rose crosses, standing sprays and sympathy baskets, flowers in hearts and the occasional floral angel with a collection of indecipherable white rose letters no doubt spelling out a recognisable loved one's name when finally assembled.

'No, I think we may be in a sort of wholesale funeral florist market,' I said, 'it does seem very, well, funereal.'

It was indeed a sombre place.

I doubt if two tourists have ever looked and felt so out of place and embarrassed. I turned to Helene, 'I think we better go.' She'd gone.

We caught up with Eva and Erik who now felt it was time to ascend the mountain in the city.

'But we'll pay today,' she said, 'it's too cold to walk.'

'We will driving up the mountain,' Erik confirmed.

The Chileans are, perhaps surprisingly, but I'm not sure why, a very health conscious nation. All the food packaging is marked with black no entry signs where either the salt, sugar or fat levels are too high. The government has an *"eat and live healthy"* initiative and the city centre parks on a Sunday are full with fitness classes for all ages and abilities. They are also lucky enough to have a large hill in the middle of Santiago rising 300 metres above the city called Cerro San Cristobal where the locals are encouraged to cycle, walk or jog to the top for the stunning 360 degree view of the city, surrounded on all sides by the snowcapped mountains. There is a road to the top but drivers are charged, or perhaps fined, at the entrance to encourage them to be more active in reaching the mirador.

We wound our way up the hill deeper into the mist and the smog hanging over the city.

'We have arriving at the top,' Erik announced, and Eva gave us a short, potted history of the San Cristobal as we watched the rain drizzle down the windscreen and the windows steam up. It rises to 850 metres above sea level, its original indigenous name was Tupahue and was renamed after St

Christopher by the Spanish Conquistadors in recognition of its use as a landmark for travellers

They were both clearly very proud of their hill so the least we could do was huddle under an umbrella and peer over the edge into the grey murky gloom unsure what was leaden sky and what was dreary mist.

'Must look good on its day,' we both agreed, 'maybe tomorrow.' With sights unseeable we opted for culture for the remainder of the day.

Santiago is a culturally rich city with far too many galleries for us to visit during our short stay; we managed three, including a rather odd exhibition by a Chilean contemporary artist. His subject was the *Search for Paradise* by the many revolutionary groups in South America. They didn't find it. It comprised of a dozen or so silky boxers' capes in red, gold and glitter.

The best was the Warhol exhibition with the famous Marilyn paintings and cans of Campbell's Soup. Did you know that his famous silver titanium hair was a wig? I didn't. Apparently, he had forty for different occasions.

The following morning, we awoke to a completely different city; Santiago in the sun. We took the cable car to the top of Cerro San Cristobal to see what we had been missing, and my goodness no wonder Eva and Erik had eulogised over it. The sprawling city looked glorious surrounded by the snowy mountains towering above the stubborn cloud; we stayed most of the day and watched the peaks turn orange and fiery red in the sunset. We were both so pleased Santiago gave up its secret before we left.

Well, that was Santiago, I returned to the hotel to put my smalls in the shower with me, that's what you do when you're on tour apparently, and repack for Easter Island where the temperature was 20 degrees higher than the deep winter of a cold Chile in July – different zippy-uppy bags I guess.

I didn't know the island was so far, or so remote, about a third of the way to Australia from Chile in the Polynesian Triangle of over a thousand islands – New Zealand, Easter Island and Hawaii make up the three points of the triangle – we were due to visit all three.

We had been really looking forward to meeting the Moai to find out who put them there, how, why, when and extraordinarily why there were over 900 on an island only 25 km across at its widest point. It's actually 899 because the British stole one for Queen Victoria and put it in the British Museum.

Should be both fun and intriguing.

CHAPTER 2

DAY 6 to 10: CHILE
Easter Island

'I am Rapa Nui'

Easter Island or Rapa Nui as we now know it, is one of the most remarkable places I have ever visited and has an equally incredible story to match.

So, let's get some brief context here. The island rose from the sea by volcanic eruption three million years ago so the landscape is covered by dormant lush green volcanoes. It is the most remote island in the world, situated in the Pacific Ocean on the eastern corner of the Polynesian Triangle 3,700 km from Chile in one direction and 4,200 km from Tahiti in the other. It was discovered on Easter Day by the Dutch 50 years before Cook arrived in 1774 hence the name, and there is only one town on the island where most of its 6,000 inhabitants live, from just thirty-six ancestral families. Although it is Chilean, I believe a principality would be more accurate – they are governed by Chile but the laws appear to be more guidelines than regulations, and they pay no tax.

We arrived after an early start and a 6 hour flight, but well rested from the flat bed comfort of a Dreamliner, into a typical Polynesian airport come shack; a tiny place with virtually no security apart from the sniffer dog having fun trotting along the moving luggage carousel. We should remember that being such a remote island everything needs to be brought in by plane, so the carousel itself was a version of Bruce's conveyor belt: a microwave oven, two rugs, an ornamental light, assorted pots & pans, sugar, a large sealed brown box (sniffer dog in), a coffee machine and so it goes on. Thankfully there was no sign of the cuddly toy.

The runway however, is one of the longest in the world, which is an odd claim for one of the smallest islands in the world, all sorts of conspiracy theories and Close Encounters stories here. The landing strip stretches from one coast to the other in the southwest tip of the island and the real reason for its existence is that it was built by the Americans and funded by NASA as a potential landing place for Challenger back in the 80's. It was never used by Challenger during its nine flights and the fateful tenth, and of course who needs a sophisticated airport for the Space Shuttle, just a very long runway.

We were greeted with garlands by our guide for the week Tito, a man whose descendants he claims he can trace back over a 1000 years, and who has just as many stories. He is a thickset man with a traditional top knot in his hair and was immediately engaging and entertaining.

'Come and meet our show vehicle for the week,' he announced, putting the garlands around our necks and taking all our bags on his shoulders.

'Show vehicle?' I whispered to Helene. 'What show?'

Tito introduced us to our vehicle for the few days' excursion; a flatbed truck with an open back upon which were three rows of four comfortable seats constructed like a theatre, each row behind and slightly higher than the one in front. What a perfect way to experience the island, far better than in a metal box cut off from the elements by toughened glass.

'The show is my island,' he said, climbing into the front as we perched ourselves on one of the rows at the back, feeling very much on-show.

Our hotel was Hare Noi – *A dream hotel for a magic island* located on a hillside with nine separate lodges overlooking the Pacific. They are constructed and furnished almost entirely from the natural materials available on the island: tree trunks and rocks – we had a huge boulder in the middle of our room, to hang things on I suppose – woven reeds and branches to form the railings on the terrace. Very rustic, very well designed and extremely comfortable.

And so to the remarkable story of the Rapa Nui population and their wonderful Moai, pronounced Mow-eye that adorn the perimeter of the island, all 900 of them, less the one the British stole. This is their story that unfolded as we discovered this incredible island during our 5 day visit.

We need to go back to around 400 AD when legend has it the founding Polynesian king of the Rapa Nui people first set foot on one of the two beautiful sandy bays on the island. The remainder of the coastline is the result of the volcanic eruptions with huge boulders transported by the lava then petrified in the sea forming a violent seascape with 5 metre waves thundering onto the rocky shore. It was over overlooking this stunning shoreline that we picnicked in the care of our guide Tito as he began to recount the history and legends of his people and the island.

When the founding king died he was not cremated like other mortals but had his organs removed and the remains left to dry on a stone platform. His bones were then buried underneath the first Moai hewn from the mother rock and erected on a platform of stones to observe and protect his future subjects.

In simple terms, this started a trend where the various tribes marked the passing of their elders in the same manner. The Moai were constructed as tributes to their ancestors and erected to watch over and safeguard the tribe, which is why although almost all are on the coast they face inland where the communities lived. Over the following thousand years they created the 900 Moai, so I guess it takes roughly a year to carve, extract from the "mother stone", transport and erect one Moai successfully.

The population of the island had a pretty good life with a healthy diet consisting of fish, chicken and the abundant fruit and vegetables of the island. Cows, sheep, pigs etc. came a lot later from the "invading" Europeans. Their communities based themselves on the coastline where the fresh rainwater from the volcanoes met the sea and food was plentiful. Houses were built only for sleeping in, the rest of the time was spent outside in the perfect climate and beautiful volcanic landscape with stunning views over the emerald sea – why wouldn't you? I was reminded of our contemporary artist in Santiago studying the South American terrorist groups and warring factions trying to find their utopia in paradise and failing. Well I guess these peaceful simple souls on Rapa Nui some 1,500 years ago got a lot closer without really trying.

We visited the quarry where all the Moai on the island were excavated from the side of the Rano Raraku volcano in the northeast of the island. We hiked there with Tito and during the steep climb listened to the stories of his ancestors; it was well worth the effort climbing the volcano with fabulous views into the crater lake at the summit.

The Moai were chiselled from the earth and taken to their final resting place up to 25 km away. At that point they were given their eyes, made from white coral and obsidian, a black glossy and shiny mineral symbolising the pupil. The Rapa Nui people believe it is only then that they transform from rock to the ancestral protectors of their future families. I guess Rapa Nui people also understood that the eyes are the window to the soul.

The next bit requires some imagination; once they have their eyes they act as a conduit if you will, for Makemake to protect the future of the tribe. Makemake is the most important god, he is the main man, there's another four but he is the boss.

We visited the only Moai on the island with eyes, it was restored a few years ago, and to me although it looked powerful and domineering – as it should do defending and keeping check on the behaviour of its future family – its face looked almost comical, cartoon like. They are so much more enigmatic and mysterious as blank faced, hollow eyed effigies.

As it is in any culture and society we all want to keep up with the Joneses and so it was with the Rapa Nui. The first Moai for the king was 2m high weighing about 6 tons.

'But you don't want just that for your recently departed ancestor.' They may have said, 'Let's go higher and bigger and show those other tribes exactly how important our recently departed elder was.'

So, the larger the Moai the more power and prestige it demonstrated. The average Moai was 4m high and weighed in at 12.5 tons but as the competition to erect the biggest and best intensified so their size increased. The largest we visited on the island is 20m high and estimated at 60 tons, although it was never fully excavated from the ground, we found out why later.

Helene asked Tito the obvious question.

'We know how the Moai were created and we know why, but how on earth were they transported from the Rano Raraku volcanic quarry?'

'They walked,' said Tito.

Their sole purpose was to watch over the communities and provide protection courtesy of the god Makemake so they had to be moved from the quarry for up to 25 km to the selected village, most of which were on the perimeter of the 163 sq. km island.

We were to interrogate Tito's curious answer on a visit to another Moai platform where we bumped into the world's leading authority on the subject, Terry Hunt – now he should be able to provide a sensible answer to the question about how they were moved.

'They walked,' said Terry.

Over the years there have been many theories; were they simply dragged by hundreds of men, or mounted on a wheeled sled, perhaps lifted by a rudimentary wooden crane or pushed on rollers? None of which seemed feasible to Terry. He explained that brute force would never shift the 12 ton load and the weight would simply crush any wooden sled or rollers.

'Anyway, the wheel hadn't been invented here at the time of the Moai,' explained Terry.

'So, what was the solution?' asked Helene.

'The scientists should have listened to the Rapa Nui people,' said Terry. 'The answer had been passed down through the generations but ignored by the scientists. The Moai walked.'

'That's what Tito said,' replied Helene, 'it sounds as far-fetched as the UFO theory.'

The idea that extraterrestrials visited the island has been around for decades, a theory most prominently promoted by Erich von Daniken, author of the best-selling classic work *Chariots of the Gods*.

'This is not science fiction, Helene,' said Terry, 'the Moai actually walked, I proved it.'

Terry had indeed listened to the locals and solved the conundrum in 2012 by explaining how they "walked" from the quarry to their resting place overlooking the community they were to protect. Once sculptured from the rock on their backs, holes were made in the last remaining spinal ridge left in place from head to toe on their backs. Okay, they don't have toes so let's say head to thigh. With ropes attached they broke away the spinal ridge to allow the Moai to be freed from the earth and pulled into a standing position.

Three ropes made of woven banana plant were tied to the head, one held by men behind, one on the right and one on the left side of the erect Moai.

'Now for some audience participation,' said Terry. 'Stand with your arms flat against your sides and lean forward slightly. Don't bend your knees but take a pace by swinging one leg from the hip then the other in a pendulum action.'

The two of us did as instructed as a small crowd gathered. We swung our legs in turn and started to waddle across the field, how odd.

'Now you're walking like a Moai!' shouted Terry, much to his and Tito's delight.

Terry discovered that the base of the Moai was chiselled away to allow it to lean forward slightly, as we do when we walk Helene pointed out, which allowed this pendulum walking action. The teams on either side would control the swaying motion as it walked pivoting from side to side and the team at the back stopped the edifice from toppling over. In 2012 he proved his theory with a 5 ton replica and with just eighteen men "walked" the Moai 100m in just 40 minutes. His discovery was the subject of a TV film and won him the front page of the National Geographic. That's his mobile screensaver today.

It wasn't easy, the volcanic quarry and paths leading to the coastal resting places are scattered with fallen Moai. After months carving the Moai from the rock face over a third didn't make it and were left where they fell – but at this stage they were just rock, they didn't have their eyes, so had no soul and could be abandoned.

Those that did make it were walked onto 3m high stone ramps, known as Ahu so they must have really dominated the tribe, quite intimidating I guess with your ancestors looking down at everything you do. They were polished with coral and had their black and white eyes inserted to give them the soul of the ancestors they represented, but they were not complete yet.

The Rapa Nui people had a top knot in their hair then, they still do, like Tito's, and it is known as a Pukao. So, not content with spending a year creating, walking and erecting the tribe's own Moai they then chiselled huge Pukao to be lifted onto the Moai's head. Not from the same quarry, that would be far too easy. We visited the other ancient quarry where the huge Pukao, around a metre across and a metre high shaped like a bottle stopper, were made from the red volcanic rock and rolled to the village to be hoisted onto the Moai head.

But sadly the story does not end there. As the challenge to create the largest and therefore most powerful Moai intensified so the tribal competition became more passionate and finally violent. Rather than focus their energies on creating the biggest and best they started to sabotage rival tribes' Moai by pulling them down and toppling them over. Inevitably, tribal war broke out until all the Moai on the island were destroyed and left fallen on the ground. What a sad sight it is, knowing the story of how and why they were erected.

After the Moai had fallen the Rapa Nui people believed they were no longer protected by the souls of their ancestors, and so it proved. The tribal fighting continued while Spanish and the mainland Chileans came to the island and took many Rapa Nui people as slaves, leaving behind disease, sickness and infection. By 1888 the 20,000 population had been decimated to 111, yes only one hundred and eleven survived without the guardianship of the Moai.

As we toured the island Tito told the story of the fallen Moai we visited, so it was difficult not to experience the devastation they must have felt when the final proud Moai was pushed to the ground. It wasn't until 1956 when Thor Heyerdahl who sailed the Kon-Tiki expedition came to the island and restored and re-erected the first Moai at the beach where the Polynesian king first came to shore. Since then some of the Abu platforms have been recreated and Moai returned to their dignified position protecting the remaining Rapa Nui people on the island.

So, as our plane off the wonderful island was delayed by 9 hours, we were left to reflect on an incredible story of gentle people who tried to pass on their paradise to future generations under the watchful eye and protection of their ancestors. And, the story lives on today, as Tito said, 'I live on Rapa Nui, I speak Rapa Nui, I am Rapa Nui.' I was spellbound, may their gods go with them.

CHAPTER 3

DAY 11 to 14: CHILE
The Atacama Desert

The Sweetest Death

'Doavid, we're going to miss the plane!' shrieked Helene, as *Gate Closing* flashed up on the Departures screen for the flight from Santiago to Calama.

'When you're an international jet-setter,' I said pompously, 'you get to know the herding process at airports; that simply means prepare to queue,' I reassured her as I was dragged along the moving walkway.

Chile has taken queueing to a completely new level of ineptitude at one of the largest international hub airports in South America. Following a 9 hour delay from Rapa Nui to Santiago due to planes being in the wrong place (9 hours – goodness, they must have really been in the wrong place), we arrived to complete chaos with thousands of families on the first week of their winter holiday all trying to board domestic flights. Forget priority fast track this was every man for himself, women and children last.

'It's now flashing *Last Call*, and it's in red!' said Helene. This may be a bit more serious.

'Keep calm and keep walking,' I advised, increasing the pace and with perhaps a little more panic in my voice than I intended. It appeared we were about to get our own personal tannoy invitation onto the plane as we arrived into complete chaos, or Departures as LATAM know it.

There were two flights exiting from the same gate at the same time. I wonder how many finished up on the wrong shuttle bus, the wrong plane and perhaps in the wrong city. There were gates either side of the departures lounge so we started queuing, as you do, at Gate 32 for Calama with Gate 34 behind and opposite us.

Bing Bong!

'Will all those queuing at Gate 32 go to Gate 34.' So everyone simply turned around. Those at the back were now at the front in Priority Boarding and we, who were originally at the front, were now, well, pretty pissed off. Didn't matter though, 5 minutes later they cancelled the flight altogether and put us on one 9 hours later. Oh, the delights of international travel!

We could have ventured into Santiago to kill some time but after those elections we flew into the previous Sunday – the no alcohol day – there were riots in the streets with the armed police out again and all the taxi drivers were on strike protesting against Uber. So, with a generous $10 dollars credit each from the airline (LATAM, if you ever want to ignore them) which could only be spent at McDonalds or Starbucks – or put another way, nothing Helene can eat – we queued to get into the VIP Lounge. Yes queued, it's what you do in South American airports.

When we finally went through Priority Boarding and down the extended walkway gantry, the door to the plane was still closed.

'What do we do now?' asked Helene.

'I'll knock,' I suggested.

'No, we'll just wait; it's bound to open soon.'

'Just wait? Open soon? It's 9 hours late!' I banged my fist on the plane door. 'Is there anyone there?' I shouted.

There was a hiss of mechanical air as the door slowly unfastened itself and was sucked into the fuselage to reveal a smiling air steward. 'Buenas Noches,' he greeted us. LATAM at its very best.

We arrived at the Atacama Desert Hotel exhausted at about 1:30 AM after the 9 hour delay trying to get into Santiago due to planes in wrong place, and a 9 hour delay trying to get out due to fog, or as the locals call it, smoke.

After an hour's drive into the desert a wonderful receptionist processed our arrival quickly and we fell into the widest, warmest, whitest bed we had been in, to wake rested, refreshed and ready to meet our guide for the next few days. A local geologist named Marcella and our driver the wonderfully named Nelson. After a quick breakfast and a wander around the Hacienda constructed in red desert stone, what else, we were ready for our first expedition into the desert and the Luna Valley.

Audley had advised that we dress in layers because the temperature changes from absolutely freezing in the early morning to extremely hot by midday. This was a confusing one for zippy-uppy bags and very odd packing our backpacks for the day with gloves and a woolly hat alongside sunscreen and a floppy hat, slave to fashion me, but my goodness they were right.

The desert challenges my descriptive abilities and would exhaust a Thesaurus of superlatives, but let's give it a go. The Atacama is the driest in the world; some parts have never seen rain. It is the oldest in the world at 150 million years, and the highest in the world; we visited some parts at 4,600 metres. It is also simply huge at 1,500 sq. km and has many varied landscapes from salt flats and deep canyons to moonscapes and sand dunes – we visited the lot!

Our town was San Pedro de Atacama just 30 km from the Bolivian border and just over the mountains from Argentina. Every view we had, and there are some stunning ones, had the backdrop of snowcapped mountains, the highest at 6,739 metres.

Probably worth mentioning altitude sickness here, it can make you breathless and a little light headed, and doesn't distinguish by age, gender, fitness or build – some people suffer others don't. The advice is to drink plenty of water, acclimatise slowly and go easy on the alcohol, although Helene's natural remedies seemed to be doing the trick for us so far. My only symptom was that I fell asleep in Nelson's car at every opportunity; Helene called it my "altitude sleep".

San Pedro is a town straight out of your favourite Western. With its single storey red sandstone buildings built on dusty tracks, we expected Butch Cassidy and the Sundance Kid to charge out of the Banco de Chile guns blazing, at any minute. In fact, I was going to the saloon tonight; "gimme a red eye in a dirty glass". The shot glass would come sliding down the polished bar to stop right in front of me. "Can I have some lemonade in that please?" Well maybe I'm not cut out to be a cowboy after all.

In the Atacama there are dozens of different landscapes and as many stories behind the scenes, as it were. The Valle de la Luna is aptly named; it's like nothing on Earth I've ever seen. The mountain slopes glitter with what look like diamonds,but are actually gypsum. There's volcanic rock alongside sand dunes hundreds of feet high with valleys of white salt and a backdrop of mountains with gleaming white snow – quite breathtaking. It is dry and arid so virtually nothing grows but still there were flocks of screaming green parrots flying above us as we walked the ridge looking down a sheer drop off our narrow path to the salt flats below. A little intimidating but far too spectacular to worry about the vertical drops either side.

It was on the platform at the end of the ridge while we were taking a well-deserved rest that Marcella our guide told us the story of the "sweetest death" on the sacred mountain Llullaillaco, pronounced Ju-jay-jaco. We sat on the peak marvelling at Llullaillaco, the second highest active volcano in the world at 6,700 metres towering above the horizon between the border of Chile and Argentina, as she began her captivating story.

The Incas believed the mountain to be sacred, the home of their gods and a place where annual sacrifices were made, astonishingly these sacrifices were children. The most exceptional children in the tribe, either the most beautiful or the most gifted were the chosen ones. They were selected at a very young age and taken to be educated separately from the others in the tribe, not all made it to the ultimate sacrifice however.

Around 1,500 AD three children were selected from the "school" two girls, aged 15 and 8 and a boy aged 6. They were escorted on foot by their families and the Inca elders on the lengthy journey to Llullaillaco. Their job was to keep the children alive on the long trek up to the 6,700 metres summit; our highest was 4,600 metres and it was tough at times even in Nelson's chauffeur driven vehicle.

At the end of the journey there must have been all sorts of rituals performed before the children were given hallucinating drugs and alcohol to help them sleep – at 6,700 metres you don't wake up. This was known as the "sweetest death". Can you imagine how the accompanying parents must have felt? Pride perhaps that their children were selected to be sacrificed to the gods and ultimately to become gods themselves, but the devastation any parent would feel in losing a son or daughter.

In 1999 the children's mummies were discovered on the mountain and are considered to be the best preserved Inca mummies of all time. It was quite a story to reflect upon as we made our way back down the Valle de la Luna.

Flamingos in the driest desert in the world and at 3,300 metres, how does that work? Well, no one is really sure, but there they were on the salt flats with necks like crooked drainpipes and pink as you like against the clear blue skies and sparkling snow topped mountains, what a picture. We picnicked and watched the sun go down as flocks of flamingos sailed above us, pink necks and legs outstretched silhouetted against the matching sunset. Wonderful!

The salt flats supported a huge economy in the region, not for domestic salt, it has far too many other minerals in it for that, but salt that was sold to the copper mines for use in the refining process. Copper was and still is the foundation of the Chilean economy accounting for nearly 50% of exports. The salt mines depended on the thriving copper industry so towns sprung up, the Brits came over to build railways and as always neighbouring countries like Bolivia and Argentina tried to get on the bandwagon – Bolivia even moved its border by 50 km to claim mining rights. All was well until the mid-1980's when technology moved on and found a new way to process copper without salt. Overnight the market for Chilean salt crashed and the mine owners, their workers and families upped and left leaving ghost towns, Marie Celeste style, across the Atacama Desert.

While on the subject of technology let me digress for a moment to highlight an astonishing fact, so astonishing that I still find it difficult to believe. On Rapa Nui we investigated the alternative theories of how the Moai were moved from the quarry to the villages; as Terry said there was no mention of a wheel. Incredibly Chile and therefore Easter Island did not have the wheel until the Spanish arrived in 1535 – somebody just forgot to invent it. Compare this with the oldest wheel found in the UK, from the Bronze Age some 3,000 years BC and it does seem bizarre that it took the Chileans that long to discover what we may consider to be as rudimentary and essential to life as fire.

Back to the Atacama adventure, next up was a 2 hour hike up the valley, and I mean up, it was hands and knees at some points in the narrow and steep gorge. But what awaited us at the top of the ravine were the hot mineral pools of the river we had been climbing. It didn't take Helene long to de-robe. On went the fluffy white dressing gown and slippers brought to us by Nelson along with a scrumptious picnic that Helene could eat and a well-deserved beer in another most unconventional setting.

You may be getting the idea that this country has a huge amount of awe inspiring landscapes and scenery, and you'd be right but we were far from finished yet.

We visited the Rainbow Valley, you can probably guess what's coming, but if you can find a more incredibly stunning natural panorama then let us know and we'll be off. The seven colours making up the rainbow of rock we found in the valley included mountains of green crystal, red volcanic rock exploded from the very core of the Earth, white volcanic ash slopes, purple ridges and minerals of black, silver and gold. Goodness me what a sight, it moved Helene to tears, a Magic Kingdom Moment as the kids call it.

I should explain. It was on our first visit to Disney's Magic Kingdom as a treat for Charlotte and Elliot some years ago that Helene walked onto Main Street, saw the view of Cinderella's Castle and promptly burst into tears.

'Oh, Heleneeee,' as they like to call her – the E at the end of Helene is silent, but they love to emphasise it – 'what on Earth is the matter?' they asked, as they laughed and danced around, hugging her waist. 'I'm just so happy,' she blubbered through the tears. The "Magic Kingdom Moment" stuck and is always used to describe Helene when the emotion takes over.

We waited until our final day to tackle the 4,600 metre high trip to the El Tatio Geysers to ensure we were fully acclimatised. It was up at 5:00 AM to allow us time to see the sunrise.

'Not enough layers,' Helene instructed as we prepared for the early morning expedition.

'But that's four including a thermal vest,' I protested.

'Not enough, we were warned it was going to be a bit chilly up there, but the forecast is minus double figures.' Unsure of exactly what that meant I retrieved another zippy-uppy bag.

'Not enough!' cautioned Helene again.

'Basically, what you're saying is remove everything from my wardrobe and put it on,' I complained.

'Yes, and don't forget your scarf and gloves,' she said, slipping on another warm top.

We were eventually ready, but with Helene (eight layers) and me (six layers including two pairs of trousers) we were barely able to bend to pick up our backpacks.

The advice was good; minus ten on the summit, it had been minus fourteen earlier in the week and minus twenty the previous month, June. It was, as promised, a stunning sunrise over the mountains, with bursts of steam rising from scalding water in the snowy ground into a clear blue and pink sky.

The water at the surface of the geysers is at boiling point, packed full of minerals and some rare bacteria that makes oxygen and can actually create life. In fact, if, or perhaps when, there is Armageddon on planet Earth then here is one of only three places around the globe where scientists believe life will begin again, a sobering thought and difficult to believe in this desolate harsh environment.

Nelson's picnic that day was breakfast, and what a fine occasion it was as the sun rose into a clear blue sky illuminating what appeared to be a prehistoric landscape, finally raising the temperature to a more bearable balmy minus two. Hot coffee, cold meats and cheese, fruit and crusty bread, and even a gluten free version for Helene. It reminded me of the Varsity Match picnics in the car park at Twickenham, always freezing as we attempted to eat soups and stews with huge ski gloves on.

Before we left we walked around a lake just beginning to thaw out to observe the varied wildlife tottering around on thin ice. The coots really were on thin ice, if they didn't move around while the temperature dropped in the evening they were frozen solid in the lake with no way of escape until the morning. They just sat there looking vaguely embarrassed. This made a frozen ready meal for the foxes who just waited for the lake to freeze over and then off mum fox goes to "Iceland".

We had a slow descent out of the unique and snow covered landscape, into bright sunshine with not a cloud in the sky. We arrived back to what we had begun to call home and removed layer upon layer of clothing to be replaced by shorts and a tee-shirt, and enjoy a beer around the pool. And that just about sums up the Atacama Desert, a place of amazing contrast from salt flats to towering volcanic peaks, barren and parched lunar landscapes to warm mountain pools and hillsides that sparkle at you. We loved it.

CHAPTER 4

Day 15 to 17: CHILE
The Casablanca Valley

Hello Luchito

W̶e readied ourselves for another LATAM flight, this time from Calama back to Santiago – but only endured an hour's delay this time, pretty good for LATAM. *Last Call* was before our incoming plane had actually landed, excellent. As usual we queued and waited, although that's not what they do here, LATAM devotees know the form. On arrival at the gate they put their case in the queue and go for coffee. Security clearly wasn't an issue there then, but imagine what would happen at Heathrow.

As we waited on our own in the queue of luggage I noticed a group of young trendy twenty somethings in the lounge. All loud and confident, boys acting the fool and girls giggling and I began to wonder where and when fashion changed. Back in the day, if your jeans were ripped you threw them away, if your pants were showing you pulled up your trousers, if your collar was up your mate pulled it down and if your shirt was hanging out you tucked it in, so when did they become fashion statements? Slave to fashion me, but "dignity always dignity", to quote Don Lockwood.

Back to the adventure. After a full-on few days in the desert, it was time for something completely different, three days' rest and relaxation at the Vina Matetic Vineyard in the Casablanca Valley, about 100 kilometres northwest of Santiago in the middle of Chile's quality wine region. It is best known for its Sauvignon Blanc. Lovely, it's the Chilean Sauvignon Helene drinks at our local, gosh that felt like a long way away, and Chardonnay, not a great fan but I was hoping it wasn't the oaky sweet syrup the Southern Hemisphere usually serves up. And Pinot Noir, our favourite, is also grown in these cooler climates near the coast.

This beautiful country house known as a *casa de campo* of the Matetic Vineyard has just eight rooms, two restaurants and a wine bar for tastings, all designed in a British Colonial style complete with roaring fire, spirits "honesty bar" and an old pool table with red baize, in the library. It's the perfect place to relax, unwind and re-live the extraordinary trip to Atacama – we couldn't stop talking about it. Each room was named after the red and white grapes used on the estate in their wines. Which room were we provided? Pinot Noir of course.

Interesting thing about Chile, they seem to consider wine as a soft drink. In three of our hotels where we were on full or half board it included all soft drinks and wine. Nice, odd, but nice.

The vineyard is situated in the Rosario Valley sandwiched between the Pacific and the Andes so the vines are constantly refreshed by sea winds to give the wines a pleasant mineral salty taste. The 10,000 hectare winery is based on purely organic and biodynamic farming, no pesticides or chemicals just natural ingredients and compost.

They also farm alpacas, sheep and cows and use their manure as fertilisers, or as the wine makers call it "Ingredient 501", more scientific than alpaca shit I suppose. Interesting thing about pure organic wines, they don't give you a hangover apparently, it's the chemicals added to other wines that give us the sore head in the morning. Thought we better put that theory to the test, purely in the name of research you understand.

One of the examples of organic wine production we discovered when touring the winery on our tasting tour was that to increase the plumpness of the grape they crush quartz crystals, mix with water and spray onto the leaves. The small crystals then act like solar panels to aid photosynthesis and increase the size of the fruit. Quite interesting I thought.

The wines from this vineyard are distributed internationally but given they only produce half a million bottles a year (some Chilean vineyards will do that in a week) they can only be found in restaurants, not at retail. So, if you spot Corralillo from the Matetic Vineyard give it a go, the Sauvignon and Pinot Noir are definitely the best of their offering.

On the label you will find a fairly primitive drawing of an alpaca, this is Luchito, he was abandoned at birth so the orphan is cared for by the vineyard staff and is as domesticated and tame as a dog. As Helene was about to find out.

On the day we arrived in Santiago they had the first snow for 25 years and the city was at a standstill – no change there then. Although the guys at the winery were a little concerned about the consequences of the low temperatures on the vines the snowy mountainous terrain looked spectacular from our country house at the bottom of the Rosario Valley.

The day started with a bright chilly morning of blue skies and plenty of sunshine, a great day for a hike along the valley to the winery, about 10 km up the valley from our Casa. Kitted out in our puffer jackets and walking boots we set off on a beautiful walk, a bit damp underfoot as we traversed streams and puddles but we were escorted by a variety of wildlife on the way with swifts, lapwings and finches keeping just a few feet ahead of us as we walked.

About 10 km into the walk we arrived at the Matetic winery cheese shop. As I investigated the area to find the onward path I had that sinister feeling we were being watched. Indeed, we were, off in the distance behind a locked gate about 100 metres away was a dark four legged shape staring straight at us.

'Is that a donkey?' Helene asked, pointing up the track.

'Possibly,' I said, unsure exactly what was taking such an interest in us, 'but whatever it is it's behind the gate so it'll be fine.' It looked, and came a bit closer, looked some more and came closer still. Helene by this time had found a way around the gate and was checking out a possible path past our new friend.

'This seems to be the way,' she said. And still it came closer. I watched as Helene decided to return to the assumed safety our side of the gate, but this particular beast knew his way around.

'It's coming closer,' she said with slight panic in her voice as it slowly dawned on her that if we could find a way around the gate so could it.

As it negotiated the gap between the gate and the fence Helene increased her stride across the empty car park, only to be met pace for pace.

'It's really close now!' she yelled, as she jogged towards me followed by some trotting behind her. 'David, I'm being chased by an alpaca!' will no doubt go down in family history.

It was of course Luchito, the orphaned alpaca, pet of the winery and star of the Corralillo wine label. He only wanted to say "Hola" and enjoy a gentle stroke I guess, but he sure gave Helene a bit of a scare. My, how we laughed about it over dinner, well one of us did.

Our trip back to Santiago was a very early start and the beginning of a long day of travelling; Santiago to Bogota the capital of Columbia and a connecting flight to Quito in Ecuador. We had both been looking forward to this part of the itinerary, a stay in the Ecuadorean rainforest at Mashpi Lodge. We had seen the documentary on TV when Monica Galetti the chef from Le Gavroche and TV's Masterchef visited there, it looked incredible, and we were about to find out for ourselves.

CHAPTER 5

Day 18 to 22: ECUADOR
Quito and Mashpi Lodge

Hugging, Howling and Humming

O ur flight to Quito was on time, well an hour or so late again, but over there that's positively early. The highlight of the short onward flight to our final destination was my wonderful travel companion sharing our three seats, a tiny and extremely old and frail nun. She sat herself down on the aisle seat and pushed me over to gain access for the multitude of carry-on bags she had, I guess aircrew don't challenge a nun. The rest of us had our bags measured, weighed and scrutinised before we could take them on as hand luggage. With rosary in one hand and iPhone in the other, she made a variety of calls, no doubt to her various "sisters" and continued to receive them until the stewardess lost patience. You'll never guess what her ring tone was.

We arrived in Quito the capital of Ecuador, which is exactly what I would expect Rio to look like; small brightly covered houses crammed together and perched on the hillside overlooking the old town. So, what do we know about Ecuador? Unlike Rapa Nui it no longer has any pure indigenous population; they died out a few years ago. The Spanish, Moors, French, Americans, and Peruvians to name a few have all at one time invaded, owned or settled in Ecuador. So, the country's population is a great big melting pot. Beyond our charming three storey hacienda centred on a rustic courtyard we found the streets of the old town and met the round faced, olive skinned and quite short locals, playing music in the street or inviting us into their small family run restaurants, more like their kitchens, to sample the local dishes – lamb stew with rice, plantains and salad was a favourite of mine.

The old town in this vast city slowly creeping up the mountains was inaugurated as the first UNESCO world heritage site in 1978 when frankly it was little more than a slum until an entrepreneurial mayor took over in 1994 and renovated the area to attract globetrotting travellers. Tourism, oil, roses and shrimp are now the main exports for the country, an eclectic mix. One other worth a mention is the Panama hat; not made in Panama but in Ecuador from the local palmata plant, you can buy them there from around $20 up to a whopping $32,000. Apparently Sylvester Stallone had recently bought one for $25,000.

But of course, the one thing Ecuador is known for and named after (the whole country used to be called Quito until its independence in 1822) is the equator. It is in fact the nearest land to the sun, forget Everest, we're already at over 4,000 metres before we even look at the soaring active volcanoes in the region. And, of course the world is not entirely round, Isaac Newton called it an oblate spheroid, I call it a sphere that's squashed at its poles and swollen at the equator.

'Let's visit the equator,' I said to Aldo our guide, a young university graduate still deciding upon his career.

'Absolutely, which one?' he asked. That flummoxed me slightly, I'm sure there was only one.

'Well, how many are there?' Which I thought was a fair question, despite some tutting from Helene.

'Four, which one would you like?'

'Are they all on the same equator line?' It seemed reasonable that anyone sitting on the equator around the globe could stake a claim for commercial use.

'No, they're all at different latitudes.' I appeared to be getting out of my depth now. The voice of reason stepped in.

'Take us to the one that's most accurate, Aldo,' said Helene.

Although all four claim to be the accurate equator, apparently two simply miscalculated; the latest in 1982. One established in 1736 got fairly close, by about 150 metres, not a bad guess with 18th century technology, or lack of it. But in 1991 with the aid of GPS the accurate equator of latitude 0° 0' 0'' was defined. That was the one we should visit.

As we are all taught at school, it never rains on the equator; it poured. A miracle, our guide Aldo called it, bloody wet I called it.

We were escorted around a rather commercialised, but great fun, display exhibit allowing us to try some unique tricks only possible on the equator. We've all heard about how water in a sink goes down the plug hole with a vortex in different directions in the north and south hemispheres, and straight down on the equator. But to see it demonstrated first hand no more than 2 meters either side of the equator was pretty impressive – a mobile sink in case you're wondering. Trying to walk the "red line" of the equator with eyes closed and arms out was fun, impossible but fun; the magnetic forces completely upset your equilibrium. And balancing an egg on a nail directly over the equator was a challenge, not sure about the science behind that one, but we all had a go.

A thin red line stretching across the small show area reveals the true centre of the Earth. Our companions on this brief tour were photographed straddling the red equator line, a foot on either side.

'Come on, Helene, we can do better than that,' I said grabbing her in an embrace.

'What on Earth are you doing?' she asked, as I stepped back across the red line.

'Hugging across the hemispheres,' I said, as we both reached to each other and hung on.

Much to the hilarity of the watching crowd we did indeed hug across the hemispheres, her in the north and me in the south. There were some "ah's" and clapping from the onlooking women and some groans from the men, probably because we thought of it first, but it was great fun.

We ended our couple of days in Quito with a delightful walk around the city accompanied by Aldo followed by dinner at one of the oldest restaurants in the city, full of gnarled old locals of course. The following day was to be the main feature of our time in Ecuador and one of the highlights of the whole adventure, the trip to Mashpi Lodge in the Amazon Rainforest.

It was a fairly sedate start to an astonishing 4 hour journey as Aldo and our driver Richard collected us at 8:30 AM for our drive to the rainforest. Quito is yet to have a subway system and the public transport is poor so the city hosts 18,000 yellow taxis New York style. This meant we started our journey in an hour traffic jam, but once out of the city we started the climb up the surrounding mountains. Up to 4,000 metres, down to 2,000, back up to 4,000 and down again, ears popping all the way as we twisted and turned around the inclines.

The air began to change from chilly and dry in the arid and barren lower slopes outside Quito to hot and humid in the lush green mountainsides with banana plants, fruit trees and ferns populating the vast valleys we were circumventing. As we ventured farther into the beginnings of the rainforest the landscape became more extreme with palms, sugar cane and exotic plants, some of which we recognised from home but these must have been on Baby Bio with Speed, they were huge, it was like being in Lilliput.

We continued winding our way up and down the peaks and had occasional sightings of hummingbirds, and butterflies the size of your hand. Above us were half a dozen vultures circling around the carcass of who knows what, or perhaps they were deciding what to do next; "what do you wanna do?" "I dunno what do you wanna do?" Maybe not.

Still no condors yet though. The largest flying bird in the Western Hemisphere, the condor's length is around a metre but their massive wingspan can often be over 3 metres. It is also the national symbol of Ecuador and just about every South American country, and is classified as Critically Endangered. In Ecuador there are estimated to be only a hundred remaining in the wild yet still farmers kill them in the mistaken belief they are a threat to their animals, they are not, they feed on carrion. Last year a misguided cretin was jailed for hunting and killing one of these magnificent birds – the idiot put a picture of himself and his "trophy kill" on Facebook. He didn't pass Go.

After 3 hours the road ran out. We were now pretty deep into the rainforest and continued on a bumpy old stone track doing its best to break our suspension. After miles of nothing apart from the forest attempting to take over the narrow route we were navigating, we arrived at a one road village. Homes of brightly painted multicoloured, single storey houses constructed from local tree trunks, a hotchpotch of wood presumably gathered from the forest and corrugated metal, all wedged in against each other.

There was a tiny chapel which for some reason had been painted bright sky blue and a few shops, really nothing more than market stalls in their front rooms, bizarrely one had a poster for the local mobile provider. Even the Amazon Rainforest can't stop the advance of technology, and advertising I guess. Another isolated little tumbledown shack some miles out of the village had a hand painted wooden "Se Vende" sign hung on its front door and a mobile number; it did come with your own 59 hectares of rainforest though.

We finally arrived at the entrance to the Mashpi Reserve, 3,213 acres of privately owned rainforest reserve bought by Ecuadorian entrepreneur and former mayor of Quito, Roque Sevilla from the Dutch loggers who had decimated vast areas of this wonderful environment. The twenty-two room Lodge was created with the sole purpose of protecting the region from any further devastation. All the money raised from tourists, he calls us ecotourists, goes back into the conservation of the rainforest and care for the biodiversity of its ecosystems.

The entrance to the reserve clearly resembles the gateway into Jurassic Park, two huge wooden gates well over 6 metres high were slowly opened by one of the Rangers, a salute and a wave and we were in, but still a long way from Mashpi Lodge itself.

The track the other side of the gates made the previous few miles feel like our long forgotten A404 at home. We now had a sheer drop on one side, Helene's and the spectacular impenetrable rainforest on the other. Goodness me, the scenery had just gone up another notch or two.

Bamboo as thick as your arm towering into the distant canopy.

Single leaves the size of a table for two.

Soaring trees competing for the first of the rain and the sunlight 50 metres above us.

Plants and fauna clinging to the rock face and life.

A fruit tree with what looked like individual boiled eggs hanging from their own branches. I later discovered this was the highly toxic Tomato Tree and then discovered a jam made from it at breakfast, who knows.

Exotic plants of deep purple, golden yellow and pillar box red neither of us could identify.

Every centimetre covered with plant life and others that can't find space on the ground living off another tree.

Extraordinary stuff, this was looking to be some adventure.

The Lodge was not at all what I was expecting; I imagined a property constructed in wood – like a safari game reserve I guess – but think Frank Lloyd Wright, a breathtaking creation of steel cubes in glass and stone with straight edges and tall ceilings. If you know his famous Fallingwater residence then it's pretty close. The architect was Diego Rivadeneira who intended to create a space where guests could be immersed in the rainforest while making minimal impact on the surrounding environment. He achieved it.

The manager, a lovely guy named Alfonso, greeted us with his team to dispense hot flannel towels and a refreshing unknown fruity drink. Our luggage was whisked away and we were introduced to our guide for our first excursion into the rainforest. Blimey, that was quick, but why not.

'We need to get you togged up,' our guide Juan told us, 'and you'll need these,' he said handing us some industrial heavyweight binoculars that would have been more at home with the Gurkhas.

Juan, a young man who looked barely old enough to be out on his own in the forest, was dressed from head to toe in green camouflage and carried a larger pair of binoculars, a thick stick almost as tall as him, a huge jungle machete and an iPad.

'First you'll need boots,' he advised, as we followed him into the "togging up" area.

'We've got boots,' Helene whispered to me.

'Apparently not, look.' Dozens of upturned black wellies, upturned to keep the spiders out we later learned, were lined up next to benches of silver water bottles and rows of thick pine walking sticks with rubber grips just like Juan's.

'Do you think we get a knife like his too?' I said, excitedly. 'I'd like a knife like his.'

We were measured up for walking sticks and boots, sadly no machete, handed a Mashpi Lodge silver water bottle and off we set trying to keep up with Juan.

'Why are we wearing big black wellies?' Helene asked.

'Dunno, probably to protect us from snake bites around the ankles.'

'I'll ask Juan,' said Helene.

'It's a rainforest,' he said, 'it's wet.'

As novices in the rainforest we were unsure what to expect but guide Juan guided us well, stopping every now and then when we heard the squawk or scream of a bird or a rustle of something unidentified in the undergrowth.

The reserve actually has two ecosystems situated either side of the mountainous valley and the Mashpi River. One is fed by the cloud advancing down the valley from the Pacific; the other is on the high peaks and creates its own clouds and convectional rainfall. It also has both primary and secondary rainforest. Primary is the established part which has been untouched for hundreds, maybe thousands of years. Secondary is where there has been human intervention, mainly from the timber companies, and has over time re-established itself. Both are stunning and to be honest it's difficult to see any difference apart from some of the colossal trees. Interestingly, the rainforest is recognised as having only two seasons: summer and winter, identified by the longest and shortest days – I always prefer spring and autumn myself but there you go.

Alfonso met us after our excursion to demonstrate our room; I say demonstrate because it was all theatre. As he opened our door the floor to ceiling, wall to wall curtain whirred into motion lifting to reveal a window the full height and length of our suite with the rainforest behind it; my goodness that was impressive.

But there wasn't time to admire the view for too long, as we were soon invited on our next walk out to the Lodge's Life Centre to spot some exotic birds and visit the butterfly aviary. On the way we first heard, then met a family of Howler Monkeys playing above us. The little ones were riding on the backs of their parents as they sprang from tree to tree; what a sight, what a sound – they do actually howl to warn off other families competing for their territory. You may have heard them, they provided the "voice over" for dinosaurs in the Jurassic Park movies.

Our guides pointed out toucans and brightly coloured birds of paradise in yellow and black, green, orange and kingfisher blue, a huge diversity of birds. Then the butterflies, bigger than your hand fluttering around our heads, one looking exactly like the face of an owl, another with electric blue and silver wings, it was great getting up close and personal with these fragile creatures.

This was also to be our first night expedition.

'Where's your head torch?' asked Helene.

'On my head.'

'Well turn it on!'

'Have you seen all the midges attracted by these lights?' I protested. 'We'll get eaten alive!'

'You should have put on the Moskito Guard I gave you, it cost a fortune!'

'I know that's why I'm not using it.'

Head torches on, flashlights in hand, sleeves rolled down and insect repellent now sprayed on, we were prepared for what our guide announced as "a hunt for spiders and snakes". Now, I'm with Jim Stafford on this one, if it stings or bites it's probably left well alone under its rock or behind its leaf, but no, we were barely 5 minutes in when there was great excitement from our guide beckoning us over and pointing into the undergrowth.

'Quick, before it disappears!' he said. 'If I poke it with this stick it might come running out.'

'That's okay, no need to aggravate it,' I virtually begged.

'Shall I take a look first?' offered Helene. No argument from me. 'Ooh, that's big and furry!'

I've seen the Bond film and I've watched in horror as David Attenborough allows a large hairy tarantula to walk up his shirt sleeve but this was a beautiful elegant graceful specimen. I'm joking it was horrible! Huge, leggy and dark purple under the torchlight it watched us watching it before getting bored and sloping off into the ground cover.

With moths whirring round our head torches and a variety of oversized arachnids being unearthed by our guide the soundtrack of the rainforest began to play out. Squawks, screams, whistles, yelps, squeaks, shrieks, howls and wails; it had it all, I'm sure I heard something laugh as well. The loudest turned out to be from a small frog blasting out a sort of quack with a belch.

Hot showers, steaming goat stew and a beer or two had us collapsing into our bed exhausted but enraptured by our experience. We left the huge curtain blind open to allow us to be woken by the misty rainforest in the morning. What a day!

The following days brought more excursions deeper into the rainforest with our personal guide and trusty whittled walking sticks – they really were surprisingly useful in helping us scale the steep ravines and rocky rivers. The guides all had degrees or PhD's in biology, environmental sustainability or suchlike, so were incredibly knowledgeable about the plants, animals and ecosystems. In fact, our guide Juan Carlos was responsible for identifying a new species of tree; after 2 years of research and articles to prove it was unique he named it Mashpi Magnolia. Surprisingly, technology and nature are good companions and he had a clever app on his iPad that not only identified birds by recording their song but also played the mating call back to attract them towards us, a sort of ornithological version of Kazam, for those under 25 years of age.

One of the most fascinating anecdotes Juan Carlos told us was about the "walking tree". We'd heard about the walking Moai from Rapa Nui now we had the walking tree. When the tree is beginning to establish itself, it grows towards the sunlight, but the canopy is ever changing so its original location may now be in the shade, so it just moves itself to a better spot. It throws down a root from its trunk and once it hits the ground uses the root as a pivot to move the whole tree to a place where it can once again reach for the sun – the whole process may take 2 years but what a clever soul Mother Nature really is.

We swam in waterfall pools in the middle of the rainforest valley, we walked up and down mountain streams that would eventually find their way to the Pacific, we crossed the valley in an open caged cable car for four and traversed the ravine on a tandem suspended 80 metres above the rainforest floor. We heard the Manakin bird that sings with its wings and dances like Michael Jackson, and watched hummingbirds hover right in front of our face like the snitch from Harry Potter. What an experience.

We said our goodbyes to our new-found friends we will never see again and I felt privileged to have spent just a few days in the company of some great people, amazing wildlife and the incredible rainforest. As Helene became a little tearful on leaving I thought; well that really is a Magic Kingdom.

CHAPTER 6

Day 23 to 27: ECUADOR
Hacienda Zuleta

That Condor Moment

O ur next venue was back up to 3,000 metres and our interpretation of that great Billy Crystal film "City Slickers" at a working Hacienda ranch. On arrival it looked more like the "High Chaparral"; I expected to see John and Victoria, Buck and Manolito extricating Blue from his weekly catastrophe.

Hacienda Zuleta is a working farm about an hour into the mountains the other side of Quito from Mashpi with around 2,000 hectares and a very different landscape to our previous week. It is green and fertile with pine trees, a eucalyptus forest and lush pasture for the large farming community in the beautiful Zuleta Valley. It even has its own pyramids. Constructed in the 13th century, pre-Incas, they look like pyramids with the ever-decreasing steps up, but then imagine the top third sliced off. There are seventy of them in and around Zuleta and look a lot like the famous Aztec pyramids of 200 years later, maybe that's where they got the idea from. We met the archaeologist investigating these odd formations – her daughter Jess works on the ranch – and to be honest I'm still not sure why the Zuleta pyramids are there – I don't think she knows yet either.

The Hacienda is the family home of two ex-Presidents of Ecuador; Lasso Senior and then his son Galo Plaza Lasso a remarkable man. He was a bullfighter, a farmer, a diplomat and then the President from 1948 – '52, the first to stay in office for a full term since 1928. There are some great photos of him in the library with Nixon, Truman, Roosevelt, Kissinger, Golda Meir, the Pope and standing in the front car of a cavalcade with full military honours bringing New York to a standstill. He also introduced the tractor and Holstein Friesian cattle to the country, showcasing them at the Hacienda and then revolutionising farming in Ecuador.

The Hacienda has been in the family since the mid-19th century so on Galo Plaza's death in 1998 he bequeathed the estate to his six children each of whom owns equal plots of the farmland, some well-kept, some not depending on their wealth, and they jointly own the Hacienda. His grandson Fernando is manager of the operation.

The family often stay, as they were during our visit, but it's good to know they have to pay as well, but with a substantial discount I heard; fair enough. The Hacienda only has seventeen rooms, each with a wood burning stove lit at 5:00 PM each evening by the maid, and re-fuelled at 7:30 PM when the beds are turned down with hot water bottles placed in either side of our huge bed. Our equally large double floor-to-ceiling arched windows overlook our private garden and down the valley to where the condors fly.

Part of Galo Plaza's legacy is that every member of staff is given a cow they can keep on the ranch, have it milked twice a day and sell the milk with the rest of the co-operative to Nestle whose factory is just 15 km out of town. Not surprisingly there are Nestle chocolates available everywhere in the hotel, almost as many as there are roses.

You'll remember one of Ecuador's largest exports is roses and their farms (far bigger than nurseries) surround this area, the locals call it "the rose capital of the world". Helene discovered that if you buy direct from the greenhouses in the morning you can get seventy-two stems for $5, it's kind of a floral version of our trips to Billingsgate for fish I suppose.

Apparently, there are seventy varieties of Ecuadorean roses and if you want reds, the most popular of course, there are fifty to choose from – that would be "Fifty Shades of Red" then. At lunch one afternoon we met a Swiss couple who own one of the largest rose farms in the area, apparently the roses can grow all year round in the sunny and moderate climate and have thick stems and much larger heads than we see in the UK. Last year their farm alone produced 24 million, mainly for the European, and particularly the Swiss market. Their largest competitor in the global market for roses? Kenya! How odd.

In every room of the Hacienda there are crystal vases and china bowls stuffed full of broad headed roses, including some beautiful yellow and whites in our bedroom. Sadly, as I wrote this next to a roaring open fire sipping a chilled glass of Sauvignon, Argentinian this time, Helene encouraged me to count the number of roses in the lounge; 204 – that would be about $14 dollars' worth I guess.

There was plenty to do at Zuleta Hacienda including hikes to waterfalls and ridge walks – each route is given a name: Fox Trail, Rabbit Trail, Bear Trail, (yes there are bears) – mountain biking, condor spotting, the condor reserve, horse-drawn carriage riding, helping out milking cows or rounding up the horses each day. There's the cheese factory on site, cookery and local artisan embroidery lessons and then there is horse riding.

'Good news, I've booked us on a hack tomorrow,' I announced to Helene.

'Excellent,' she replied, 'what's a hack, something to do with computers, or logging, logging on?' she laughed.

'Horses.' The laughter disappeared.

'I hate horses. They bite and kick, and probably smell. And they're really high.'

'I'll get you a small one, a pony; you'll love it, like being a cowboy.'

'Girl.'

This may take a little more persuasion.

The Hacienda was the first to bring purebred horses to Ecuador and introduce a cross between Andalusian, Thoroughbred and Quarter Horse, called the Zuleteno Horse, the Hacienda's own special breed. I wasn't sure what all that meant for our hack but they looked healthy and fit – should do, all twenty are ridden at least once a day.

Helene was a little quiet over breakfast before we met our guide for the morning, Rodrigo. He was a rugged man, browned by the sun and weather-beaten from an outside life on the farm, who clearly preferred the company of horses to humans. He was dressed from head to toe in old stained leather and carried a fierce looking riding crop, which the horses seemed to be keeping a wary eye on.

'Zese are ze chaps, put zem on 'ere,' he said, clutching his leather bound calves.

'There we go, Helene we've got chaps and everything,' I said.

Not a word.

Fernando joined us, the manager of the estate, looking just like his young grandfather from the presidential pictures in the library.

'Hi, Fernando, any tips for Helene, it's her first time on a horse?' I asked.

'Make sure you're facing the right way and talk to your horse,' he laughed.

'Talk to the horse,' Helene replied, 'what do I say? And does it have to be in Spanish?'

'I think he means show it who's boss,' I said.

We collected the rest of our tack, put on our chaps and were allocated our horses by Rodrigo, who may have been up to a little mischief. Helene's 15 hand horse – a pony is under 14.2 apparently – was a fiery looking beast doing its best to ignore her as she stared up at its dignified head held high above hers.

'Zis is Rebeldia, ze 'orse for you,' he said to Helene, handing her the reins.

'How on earth do I get up there?'

'It means Rebellion,' said Rodrigo, turning away, I'm sure to hide a smirk.

At this point you may be able to guess where this one is going.

'She's strong willed, assertive and likes to control the situation,' said Fernando.

'I know,' I replied. 'What's the horse like?'

It was a delightful ride through the village and up a cobbled bridleway with vegetation of some sort either side, vegetation that Rebeldia really liked. There was, let us say, a conflict of interest between rebellious horse and determined rider. As Rebeldia made for the lush grasses of the bank Helene was straining on the reins to literally get her back on track. Halfway round I heard Helene capitulate.

'Oh go on then, I know you want to,' as her rebellious horse sunk its head into the roadside greenery.

'Kick ze 'orse, lady, kick ze 'orse!' shouted Rodrigo.

'I can't, it's got its bloody head in the bushes,' Helene screamed back.

I would have helped if I could, but the tears of hysterical laughter were rolling down my face making any attempt at conversation entirely impossible.

After a great couple of hours we returned to the stables to de-tack or whatever the correct equestrian term maybe.

'Let's thank our horses,' I said and gave my nag a pat and a stroke. Helene approached her not so trusty steed to give the same appreciation only for Rebeldia to turn her head away in disgust. Oops, pissed off horse! It had been a battle of wills. As Helene described it later, 'I wanted to hack, the horse wanted to eat.' Horse won.

But I was very impressed with Helene's approach to riding and the whole escapade. She had said she would try anything on the adventure and so it had proved. In the rainforest she tackled the pretty formidable hikes with ease and we'd been on some extremely high and intimidating passages across the valleys. She had engaged with the wildlife and conquered her fear of horses; I was very proud of her.

As I was counting roses in the lounge an extremely elegant lady with a large glass of wine in hand joined the two of us on the sofa and introduced herself.

'I'm Margarite, daughter of the late President,' she said, straight to the point, what a charming and distinguished lady.

The three of us sat around the fire for half an hour or so before dinner discussing her family, the Hacienda, the valley and despite her saying she is not allowed to discuss politics the conversation kept drifting back to current affairs. But it was the family that intrigued me most, Galo Plaza and his wife Rosario had five girls and a boy – almost an Ecuadorean version of the Mitford family – and Margarite hinted at the fact that there was more scandal in her family than any Downton Abbey plot, but sadly this genteel lady was too discreet to go much further.

But as colourful as the family and the guests were, we were there to enjoy the countryside, the scenery and the ranch. So, despite the unusual rain – it was supposed to be the dry season, the locals couldn't understand it, another miracle perhaps – we togged up with boots, hats and waterproofs to hit the rabbit, fox and bear trails. We visited the condor sanctuary where Jan, the condor man, okay, highly educated French biologist, introduced us to his four residents.

There are only eighteen in captivity and a hundred wild in all of Ecuador. His four were all rescued; would you believe that one was kept on a lead as a pet in someone's yard. None of them would survive if let loose to fend for themselves, they are now just too reliant on man. One pair was taking it in turns to sit on their egg, the only known condor egg in Ecuador. Jan was trying to keep it a secret from the media who turned up in coach loads to this tiny sanctuary in the middle of nowhere when the last one hatched 2 years ago. It died a day later.

They really are striking birds with their turkey-like heads, white collar ruffs and huge 3 metre wingspan which they showed off to us as the sun broke through and they could dry their feathers. Surprisingly, they are not all black as I expected but have large swathes of white feathers underneath their wings. The wings themselves are unmistakable; the condors look as if they're carrying a door across their shoulders when they fly. They start very high up at the neck and fan straight out at right angles to their head, like a glider, because that's exactly what they are. At the end of their wings they have hands of feathers, "fingers" pointing straight out, to help with the aerodynamics, it also makes them easy to recognise in flight.

Jan was still suffering from the after effects of fighting a forest fire at the end of the valley very close to the sanctuary. He said they were only minutes away from evacuating the site and fleeing for safety back down the valley to the Hacienda. His only option would have been to bag each of the condors, steering well clear of their razor sharp beaks. Their claws are not a danger because they cannot clench them like a bird of prey; they are more like large chickens' feet. Can you imagine this tall, ponytailed French biologist with a bagged condor under each arm running for his and their lives down the river valley towards the safety of the Hacienda? Luckily the firefighters arrived by helicopter and disaster was averted.

It was not until the last day, when I had a crick in my neck from constantly scanning the sky and we were on our final walk with Carlitos, our dog for the week who accompanied us on every hike, that we finally spotted a pair of condors. They were quite low in the sky at the end of the valley no more than 50 metres away, it was a wonderful sight. They may have appeared a little clumsy on the ground but my goodness they were majestic in the air, gliding over the landscape and riding the thermals. We stopped and watched as they spiralled above us, what a privilege to see. This was our "condor moment".

There was one last magic moment before we left Ecuador, slightly weird and eccentric, but nonetheless well intentioned. On our way to the airport and after a pleasant lunch overlooking a lagoon and the mountains we had recently traversed, Aldo our guide invited us outside. We were introduced to a girl in traditional Ecuadorian dress who sung to the two of us a lilting ballad no doubt about her homeland, family or ancestors perhaps. It was a touching moment but still rather odd being serenaded next to a minibus in a tarmac car park.

We loved our time on the ranch at the Hacienda, it was so different from any of the previous experiences over the past month, it was incredibly relaxing and stress free, a real bubble. But we probably needed it, next up was the Galápagos.

CHAPTER 7

Day 28 to 34: ECUADOR
The Galápagos Islands

Lonesome George and other New Friends

It was an early start the next day to catch the 8:10 AM flight from Quito to the Galápagos Islands, and a fond farewell to our personal guide Aldo and driver Richard who had been with us on and off for the past 10 days or so in wonderful Ecuador.

I knew we would learn a great deal on the Galápagos, but this was an early one; it has the first ecological airport in the world. The consultant was Pierre Yves Cousteau, grandson of the famous Jacques; we hoped he had more luck with his baby dolphins.

A rather battered coach, which looked as if it had spent too many day trips from the East End of London to Margate, took us the short distance to a small port where the RIBs were waiting to ferry us to La Pinta. A twenty-four cabin cruiser known as one of the best of the Galápagos fleet according to our agents, Audley Travel.

'No one seems to have much luggage,' said Helene, as a few small bags were thrown onto the RIBs by the crew.

'Well, I've never done a cruise before, maybe you don't need much,' I replied as the crew began to struggle with our huge cases, much to the amusement of our fellow guests.

'We're not really cruising though, we're exploring. Perhaps one only needs an explorer pack,' she whispered, as we pretended not to be the owners of the weighty matching luggage.

'What's in an explorer pack?' I asked.

'I have no idea but we've probably got all of it.'

We did indeed have the most luggage by far – I made a mental note to let people know it was not all for our few days on the Galápagos – apart from the five man film crew accompanying us to make a documentary about the impact of tourism on the islands. We appeared to be in the first edit. One evening I asked the head cameraman to take a photo of us against the sunset, nice shot if you like your heads chopped off, should be a good film.

Our cabin was a delight so we unpacked more clothes from our zippy-uppy bags than we had in any other location and I looked for somewhere to store the oversized cases; it seemed the cabin was designed for "explorer packs". I somehow expected portholes and bunk beds, but far from it; a large bed and bathroom, seating area to watch out for a variety of sea birds, dolphins, rays and possibly sharks, moonfish, or even whales, and a huge bedroom window providing beautiful views of the sea and islands. Like Mashpi, we left the blinds open to be woken by the sunrise over the Pacific each morning.

The first evening was an introduction to the captain, his small crew, our three marine biologist guides, and of course, our forty-six fellow guests sharing our adventure over the next few days. It's always good fun pre-judging your holiday companions in a hotel but even better in the confined space of a boat. Give the loud American couple in matching jungle gear and binoculars a wide berth, try not to get stuck on the table with the two girls who won't stop giggling and leave the couple not talking to each other with the nightmare son to sort themselves out. The guy in the Boater looks fun though. He was, Mario, a New York architect.

But we were here to investigate other species entirely and spot the Galápagos Big 15. It is indicative of the diverse wildlife on the archipelago that safaris have their Big 5 but the Galápagos has its Big 15. They are to be found on 16 volcanic islands and hundreds of islets in the middle of the Pacific Ocean straddling the equator 950 km from the South American coast. The largest island is Isabella shaped like a seahorse; it has a vast crater 6 km wide. We were to visit Isabella and eight of the other islands in this unique ecosystem sitting on a volcanic hotspot measuring 4 km across and over 1,000 km deep towards the Earth's core.

As a footnote to our voyage, exactly a month after we left the Galápagos, La Cumbre the volcano on Fernandina Island erupted sending a column of water vapour and magmatic gases 4 km into the sky above the islands. All ships were called back to port.

Let's get the Darwin Theory out the way before we move on. He was just 22 when brought in as first reserve to join the ship Beagle as an unpaid naturalist for a 5 year voyage starting in December 1831. He was seasick all the way and tried to jump ship at Tenerife, but they wouldn't let him. He had been toying with the idea of evolution by survival of the fittest, or "natural selection" (or *Hunger Games*) for some years before he visited the archipelago in 1835. In fact, many argue it was not his theory in the first place.

My precis of his 500 page book *"On the Origin of Species by Means of Natural Selection"* is this: creatures that are best equipped to their local environment refine and pass down their most important characteristics to the next generation to equip them for survival. Those creatures without the traits needed for their local conditions, die. His theory was that the refinement of these characteristics needed for the best possible chance of survival would eventually create a new species.

Impressed with my simplified version from the afternoon lectures I tried it out on Helene.

'Not bad, darling, but here's the tee-shirt I bought at the airport.' She held it out for me to read:

"It is not the **strongest** of the species that survives, nor the most **intelligent** that survives. It is the one that is the most **adaptable to change**."

'Oh! That's even shorter,' I said, somewhat crestfallen.

'Yes, and clever, and concise, but never mind, I bought it for you anyway,' she said with a smile and a kiss.

To expand on the tee-shirt principle, the finches on the islands for example, had to develop different bills, more like beaks, to be able to feed on the nuts and shelled fruits on the islands. If they didn't adapt by evolving this beak they starved and died. Interestingly, their beaks continue to evolve each generation to adapt to the foods available determined by the level of rainfall the previous generation experienced.

Another example are the beetles, one of the first species to colonise the new islands, they had small wings and could travel, wind assisted, from the mainland. Once they had established themselves on the islands and had sufficient food and protection they lost their wings, they simply didn't need them. Same with the cactus, they have evolved on the islands unlike those found elsewhere, by growing hard wooden trunks below a metre in height otherwise they will be eaten by the tortoises and iguanas, and of course their leaves have evolved into sharp needles to protect the fleshy pads – clever old Mother Nature again.

Our first excursion was with Grace, our favourite of the marine biologist guides, and we were in for a rare and privileged treat. Grace was a small German lady barely visible under the largest floppy khaki sun hat you can imagine.

'It's protection, darlinks, protection,' she would say from somewhere under the canvas folds.

She certainly had a Germanic efficiency as she herded our small group military style off the RIBs to the islands. As we walked, surrounded by seals and marine iguanas, we heard a cry in the distance.

'What's that, Grace? It sounds like a lamb?' I asked.

'Not on these islands, darlink. Hurry, hurry keep walkink, faster I'm thinkink,' she replied.

Its source was a baby seal born only a few moments ago. Its mother, with the umbilical cord still attached, was licking the newborn.

Helene knows about these things from her role as a mother and baby therapist, so she explained to the group that mum was commencing the bonding process immediately to allow her to recognise her offspring. Grace agreed; Mum needs to find baby easily when she returns after a full week feeding, leaving the baby seal to fend for itself. This may seem odd, even cruel, but it is how a seal's life is; they fish and eat for a week then sleep in the sun on an island for a week – not so bad really.

But of course, they have no predators on land, very few of the indigenous species do, that's partly why we can interact with them so easily. To say they are tame gives the wrong impression, because it suggests they have been "broken in" or trained, clearly this is not the case. They have just never learned to be fearful of humans – there's a bit of Darwinism right there I guess. As an example, while we were watching a mockingbird it walked over the feet of one of our party, we are not seen as predators, I'd like to think just friends.

It would be possible to touch or pet the seals, birds, iguanas and others, we don't of course, no human intervention is permitted. I was surprised to learn from Grace that she and her colleagues always let nature take its course. Even if the lava started to flow again threatening some of the animals they would not intervene to save them. The one exception is if we humans have created it, such as when a seal was caught in a discarded fishing line that Grace unwrapped to free the animal.

Next up were the "Blue Footed boobies", number two of the Big 15. Huge birds with, well, bright blue feet due to the collagen in their fish diet – there is another variant with red feet, guess what they're called? They are spectacular to watch as they dive from 10 metres or more, entering the water at 60 mph to catch their prey, they have air sacks in their head to cushion the impact with the water. Living side by side with the boobies are literally hundreds of frigatebirds, wonderfully named the "Great Frigatebird" and "Magnificent Frigatebird". These guys have the distinctive red pouch on their chest they inflate to attract females. They are large birds with black plumage to really show off their red pouch, forked tails, long hooked bills and a 2 metre. wingspan. They are able to soar for weeks on wind currents, and they can sleep on the wing. Remarkable.

'Snorkelling today, Helene,' I announced cheerily over what they call an international breakfast on board. I knew this was going to be a hard sell.

'Last time I went snorkelling I was bitten by a Trigger Fish in the Maldives.'

'Nasty place to get bitten,' I joked, hoping to lighten the mood and encourage her back on the horse as they say.

'It's not funny. And it looks very cold out there.' This was going to be tougher than I thought.

It was a squeaky climb into wetsuits and onto the RIBs, full of expectation and anticipation. The Galápagos didn't let us down, no sooner had we entered the clear blue water with sun streaming through the plankton in hundreds of pinprick spotlights than we were met by the Galápagos green turtles, what fun they were. It didn't get any better for Helene, she was stung by a jellyfish, but did it put her off? No, she was back in after a spray of something from the explorer pack, to play with the turtles.

After another delightful lunch of fish, salad and a local cakey thing Helene couldn't eat, it was onto the RIBs again for the short crossing to an island the good ship La Pinta had sailed us to and anchored off overnight. This was to be an excursion onto the volcanic island to visit the iguanas. Hundreds and hundreds of marine iguanas tightly packed together to keep themselves warm as they waited for the sun to appear from behind the clouds and heat the black volcanic rock upon which they like to sunbathe.

There are three iguanas in the Galápagos Big 15: the land iguana, the larger Santa Fe land iguanas looking like dragons and the very prehistoric black marine iguana. Funny thing about these, there is a misconception that they spit and when you have a carpet of them in front and around you it's easy to believe they are doing exactly that. On closer examination they're not, they are sneezing salt. With the fish they eat they obviously consume a lot of salt water as they swallow their prey, the salt is filtrated and held in glands behind their nose, they then lie on the rocks sneezing, thereby propelling their salty snot all over their companions on the warm lava stone. Nice.

Bing Bong.

'Ladies and gentlemen there will be a short presentation on tomorrow's excursions at 7:00 PM over cocktails, and dinner will be served at 7:30,' announced our captain.

'Oh, Gawd! I'm beginning to like cruising, Helene,' I said.

Over an extremely agreeable three course dinner with fine wines we exchanged stories of the day with our fellow passengers, and then it's a couple of drinks on the top deck and bed around 10:00 PM. I absolutely adored being gently rocked to sleep by the incredibly quiet boat knowing we would be woken by the sun streaming into our cabin offering a new view for the start of another intriguing day. Did I say I like cruising? I really like cruising.

After a hearty breakfast – full English if you want it, cold meats and cheeses for the Germans and everything for the Americans – it was the start of another adventure to meet more of our Big 15. Today was the turn of the land iguanas, beautiful looking creatures in gold, orange, yellow and red about a metre long, maybe more. They usually sit completely still soaking up the sun looking intently at observers in an inscrutable way, until they decide to go walk about.

Floppy hatted Grace was our guide again and was in her element.

'Quick, don't be missink this please,' she said, as we were ushered forward and then abruptly stopped by her arms held out wide holding us back.

'Lettink them go first I think,' she said as two huge iguanas walked side by side on our path like an elderly married couple. On these islands iguanas have the right of way, so our party had to back up and make way for Mr. and Mrs. Iguana; quite right too, they were here first.

On that point there was a fascinating talk given by the biologists that posed an interesting question. The islands in the Galápagos archipelago were created out of the sea by volcanic eruption and very few have been inhabited by humans. Obviously, birds can fly to the new islands but how on Earth did the mammals get there?

They walked. I'm joking; we've had the walking Moai in Rapa Nui and the walking trees in Mashpi Rainforest but walking mammals between islands? That's ridiculous.

No, they didn't walk, they sailed.

These islands were created between five hundred thousand and four million years ago, the eldest nearest the mainland. Over time the mammals like the land iguanas and tortoises were occasionally cast adrift on reeds or some kind of vegetation raft that drifted across the water on the two trade winds from South America and the Caribbean to a newly created island in the archipelago. Still today islands have species that are unique to them such as the Sante Fe iguana only found on the small island of, well, Sante Fe. And the tortoises, although as a single species they all "sailed" from the mainland originally inhabiting fifteen different islands each with their own habitat, as Darwin's theory goes they adapted to their different environments. There are now tortoises on only eight islands but each of them is a completely different and unique species.

The Saddleback tortoise is a good example. The traditional tortoise we think of has a dome shell, adapted for wet zones where the food is plentiful and close to the ground. But those ferried across to an island where the terrain was just dust quickly devoured the low hanging fruit of the cactus and were unable to reach the branches, or pads, higher up. Mother Nature stepped in and adapted their shells to remove the back collar to allow their neck to reach further up the cactus; she also evolved longer legs to provide them with greater height to get above the wooden trunk of the cactus. They adapted to their environment and survived as a completely new species and are of course unique to just one island in the Galápagos.

I digress, our day was completed by a panga ride in the RIB – panga meaning no dry or wet landing on the islands – to hug the craggy coast line just feet away from the rocky cliffs and get up close and personal with the island's wildlife. Or as Grace put it in her eloquent and straightforward way, 'Keep lookink, keep lookink, it's what you're here to see. Are you thinkink this is a holiday?'

We looked and saw Nazca boobies, a beautiful white bird with a long pink bill and bright yellow eyes, flightless cormorants, poor things look so sorry for themselves with their shrivelled wings, Darwin again. Marine iguana clinging to the cliffs in any sunlight they can find, sea lions and Fur seals sunbathing or fishing and penguins, yes penguins on the equator. One species not in the Big 15 but an absolute delight is the storm petrels, large groups of these birds dance on the water, their feet just touching the surface as they pirouette across the waves looking for small floating insects. Somebody should really put them to music.

On our return to La Pinta at the end of each day it's off the RIBs for snacks and local delicacies with exotic fruit drinks on the sun deck. Or a Cerveza and a Sauvignon, Chilean this time, if you've got to know Felipe our friendly head waiter, who always had our two glasses chilled ready for our return. Then we would often watch an amazing pink and orange sunset against a darkening blue sky as the sun disappeared over the Pacific to mark the end of another glorious day.

Nine out of the Big 15 so far and still much to see as we cruised overnight to Rabida a small island great for snorkelling. An introduction by Dries our Naturalist Guide included the chandelier cactus, a great name and you can imagine what they look like. Then the killer trees. They look like an apple tree and bear similar fruit, but the fruit is poisonous, if you touch the leaves your hands will swell and itch for days and the bark will bring you out in welts. Tortoises love them.

A brief yet extremely entertaining interlude followed, Dries ferried us by RIB to Post Office Bay to mail our cards and collect post from previous visitors that we could deliver by hand on their behalf. This was a custom dating back to the 18th century when whalers kept a wooden barrel on the island for precisely that purpose. As they journeyed through the islands they would place their letters in the barrel to be collected by other sailors on their passage home and delivered by hand. No stamps required. The tradition continues today.

So, while we were writing our cards home Dries stood on a rock and read out the addresses of those cards already in the barrel, anyone recognising a location took the card to deliver personally when they returned home. Helene was a little ambitious.

'We're going there,' she said, to almost every second card Dries pulled from the barrel.

'Helene, we're going to Auckland but it's an awfully big place,' I cautioned her.

'We're going there,' she said, as an address in Brisbane was announced by Dries.

I was able to negotiate her down to three, one for Hawaii and one each for New Zealand and Australia in cities we would eventually visit, although how far these deliveries may take us off our planned route I had no idea.

When we returned to the sandy red beach for snorkelling along the volcanic perimeter of the cove we had been joined by five sea lions with the same idea and wanting to play. We sat squirming on the soft sand trying to squeeze into our wetsuits and ventured out into the clear water to swim with shoals of pink fish and oversized parrot fish in greens and blues, with one that was so electric blue it looked like it had a swallowed a halogen light. Sure enough, out came the young pups to play a game where they swim up to your mask take a look and frighten the life out of you, then disappear.

Later we came across an odd creature on two legs. There's a funny thing about the Brits abroad, we're on a tiny remote uninhabited island in the Galápagos thousands of miles from home in our group of eight or so walking a narrow dusty trail with our guide, when another smaller group approach from the opposite direction. We let each other pass with lots of shuffling and apologies and the only word spoken? A bright and cheerful "Morning!" as we pass.

It was one lunchtime while we were enjoying a sharpener on the deck when Helene spotted a whale not far from the boat, and as you can imagine this caused a bit of a commotion.

Bing Bong.

'Good afternoon, ladies and gentlemen, a whale has been spotted off the starboard bow.' Around forty-eight guests, various marine biologists and the film crew rushed for the small forward deck, binoculars flying around their necks and cameras, with lenses only the paparazzi should have, held aloft. Priceless, no further sightings, at least not that day.

One of the most distinguished residents of the Galápagos is the Giant tortoise, what an elegant and charming amphibian it is and my goodness what a struggle they have had over the years. After their "voyage" from the mainland to settle on fifteen islands some simply failed to adapt and died, unable to survive in their new environment. Then came Darwin and the sailors, they discovered that tortoises could survive without food or water for 6 months or more, and they tasted good. Hundreds of thousands of them were taken by the mariners as fresh food for long trips.

Next up was further human intervention. As Spanish, Ecuadoreans and oddly Germans started to populate the islands, they brought with them pets, livestock and inadvertently rodents, all of which threatened the tortoise community. Rats, cats, pigs and ants ate the eggs, and goats and donkeys found the tortoise's meat to be a delicacy, much like the sailors.

The tortoise population was decimated and was close to extinction, one island went from thousands to just fourteen. They became a protected species in the 1960's when a research centre was set up and the newly introduced predators were killed off or removed from the islands where they were not indigenous.

And so, we come to the sad story of Lonesome George, and further evidence of Darwin's theory. There is a small uninhabited island at the north of the archipelago called Pinta, our boat was named after it, and like the other islands it developed its own species of tortoise. By the time this island was investigated by the newly formed protection centre in 1971 they found just one remaining tortoise; George. Not a particularly Ecuadorean name but he became a national hero – the last one remaining on the island, the last of his species.

Grace was a volunteer at the time and helped the centre scour the world for another of the Pinta species and hopefully a mate for George, but without luck. It was a slim chance that one of the species had been taken and sold to a zoo or a private collector, but it was not to be, George was on his own. In an effort to preserve the species George was retired to the protection centre and introduced to some female tortoises from other Galápagos islands , but he was not interested. As Grace explained,

'I'm introducink George to some of the prettiest and most beautiful lady tortoises for matink but none of them could seduce him.' Poor George.

As we discovered earlier, the principle of protection on the Galápagos is no human intervention, even if the creature's life is in jeopardy, or in this case a complete species. So, artificial insemination from George was not an option. After 40 years of steadfastly maintaining his virginity George died aged 106 on the 24th June 2012.

'So, what happened next, Grace?' I asked.

'George was taken to America for stuffink,' she replied.

Now I'm as sentimental about these things as the next person but while others in our party exhibited a far more sombre and respectful demeanour I was trying not to laugh.

'David!' hissed Helene elbowing me in the ribs. 'I'm sorry, Grace, do go on,' she said.

'We are visitink George today,' she announced, 'he is livink here, dead.'

'I'm sorry, I don't quite understand, I thought he was stuffed and in America?' I asked.

It turned out that during the taxidermy process, which I can only guess took some while – he weighed in at over a quarter of a ton – a final resting place was built specifically for George in the tortoise sanctuary at the research centre. It is open to the public if you book some time in advance but given Grace's involvement with the project we were apparently privileged to be invited to take a look at poor old stuffed George on display.

The house of worship for Lonesome George, for that is how it felt, was a wood and steel structure about the size of a large double garage. Bizarrely, to enter and exit you have to stand in a small airlock chamber that brought the temperature up or down, I didn't notice any difference, to the ambient temperature in the final mausoleum.

A very solemn and melancholy young man in an *"I love Lonesome George"* cap ushered us into the far too small airlock.

'Squeezy, squeezy please,' he instructed as we all shuffled in close to each other. I'm afraid that was nearly it for me. Our young guide then drew our attention to the sign above the airlock door.

'Six minutes only please, six minutes only,' he advised. Not seven or even rounded down to a manageable five, but a definitive six. Presumably some poor sod with a spreadsheet worked out how many people may attend this reptilian Mecca during the year, divided it by the opening times and hey presto it's six minutes. I should add we were the only group showing the slightest interest in visiting the remains of old George.

Once inside the darkened room with the doors firmly shut to protect the carcass from any outside contamination there was a still peacefulness as our young man gently whispered something in Spanish. With a flourish he pulled a switch to reveal a huge glass cube in which our stuffed Lonesome George was serenely lit with beams of soft light.

'No photos please; no photos.'

You could have heard a pin drop, had it not been for the stifled guffaws from one of our party. Another switch illuminated a beautiful artificial backdrop of what was presumably intended to represent George's home on Pinta many years ago.

Having paid our respects for 6 minutes, frankly 60 seconds would have done me, the radiant glow in George's glass box was abruptly switched off and it was "squeezy, squeezy please" into the exit airlock to be released back into the real world. What a hoot!

We left La Pinta for the flight to Guayaquil and then a connection on to Lima the capital of Peru, but I should allow the Galápagos Islands themselves to provide the last impressions. There had been so many wonderful, magical moments in such a short space of time and my goodness we'd learned a huge amount about the wildlife and its evolution by Darwin's natural selection.

So, two to finish with. A small group of us sat on the rocks in a bay on our second day waiting for the RIB to return us to La Pinta, there was a silence amongst us as we stared in awe at the beauty of these islands, their landscape and of course their inhabitants. We began to list what we could see just from that spot – turtles, penguins, sea lions, dolphins, boobies, pelicans, frigatebirds, flightless cormorants and marine iguanas all from that small cove, incredible.

On our final day Helene and I sat on a lookout platform with our friend Grace high above a rocky cove where we had been kayaking with seals and turtles in the morning. As we looked out to sea admiring the panorama and listening to more of Grace's wonderful stories about the wildlife, there was what looked like a large black arm thrust out of the water followed by a huge splash, then another smaller one. We grabbed our binoculars in time for us to see it repeated, bigger this time as the body of a Humpback whale and its calf soared out of the sea and crashed back down. Wow! The three of us watched for 5 minutes as mum and baby played in the Pacific. It was quite emotional, but that's what the Galápagos does to you, it is a beautiful and emotional experience, I wouldn't have missed it for the world.

CHAPTER 8

Day 35 to 42: PERU

Lima, Arequipa and Colca Canyon

Dancing in the Streets

After an active and spectacular week on board La Pinta we were looking forward to a couple of days rest and relaxation in our fourth South American major city; Lima the capital of Peru, a city with a colourful past and a pretty vibrant present.

Our flight from Baltra airport was on time and without incident although we very nearly blew it when we reached Guayaquil for our transfer to Lima. We made ourselves comfortable in the VIP salon with plenty of time for the connection, or so we thought. After a light lunch and a glass of Sauvignon, Peruvian and surprisingly good, compliments of Priority Pass, we settled down to discuss our "bestest bits" from the Galápagos Islands, not an easy task for either of us.

'That's odd,' said Helene, 'why is our flight number flashing *Gate Closing* on the screens? And why are there no other flights showing before ours?'

'No idea. We've plenty of time,' although it slowly began to dawn on me that there was an hour difference between the mainland and the Galápagos; well you don't expect it on a domestic flight do you? We made it, just, but as we now know, Gate Closing means you're about to get a personal tannoy invitation to board the plane.

Lima – *an animated lively city with much to offer and many surprises.* The first surprise was that it is a city with no weather. It is consistently 18 degrees almost all year round, always overcast and it never ever rains. There are out of work weather forecasters driving taxis and serving in bars all over the city, it just doesn't differ from 18 degrees, overcast and dry. Perhaps that's not surprising as it was only the second city to be built in a desert after Cairo.

It was known as the City of Kings when it was the political, commercial and religious capital of the Spanish, with influence all over South America. It was also reputed to be the most beautiful and cultural city in Spanish America for 200 years until a colossal earthquake in 1746 triggered its decline.

It is also massive, 140 km wide with a 10M population, a third of Peru's total, it's big, and once had inflation to match, would you believe 5,000% in a year. How they coped with that I have no idea but our guide Helen said there really were doctors and lawyers driving taxis and serving in bars when the economy went pop. After two new currencies, a military coup and a new government the economy stabilised, inflation is now a manageable 3% and the city is thriving and fun.

In 1920 they claimed their independence and were presented with celebratory gifts from all over the world. The British gave them a football stadium, of course. Still the national stadium today, never won anything though.

'Good grief,' said Helene, in a surprised voice, 'what on earth is that thing?' She was pointing at a dog walker, or more specifically the thing at the end of the dog walker's lead.

'Ah, that,' said guide Helen with pride, 'is the ugliest dog in the world. And that's official.'

'Why would you want an ugly dog? Don't they say a dog always resembles its owner?'

'But it's adorable and affectionate,' Helen argued.

'No it's not, it's unsightly and unattractive.'

This was going nowhere. 'Beauty is in the eye of the beholder, I suppose, even if it is hairless with a Mohawk,' I suggested, trying to diffuse the growing tension.

To be fair it deserves its accolade, it's like a small skinny whippet and appropriately called a Peruvian Hairless dog. It was on the verge of extinction but the government stepped in and it's now protected. Revolting little mutts if you ask me, it seems Helene agreed.

Another surprise about Lima is that there are a lot of dead bodies...

Guide Helen didn't appear to be talking to Helene after the comments she made about their national dog, but she took us to an archaeological site right in the middle of the city, in fact strangely it has a main road running straight through the middle of it. The tide of tarmac waits for no man however old. These men were over 2,000 years old, way before the Incas we all associate with Peru.

Helen showed us around an enormous flat-topped pyramid, similar to the ones near the Hacienda Zuleta, but this was vast and surprisingly built with cement and bricks. The bricks are called Adobe, about the same size as a house brick, but are arranged vertically not horizontally, and the cement is made from sand, crushed shells and weirdly egg white. The whole structure is larger than a football stadium and has seven layers rising to about 30 metres. Very impressive and most peculiar to find in the middle of a noisy cosmopolitan city. They are still excavating, but to date they've unearthed sixty-seven bodies from under the pyramid, all female, all sacrificed to the sun, the moon or Harry, or whatever their god was then.

Fast forward 1,500 years or so and they still seemed to have this issue with burying their dead. In 1945 they discovered the catacombs under the impressive Lima cathedral where they found over 30,000 bodies, or at least thousands and thousands of bones once belonging to 30,000 bodies.

As we learned from Rapa Nui these things tend to start at the top of the social demographic with the elite and filter down to the commoners, so it was in Lima. When senior members of the church died they were buried in the mausoleum under the cathedral and as time went by more, not quite so senior people, were buried in the same place until almost everyone whether distinguished or not was buried there. Buried, may not be completely appropriate though; they let the bodies decompose in baths of lime then, when only the bones were left, they were thrown into a selection of large wells dug deep in the catacombs. When excavated one well was found to contain bones more than 10 feet deep. This went on until 1820 when some bright spark decided to build a cemetery, if building is what you do to create a cemetery.

'I know someone who would kill to get their hands on these bones, if you know what I mean,' said Helene.

'No, what do you mean?' asked Helen. They seemed to be talking again having buried their differences, so to speak.

'Bones are really expensive back home and I have an anatomy teacher who never has enough to go around at training sessions.'

'Well there's plenty here, but we like to display them to honour the dead,' Helen said pointing at a bizarre exhibition area.

Strangely all the bones had been sorted into types and are now displayed in the catacombs in what I suppose are meant to be artistic arrangements. There was a tall pyramid of skulls in one corner, a large circular fan of femurs in another, a delightful rack of rib cages on a wall and a sizeable selection of sacra. Surreal, one might say.

Despite the rather macabre nature of the city's past we had great fun walking the streets watching it all go on. A highlight was visiting the frenetic food market. Quails' eggs, sweet corn and mussels seemed to be popular with the locals along with some fruits which neither of us could identify and every conceivable colour and shape of potato, there are over two thousand varieties in Peru with some growing wild. And of course, chillies: fresh, dried, chopped, sliced, whatever takes your fancy, there are two hundred varieties to choose from and fifty-two different types of corn, including black corn that looks awful and tastes unexpectedly really good.

Peru has also been voted the Best Culinary Country in the world, not for just this year but for the past 5 years, this we had to take advantage of.

'Helene, I've booked us on a culinary tour tonight,' I announced enthusiastically.

'I'm not eating Guinea pig!'

'Cuy Chactado,' I corrected her.

'I don't care what it's called, I had one when I was a child and I'm not eating a pet.'

'But it's been a delicacy here for 5,000 years and it tastes like duck, you like duck,' I argued.

'That's even worse, he was called Chucky and I'm not eating his cousins.' This wasn't going to happen. We agreed to go on the tour providing Chucky was off the menu.

It was quite an experience visiting half a dozen very varied restaurants starting with a Pisco Sour, the national drink of Peru; it even has its own national holiday. Then a course or two in each restaurant including an excellent ceviche, Helene's favourite, followed by lomo saltado, a stir-fried beef in onions, tomatoes and fiery yellow Peruvian chillies called aji amarillo which you're not allowed to touch, you crush them in the dish then remove. And beef heart, seasoned with garlic, cumin, chilli and grilled. No Cuy Chactado served thank goodness, she'd never have forgiven me.

We finished the 5 hour tour at a party in one of the squares where a wonderful Peruvian band full of pipes and guitars was having fun as the locals danced a sort of Peruvian jig. It was unwise to prevent Helene from joining them and dance the in the square, so we all joined in.

We then attempted the walk across the Bridge of Sighs. Custom has it that you hold hands and hold your breath and then walk across with your loved one. If you can both hold your breath all the way across your wishes will come true. On the third attempt we made it and found our way back to the hotel rather full of wonderful local food and somewhat tiddly pom pom.

One last impression from Lima before we moved on to Arequipa in the highlands was a walk in the park. We walked through the park in the centre of Lima on a Sunday when there are the usual street food vendors, artists with their dubious creative work hanging on the perimeter fence, just like they do on a Sunday in Hyde Park and families on their post luncheon constitutional. Then we heard the unmistakable rhythm of salsa. Uh-oh!

When Helene's legs and arms start to sway to the tempo I know I'm in trouble, they didn't call her snake hips in her younger days for nothing.

'C'mon this is for us!' she said and grabbed me firmly by the hand.

'I'm not dancing in the street again,' I protested, to no avail as I was marched towards the music.

'It'll be fun, just do your normal bouncy thing you do.'

'Bouncy thing? I thought you liked my dancing?' I complained.

'I do, well not so much like, but it makes me laugh.' Oh good.

In the middle of the park was a circular amphitheatre about twelve rows deep, across its 30 metre diameter, it was packed full of locals clapping along to the music and cheering those on the dance floor below. They seemed to be having a lot of fun so we joined the elderly citizens all swinging to the music, a damn sight better than we could do.

I relied on the old repertoire of a cross between jazz, jive, rock, ceroc and salsa, or a bouncy thing as I now know Helene calls it. I thought we contributed to the Sunday afternoon version of Strictly Peru quite well and the locals were very respectful in stepping back and giving us room to take centre stage on the outdoor ballroom. As we climbed the steps back up and out of the amphitheatre I'm sure I heard someone say "a-maz-ing", but perhaps it was drowned out by the laughter.

The following day was another chaotic domestic flight this time from Lima to Arequipa 1,000 km southeast back towards the Atacama Desert. But what a wonderful city, a complete contrast to Lima, more like a village, even though it is the second largest city in Peru with a million inhabitants. It is known as the White City, either because it is built entirely in pearly white volcanic stone, or as the locals believe, the name originates from the high-class Spaniards who used to live there and didn't allow any mixed race. Frightfully non-PC by today's standards and understandable why the folklore was changed.

Arequipa means "stay here" and we could see why. Helene and I fell in love with the area immediately, it is a beautiful town full of music and surrounded by active snowcapped volcanoes. In fact there are 183 in the region and 30% of them are active, as we were about to find out.

Our hotel dated back to 1794 and was conveniently situated just off the impressive main square that was full of bars and restaurants. It was originally the mint and had high vaulted barrelled ceilings with the remnants of original frescoes and an impressive open air courtyard where breakfast was served to the sounds of a Peruvian harp played by a friendly old gnarled local.

As we made our way up to the square to explore, always my favourite bit when we arrive somewhere new, we heard the distinctive sound of Peruvian pan flutes, drums, guitars and ukulele. I'm a sucker for these groups in London let alone in their homeland so it was onto the bar terrace overlooking the square and with a little encouragement and a handful of Sols, the local currency, we could enjoy traditional Peruvian music.

Like Simon & Garfunkel's "El Condor Pasa – *I'd rather be a hammer than a nail*", that old Peruvian classic "*Paloma Blanca*" and the definitive stanza "*Guantanamera*". Come to think of it I did vaguely recognise a couple of them from a dodgy wine bar in Paddington, quite appropriate I thought given we were in Peru.

Later that evening we returned to the square for dinner to be greeted by a full orchestra, probably eighty or more, supporting a massive choir, all dressed in black and lit in red against the white cathedral, very grand. We acquired a front of house table on the third floor overlooking the show and enjoyed an eclectic mix including Handel's Messiah, Star Wars, the theme from The Omen and some odd local fare requiring the orchestra to perform Mexican Waves by holding their instruments in the air, strings first, then percussion, brass etc. Odd; fun, but odd.

The following day our tour around Arequipa with our guide Victor and our driver coincidentally also Victor, included a food market with fruits we were still unable to identify, vast displays of quails' eggs, mussels, black corn on the cob and potatoes in blues, white, red and every size and shape imaginable.

But the culinary highlight for me was the visit to the cathedral, or more specifically one particular 18th century religious frieze some 10 metres across above a momentous tomb.

'Is that what I think it is?' asked Helene as we approached the artwork high on the wall.

'Yes,' said Victor, 'it's our Last Supper,' waving his arm dramatically as if introducing the real thing.

It was indeed a version of The Last Supper, but with one interesting variation.

'Can you spot why it's Peruvian?' he asked.

'Well, there's Jesus in the centre holding court,' I said, 'and his Disciples either side, in various unnatural poses like the original.'

'Yes,' said Helene, taking over. 'There are the flagons of wine, cups, cutlery and salady bits, but what on earth is that?'

'I think that may be Chucky,' I said, barely able to control the laughter.

There in the middle of the table for the main course of the feast was Cuy Chactado, roasted Guinea pig. Well there we are; who would have thought that Jesus would have selected the national Peruvian dish as his last meal?

I may have been a bit harsh on Arequipa because we did love it, the views were spectacular, wedged as it is between two enormous active volcanoes – caught between a rock and a hard place. It was comfortable, relaxing, full of music and had some great restaurants and bars. Next up was the trip to Colca Canyon and getting a little too close to one of those active volcanoes for comfort.

Arequipa was at 2,300 metres, and to get to Colca Canyon we had to go up to 4,910 metres, across the top of the mountain range and then down to Colca Lodge our hotel in the canyon at 3,650 metres. As we have already discovered altitude is a tricky customer and can do some funny things to you. Breathlessness, headaches and dizziness are common, some people faint, like our guide Victor, although he managed to keep with us this time, and others go a bit doolally, particularly those who spend weeks in the observatories on top of the highest mountains, apparently.

'Why does Victor keep looking at my hands like that?' Helene whispered to me in the back of the car.

'Which one?'

'Both of them I think.'

'Both Victors?'

'No, both hands, look he's doing it again,' she mumbled, 'now he's looking at yours.'

'Victor, why are you looking at our hands?' I asked.

'I'm checking for signs of altitude sickness,' he answered, as we both started to inspect each other's hands looking for anything that might be a little out of the ordinary. 'It's your nails and lips. If they go white we may need to give you oxygen.' This seemed a little alarming.

But we were okay thanks to a variety of preventative remedies including Helene's homeopathy tablets, bottles and bottles of water, chocolate, chewing on a cocoa leaf and half a pint of steaming hot Inca tea. An infusion we were served at about 4,000 metres in a shack perched on the side of a mountain in the middle of nowhere. This concoction of herbs, leaves and unknown greenery stuffed into a glass of boiling water may have done the trick and apart from bloody noses when we sneezed into a tissue we seemed to be coping pretty well so far, but we were to be at altitude for some while yet so we'd have to see how it went.

On the road across the mountain tops, a surprisingly good road actually, Victor spotted an ash cloud on the horizon, the horizon we were headed towards.

'I've always wanted to see an active volcano,' I said.

'Be careful what you wish for,' came the voice of reason from Helene. The plume of volcanic ash spiralling into the sky became wider, thicker and darker as we approached, but it was some way off, it'll be fine. It was then joined by a tornado. And another a bit closer.

'I've always wanted to see a tor…'

'Oh, do be quiet, David,' said Helene.

Over the coming days, Ubinas as the volcano is known, continued to spew ash and the smoke became thicker and darker. The volcano watch in the mornings was always intriguing as we planned our day.

Colca Canyon is the deepest in the world at over 3,000 metres from ridge to river, more than the Grand Canyon, which was surprising, not so grand now then. The hills around the canyon are intricately laced with terraces built by the Incas to grow food in the fertile volcanic earth of the steep elevations; it was quite breathtaking looking down into the scarred terraced valley as we navigated the mountains.

It was also flipping freezing, the temperature falls as the sun goes down, and just keeps going. But the hotel had underfloor heating, which was so hot we had to use those soft towelling slippers some hotels provide, just to walk around the bed. Helene took full advantage, using it as an improvised steam room of some sort. I arrived back to what may have looked like the end of a rather good party from the swinging sixties; there was underwear strewn all over the floor. Lingerie, smalls and some might say scanties, were displayed and spread everywhere; I didn't know where to tread. It looked like a winter sale at Rigby and Peller.

'What's all this then? Our smalls seem to steaming on the ceramic.'

'You should be thankful, I've washed them all and now they're drying on this hot floor. Needs must when you're an intrepid explorer you know.' Yes, Helene knows about these things.

Our hot hotel for the few days in the canyon was Colca Lodge a largely wooden construction perched just above the winding ribbon of silver that is the Colca River. Only about 20 metres across, fast enough to have fun in the canoes but sufficiently shallow to get out and push if the need arises. It also has its own alpaca and lama farm, stables, a zip wire across the canyon and volcanic hot springs. There are also four large, stone built, deep pools alongside the river at a warm 36 degrees with a bar where the staff bring you drinks in your selected volcanic Jacuzzi. Just what we wanted, to wallow in the mineral rich waters and recount sights and stories of the past few weeks, including the slightly disturbing story about Peruvian hats. Hats are not often disturbing, but this one was.

During our sometimes quite hairy drive around and over the volcanoes to Colca our guide Victor and our driver Victor – odd, doesn't sound like a traditional Peruvian name – recounted the tale. In fact, to digress a moment before we get onto the exciting story about hats, guide Victor used to play Division 1 football in Peru and was due to be transferred to Newcastle Utd when he injured his back and was advised to give up the game.

Anyway, potential Magpie Victor recounted the reason why the diminutive women in the area, they really are rather small, makes 5ft 2" Helene look like Uma Thurman, wear either an elaborately decorated boater or a pointed embroidered textile affair.

Some time ago, but post Inca, there were two tribes in the area, both of whom claimed their heritage, culture and traditions were the founding ones, and this goes on today represented by their headgear. Now, we are all familiar with the Peruvian Bowler Hat the older ladies generally wear. A sort of brown bowler with the wide rimmed turned up, but in the Colca Canyon society one dynasty wears a heavily embroidered white boater and the other a tapered coned shape material version of a bobble hat.

The decorated white boater was a silent signal to the men in the village using the embellishments of silk flowers on the sides. One flower meant "I'm young, free and single, and could be interested in a night out counting alpaca". One flower on either side meant "hands off I'm married with a husband and alpaca", and a black floral decoration meant "I'm in mourning and know how many alpacas the old fella left me".

The second group's hat has evolved from a rather alarming and misguided tradition. To prove they were the real natives of the mountains they decided to make their heads pointed like the volcanoes that surrounded them. Not sure what cactus juice or Pisco Sour they were on when the elders conceived this ominous task but, as seemed to be fairly common in their culture, they made the children pay the price for their advancement. At birth they "trained" the baby's head into a more pointed shape by strapping wood to its head in a pyramid shape, can you imagine the damage this must have inflicted on skull and brain? Towards the end of the 19th century this barbaric custom was prohibited but the pointed headwear required for a pointed head continued. Hence the two types of hat favoured by the Colca Canyon women today dependent on their ancestral heritage.

We had enjoyed our "condor moment" at the Hacienda Zuleta, but both Victors assured us that Cruz del Condor was simply the best place in Peru to watch them. We left early in the morning for the best sighting because as the land warms the condor start to ride the thermals soaring higher and higher up the canyon towards the onlookers on the ridge. We had been told that once they ascend to the top of the canyon they put on an aerobatic show for the sightseers flying at eye level just a few metres away. We could not miss this.

And we were not disappointed; in fact it surpassed our expectations. As the bright morning warmed the air sure enough we looked down the canyon to see the condors searching for the thermals that would bring them up towards us, waiting some hundred metres above. We followed one pair to a ledge just 20 metres below us, and with the help of the binoculars we were privileged to observe a group of six magnificent birds including a chick no more than a couple of months old.

We watched for about an hour as this family tended the young one and preened their feathers in preparation for their morning flight. When the thermals were strong enough, just as the Victors had promised, they brought these mighty birds level with the canyon ridge allowing them to soar and glide, dive and ascend above our heads. What a treat, what a treasured memory.

Three unique and distinctive locations visited over just a few days. Cosmopolitan, vibrant Lima with its many surprises, beautiful Arequipa with its own soundtrack and the quite astounding Colca Canyon a dramatic and formidable landscape tamed by the Incas but still volatile and threatening. Impossible to choose a favourite, we enjoyed and appreciated all three.

CHAPTER 9

Day 43 to 50: PERU
Lake Titicaca, Cusco and the Sacred Valley

The Incredible Mr. Pachacutec

There is only one way to get from Colca Canyon to Lake Titicaca, that's the rollercoaster road we were becoming so familiar with. So, it was back up over the volcanic mountains to 4,910 metres and down into Puno the elegant city on the banks of this enormous lake. Due to "volcanic activity damaging the main road" as our driver Oscar explained, our journey was prolonged even further as we were forced to take a diversion via Juliaca, a city doing its best to impersonate Hong Kong, Helene thought. Bizarrely every other store on the narrow bustling streets was a photocopying shop, and they all looked busy.

The beautifully named Lake Titicaca, meaning Puma Mount, is the world's highest navigable body of water at 12,500 feet above sea level and is famously still. It covers 1,800 sq. km shared between Bolivia 40% and Peru 60%; Peru owned it all until the war in 1820. We were beginning to learn that these South America countries have had multiple ownership over the years and boundaries move with regularity as Bolivia, Peru, Chile, Ecuador, and Columbia are in continual conflict. Cartographers must make a fortune.

Our hotel was wonderfully situated in the centre of the old part of Puno, probably the most classical Peruvian town we'd visited so far. It was full of women in traditional dress, including the bowler hats we discovered in Colca Canyon and tiny shops in equally small cobbled streets selling mainly scarves, gloves, jumpers and all sorts of blankets we didn't know we needed, made from the famous alpaca fleece.

We were still at altitude, around 3,800 metres, which makes the very existence of Lake Titicaca even more impressive and the need to keep an eye on lips and nails for altitude sickness even more important. The advice includes eating only a little in the evening so it was an early night for us, well almost.

There was a rapid knocking on our door.

'Scusey, scusey. Two oxygens,' we heard in the hall.

'Oxygens? Did you order a cocktail, Helene?'

'Of course not, it's bedtime not party time.'

Standing in the doorway was a porter in full formal livery with a gas cylinder on a trolley in front of him. He pushed his way in, trolley first.

'Free ten minutos please,' he announced, wheeling the contraption to the bed rather to the surprise of Helene doing her best to pull up the covers.

He turned some taps, stretched some hoses and handed us a hissing mask each.

'Free ten minutos and leave by door,' he instructed and vanished as quickly as he had arrived.

What an odd scene we must have made tucked up in bed reading our books with masks on as the oxygen cylinder bubbled away beside us. My goodness it worked though, best night's sleep we'd had had in ages.

The morning was blue skies, bright sunshine and chilly for our first excursion on the lake with our personal guide Hilda, born and bred in Cusco, you can tell by the name. She had arranged a skipper and a boat for forty-eight with upper and lower decks. There were just the two of us, and Hilda.

Despite the size and width of the lake all traffic is siphoned through a narrow canal between acres of reeds to access the huge expanse of open water. Once through we approached Uros, a cluster of floating islands sounding like something out of Dr Doolittle. Around a hundred of these islands make up the community with 3-5 families living on each. I asked Hilda how on earth these people finished up with nomadic floating homes.

When the Spanish arrived to displace the Incas in 1535 some of the native population fled. Finding themselves on the reeds they began to eke out an existence using the local vegetation for food, shelter, boat making, weapons, in fact their whole life was based around these incredibly adaptable reeds.

The dried out tangled reed roots and mud are fashioned into large bricks about a metre square that are extremely buoyant, they then bind up to five hundred of them together to make a floating platform. Bundles and bundles of the tall reeds are cut and arranged a metre thick on the platform to provide a solid and comfortable flooring. More reeds are used to build shelters and the kitchen area is covered in the lakes mud and silt to prevent the whole thing from going up in smoke. A simple reed rope and heavy stone tethers it and there is your liveable floating island.

It's an odd sensation standing on the island when the wake from a boat starts to gently sway the whole construction, but that's exactly how they live today. As we were shown around by a family on their floating island built as it would have been half a millennium ago, I couldn't help but notice the solar panels powering the colour TV in the family's reed hut.

But it is a community, they have floating schools, floating clinics, a floating market to trade their crafts and they build large rafts not dissimilar to the Viking boats that invaded Britain. One key difference is that the Uros people use empty litre size plastic coke bottles on the inside of their reed hulls for buoyancy. There's progress. They have a simple but it appears rewarding life living off the tourist trade and a healthy diet of fish and what they call water chickens – coots.

After Helene negotiated the purchase of a cushion cover made by the family we were visiting, we ventured out of the Uros floating islands farther into the lake. It opened up into a vast expanse of water and after a couple of hours enjoying the boat to ourselves, not forgetting Hilda, we berthed on a rarely visited island called Llachon.

'Lunch is with a local family,' Hilda informed us. 'He's experimenting being a chef,' she added.

'Experimenting?'

'Yes, his hat business was doing well but it's beginning to fail now because of the lack of available women.'

'Not great when hats peak,' I offered, to the tutting of Helene.

'What's it got to do with available women?' she asked.

'He specialises in the woven hats young unmarried women wear around here, but either the girls are spoken for or they've gone to the cities,' Hilda said, with sorrow in her voice.

We strolled along the beautifully sandy deserted beach until we met a farmer and his wife cultivating a patch of sand in front of their rather ramshackle house – with one of the best views in the world – funny how value and worth can change across different cultures. Their seashore allotment was being prepared for planting potatoes. Potatoes grown on a beach? Well, that's one of the 2,000 varieties accounted for.

We met our local Llachon family for lunch and as Hilda had promised we were the Guinea pigs who were invited to test out the old man's culinary skills. Let's hope they're not on the menu. A lovely old fella definitely in the gnarled-old-local category served us more food than we could possibly eat. We enjoyed quinoa vegetable soup, grilled trout caught from the lake that morning, accompanied by rice and a few potato variations plus his garden vegetables, all washed down by lashings of Muna tea. It was excellent; his diversification from virgins' hats to home cooking was an inspired decision. As we ate in the family kitchen we made encouraging noises and positive gestures about his cooking and watched the occasional colourful fishing boat bob by on the beautiful lake. I think he and his family will do just fine.

After lunch he invited us to watch the skills he used in his day job. We entered his workshop where he demonstrated how he dyed alpaca wool with local herbs, spices and vegetation to make the yarn for the colourful hats. Helene enjoyed modelling them for us, much to the delight of the owner, although I assured him she was not available.

The following day we visited the first of what were to be many Inca sites. This one called Sillustani was a burial site where initially the elite in their society were laid to rest and towers, constructed from large boulders and stone transported from a quarry some miles away, were built above the graves. Smaller edifices were later constructed for the less powerful in their society as the commoners attempted to imitate their more senior neighbours. I'm thinking Rapa Nui and Lima Cathedral here. Interesting how different societies behave in similar ways.

We flew from Juliaca to Cusco, surprisingly uneventful, apart from me nearly getting arrested. Following our 'ten minutos' of bedtime oxygen and a wonderful sleep I hadn't experienced at altitude, Helene found a rather dubious looking shop that may have struggled to call itself a chemist. It did however sell canisters of oxygen, we think. The shopkeeper spoke no English and the canisters seemed to be labelled in a dozen languages that didn't include English or French, or Spanish. So that exhausted our opportunities of deciphering the description or instructions.

'I guess you just strap on this mask thingy and press the aerosol button,' was the best interpretation Helene could offer.

'We'll give it a go then, what could possibly go wrong?' I agreed. We packed and left for Juliaca airport.

Bing bong.

'Would Mr. David Charles please report immediately to the security desk?'

'I think they mean you,' said Helene, 'what have you done now?'

'Nothing! I wasn't there, I didn't do it. I'll deny everything.'

'It's not funny, David, you don't want to get locked up in Peru, well anywhere I suppose. You'd better see what they want.'

At security I was greeted, more collected really, this was not a "greeting" situation apparently, by a security guard, an airline officer and a plain clothed gentleman who frightened the life out of me – it's always the silent ones.

'What explosives you have?' said the uniformed security guard.

'What? None.' I stared at them blankly.

'You follow me, wear this,' he instructed, as the airline officer thrust a bright yellow high-vis jacket in my hand. My three companions marched me through security, out of the terminal and on to the airport tarmac. The silent one led the way, me in the middle, as our small procession filed across the roadway passed those odd vehicles you only ever see at airports and the dormant planes awaiting their crew.

I looked around to see Helene's face pressed against the window, arms out wide and palms showing in that "what on Earth is going on?" posture.

We arrived at a portacabin and entered to find two more security blokes standing around my case that I presumed was now in the hold, this was getting a bit serious.

'What explosives you have?' one of them asked.

'As I've tried to explain to your colleague here, I don't have any explosives,' I replied patiently.

'You open case,' he said, I'm sure I detected a small step back away from me.

I rummaged around and pulled out Helene's oxygen canister, at which point they all stepped back.

'It is forbidden!' security number one bellowed as security number two relieved me of the offensive weapon.

Of course it was, how foolish of me, it's a pressurised can. I bet we'd all laugh about this later.

I was marched back to the terminal to find Helene, hands on hips, waiting for me perhaps not as patiently as I would have hoped for. She had already guessed at my misdemeanour.

Cusco is another beautiful city of cobbled streets, pretty plazas and dramatic squares where much of the bustling life takes place. No hairdresser though, and I was beginning to look like Shaggy from Scooby-Doo, maybe a Rapa Nui topknot would suit me. Cusco is more touristy than we'd been used to but it was to be expected as it's the start point for the expedition everyone wants to take, to Machu Picchu, the Lost City of the Incas.

And so to the Incas, what a story. They were one of the most sophisticated and prominent civilisations in history and yet I knew so little about them compared to the Roman and Greek cultures. I was surprised to learn that their supremacy was in the 15th century, I thought they were much earlier. Curiously the Mexican Aztec Empire was formed in 1428 and the Inca Empire in 1438, 10 years difference between the founding of two immensely powerful and independent American and South American empires. Is it just me or does that sound too much of a coincidence? Erich von Daniken would probably have an interesting theory here, I'm sure.

Where to start? To quote Dylan Thomas "to begin at the beginning", where did the Incas come from? When we were motoring back across Lake Titicaca after our wonderful lunch with the Llachon family I had asked Hilda exactly that question. She said no one was really sure and went on to tell us a wonderful legend held in strong belief by the families who have been there for generations, especially the Uros islanders we had visited earlier that day. It goes like this.

When mankind was primitive and savage the sun god took pity on them and sent two of his children to civilise their society. Manco Capac and Mama Ocllo emerged from Lake Titicaca with a golden sceptre and were commanded to establish an empire wherever they sank their staff. They arrived at the hill on which Cusco is now built and thrust the sceptre into the ground, summoning mankind to begin the civilisation process by cultivating the land, weaving, farming etc. So, Cusco was founded with its name meaning "navel of the world". Lovely story, complete nonsense of course, but a great legend.

The factually accurate account started to unfold on our first expedition in Cusco with our fabulous guide Saiber. That's more like it, a really good Peruvian/Inca kind of name, straight out of Indiana Jones, let's hope not. Saiber was to be our guide for all our visits to the intriguing Inca sites, he was informative, fun and passionate about his subject and clearly enjoyed watching the astonishment on our faces as he revealed the fascinating stories of the Incas.

He started from the beginning. A few thousand years ago the Cusco area was visited by nomadic tribes following the llama they needed for food, clothing, tools and weapons. They ate the llama meat but discarded the organs by burying them, left nearby they would attract tigers, bears and other uninvited predators. When the llama and nomads returned from venturing south for the better climate and food, they found that the seeds in the buried stomachs and intestine had germinated and grown the very food the llamas liked of course. So, the nomadic hunter-gatherers settled in the Cusco area and became farmers growing food for themselves and the llama who no longer needed to migrate.

Fast forward to the 14th century and we have around a dozen tribes who had moved on from hunter-gatherers, to farmers, and then to warriors fighting between themselves to gain control of the most fertile land. We never learn do we? This is Rapa Nui all over again, but with a difference.

The best thing that could have happened to the warring tribes happened, they were all invaded.

As individual tribes they would have been slaughtered one by one, but some clever tribesman said "Hang on, if we stop fighting each other and combine as a single force we could give this lot a jolly good trouncing". A sort of early coalition you might say. And so, the Incas were formed, they didn't come from anywhere, they were already there.

True enough they gave their invaders a damn good thrashing, sent them packing and established a single community and eventually a new empire; the Inca Empire. As we all know, every good empire needs a good leader, and so it was with the Incas. By democratically electing a single leader for all the tribes they established a "royal family". By 1438, the ninth ruler, a young man of 22 took over from his dad the king to lead the Incas in establishing the empire across a large proportion of western South America centred on the Andean mountain range we had recently visited.

As Saiber took us to each jaw dropping site and described the origins of each one I was reminded of a Monty Python phrase; "what have the Romans ever done for us?" Let's corrupt it; what have the Incas ever done for us? Architecture, agriculture, communication, botanical R&D, transportation, medicine, brain surgery, yes, brain surgery, weather forecasting, codes, travel, irrigation and more. And all managed by our young king or, as he changed his name to, Pachacutec, which translated means "Transformer of the World". Yes, he had a bit of an ego too.

Pachacutec's strategy to build the empire was quite brilliant, using "conquest and peaceful assimilation", as he called it, or the carrot and the stick as I call it. He would send his army close to the tribe or community he intended to take over and then visit the tribe leader personally to reveal how wonderful his empire was going to be, offering them the opportunity to join. If they didn't his troops invaded and they joined anyway. The conversation may have gone something like this:

P: Hi, I'm Pachacutec and I'd like you to join our Inca Empire.

TL: No thanks we're farmers and textile makers, and we're happy as we are.

P: We have new technology that would increase your crop yield and you could use our roads to sell your textiles to new cities.

TL: Sounds interesting but no thanks.

P: See those thousand men armed to the teeth on that hill over there, that's my army.

TL: Oh!

P: And of course, as a former tribe leader you would get a valuable job at my new Administration Centre just outside Cusco.

TL: When do I start?

Young Mr. Pachacutec was indeed a warrior but he was also an accomplished statesman, diplomat and politician as well as an inspirational leader and an innovative thinker. During his relatively short period on the throne 1438 – '71 he developed some truly original, imaginative and inventive creations requiring a level of sophisticated thinking the world had not as yet seen – all this and they still hadn't invented the wheel.

In just 100 years by the 1530's the Inca Empire had expanded enormously out of its cultural home of Cusco, it stretched the length of the Andes from Ecuador to Chile a distance of 2,500 miles, with Pachacutec's strategy, innovations and I guess personal charisma they had conquered 300,000 square miles and developed an empire of 12 million Incas. Now that's impressive by any standards.

Saiber introduced us to more of the Inca sites and explained how this complex society developed under the watchful eye of its young ruler. I have to say Helene and I were completely absorbed in this part of the excursion; it was fascinating to hear the story unfold and see it reveal itself at various sites. Saiber was in his element and we were mesmerised by his narrative, what was supposed to be a 3 hour tour became 6 hours; I'm not sure who enjoyed it the most, we were all thrilled and inspired by it.

Oddly, I feel almost a responsibility to pass on the story of the incredible Mr. Pachacutec and his innovations, it is well worth retelling.

Pachacutec believed control was vested in communication so he created the Inca Trails, an incredible 25,000 miles of roads. They had two uses: for transportation of goods on the backs of llamas and alpacas and more importantly for his runners known as chasqui, for relaying messages; there were no horses there yet either, so on foot it was. He had built "communication centres" every 30 or 40 kilometres to allow the runners to rest and pass on the message to the next in the relay. Interesting that the distance between these resting points is about the same as a marathon from the Greek Empire.

He also realised that if the messages were sent verbally they may fall foul of Chinese whispers – we've all heard the story of the WW1 message "send reinforcements we're going to advance" finally delivered as "send three and four pence we're going to a dance" – or the baddies could capture the runners and beat the message out of them. So, a code was needed, but they couldn't read or write, problem. Not for Mr. P it wasn't.

He, or his Comms Team, probably over a marketing department lunch, developed such a sophisticated code system for his messages that despite UNESCO and the Peruvian Government funding a team of scientists, anthropologists and code breakers they can still not be deciphered. The code was in a series of different knots tied into a number of variable lengths, thicknesses and colours of twine. When Pachacutec's stunning Machu Picchu was excavated they found hundreds of these messages or quipu as they were known locked in a wooden casket, some as long as 8 metres. With the number of variables, it's little wonder they cannot crack the code, but when they do who knows what this Pandora's Box may reveal.

Next up for us on this enlightening day were the Inca's weather forecast station and their surgery. When the area was excavated in the 1970's the archaeologists found a stone built pool or reservoir which they first believed was for either irrigation, bathing or food preservation. They were thinking far too basic for Pachacutec's Incas. Once they discovered the bones of catfish and frogs strewn across the baths they began to think at a higher level. Local knowledge provided the answer; frogs leave their eggs in a linear fashion only when it's about to rain, catfish leave their eggs deeper if there is to be little rain over the coming months. The Incas had effectively created a short and long term weather forecasting solution for their agriculture.

On the same site about 10 metres deep in a cave we found the surgery, complete with operating table, anesthetiser, antibiotic and surgical lighting. Remember we are talking 15th century here. Helene and I were astonished by the sophisticated thinking and rudimentary solutions in the development of the Inca's hospital, for that is what it was. The thick slab of granite providing the operating table was so cold to the touch that it would have served as a more than adequate antibiotic. The anaesthetic was alcohol and coca leaves the raw material for cocaine and now chewed to prevent altitude sickness. The small opening above the "theatre" once held a simple mirror when, at the right time of day, would reflect the sun and shine a bright light onto the patient, much as surgeons do now. One of the most common procedures was trepanning or bloodletting from the skull, mainly because the most common injury at war was to the head. Instruments adapted from their weapons drilled into the skull to relieve blood clots and pressure. From the skulls found having had this type of treatment they calculated that the brain surgery was over 70% successful. Astonishing.

I could go on and talk about the enormous Administration Centre he created, the ingenuity of their ornate architecture, the sophisticated 10 metre stone clock and calendar, or the aqueducts and brilliantly designed frost free irrigation systems on the terraces, but I should save some for you to discover, you will be as blown away with this as we were. Promise.

'Today,' announced Helene, 'I've booked a Peruvian cooking course for the afternoon.'

'What fun. Any Guinea Pig on the menu?'

'Definitely not. Our teacher is Chef Chris.'

'Not very Peruvian.'

'He's a Cordon Bleu chef trained in Paris and Australia, with his own cookery school and restaurant in Cusco. We're meeting him at the food market.'

'Excellent, Cusco Chris here we come.'

I loved the food markets we visited in the cities and towns on our itinerary. The smelly fish markets, the fruit and veg we barely recognise and meat fresh from the abattoir being hacked into pieces for restaurants or home, it was all great fun.

We met with Chef Chris, who turned out to be from Shrewsbury and was not quite sure how he landed up in Cusco, but he seemed to know everyone in the market and helped himself to samples from various stalls for us to taste.

Our job was to buy all the evening's ingredients for our cooking course but it also gave us an ideal opportunity to put a name to some of the fruit and veg we had yet to identify. My favourite was an ugly green lumpy pocked thing, pliable to the touch and the same size but heavier than an orange. Inside the white, gooey flesh is in creamy segments with black stones about the size and shape of small olives. Chris told us it was a Custard Apple, it has a dull aroma but my goodness the taste is divine, it tastes like, well surprisingly, sweet custard mixed with cooked apple.

The three of us spent a wonderful hour or so selecting the ingredients for what was sure to be a food fiasco given my culinary skills, or lack of. It was enlightening to watch a professional pick out just the right strength of chilies and texture of cheese, the freshest herb sprigs and the perfect potatoes. My goodness we did have a lot to choose from, row upon row of different shapes, colours and sizes, as we had discovered already they have 2,000 varieties. We were to find out why the next day, would you believe it's that man Pachacutec again.

With the best bartered for, bought and bagged it was off to Chris's Cusco Culinary School with our ingredients to meet his sous-chef for our hands-on lesson.

'Before preparing any food,' said Cusco Chris, 'you have to learn how to make the perfect Pisco Sour.'

'I think I may be able to help here,' said Helene, who to be fair had become quite an expert on the nation's favourite drink, so now knows about these things. This was a fine start to the afternoon's cookery course and after a few attempts we got it right.

'The secret,' Chris informed us, 'is the egg white and three drops of bitters. So many people don't bother with those ingredients, but they are the making of a good Pisco Sour.' We tasted with and without and he was absolutely right.

He went on to tell us about the origin of the Pisco Sour. When the Spanish took over in the 1530's they introduced vines to produce their wine, Pinot Grigio perhaps, but the climate and soil created very poor wine. Oh! It was Pinot Grigio. So, rather than ferment the grape juice they distilled it, thereby creating pisco, grape brandy, the base ingredient of the Peruvian national drink Pisco Sour.

'Ceviche!' Chris announced in a Peru meets Shropshire flamboyant way.

'I love ceviche,' said Helene.

'Good, then we will try not one but three types of ceviche,' he proclaimed, pulling out the fish we had bought from the market.

'I can fillet fish,' I said, joining in the fun. This was indeed Helene's favourite restaurant dish so far in Peru and she seemed to know exactly how to prepare it, so my filleting had to be good.

I carefully sliced it into wafer thin pieces to be "cooked" with either lemon juice, passion fruit juice or another citric juice, I can't remember. I blame the second Pisco Sour. We added coriander, a few finely chopped chillies and something else (Pisco Sour three) and voila, as we Cordon Bleu cooks say.

We prepared and cooked potato cakes, a quinoa risotto and a dessert using those wonderful custard apples I found, all under the guidance of our tutor and chef, Cusco Chris. With each course complete he served it to us on our chefs' table as the afternoon and evening flew by, what great fun.

On our way home, we passed the five star Marriott Hotel; well actually we didn't pass it we went in. It had an ornately impressive courtyard in the centre of the building with fountains, heaters at each table, buffet style nibbles, fire pits with whopping marshmallows to toast and as it turned out Peru's number one award winning cocktail mixer – *here for one night only*. We were warmly greeted and invited to try his version of a Pisco Sour based on a gold leaf Pisco the Marriott were promoting. With our new skills we could have taught him a thing or two, but he did a pretty good job, even including the egg white and bitters. A couple of drinks later and we giggled our way home.

The following day it was up early for mountain biking in the Sacred Valley of the Incas, from Chinchero to Maras and Moray. We were collected by Saiber who was dressed in full Chris Hoy ensemble complete with padded cycling shorts, helmet with pro cycling camera and a yellow jersey with his name embroidered elaborately on the reverse. The backup vehicle was just as well equipped.

'Backup vehicle? Blimey, what are we letting ourselves in for?' asked Helene, with more than a touch of concern in her voice.

'I'm not entirely sure, but we promised each other at the start of this adventure we'd try anything, maybe only once, but we'd try it. So, let's give it a go.'

'But Saiber looks like Superman on a day off,' she said, 'look at all that kit he's wearing. We only have shorts and tee-shirts.'

'Maybe that's what the backup vehicle's for?' I suggested, not very convincingly.

It was quiet in our vehicle as we climbed the mountain, backup vehicle following closely behind.

'We're going up,' I said, 'maybe the cycle ride is all downhill.'

'Yes, but how steep?' asked Helene. 'And why is Saiber so quiet?' she whispered.

'Dunno, maybe he's getting in the zone for the downhill descent,' I said, trying to lighten the atmosphere. It didn't.

'What have you got in your bag,' Helene continued to whisper, 'we should at least try and look the part?'

We continued up the mountain clinging to a road with switchbacks, hairpins and S bends as we ransacked our sacks for more appropriate cycling gear. With lots of shuffling and groaning as we squeezed and pulled on clothes while being thrown around the van at each bend we redressed ourselves. On came the Lycra shorts I thought were in a zippy-uppy bag somewhere, a cycling vest I use around the National Trust tracks at home – that should impress Saiber – and a baseball cap with a Harlequins Rugby logo. Helene opted for a gym outfit she had brought along – that really should impress Saiber – and a gold headband, I had no idea why or where that came from. About 1982 I should think.

Up we went some more to the plateau at 3,500 metres – hoping the van had oxygen on board – great scenery and a clear bright day did little to dismiss our fears of the Tour de Peru.

We were provided with 24 gear, fork suspension mountain bikes with saddles that could split your differences, a pair of gloves without any fingers – seemed quite warm to me – and go-faster helmets. To say the first bit was tricky maybe an understatement, particularly if you ask Helene. The terrain was not dissimilar to a dried up river bed and the gradient descended at about 1:4 for half a mile towards the mountain lake we were promised would make it all worthwhile. We slipped and slid, plunged and plummeted our way down.

'My brakes aren't working, Saiber,' she complained, as her bike barely moved down the steep incline.

'What do you mean?' I interrupted, 'any slower and you'll be going backwards.' That helped.

'They're not coming on evenly.'

'Are you squeezing them at the same time, together?'

'Of course I am, but the front's coming on before the back, unless I judder them a bit.' That would have foxed Bradley Wiggins – but with a bit of reassurance from Saiber she made it.

He was right; the lake was spectacular and gave access to a mountain track, on the level that took us across the plateau amid some striking scenery of glaciers gently wrapping themselves around the mountain's crevasses. One impressive peak called Veronica had a glacier known as the silver tear, how lovely. The next 2 or 3 hours mountain biking was an absolute pleasure of relaxation and enjoyment as we descended 1,000 metres serenely into the village of Chinchero for a picnic lunch.

With bikes perched precariously on the support van roof we drove to our next destination, Moray in the Sacred Valley and a return to Pachacutec's sheer brilliance and imagination. See if you can out guess this, we couldn't. On first sight of these visually stunning Inca ruins, the circular terraces look like a vast round amphitheatre set in a natural crater, and in fact when it was first investigated in the 1970's that was exactly what the scientists, archaeologists and anthropologists thought it was. Wrong, once again the researchers were underestimating the sophistication of Mr. P's thinking; he was way ahead of his time.

To put it into context, on the sides of the cone shaped deep bowl there are about fifteen circular terraces that look like seating, the top one measuring over 50 metres in diameter the bottom one no more than 10 metres, all surrounding what looks like a circular stage. Clue; the difference in temperature from top to bottom is 15C degrees as the crater provides more shelter in the deeper parts and acts as a sun trap. It is no coincidence that these differences in temperature represent exactly the climate at sea level farming and at mountain farming.

Behind the circular terraces were about twenty conventional laddered terraces, the type we have seen all over this area of Peru for farming. So, what was Pachacutec up to? Unbelievably, he had built an agricultural laboratory and research centre.

The Incas used this "greenhouse" to experiment, test and incubate different crops. The microclimates at the different levels depended on their orientation to the sun, exposure to the wind and the amount of irrigation they were provided. The Incas could therefore reproduce the varied geographic and climatic conditions from across the empire; the researchers even identified soil on some of the terraces only found miles away on the coast and other distant regions.

The Incas began to create hybrid crops that were modified to the farming conditions available across the Empire. With a hardy crop developed and incubated they could reproduce the right recipe of sun, wind, water, soil, fertiliser etc. for a particular region and test the new crop, then finally release them for mass production in the regions. They even took wild crops and adapted them to make them fit for human consumption by experimenting and playing with the science we know today as molecular biology. This Pachacutec was indeed a visionary.

One of the wild crops they experimented with was the potato, which is why Peru has more than 2,000 varieties today. There's something quite gratifying to see his influence 600 years later when we visit the markets and see so many variations of the potatoes Pachacutec researched and cultivated.

For the next few days we were staying in Urubamba at the Sol y Luna Lodge and Spa part of the Relais & Chateaux group and wedged in the Sacred Valley of the Incas allowing us to catch the train to Machu Picchu. But first it was time to relax and indulge ourselves in their outside pool and Jacuzzi, spa, extensive gardens, riding stables and two restaurants and bars; it even had a gym somewhere, apparently. The owner, a lovely French lady we met while she was being filmed by the Disney Channel created the hotel to fund the school she had built next door. How enterprising, how lovely.

The forty or so individual bungalows are entirely round constructions with overlapping roofs perched on top like a lid; it's like walking into a large mushroom. The hotel is nestled in the bottom of the steep valley so there are some great views from our sun beds around the pool; almost vertical, barren slopes soar either side of us with snowcapped mountains in the distance, quite idyllic. Every lunch time there is a show in the gardens outside one of the bars with dramatic Peruvian music and dancing horses followed by a couple in traditional dress dancing what looked like a paso with the horses.

We strolled into the local town, a real Peruvian working town without a thought for tourists. We saw only one other touring couple, young backpackers looking slightly lost and bemused by it all. The main road into the square was nothing more than a dusty track with occasional pavements and my goodness it was busy. Hundreds of brightly painted and colourfully personalised tuk-tuks thrashing around the place, one had a mounted spoiler on its roof, goodness knows why, they're three wheelers and can't do over 20 mph.

There were dogs, sheep, llama, bulls and chickens in the street competing for space with the vehicular and pedestrian traffic, neither paying any attention to the other. It was hustle and bustle everywhere with the locals all selling or buying something they were carrying, usually foodstuffs of some kind. We saw a dog run by with the top of a bull's head complete with horns, almost as big as itself, hanging from its jaws, the kids in beautifully turned out school uniform were marching home and dozens of street food vendors added a hot steamy aroma to this colourful town.

We found the local food market and hesitantly ventured in; this was unlike any market we had seen so far. The stalls were jammed together and every square inch of the floor was covered with the contents of the surrounding sacks of fruit, vegetable, beans, pulses, corns of all sorts of colour and sizes, herbs, spices and of course potatoes.

Strangely every one of them was manned by a woman – if that's the right expression – there were simply no men either buying or selling in this vast theatre of food. And, if there were no stalls available the elderly women simply placed a large colourful tablecloth on the stone floor to display their meagre offerings of a few dozen potatoes or some root vegetable around themselves. We bought some chocolate and nuts from a delightful local on one of the crammed stalls. She took great delight in offering us all sorts of local foods to taste; I guess we were some sort of novelty in that very parochial environment.

We arrived at the town square, more street vendors with school kids helping their mums or helping themselves to whatever she was selling, as their after school tea. The centrepiece of the square was a tall column of white marble ornately carved and protected by a low chain railing; this was obviously a feature of some importance in the town. Sitting proudly on the top of the pinnacle was a meticulously sculptured large maize of sweet corn. I guess food is the most important component of life in these parts.

It had been a wonderful few days of adventure and discovery, and I wondered if it might be about to go up another gear as we packed up and moved on to one of Pachacutec's most famous legacies, Machu Picchu. I couldn't wait.

CHAPTER 10

Day 51 – 55: PERU
Machu Picchu

There's a Hidden Castle in the Sky where the Kings Live

A nother early start, but that's okay this was Machu Picchu, one of the seven wonders of the modern world. Our wonderfully informative guide Saiber collected us at 6:00 AM and made sure we had our passports for the couple of days we were to spend in the town of Machu Picchu – yes it has its own town – but why passports?

There is no road to Machu Picchu, so we were booked on the Perutravel Vistadome train – *providing a journey for your senses with a panoramic view beside and above your seat to bring you closer to nature and making you feel as if you're somehow part of the nature that surrounds you.* Government owned and desperately in need of a new copywriter. The 7:05 AM from Ollantaytambo to Machu Picchu sure beats the 7:58 AM from Maidenhead to

Paddington, but the station was just as busy. I say station; it's actually just the tracks with a cabin to provide shelter from the sun, no platform.

Our passports and tickets were checked as we were pointed in the direction of a throng of confused tourists. It was rush hour and all manner of trains were passing through blowing their whistles and horns to attract the attention of the hundreds of bewildered waiting passengers. Thank goodness for Saiber, but we still had to run down the track to catch our train before it departed. We presented our passports again, this time to extremely well-dressed guards, men and women in Perutravel uniform and boarded the bright blue carriages with, as the blurb promised, glass sides and roof.

'Goodness,' panted Helene, 'we only just made that.'

'Well, it saves queuing I suppose.'

'Oh! They'll be plenty of that later on,' said Saiber, 'but leave that to me.' Fair enough. Teas and coffee were served at our soft "armchair-comfortable" seats along with a cakey snack thing Helene couldn't eat.

The journey was 90 minutes and to be fair to the copywriter, took us through an ever-changing dramatic scenery as it hugged the torrent of the Urubamba River that snakes its way through the narrow Sacred Valley.

We left the barren mountainous slopes and the vegetation became green, lush and lofty, forming a tunnel around our train as we entered the humid rainforest, very reminiscent of Mashpi Lodge. After passing some teaser Inca ruins we entered the town, and I mean entered, the train stopped right in the middle of it, no station just the market on one side, shops, restaurants and hotels on the other.

'From here it's straight up by bus to the Inca's Lost City,' said Saiber, pointing at a procession of tatty old coaches that were more like museum pieces, in fact, they probably weren't in a good enough condition for a museum.

'Don't sit at the back,' Saiber advised us, 'it's too bumpy with too many bends and they drive too fast. You'll fall on the floor.' Okay, good advice. We dumped our cases at the evening's hotel for the day and headed for the bus station, or queue as it's known over there. A huge queue.

But Saiber was good to his word.

'You go for a drink at the café at the front of the queue, I'll pick you up there,' he instructed.

'Surely, Saiber, you don't want to…'started Helene.

'That's fine, Saiber,' I interrupted. 'Come on, Helene, let's find the café,' I said ushering her down the row of thousands of tourists, all wondering why we were queue hopping.

'Apparently when you have a guide they queue for you, Helene, it's part of the job I guess.' This was to come in very useful.

After a coffee or two and a cakey thing Helene could eat, Saiber appeared in the queue in front of the café. He had the tickets; we had our passports so we were all good to go up the 1,000 metres to 2,430 metres and one of the highlights of our Peru trip.

The night before we had been chatting about bestest bits again and started to wonder whether Machu Picchu could really deliver given the sights we'd seen and experiences we'd had so far with Saiber and indeed Pachacutec, who felt like part of the team now. But as the speeding bus bounced and zigzagged its way up the mountain track towards the site we began to have glimpses of what would clearly prove us wrong, this was going to be the experience we both hoped it would be.

After jumping the queue on arrival (Saiber our professional queuer is rather good at this), we presented our passports again and began the climb to the plateau for the first sight of the ruins in the classic image we have all seen in books and on websites.

Saiber let us go ahead to stand on a grassy ledge looking down on the remnants of the citadel and across to the Piton shaped mountain known as Huayana Picchu (young peak). I guess he knew what was coming. Helene burst into tears, this was a full on Magic Kingdom Moment.

'I'm so sorry, Saiber,' she sobbed, as I held her tight.

'It's fine,' he said, 'it happens all the time. I had the same reaction the first time I saw it as a student. Its beauty is breathtaking and often quite overwhelming.'

How right he was. I have to say none of the pictures can prepare you for it, and it was certainly an emotional moment for us. I'm not sure completely why, maybe it was the serenity of the place, the view itself, the sad story behind Machu Picchu or that it represented exactly why we made this decision to give up our comfortable lives and take on this extraordinary adventure.

Helene was pretty much inconsolable for the next half an hour or so as more and more of this absurdly impossible and spectacularly beautiful place and its history revealed itself, both visually and in compelling narrative from Saiber. I will not attempt to describe Machu Picchu, it is somewhat indescribable but let me try and provide some of the story line to the images, I found it just as fascinating.

While Pachacutec was launching initiatives that were years, if not centuries, beyond his time and while he was busy building the Inca Empire across six different countries, he also had the foresight to create a defensive strategy. What if they were to be invaded by, let's say the Spanish for example, who had been planning their visit to America with Columbus and probably had their greedy eye on Mexico and then South America?

Typical Pachacutec vision I reckon. He instructed his R&D department to scrutinise the area within 100 km of the capital city Cusco to identify a defensible area they could retreat to if there was an invasion. Seems to me Pachacutec was thinking when, not if. His brief had three strategic requirements: it must be geographically impregnable, provide a natural water supply and have innate resources to enable them to build a small self-sufficient city.

Machu Picchu met all the criteria. Firstly, it was at an elevation of 2,500 metres at the end of the valley, so it could only be approached via a very narrow and exposed trail through the gorge where our train had taken us, then almost vertically up to the plateau. The plateau itself was wedged between two mountains north and south with sheer drops of 300 metres and 400 metres on the east and west down to the river that almost formed a full 360 degree moat.

Pretty tough to conquer even for the Spanish Conquistadors. The natural and plentiful water supply came from the mountain springs. Of course, Pachacutec took full advantage creating viaducts across the citadel, his own private spa, sixteen showers for villagers and the first en suite, as Helene pointed out, in the royal residency. Finally, the plateau when found was strewn with giant boulders of granite, ideal for the construction of the various buildings required for self-sufficiency. Mr. P signed it off and construction started in 1450.

The citadel itself took 30 years to build so Pachacutec sadly did not see the nirvana he had envisaged finally completed, but his unmistakable influence is all over it. Before we entered the site itself we hiked to the Sun Gate, an hour's climb on an original Inca Trail that ascends through the old agricultural terraces high in the mountains to what was once the main and only entrance to Machu Picchu. It's narrow, with a sheer drop on one side hundreds of metres down to the river and was busy with huffing and puffing trekkers and resting and relaxing llamas blocking our path every so often. They're big lumps to move but with a bit of encouragement and shoving we found our way around the idle brutes, and the llamas. What a view looking back from the Sun Gate, Pachacutec certainly new how to deliver theatre to his guests.

We spent an intriguing morning wandering around the citadel, the sanctuary for the chosen few. But it also had to be supported by labourers for building and farming, and gifted architects, engineers and craftsmen so there are three very different styles of construction. The impressive royal residency and temples are constructed of intricately cut and shaped stone, whereas the labourers had homes built of any shaped rocks and boulders forged together in a haphazard way. The accommodation for the skilled workers were a sort of half measure of both, the class system was clearly very important at that time.

There is an upper and lower town of about two hundred buildings so the population is estimated to have been about five hundred. The top part of the citadel was for the elite of society with the labourers in downtown Machu Picchu. Perhaps the most important structure was the Temple of the Sun where only priests and higher nobles were allowed to enter. It is a semi-circular building sitting on a vast granite boulder, with its two windows aligned to the summer and winter solstices.

The Temple of the Condor was equally impressive. At first you see a low altar of smooth flat rock shaped in the head of a bird, this was used for sacrifices of llama. Then, as you take a few steps back from the altar you begin to make out the vast wings of the condor formed naturally by two diagonal outcrops of rock towering 10 metres over the temple entrance. Saiber told us that mummified human remains were found there, it was believed then that the condor soaring high in the sky took the souls of the recently departed to heaven.

Can you imagine when the sacrifice was made and the condors picked up the scent of the carrion, circling high in the air above the monumental temple, with the priests offering the souls of the dead to be taken to heaven by the magnificent airborne creatures? What an event that must have been.

A couple of other fascinating structures. The Southern Cross stone was the Incas early attempt at astronomy and cartography. It is shaped exactly as the constellation we are familiar with in the night sky or on the Australian flag and positioned to identify precisely where the five stars will appear on the horizon.

Their fascination with the stars could also be seen in another building at the highest point in the citadel where Pachacutec had an astronomical observatory built. Clever. Two custom cut stones about a foot in diameter and shaped like shallow bowls were lined with metal, probably silver, and filled with water. The priests would then observe the stars and celestial bodies in the reflection.

This intrigued Helene, who knows about these things, especially because on the day we were there a solar eclipse, was due across parts of southern America. She took a photo of the sun reflected in the water but it was not until later, on the train home when we were examining the photograph that we realised we were actually looking at an eye.

The reflected sun was the pupil, the circular shaped bowl was the iris and then quite clearly, we could see an oval shape carved into the outer rock.

'Look at this, Saiber,' she said, showing him the image. 'You do know this is an eye, don't you?'

'Well, I've never seen that before,' he replied excitedly, 'of course it's Pachacutec's eye to the heavens.'

He was, to put it mildly, extremely animated, holding it up for all our fellow passengers to see and describing the elements making up the eye. He told us the Inca Observatory had only been discovered in 2013 and I think Saiber was about to put his name to Helene's discovery.

I have touched on a very small part of what fascinated and enthralled me on our 2 day visit to Machu Picchu. There were many other surprises and probably many more yet to be discovered; only 4 years ago another Inca Trail to a platform opposite the citadel was discovered by some naturalists. It is still not completely excavated or understood.

But the story of Machu Picchu and indeed the Incas ends almost as impossibly as it began. Sure enough as Pachacutec predicted the Spanish arrived in Peru in 1532 led by Pizarro and his entourage of Conquistadors in search of the gold and riches he believed, quite rightly, the Inca Empire owned. It was the first time the empire was seriously threatened, not just with war but by the infectious diseases the Spanish brought with them. Rampant disease spread throughout the empire causing the single most devastating loss of life in the Americas, with the Inca population reduced by two thirds from 12M to just 4M.

In fact, the Spanish conquest was accomplished without massive battles and warfare due in part to the disease, but also the naivety of the then Inca emperor Atahualpa. He promised the Spanish "two rooms of gold as high as a man's outstretched hand" in return for his freedom. He delivered the $50M (in today's money) and was promptly killed to allow the Spanish to raid Cusco where they thought they would collect the rest of the treasures.

But the Inca royalty and elite had retreated to Machu Picchu and shut up shop, just as Pachacutec had intended. They should have been safe there for years with the natural defences and self-sufficient life he had created in their secret hideaway. The Spanish knew the legend of a hidden castle in the sky where the kings lived but had simply failed to discover it, just as Pachacutec had planned. But in 1572 there was a rumour that the Spanish had identified the location of the citadel and were on their way in. Machu Picchu was abandoned.

The small population deserted their utopia by creating a trail "out the back door" with a bridge constructed over the valley and its 400 metre drop. They took what they could and having crossed the bridge destroyed it and retreated into the mountains.

We hiked to what little is left of the bridge and the Incas' escape route. It looked intimidating to us even with the introduction of steel handrails to grasp hold of and keep us away from the edge. It must have been terrifying for the five hundred or so making their getaway with as much as they could carry. The trail we hiked, as the Incas had all those years ago, had been built into the side of the mountain about a metre across and ended of course at the collapsed bridge. We could see where it picked up again across the valley and disappeared into the craggy mountains. Nothing much would have changed in the 450 years since they fled and retreated into the mountains, it was quite possible to visualise how they escaped, ending their days at Machu Picchu and extinguishing the last glimmer of the glorious Inca Empire.

As we stood on the path where their escape bridge had been, Saiber recounted the denouement to the 4 day story he had enthralled us with. The unbelievably poignant and sad end to this story is that Pachacutec had, as always, done a wonderful job. The Spanish never did find Machu Picchu, it was abandoned needlessly. The hidden castle in the sky became the Lost City of the Incas and was left to be reclaimed by the jungle, not to be seen again for nearly 350 years. How dreadfully tragic.

I was saddened beyond belief. How could this have possibly been? What a desperately disappointing end to an incredible story.

It had been a wonderful couple of days in Machu Picchu, beautiful, intriguing, astonishing and overwhelmingly sad, but it was the highlight we hoped it would be. We jumped the queues and sat in the middle of the rickety old bus that wound its way round the mountain down to the village. As we came to the first hairpin bend I saw Pachacutec.

'Helene, I've just seen Mr. P on the bend back there,' I said.

'You've had too much sun, or it's the altitude. If you hadn't had that canister...'

'No, seriously, he was on the side of the road.'

'Of course he was, have some water and chocolate.'

'Look! There he is again,' I shouted pointing out the window as we navigated our way around another hairpin.

'Good grief,' said Helene, 'now I'm doing it, pass the chocolate.'

A young boy of about 14 dressed head to toe in what we assumed represented Pachacutec's warrior wear and carrying a spear twice the size of him, was standing to attention on the side of the road.

We looked out of the back window to see him race straight down the mountain as we continued our descent via a number of loops and hairpin bends. Two hairpins later, there he was again standing perfectly still as the bus slowly manoeuvred around the bend. Once again, he ran off straight down the mountain to meet us at the hairpin after next. This was great fun and lightened our spirits as we all cheered and waved every time he beat us to our next hairpin bend. We met him at the coach station, such that it was, and made sure he was handsomely rewarded for his Herculean efforts. I think Pachacutec would have quite enjoyed that.

The mystery of Machu Picchu continues to this day and Pachacutec is still keeping us all guessing over 100 years since its modern day discovery. The Yale sponsored and wonderfully named Hiram Bingham III found the Lost City on 24th July 1911. After years of searching, certain that there must have been an exit for the Incas from the invading Spanish, he came across a young family at the bottom of the mountain and asked about any local ruins. Their son Pablito said something like, "Oh! Yes, there's a town of tumbledown houses up there where I play all the time."

Led by the local farmer Melchior Arteaga and young Pablito, 339 years after the Incas left, the Lost City was found and Machu Picchu was rediscovered, what a moment that must have been. It was in surprisingly good condition having had the jungle largely protect the buildings from the weather. In fact the restoration only accounts for 35% of what we see now.

Hiram Bingham III removed all 200,000 priceless artefacts left behind at the Inca exodus promising to return them to Peru after analysis. Unfortunately, the contract was lost and over a 100 years later Peru is still asking for its property to be returned.

But you can't keep a good man down. Even if he is buried. Somewhere.

Pachacutec died aged 90 and although it may seem blindingly obvious to us, the real identity of his resting place has been the subject of much debate and controversy for many years. There is a story that he was entombed in Cusco Cathedral and the Spanish, frustrated in not finding the riches they expected, took his body out into the square and burned it in front of his Inca subjects. I do hope that's not true.

Some believe he was taken to Huayna Picchu the peak opposite Machu Picchu and buried there overlooking his creation. Although this is largely based on the assumption that everything had been excavated, researched and studied at the citadel. I've even heard his body was taken to the new capital Lima, but I don't believe that can be true.

In February 2010 French engineer David Crespy was taking some measurements on a small path never used by tourists or the archaeologists, when he noticed the presence of what appeared to be a "door" sealed with rocks, at the foot of one of the main buildings.

"This is a door", Crespy immediately thought, clever engineer. He claims to have been unaware that someone, a funny or bright tourist, or an archaeologist with a sense of humour (doubtful), had written on a stone above the entrance the word "treasure" and drawn an arrow pointing downwards. Bizarre but true.

Crespy and Thierry Jamin, an explorer and historian, a sort of French Indiana Jones – he even has the same hat – applied to excavate the sealed entrance. The Cusco branch of the Ministry of Culture responded with a clear "ninguna possibilidad".

So, they used geo-radar and electromagnetic sensor equipment to investigate behind the blocked doorway, technically not excavation I guess. They discovered the existence of a large burial chamber, with a considerable amount of gold and silver, and a whole underground structure that housed a dozen cavities they believed were family graves. They were convinced they had found Pachacutec's tomb.

It seems like the best kept secret in Peruvian history had been solved, making it the largest and most important discovery ever at the world famous site. The Director of the Ministry of Culture gave his permission for Crespy and Jamin to carry out observational studies at the site and by 2016 they were ready to excavate the tomb. How exciting. The Cusco branch of the Ministry of Culture responded with a clear "ninguna possibilidad".

Or put another way, as the Director of Culture said, "Permission was given to carry out observational studies. But when they proposed to excavate based on some hypothesis that a laser scanner may have detected an Inca tomb and there were some steps lined in gold, it has been completely denied because this goes against the reality".

Or put another way, the politicians want the discovery to be 100% Peruvian. Who can blame them after that scoundrel Hiram Bingham III ran off with all the treasures last time?

During our visits we saw red tape and "no public access" around new construction areas at the site and the Crespy / Jamin project is still being pursued although being met with much controversy and resistance from the government. As Saiber said, 'Hopefully this mystery will be uncovered soon,' but I'm not sure I agree. I like the idea that Pachacutec still has the upper hand 500 years after his death. Maybe just like the Spanish never found his Machu Picchu, it's right we should never find him.

It was late in the day but Machu Picchu and possibly Pachacutec were not done with us yet. On the Vistadome home after coffee and cake, that Helene couldn't eat, a commentary began in Spanish followed by rousing music. A costumed dancer appeared from behind the curtain complete with colourful mask and flowing skirts. He waved a golden sceptre and charged up and down the gangway grabbing the more attractive girls in the carriage to dance with in the aisle. Luckily, Helene had a window seat next to me so she couldn't be reached, given half a chance she'd have been up with him though, rather a lot of that going on in this escapade.

I'm guessing our multicoloured animated dancer was supposed to be impersonating Pachacutec, dancing had not been in the repertoire of his varied skills we had seen so far, but it was quite a performance for 15 minutes or so as we crept along the Sacred Valley.

There was more to come that also fitted comfortably into the "bizarre experiences in South America" category. No sooner had our dancer pranced off behind the curtain at the end of the carriage, leaving a few slightly embarrassed girls with mouths open readjusting their hiking wear, when a new, completely unrelated show began.

A new soundtrack of a slightly more dignified nature was broadcast and the carriage aisle was converted into a fashion catwalk. Out came the first model showcasing a versatile reversible cloak in black and red alpaca wool.

'Hang on,' I said to Helene, 'hasn't she just served me coffee and the cake that you can't eat?'

'Yes, and that's the guy who checked my passport, how odd.'

'I rather like that tunic of greens and browns with detachable collar, gold trim and buttons to match, though,' I said. I may have taken too much interest here.

'David, you'd look like something out of a Freeman's catalogue,' said Helene, 'but that wrap's fun.'

They sashayed their way up the aisle between bewildered passengers, hips swinging and doing that funny model walk thing where they throw one foot over the other to execute a step. There was a twirl at the end of the corridor and a demo of the finer design elements of the belt or wraparound integrated scarf, then it was an about turn and a purposeful stride to back behind the curtain for a quick change into the next ensemble.

Oddly we all clapped. Having completed their show, they converted back to the train assistants they actually were. With outfits slung creatively over their carts where coffee and cake had recently been they attempted to persuade the awestruck passengers to part with a few hundred Soles for the designer garments. Surprisingly, there were some takers, still in shock perhaps.

That night we had dinner with Saiber and reflected on what we had seen and heard, still making me swallow hard when I think of the past glory of Pachacutec, his people, what they had achieved and the tragic end. I wondered how different the world would be if the Incas had been allowed to flourish, they achieved so much in such a short time. I have developed a huge amount of admiration for a civilisation I scarcely knew; I guess that's what this adventure was all about.

It was a sad goodbye to Saiber, we had enjoyed his company so much and I will always be grateful to him for introducing us to the Incas and the wonderful Pachacutec.

The following day we made our way back to the Sol y Luna Lodge for a couple of days' rest around the pool in preparation for our trip into the jungle; should be a right carry on.

CHAPTER 11

Day 56 to 60: PERU
The Amazon Jungle

Intrepid Explorers

The Amazon has thousands of tributaries so both Peru and Ecuador claim the source of the river. Peruvians believe it starts from Arequipa, the White City with the odd Peruvian Last Supper. It's also claimed by the locals to be the longest at nearly 7,000 km, longer than the Nile, but that's up for debate. It runs west to east across South America emptying its vast contents into the Atlantic in eastern Brazil, and we were on our way to meet it.

First, was a stopover back in Cusco where we had an enjoyable yet comical evening in a tiny restaurant run entirely by an old gnarled local fella. Sadly, his wife, the chef had left him the week before so he was trying to be cook, sous chef, waiter and washer upper; it was a little on the slow side. He obviously had yet to really understand culinary procurement – or visiting the local market for the provisions required for the evening. Every so often after taking an order he would rush out of the front door leaving the diners on their own, to return 5 minutes later with either a small vine of tomatoes, a single avocado or perhaps a bunch of coriander.

On one occasion while he was off searching for another ingredient the evening's "turn" arrived. In came the Peruvian combo with guitars and pan pipes and clearly couldn't believe their luck, a mix of Germans, Brazilians and Brits with no restaurant owner. They plugged their instruments into an old amplifier completely blocking the entrance, perhaps to stop us leaving and launched into *"I'd rather be a hammer than a nail"*. After a couple of other classic traditional Peruvian songs and still no sign of the owner one of the troubadours took the opportunity to test his cabaret skills. He approached each table with the same questions in broken English.

'What's your name? Where do you come from? Oh! Yes, know it well, Manchester United and Windsor Castle. Del Boy, yes?'

We finally ordered and the owner went off to negotiate the purchase of a carrot. To be fair the meal was pretty good, Chicken Milanese for me, that's where the carrot came in, and a fishy gluten free stew for Helene. After an hour or so the Germans and Brazilians left and so did the owner. Exhausted he put an unlabelled bottle of red wine on our table and went out for a good sit down and a smoke, leaving us alone in the restaurant to plan tomorrow's adventure.

The flight from Cusco to Puerto Maldonado took 30 minutes, the queuing took 2 hours. We were met by our driver and transferred to the banks of the golden brown river where a myriad of porters in khaki jungle uniform took the small luggage to load onto the boat, a long motorised junk with a tarpaulin roof. The large cases were taken into a hidden safe and secure storage facility, we didn't get to see. Sometimes you just have to trust it and go with it.

I should mention we were limited to a small hold-all each for the 5 days in the jungle so we restricted ourselves to trousers (long, one of) shirts (long sleeve, four of), smalls (small collection of) and a vast quantity of sun cream and insect repellent. We had decided not to take the Malaria pills having read the huge list of side-effects including hallucinations, severe vomiting and violent diarrhoea. Just what you need in the jungle, blimey I'd rather catch Malaria, maybe not. As it turned out there were barely any mosquitoes in the dry season and they had not experienced a case in the area since the Reserve opened years ago.

Thirty minutes down the river we arrived to the clanging of the big brass "welcome bell" rung by a Ranger at Reserva Amazonica, our accommodation for the next few days.

'Is this what you expected the Amazon to be like?' I asked Helene, who hadn't spoken throughout the journey.

'I don't think I brought enough khaki with me. Do you think they have a shop?'

'I doubt it,' I responded quietly, 'but you're right everyone seems to be in jungle gear already.'

Our fellow explorers seemed to be better equipped than a safari gamekeeper: floppy hats with muslin netting, binoculars swinging from their necks and enough camouflage to keep Millets in business for another year.

'Welcome to the jungle, welcome to Amazonica!' our bell ringing Ranger announced.

We were immediately ushered into the Rangers' Hut for a briefing, a room with a troupe of guides, not sure what the collective noun is. One of them, the Head Ranger I guess, spoke up.

'Let me introduce you to some of our residents in the jungle,' he said, standing back to reveal a collection of large jars, the contents of which seemed to be crammed in to their formaldehyde eternity.

'Giant anacondas, the green olive snake, rainbow boa, tiger rat snake, the common viper…'

'Not too common I hope,' I suggested to the meeting. Silence.

'And other creatures that can do you serious damage and, if we're lucky, we may get to meet.'

Oh good!

Following the short safety briefing and an introduction to the exciting excursions and exotic expeditions available we enjoyed a delightful three course lunch in the grandiose restaurant, the main focus of the reserve. And of course, played the game of pre-judging our Amazon companions.

The restaurant is an impressive circular building built entirely from the fallen wood and bamboo from the jungle with a 5 metre high fine mesh "window" around its full circumference allowing us to keep an eye on the jungle activity without it activating with us. There was also an elegant first floor walk-around bar like a minstrel's gallery overlooking the dining area, well worth investigation.

We were then escorted to our lodge. Goodness. I was reminded of that guy in another jungle, Dr Livingstone I presume. We may have a 21st century version of his accommodation but I bet he had a view like ours. The wooden, thatched lodge sat on stilts with a three sided mesh conservatory at the front featuring his-and-hers hammocks overlooking the wide river, probably 200 metres across. The bedroom has a mosquito net canopy over a four-poster bed and the shower was also partly mesh to give you the impression of bathing in the jungle. We were perched above the bank no more than 3 metres from the waters edge and had a view of the end of our Monkey Island and the continuation of the jungle on the far bank. There was the occasional working boat either fishing or illegally dredging for gold and the wildlife scream, squeak and shriek in the jungle canopy above us. My goodness it could give Mashpi Rainforest a run for its money.

It felt remote, it was remote, and we didn't have electricity throughout the whole of the day. Apart from no wifi and no mobile coverage which we haven't experienced for many years, the generator had to have a little nap from 3:00 PM to 6:00 PM and again from 11:00 PM to 3:00 AM so everything is lit by hundreds of silver oil lamps dotted around the thirty or so lodges after dusk, quite romantic Helene told me. Of course, there are no phones in the lodges so instead they provide you with a whistle, if you need something like room service you just give a little whistle or a loud blast if you're in the farthest cheap seats I suppose.

Before dinner it was a Twilight Cruise on one of the canopied canoes in search of alligators. It was pitch black by the time us newbies, about seven of us, joined our guide Paolo and his power flashlight for the night-time excursion.

'Have you seen anything yet?' whispered Helene.

'Not a bloody thing, it's pitch black out there and we've no lights.'

'Sshh.'

'I'm more interested in what we might hit than the alligators.'

After 20 minutes or so navigating around the floating tree trunks, jungle debris and shallower parts, with Paolo occasionally flashing his power whatsit, we began to pick out the reflections of golden eyes on the banks.

'Are they watching us or are we watching them?' Helene said. 'They do look as if they're waiting for something.'

'Whatever it is let's hope it's not going to happen.'

These were Caiman, a smaller relation to the alligator but big enough to take your finger off, possibly with your arm still attached to it. One of the other species we spotted was a Fishing Bat, I had never heard of them before. But sure enough Paolo picked them up in his torch as they raced across the calm water searching for small fish to feed on.

A good inauguration to life in the jungle I thought. We returned for drinks with our new jungle colleagues, a light dinner and back to our Lodge to work out how on earth you get into a four-poster mosquito net. But what a restful night; no altitude to cope with, the soporific sound of the river slipping by and the curious sounds of the jungle. Apparently, Helene was still talking as I drifted off to a contented sleep to be roused again by the waking birds and beasts 9 hours later. Bliss.

It was a quick breakfast with delicious locally made coffee before we set off by boat to our first expedition deep into the jungle. What a great trek, we met a local family farming this rugged inhospitable land. Bananas, passion fruit, star fruit, in fact all sorts of exotic fruits we were beginning to recognise from the markets, cashews, brazil nuts, cocoa and more, some of which we tasted straight off the tree, all of which were sold directly to our reserve. We quietly hiked through the jungle and were rewarded within minutes when a large group of three different species of monkey travelled directly across our path in the canopy above. Some as inquisitive as us came down to the lower branches to investigate, one of which leapt onto a fern just a few feet in front of me. I don't know which of us was more shocked as the fern gave way to leave us face to face, but both monkey and human reacted in the same way and retreated fast.

Our guide pointed out exotic birds, the sights and sounds of the creatures we were sharing their home with and unusual fauna and flora, some of which we recognised from Mashpi like the walking tree, but this was primary jungle so everything had been supersized. One we hadn't seen and neither of us were familiar with was the giant of the jungle, the Iron Tree. These things are vast, large enough to build a tunnel in and drive a car through with ease. They are also as impressively old as they are large, the one we rested by was over 600 years old, apparently others have been found to be well over 2,000. Another was the Capoc tree that grows up to 3 metres a year and never sprouts leaves, it photosynthesis from its bark. Apparently, the dead tribe leaders used to be buried under them believing they would ascend to heaven more quickly with the help of the fastest growing tree. Before you know it, I bet they were all at it, like Rapa Nui, the Incas at Sillustani and Lima.

Our trek on foot ended on the bank of a secluded creek where a strategically placed wooden kayak had been left, couldn't see any paddles though. The kayak was large enough for our party of five plus guide so we spent a glorious half an hour slowly manoeuvring our way down the shallow creek. With the jungle soaring above us and accompanied by colourful butterflies in their thousands, like confetti at a wedding, some landing on our boat and some on us for a free ride downstream, scarcely a word was spoken.

The afternoon was an undemanding trek around the jungle in the vicinity of the reserve; just four of us accompanied by Roger the guide, no not an invitation. It appeared we now had a full set of guides named after taxi call signs, as always expected: Victor, Victor, Oscar, Roger. Honest, promise.

One of the most unexpected features of life in the jungle was the early starts, we woke with our jungle beasts anyway, but 7:00 AM reveille was planned because of the intense heat in the middle of the day. Excursions usually begin before 8:00 AM returning around 11:30 AM then allowing us to dress down into shorts, loose shirts and flip flops, kindly provided by the hotel, and either swing gently in our his-and-hers hammocks or watch the river amble by from our bench on the bank. Then it was a lazy lunch before we set off again around 2:30 PM for the afternoon expedition.

One morning we joined another couple for a trip to the botanical jungle research centre and a kayak around their lagoon. Our guide this time was Jim or as we renamed him Clumsy Jim, on account of the fact that he continually fell over on the trail when pointing at something in the canopy and very nearly capsized our six man kayak attempting to pluck some exotic low hanging fruit for us.

Two minutes into the lagoon expedition we were greeted by a huge Caiman. It slowly broke the surface as if stalking its prey, a long golden snout and eyes swivelling taking a good look at us less than a metre from the boat. All the more reason for Clumsy Jim to go careful, perhaps these two have met more intimately before.

We then came across the most bizarre creature; think highly colourful exotic flying turkey with poorly applied blue eyeshadow and you're not far off the mark. There were literally hundreds of them around the lagoon providing its favourite food. They are the Hoatzin, known as the missing link between reptiles and bird, and surely look like they've crossed the time line between prehistoric times and the present day. They have multiple stomachs like a cow to process their food, make a loud grunting noise similar to a pig with a sore throat and don't have any predators because they taste like cow dung. The locals know them as the stinky bird. Lovely things.

At the end of the lagoon, rich with further unusual wildlife and vegetation, was the most unusual sight of all. Some years ago, this stretch of river was owned by a missionary and the lagoon was a free flowing creek connected to the main waterway. He converted an old iron steamship into a hospital to visit the local people but in 1952 there was an enormous flood. When the waters receded the sediment and flood residue blocked the creek creating the lagoon and marooning the vessel. The beautiful steamship was then left to rot, providing an eerie rusted memorial stranded in the jungle commemorating what the missionary once achieved.

We later learned that Ralph Nelson the celebrated film producer visited the lagoon and was so inspired by the missionary's story and the rusting steamship that he wrote the film *Wrath of God* and filmed some of the location shots there. Apparently, Robert Mitchum, playing the missionary, was a little difficult to work with.

After Jim clumsily got us back to dry land we hiked to the botanical centre where they continue to cultivate plants, herbs, trees and shrubs for medicinal purposes. The nearest city hospital is some hours away so the locals treat themselves with homeopathic remedies from the jungle passed down through the generations. We tried the bark of a tree known locally as "healthy healthy" that'll do everything from antiseptically clean cuts, cure colic and treat cataracts. The sap from another is called dragon's blood because the trunk "bleeds" a red viscous fluid that will remove skin blemishes and wrinkles and we chewed on a leaf used in crude dentistry as an anaesthetic. It works; I couldn't feel my tongue for half an hour.

Another leaf, when crushed and added to water, creates a purple dye which Jim demonstrated on Helene giving her a clumsily applied new make-up across her eyelids and with two wobbly stripes down her face, it's easy to remove apparently, after a couple of weeks.

As Pocahontas led the rest of us on the trek back to the boat Clumsy Jim's jungle utility belt broke leaving his machete and 12" macho jungle knife around his ankles.

'Jim, you appear to have dropped your big knife,' said Helene, 'let me take it for you.' Helene picked up the knife as CJ covered his embarrassment and marched ahead.

So, there she was barely recognisable from a couple of months ago with her painted face, jungle gear and machete

'I am an intrepid explorer,' she proclaimed, 'with war paint on, machete in hand, ready to take on anything in the jungle. But I've got a bit of a girly tummy at the moment.'

The evening entertainment was a night walk in the jungle with you know who. We turned up covered from head to toe in long sleeve shirts, jungle trousers, hats, buffs and lashings of citronella and insect repellent. Clumsy Jim strolled in wearing a short-sleeved jungle green shirt and matching shorts. According to our research we were supposed to dress with adequate protection against the mosquitoes, flies, bugs, insects and other creepy crawly biting and stinging things, especially after dusk – it's a jungle out there.

As we marched, and Jim ambled, into the dense forest I wondered where his backpack, walkie-talkie and first-aid kit may be, probably the same place as his machete. It took us seconds to spot our first tarantula wedged into the fracture of a tree. Apparently, they won't kill you but a bite from this gruesome looking arachnid can smart a bit. As the tarantula count rose to five we became pretty adept at spotting them with our torch beams.

'There's one on that tree,' cried Helene. It was the biggest yet, with its foul black legs extended and clinging to the bark, it even made Jim jump back, they really are quite intimidating things.

It was about 30 minutes into the trail when Jungle Jim's torch began to fade.

'Shall we walk some of the way in the dark?' he suggested.

'No!' commanded Helene.

'Oh! Come on, Helene, it'll be fun,' I said.

'No! It'll be scary and horrible. Where's your mobile? Use that as a torch.'

Jim offered a compromise. 'I'll point out the noises of the jungle rather than the sights,' he said.

'How do you point out a noise?' I asked.

But Jim was good to his word and as we made our way back with the help of my mobile, apparently Jim forgot his, he stopped us every so often to identify a screech or a yelp from the jungle. There was one particular bird with a call that is exactly the same as the weapon in the Space Invaders game, another that gives a sharp whistle with a loud gulp at the end, and a Cicada that makes a continuous high-pitched whine like an electric drill, all very odd but a great soundtrack to our jungle experience.

Dinner in the jungle was always going to be fascinating, mostly based around fish, banana or plantain and the potato of course. Our favourite was Paiche a local freshwater fish, actually the largest freshwater fish in the world growing up to 3 metres in length that remarkably has both gills and lungs, it's also very tasty. They serve it in all manner of ways, the most unconventional being in a sealed length of bamboo about a metre long. The waiter presents it to the table and ceremoniously unplugs one end to pour the contents of fish, vegetables and sauce onto the plate. Very theatrical and very tasty.

A couple of the others we enjoyed were a green plantain crusted fish with mashed uncucha (an Andean exotic tuber), dried mushrooms and orinoco apple sauce. And a special sautéed beef tenderloin with ripe banana, regional chorizo, sachaculantro (no idea), chillies from the jungle and rice served with chestnuts and coconut. With a couple of Cusquena, the local beer, and a bottle of Peruvian Sauvignon Blanc at 120 Sols, about £35, it was a satisfying way to end the day and return to bed before 11:00 PM for lights out and a rest for the generator.

The next day was the Amazon Canopy Walk. Helene and I remembered sitting in bed one Sunday morning months ago planning our trip and reading about this, both agreeing it was part of the jungle adventure we must do, both encouraging each other to do something we would normally never take on.

But first the hunt for the Penis Tree.

Two of our fellow intrepid explorers were young German girls taking a break from their careers in media PR to "find themselves" on the trip of a lifetime up the Amazon.

'Ve are to find ze penis tree, yes?' they asked Jim, who looked absolutely petrified by these two feisty girls.

'What are they talking about?' asked Helene, 'they may be on the wrong trip altogether.'

'There is a tree,' began Jim hesitantly, 'that some think is shaped like, well, like as she just said, an appendage.'

'It is big, yes?' one of the girls asked.

'Yes, it's quite large,' said Jim, 'but it's a long way into the jungle.'

'Ve go now, in search of ze big penis,' they commanded and set off on a brisk march leading the exploration.

We trekked through a part of the jungle we were yet to discover, entering near a sign reading "Do not enter unless accompanied by a guide", the girls a little more enthusiastic than me, and indeed Jim, I suspect. But after half an hour there was a scream ahead of us.

'Zis is it! Zis is ze penis I have been looking for!'

'I'm sure it is, dear, but can we keep the volume down, it's frightening the wildlife,' I suggested.

'What does she want us to do,' said Helene, 'dance around it?'

It would perhaps be a little inappropriate for me to describe what we found, apart from the fact that it was an Iron Tree well over 30 metres tall with a phallic looking extension to its trunk pointing out and towards the ground.

'You take picture of us with ze penis, yes?' they asked.

'Careful, David,' warned Helene.

'Okay, ladies if you'd like to stand either side with your...'

'That's enough art direction, David, just take the bloody photo.'

They grabbed Jim and stood either side of the herbage appendage, the girls looking exceedingly smug and Jim excessively embarrassed.

The start of the Canopy Walk, as you may guess, goes up. Jim led us to a rickety old tower with ragged steps, what seemed like hundreds of them, disappearing into the overhead covering. They would take us up 35 metres to look down over the roof of the jungle, we didn't look down until we reached the platform, and what a view. We may have missed it at Mashpi due to the low cloud but this more than made up for it.

It was only when Jim started to point out the route of the canopy walk connecting nine vast Capoc trees that we noticed the footbridges. If the tower was rickety these looked positively ramshackle. Imagine the footbridge on "I'm a Celebrity..." about 50 years after Ant and Dec have gone on to present weekday afternoon programmes for the bored, sick and elderly and that would be about right. This was not for the faint-hearted.

'Are we sure about this,' said Helene, 'it's awfully high and those bridges look really unsafe?'

'Remember our agreement, Helene,' I said, 'this was something we promised we'd do.'

Clumsy Jim led the way, this should be entertaining! The footbridges could only cope with the weight of one person at a time so I went next to demonstrate to Helene how easy it was.

'You see it's fine!' I called back in the most confident voice I could muster.

'Why are your legs shaking then?' she yelled back. This was no time for discussion.

The wooden planks less than a metre wide bounced and rebounded with every step, where they weren't broken or missing. The netting, doing its best to create sides, was frayed and full of holes, and the balustrade ropes to hang on to were slippery and unstable. Frankly, the whole thing felt completely perilous and precarious but we both made it and the next one was easier. After a few crossings between Capocs we were enjoying our jungle journey so were stopping halfway across to marvel at the views below from the canopy.

The Canopy Walk ended at another tower with a final connecting footbridge to the Jungle Tree House – available for a romantic dinner and night for two at 2,200 Soles about £600. We crossed the rope bridge, old hands at this now, to take a look at what a night would be like suspended 35 metres off the ground. Answer? Not for us really, far too small, a thunderbox for a loo and the room service! Don't ask.

As we made our way back through the jungle to the lodges we heard a thrashing in the treetops, a troupe of squirrel monkeys was crossing our path directly above us. Small, chestnut brown and incredibly agile these travelling troupes usually number a hundred or more, probably half of them came down from the canopy for a meet-and-greet with the three of us. They made no audible noise themselves; there was just the crash of ferns as they descended jumping from one branch to another. At one point they dislodged an old wooden bough and sent it clattering to the ground landing just in front of us. But what a sight this was, literally dozens of inquisitive little monkeys completely surrounding us, the nearest just a few feet away. Terrific fun and a great memory to take home with us from our days in the jungle. But it was not over yet.

The afternoon's expedition was half an hour up the river and an hour's hike to Sandoval Lake – *the most beautiful lake in South America* although I think our friends at Uros on Lake Titicaca may have a view on that. On entering the National Park, where strangely you have your passport stamped, we were advised to keep to the centre of the track as a precaution due to Bullet Ants crossing. These king-sized ants inflict the same venom as a python so best to give them a wide berth. Predictably enough Clumsy Jim had been stung by them, not once but an astonishing four times and was hospitalised each time. Didn't stop him hunting them down to show us how mean they looked though.

I may be a bit unfair on Jim, he certainly knew his stuff, and he stopped us in our tracks following one distant squawk enabling us to experience one of the rarest sights in the jungle. Two Royal Blue macaws with bright yellow breasts flew to perch in the canopy above us. I would have known these as parrots – the Long John Silver kind – white around the black beak and about a metre in length due to its long blue tail.

At the end of the challenging hike to a remote part of the deep jungle we found the creek and kayak that would provide the entrance to the lake, we also found a deserted bar. If you've ever watched "I'm a Celebrity…" when the poor celebs gamble their hard earned Dingo Dollars on some longed for treat like popcorn, then this was it. Manned by an equally brusque khaki clad individual we decided to pass on the opportunity to negotiate the price of the beer preferring to negotiate the route of the creek that would, with luck, lead us to the lake. The enclosed jungle creek meandered through the tangled everglade, and then with little warning we were disgorged into the vast motionless lagoon, it was breathtakingly beautiful.

We were not entirely alone on this secluded tranquil lake. From our small kayak we spotted Howler monkeys watching us manoeuvre around the shallows, a large Paiche broke the surface to take a look and half a dozen cormorants flew nearby inches from the surface no doubt searching for a late fish supper. But the one species we wanted to see was the otter. Jim managed our expectations advising that the lake is inhabited only by the rare Great otter of which there are less than five thousand still in existence globally and they are understandably very wary of humans.

Our luck was in though. We noticed a disturbance at one of the banks and paddled quietly closer. A family, or romp, as I was reliably informed by Jim, of six Grey otters came out from the margins to no more than 20 metres away. They have poor eyesight, using their whiskers to sense nearby fish, so in absolute silence we watched them hunt, catch and eat large fish for perhaps an hour or so. These are not the reddish brown cat sized otters we now have inhabiting some of our UK rivers but thickset and grey up to a metre or more in length with large heads and white chests.

They swam and dived together effortlessly as if part of a synchronised swimming team and once a fish was caught in its powerful jaws it would appear to stand up in the water grasping its prey while we heard the crunching and tearing of bones and flesh, all adding to this unique spectacle. As we sat quietly watching the exceptional scene and the sun sank providing us with an orange and pink sunset, the lake was to gift us with one more souvenir of our visit. High above us flying in formation across the lake were five red macaws and in the trees above the feasting otters were the infants of a family of monkeys chasing each other across the canopy. We appeared to have been transported into a Disney film.

Our last night at the jungle was also to be our last in Peru and in South America. We spent most of it trying to decipher what we had experienced over the past couple of months. We each set ourselves the difficult task of trying to create our Top Five bestest bits, but how on Earth can you compare Rainforest to Rapa Nui or Mashpi to Machu Picchu, impossible. After much discussion and justification, for the record this is where we finished up, but you'll notice we couldn't contain it to five.

David:
1. The Galápagos Islands
2. Atacama Desert
3. Machu Picchu
4. Amazon Jungle
5. Mashpi Rainforest
First Reserve; Rapa Nui

Helene:
1. The Galápagos Islands
2. Mashpi Rainforest
3. Atacama Desert
4. Amazon Jungle
5. Machu Picchu
First Reserve; Rapa Nui

Of all the places we were to visit on this crazy adventure we thought South America would probably push us farthest out of our comfort zone and it certainly did that, particularly for Helene who had risen wonderfully to every challenge. We had also seen some of the most spectacular scenery I guess the world has to offer – that's up to be challenged – and had some truly privileged experiences encountering the wildlife. Perhaps what we didn't expect was just how much we had learned about other cultures: their history and traditions, their development, society and beliefs, it has moved us and fascinated us, and we both feel the richer for it. Thanks South America.

Having been taught to walk like a Moai by Terry Hunt and Tito, Helene and I may be taking things a little too far.

Who would have thought that Jesus and his disciples chose the national Peruvian dish of Cuy Chactado for the Last Supper, at least according to Arequipa cathedral.

Helene on the Galápagos Islands with a beautiful lady giant tortoise that sadly Grace could not get to seduce Lonesome George.

After a full weeks feeding out at sea some seals just need a good lie down, any park bench will do.

Extraordinary entertainment. Dancing with horses at the Sol y Luna Lodge in the Sacred Valley, Peru.

Peruvian ladies selling their alpaca goods on the road side in the headwear identifying whether they are available.

Traditional boat building on the Uros floating islands of Lake Titicaca. Using the local reed method handed down over hundreds of years. And empty plastic coke bottles.

Helene modelling the hats made for the young unmarried women of Llachon by our local chef. His food was better.

Our wonderful guide Saiber demonstrating the quipu coded messages created by Pachacutec over 500 years ago, and still not cracked.

Pachacutec's extraordinary agricultural laboratory and research centre. Also responsible for the 2,000 variety of potatoes available in Peru today.

At the mountain lake after Saiber guided us down the dried up river bed. And no sign of the backup vehicle yet.

Jim and Helene in the Amazonica jungle – "I am an intrepid explorer, with war paint on, machete in hand and ready to take on anything."

Helene on the frightening Canopy Walk we had promised each other we would complete. But we declined the romantic dinner for two in the jungle tree house.

The hunt for the Penis Tree is over, thank goodness, with the two of us looking very uncomfortable.

CHAPTER 12

Day 61 to 78: USA

Hawaii

ALOHA!

We left the jungle slightly sweaty and possible smelly for the short flight from Puerto Maldonado to Lima. We were looking forward to a stopover at an airport hotel from 6:00 PM until midnight for a long hot shower, a change into fresh, more appropriate clothes we hadn't seen for a week and a good meal before our 2:00 AM flight to Los Angeles. Unfortunately, the hotel we had selected had no hot water throughout the building; that was okay though because our shower didn't work, and the door key failed to do its single simplest job – I checked us out within the hour.

The overnight flight gave us the opportunity to sleep for a few hours without any fat bugs in our flat beds and the wonderful Marriott in LA sympathised with our plight or our pong and provided a suite as soon as we checked in at around 8:30 AM. A hot shower and change of clothes had never felt so good.

We spent a crazy day on Santa Monica Pier and Boulevard back in the best civilisation the US can offer, and my goodness they do that well. We, well Helene, watched the sinewed boys perform on Muscle Beach and spotted the larger versions eating large dishes at Bubba Gump. We explored some ridiculously funky craft stalls and trendy shops including one where for $40 you could have a "medical marijuana evaluation" by The Green Doctors. Most people exiting the premises seemed very pleased with their examination.

The boulevard was full of music, some great street dancing and exceedingly poor street art, colourful people including pop star Tony Hadley tipping every performer he could find, and every conceivable shaped bike, skateboard and wheelie contraption you could imagine. What a contrast to a few days ago and what fun.

That evening we ate early and repacked our zippy-uppy bags for another entirely different environment; Hawaii and a flight into Honolulu. This is all a bit confusing for me. We're going to Hawaii, landing on the third largest island known as Oahu, whose capital is Honolulu also capital of Hawaii. There is an island named Hawaii but it's called Big Island and it's not the capital, we are then visiting two other islands called Kauai and Maui in Hawaii. I guess that's why Helene does logistics and I do finance.

ALOHA! Yes, we finally arrived in Hawaii, I think, on Oahu after our pleasant flight from LA. Love it or hate it, the American efficiency is something to envy, it's all on time, it all works and all the information you need you get. Impressive. We were staying at a large city hotel so swapped our unpretentious yet beautiful Amazon thatched lodge for a 14th floor homogenised hotel bedroom. You know the type of thing; big bed and TV to match, mini bar and maxi coffee machine, en suite everything and on-call room service, while knowing every room above, below and either side is exactly the same as ours. But this is what we needed to rest mind, body and soul after what had been a wonderful, if not frenetic and sometimes exhausting two months in South America.

Hawaii is just the place to relax and recharge, so a stroll around town and a visit to the renowned Bishop Museum was our first port of call. It was founded in 1889 by Charles Reed Bishop. A large picture of him hangs in the entrance, a solemn looking gentleman posing formally against a studio made rock in a frock coat and a white beard almost as long as his top hat is high. Sitting demurely next to him in a long dress of many layers is his wife in honour of whom the museum was founded. She is Princess Bernice Pauahi Bishop, the last descendant of the Royal Kamehameha family.

Hawaii still had a monarchy until the US took over in 1887 when they forced the king to sign a new charter, known as the Bayonet Constitution, eventually becoming the newest of the 50 states of the US. The last monarch was his sister Queen Liliuokalani born on September 2nd 1838 so while we were there they celebrated her birthday with a huge banquet and party at the old palace. Our invitation appeared to have been lost in the post.

In 1893 after a plot by local businessmen and farmers to strengthen her power failed, she was also forced to renounce all claims to the throne and ended her days under house arrest with Hawaii becoming a US territory in 1898. It's quite telling that there are still as many, perhaps more, British Hawaiian flags flying on the island as there are the American Stars and Stripes, particularly given that Barack Obama was born and educated in the town.

Our hotel was directly opposite the famous Waikiki beach where the royal family used to surf, okay perhaps not, but it was their private beach.

'Let's go surfing on Waikiki,' I said, beginning to sing the theme tune to "Hawaii Five-0".

'You, surf?' said Helene, not really joining in with my eagerness.

'In my younger days I was a surfer. Cornwall, Cap Ferrat, Malibu Board, the lot. I was awesome in the surf.'

'Really?'

'Yes, come on, I'll teach you,' I said with more enthusiasm than Helene was showing at this point.

Of course, Waikiki is where surfing began, or "enalu" in the Hawaiian language. James Cook's Endeavour is thought to have first discovered surfing, not sure if he tried his hand, but it certainly predates their European contact. The surfboard as we know it today however, is a relatively recent invention, the locals claim it was popularised by the wonderfully named Duke Kahanamoku a 1930's five times Olympic medallist and a law enforcement officer, an actor, a beach volleyball player and a businessman.

As we walked towards the rather loud crashing surf we came across the duke's larger-than-life-size bronze statue with surfboard in hand standing proudly in front of Waikiki beach. And his legacy lives on, no matter how early we rise we see the surfers from our 14th floor in the morning, there are hundreds of them, all bobbing on their boards waiting for **the** wave. There'd been a storm out at sea, perhaps as a consequence of Hurricanes Harvey and Irma who between them sadly wreaked havoc in parts of Texas, Florida and the Caribbean. They had also created much larger waves than usual breaking a long way out, perfect surfing conditions for the locals, not sure about me though.

'Goodness,' said Helene, 'look at the size of those waves.'

'They are a little on the large size,' I said, slightly regretting the male bravado of earlier.

'Go on then, Duke,' she encouraged, 'show me how it's done.'

'It's not just a case of paddling out with the board you know. We have to read the swell, calculate where the waves are breaking and where the riptides are. Then work out the best route to the back of those formidable breakers.'

'Maui beer, darling?'

'Good idea, maybe tomorrow.'

With a board is difficult enough but without one is ridiculous. We opted for a walk in search of the island's famous street food market near Panic Point, where the fearless and foolish body surf in huge fast waves in front of the daunting volcanic rock shore. There was a competition in full swing when we arrived with commentators awarding points for acrobatics, flamboyant stunts and I guess just how close the competitors were to being mashed on the rocks. Panic Point is well named I think.

Oahu is not what either of us expected. We anticipated arriving on an island similar to those in the Caribbean but what we found in Honolulu was closer to Dubai than Jamaica. It was a cosmopolitan city with every conceivable designer retail brand from Armani to Zara, and restaurants from high end Teppanyaki to wonderful eclectic indoor food markets, a sort of upmarket street food. Oahu is busy, vibrant and fun where the Japanese far outnumber the Americans, and the Brits are scarcely seen or heard at all.

We arrived on Labour Day weekend so it was exceptionally crowded on the beaches, full of people watching people watching surfers and snorkelers, boogie boarders, beach posers and boaters, stand-up paddlers and laid down sun worshippers, volleyball players, kayaking couples and brides and grooms. In fact, the whole island was teeming with tourists yet the bars and restaurants were so plentiful and the service so efficient that we were always well looked after. Which brings me on to service or more specifically, tipping.

Now, I believe that good service deserves a tip and the rule of thumb for me is around 10% to 15% and then rounded up, but not there it wasn't! It starts at

18% and if you're not sure they provide three options on the bill, the top one usually highlighted in yellow marker, often with a hastily drawn heart around it. So, you have to declare your hand; a miserly 18% escalating to 20% and an overly magnanimous 22%. They then calculate the three total bill options for you to choose from. Just in case we can't work out any of this for ourselves the bill, sorry check, also comes with a ready reckoner, calculating the three service alternatives for amounts from $25 all the way up to $550. Handy. This may sound hypocritical having just extolled the virtues of American service but I expect it to be good without paying extortionate fees for it, or is that just moany, miserly me?

It wasn't just the end of the meal that caught me out, we couldn't even get started.

'Can I take your order?' asked the young waiter at the beach restaurant we had chosen for the evening.

'Yes please,' I replied, 'we'll start with the drinks, a Maui beer and a bottle of Sauvignon with two glasses please.'

'No.'

'What?'

'No.'

'I may not look it but I am over 18, son.'

'David!' Helene says I get pompous when I'm in the wrong, but I couldn't see the problem here.

She intervened, 'Do you not have Sauvignon?'

'Yes, but you can't have both,' said the young waiter. 'That would be stacking.'

We looked at each other, and then turned our attention to the stubborn waiter.

'Stacking?' we both asked.

Apparently, there's a licensing law in Hawaii designed to prevent customers from "stacking drinks", that is ordering more than one drink for themselves at a time, like a chaser or shots I suppose. We negotiated the beer for me and the bottle for Helene, the kindly young waiter provided a second glass from another table.

We were intending to visit the famous Pearl Harbour site but there was a 2 hour queue so we decided to hire a car and drive the circumference of this delightful island, some of which does resemble the Caribbean island we were expecting. It is the busiest road network in America apparently but the route hugged a beautiful perimeter coast linking beaches and rocky bays to manicured green parks with brick built barbecues. You just turn up and slap on the biggest piece of meat you can buy, excellent idea, must suggest it to the Royal Borough of Windsor & Maidenhead town council for our parks.

As we discovered more of Oahu we realised that this really is an island designed for rest and relaxation, so we spent the first few days doing exactly that, strolling the length of Waikiki beach, nosing around the designer shops, light lunches at some of the hotel beach bars and restaurants, and enjoying the Honolulu version of an open top bus. These are a hop-on hop-off Trolley straight out of San Francisco with seats facing out of the open sides and a comical driver/guide Ricardo who seemed to be as surprised about the sights and sounds of up and down town Honolulu as we were.

Over the weekend we stumbled across the Okinawa Festival, the largest ethnic festival in Hawaii now celebrating its 35th year, great entertainment with traditional bands and dancing, classic Hawaiian food and local crafts. Couldn't find the beer tent but bought two walking sticks based on our Mashpi experience.

In the festival park, we discovered the famous Banyan Tree. A fig tree that is remarkable both in its extraordinary size, height and width, and the way it chooses to grow. They are epiphytes, a plant that grows on another usually by a seed germinating in the crevice of a tree. Once they have established themselves on a host they throw down "roots" from their branches and then start growing back upwards again. These create sort of accessory trunks as props for their spreading branches above and they eventually kill the host and create this marvellous edifice in their own right.

They are also believed to be sacred and mystical, children are taught never to point at a fully mature Banyan Tree for fear of offending the spirits that dwell within and apparently Filipinos always utter a respectful word or two when they pass. Somehow I get this, they really are noble creations.

Oahu was great, Honolulu was grand, and certainly somewhere to be considered for those January to March months when we intend to escape the dreadful UK weather. It was over far too quickly as we took the 30 minute flight onto our next Hawaiian island, Kauai.

We were now out of the wonderful Audley bubble for a couple of weeks, so we, okay Helene, tracked down an AirBnB apartment on a small beach complex in Kapa'a on the east of the fourth largest and oldest island. Kauai – *The Garden Isle* has a perimeter of around 150 km of secluded coastline, it promises lush vegetation, majestic valleys, captivating cliffs, tropical rainforest, waterfalls, rivers and breath taking beaches. We looked forward to seeing if that was true.

It was definitely a pleasure to be in a domestic home rather than a hotel room so we could eat-in occasionally, something we hadn't done for well over two months, although they do provide these communal barbecues dotted around the place which are really handy to whack on a massive steak or fish and eat out in the gardens watching the full moon rise over the sea.

Kauai is the result of volcanic eruption, with a crater in the centre of this almost perfectly round cone shaped island at a height of 5,150 feet above sea level, the wettest spot on Earth allegedly with 470 inches of rain a year. It's a big claim for a small island and a long way from Manchester A bigger claim is that it is Hollywood's favourite location for exotic movies: Jurassic Park, Indiana Jones, The Thorn Birds, Lost, Hook, From Here to Eternity, and South Pacific all featured the island. If there was an Oscar for Best Location Kauai would have a loo full.

After the few days in Oahu of basking on beaches and lazy lunches, I think we deserved after the jungle, we decided to hire a couple of bikes and cycle Kauai's newly established 8 km beach path along the Coconut Coast. Or tried to.

'I can't reach the ground!' shrieked Helene, balancing on the bike's cross bar. 'This is a boy's bike and could do some eye watering damage if I'm not careful.'

'Okay, we'll go to Rocky's Rentals up the road; it looks slightly more promising, but only just.'

We spotted an old shed with bikes lying scattered on the grass verge.

'Are you sure about this,' said Helene, 'the bikes just seem to be abandoned?'

'No, I'm not sure, and there's no sign of Rocky.' Rocky's rental shack seemed to be as abandoned as Rocky's rental bikes, but there was a sign on the broken padlocked front door.

'Here we are!' I called back to Helene who was gingerly testing a bike. 'It reads "Call Rocky for all your rental needs – I promise to pick up!" I'll give it a go.'

Helene found a suitable bike from the five available, she could touch the ground, no cross bar and it even had a Mary Poppins basket, so I called Rocky, he did pick up. I could almost smell the weed down the phone.

'Firstly, deposit $30 in the little black tin around the side of the shack,' he said. I'll do that last then.

'But, Rocky the bikes have locks on them.'

'No worries,' he said, 'go around the back and find the old barbecue, lift the lid, better make sure it's cold, and there you'll find a whole load of keys. Some of those will fit the bikes you want, put them back under the barbecue lid when you return, safe and happy cycling, aloha!' And with that Rocky was gone.

To be fair to Rocky the keys did indeed release the bikes, the bikes without any brakes. These were fixed wheel bikes, you sort of pedal backwards to slow down but never actually stop. Well, it's only 15 km or so what could possibly go wrong? And anyway the $30 was now in the little black box. Off we went, slowly at first, but when we found the new coastal bike path my goodness it was worth it, majestic scenery of deserted coves with huge waves crashing on to empty golden beaches. It was glorious and even Helene admitted the cycling was eventually enjoyable with the added bonus of neither of us falling off; we were only missing the 36 chiringuitos we usually pass on our Marbella cycle ride.

On our return leg we encountered a rather unusual and apparently rare sunbather on the beach, a colossal Hawaiian Monk seal gently snoozing on the shore, all 3 metres of it. Or to use its Hawaiian name "Ilio-holo-i-ka-uaua" and if you can pronounce that then hana maika'i to you. They only exist on Hawaii and were once hunted close to extinction. They are protected today but with only around two hundred and fifty on the main islands they remain on the Critically Endangered list fighting against a declining food supply and climate change. When one comes on shore for a nap after a hard day's fight the local wardens are called, who immediately seal off the area (sorry) and erect a large sign; *"Please go Around – resting Hawaiian Monk seal"*. So, we dismounted from our bikes and circumnavigated the slumbering magnificent creature, being sure not to wake him.

A great day finished off by a well-deserved swim and dinner-in with a Longboard Island lager, a beery tribute to the boards used on Waikiki beach with the inspired Ad strap line of *"Thirst's Up!"* I must say the Hawaiian air made me as sleepy as the altitude did, which was okay as we had to be up early the next morning to collect the hire car for the first of our trips around the perimeter of the island. Well, not completely around, there is really only one road on the island, it starts as a dual carriageway hugging the coast but doesn't quite make it, finishing as an unmade road easing its way onto a beach on the north side some 25 km short of where it starts. There are no roads in the interior, apart from a track with a dead end at Waimea Canyon, it's just too impenetrable.

We were staying on the east side of the island so the first stop on our tour of the north was Kilauea Bay and lighthouse, and quite unexpectedly spotting the missing No. 14 of the Galápagos Big 15, the Red Footed boobie. You may remember its Blue Footed cousin on the Galápagos. To be honest it wasn't a case of spotting, we couldn't fail to see them, there were hundreds perched on the cliff, nesting in the trees and flying above us. How lovely to be reacquainted with this delightful bird and surprisingly the frigatebird we also remembered from the Galápagos, the ones with the red chests they inflate during courtship.

Apparently not so surprisingly, we were informed by the warden that where you find one you find the other. The boobie is the one who does the work, flying up to 40 km out in search of fish they then carry back for their young only to be set upon by the frigates in an attempt to dislodge the catch, highly unsportsmanlike behaviour. We also spotted the Tropicbirds an elegant large gull with red tail streamers at least a foot long, they fly standing up in the air when courting and can be seen flying backwards to attract their mate. I thought hummingbirds were the only ones who can fly backwards but apparently not. Sadly, it was the wrong time of year to see the Albatross, or Gooney Birds as they are known due to their clumsiness on land, completely contradicting their elegance in the air, so No. 15 will have to wait.

We followed the road around the north coast to arrive at the most exquisite town of Hanalei Bay with the most expensive properties to match, would you believe $16.5M for a two bed two bath property, but it does come with over an acre of oceanfront land. Perhaps not that surprising, we were told Mark Zuckerberg had just paid $66M for 250 acres on the island and built a 2 metre stone wall around it – that must have given him blisters.

The single road continues through a golf course estate called Princeville built around the most manicured of fairways and greens. It then narrows, crossing a number of one way bridges and what my dad would call "water splashes", the vegetation evolves into a rainforest and the road into a beach. It just stops, so it's the same way home with a brief pause on one of the beautiful bays for a swim, very pleasant. Odd thing about Kauai wherever we went there were cockerels, on the roads, on the beaches, in the airport and in car parks. Colourful and brazen cockerels, nice, but odd.

Day two with the car, on the same road of course, was an expedition into the south and west side of the island with an early morning trip to investigate the Waimea Canyon, a volcanic gash running north-south over a kilometre wide, 15 km long and over 1,000 km deep – *The Grand Canyon of the Pacific.* Our new friends James and Julie, who we met on the Galápagos adventure, lived here some time ago so provided some helpful hints, tips and suggestions for our visit. This included the best route up to the top of the canyon, the one the locals use, and a recommendation to depart at 6:00 AM to beat the cloud and mist that rolls in, after all it is the wettest place in the world. We may not have set the alarm early enough.

'We are far too late,' complained Helene, as we looked for the fast route the locals take up the mountain.

'Here it is,' I said, 'next to the statue of Cook. Someone's put a garland round his neck, that's nice.'

'Don't tempt me!'

Waimea is where the explorer Capt. Cook first landed in the Hawaiian Islands in 1778, so quite fitting the town should have a statue in his honour. But it's actually a replica of the one in his home town of Whitby.

'Let's go straight to the top,' said Helene, 'we can do all these viewing platforms on the way down.'

Nothing wrong with this logic, so off we set twisting and turning to the top at an ear popping speed with the promise of spectacular coast to coast views. On our approach to the small car park at the top it began to rain.

'It's raining!' said Helene.

'Yes, and the clouds and mist are rolling in.'

'Just as James and Julie said it would. What is it with us and miradors?'

Helene was right, the lookout tower at Mashpi, the San Cristobal Hill in Santiago and now the top of the island in Kauai, all we could ever see, or not, was mist and fog. A tad disheartened and slightly soggy, we had walked to the top just to make sure and the heavens opened, so we returned to the observation posts we had passed to see if we could actually observe anything. Funny things clouds, as we descended we ducked under the veil clinging to the summit to be presented with clear views across the canyon, they were magnificent and on an immense scale.

It is said that the Hawaiian Islands have twenty-seven ecosystems and probably microclimates to match, it seems like most are on Kauai. As we drove around this diverse island we crossed rainforest, arid plains, volcanic mountains, lush plantations and tropical beaches, it's like the huge Atacama Desert all rolled into one on an island just slightly larger than Berkshire.

One of the highlights, particularly for Helene, was a visit to a coffee plantation, something she's always wanted to do, I didn't know that, and in fact the largest coffee grower in the US. Kauai Coffee – *Taste Paradise One Cup at a Time* – is in 3,000 acres with over four million trees. Following a 20 minute tour around the grounds – *from seed to bean to cup* – we were invited to a coffee tasting. Well, we've done tea tasting at a plantation in Sri Lanka, rum tasting at a distillery in Granada, beer tasting at the greatly missed Rebellion Brewery back home and wine tasting just about everywhere, so why not. I didn't know coffee could be so different, before we even start thinking about blends and adding flavours we had to consider strength of roast, drying time and bean type. Caramel Mild was my favourite; Helene's was not a decaf but Blue Mountain Dark Roast. All good fun.

On the way to a light lunch we were enticed into the "historical town of Hanapepe". This was a traditional cowboy town, more of a ghost town really; it was completely deserted, but all added to the atmosphere. The stores' facades have remained unchanged for a 100 years or so, I guess that's "historical" for the US, but instead of selling horse saddles, pistols and of course cowboy boots they now offered haute couture, pampering and of course, cowboy boots.

James had given us a great suggestion for lunch, Brennecke's Beach Broiler, the food really is better than the name suggests: fish tacos and salad, with Helene's first beer for 3 years, Longboard Lager of course, but gluten free. Later we spent an idle couple of hours watching the local boys surf and spin on some sizeable waves. We were just paddling back when a couple of seals swam up to arrive about 2 metres from us; they cavorted in the surf and showed off their skills in the shallows. The warden arrived pretty soon with ropes and "Do Not Disturb" signs in hand but the seals were more interested in performing for us in the waves than joining us on the beach.

After two days touring this wonderfully contrasting island it appeared to be another of those destinations to be considered for those cold January to March months. Our last day was to be a final time for rest and relaxation on the beach before we moved on. We were just getting our kindles and cosies together when the lights went out, all of them right across the island. But that's okay the boys were on it and an hour later power was restored, then it went again, apparently the "fix" set fire to the whole facility and the island went dark, so the shops and restaurants just shut and we all went to the beach. That's what you do in Hawaii.

The next day we moved on to our third Hawaiian island, Maui, voted Best Island in the US by Conde Nast Traveler readers for more than 20 years.

Apart from the taxi breaking down on the way to the airport the trip to Maui was short and uneventful. We checked into the Sheraton – *the most romantic escape on all the Hawaiian Islands.* Located at the end of the kilometre long Ka'anapali Beach,it was voted Conde Nast Traveller "Beach of the Year", nothing like over selling these places, but quite an accolade and a quite delightful view from our fifth floor room. There were plenty of bars and restaurants for us to discover all the way down the sandy strip over the next 4 days, and every other one seemed to be called Sandy Toes.

The hotel was exactly what we needed, acres of well-kept lawns, a huge pool and a silly lazy river passing bars overlooking the glorious beach. One of the focal points was Black Rock, a craggy volcanic spit stretching out around 100 metres into the sea and about 20 metres in height. It is a sacred spot where legend has it the souls of the departed enter into the spiritual world. Today it's the bodies of the demented that enter the water world. Yes, they jump.

Funny that things look higher when you're at the top looking down rather than at the bottom looking up, but as I climbed the rugged rock to the outcrop from which I was to launch myself into midair... of course I didn't! We said we'd try anything once but this may have been the first and last for me.

On one entertaining morning a gentleman of considerable age, well 65 and frankly should have known better, spent a full hour teetering on the top of the cliff summoning the courage to take the leap. Despite vocal encouragement from the younger Americans below he failed to take the plunge opting for the walk of shame back down the rocks. I guess the lesson is to always check your moral fibre before committing to the challenge.

Here's one; what's the similarity between a restaurant at 9:00 PM in the US and a restaurant at 9:00 PM in Spain? Nothing, both are empty. In the US, they've finished serving and in Spain they're only just opening, takes a bit of getting used to, we're just leaving the beach when they're just leaving the restaurant.

So, our last night was a late trip into Lahaina, a beachfront town for the Friday Night Art Walk, a beautiful stroll down Front Street full of open-night galleries, small designer shops, bars and restaurants. Mick Fleetwood has his rooftop music bar here, and rumours have it that he often plays live.

The quality of art and calibre of artist were impressive for this small parochial town: Chagall, Miro, Dali, Picasso and actors turned painters including Jim Carrey, Anthony Hopkins and Anthony Quinn – surprisingly good actually – along with local artists and sculptors in attendance exhibiting their skills. Enthusiastic gallery owners dispensed wine, champagne, canapés and anecdotes about their favourite artist or how they acquired a special piece and a good time was had by all. Over a dinner of shrimp and vegetable brochettes for Helene, delicious, and shrimp with macaroni cheese for me, interesting, we agreed that this was a real contender for those January to March months we intend to escape the dreadful UK weather.

We seemed to have created a bit of a dilemma here; each island had provided us with its unique interpretation of Hawaii, all attractive in their own different way.

'Perhaps a month in each,' suggested Helene. There is however, a sentiment across the islands which has enchanted, charmed and seduced us and is perhaps best summed up by "Aloha".

Although it is universally used and appears to feature in almost every sentence as an adjective, verb or noun, it is much more than just a greeting. The locals define it as a spirit or "life force" that helps to explain who the islanders are and why they are there. It is a condition, a way of life, a mind set and an attitude based upon respect, love and reciprocity. Yes, that's why we'll be returning to Hawaii.

CHAPTER 13

Day 79 to 87: FIJI

Tokoriki

Paradise Found

'Think of the points,' Helene encouraged happily.

'I'm sure we're gold, platinum or emerald on just about every airline and hotel group we've used,' I said, 'but this is really early.'

It was the start of our airline marathon. The direct flight from LA to Auckland was cancelled some time ago; they just don't offer that route anymore. So, it was a circuitous route going west to Sydney then east to arrive in New Zealand and on to Fiji.

It had to be an early start to ensure the connections worked and to catch flight number 19 of the trip Maui to Oahu. Then a bit of a haul back up to Los Angeles for a stopover and to collect the rest of our cold climate zippy-uppy bags we had stored at the hotel while in Hawaii.

As we dragged our newly packed bags into the lift we were joined by a robot, not dissimilar to R2D2 from Star Wars.

'Good grief,' cried Helen, 'what, or who is this?'

'That's Wally the hotel robot, I think.'

He wandered in, bleeped, flashed and sort of robotically stared at Helene.

'I think you should pose for a picture with him,' I suggested.

'How do you pose with a robot?' Fair question.

He graciously allowed us out of the lift first and made his way to reception skilfully avoiding other bemused guests and vacant luggage. The manager told me if we dialled 0 for room service Wally would deliver our order. How he knocks on the door and whether you tip him I had no idea, great name when he goes walkabout though.

Our body clock was about to be assaulted by a 15 hour flight leaving LA at 10:30 PM on Sunday evening and arriving in Sydney at 6:30 AM on Tuesday morning, not quite sure how that works, but has anyone seen Monday? Then a quick turnaround for a flight to Auckland, so Australia had to wait for a couple of months, and finally flight number 23 to Fiji, our destination for an island break and a cruise. I still wasn't convinced that I was ready or old enough for cruising.

We were back in the Audley bubble at Fiji's Nadi International Airport where we were met on the aircraft gantry and escorted through "Diplomatic Passports Only"; I don't know how Audley managed that, but all part of the service I guess. Our luggage was collected for us and we were adeptly ushered onto our transit vehicle heading for Port Denarau where our boat would take us on the 1 hour journey to Tokoriki our island home for the next week. We later discovered we also had the option of arriving by sea plane or helicopter, but it was a delight to see all the palm tree covered sandy islands on the way despite the bumpy conditions.

We weren't sure what to expect in Fiji, what little we knew was limited to their passion for rugby where the All Blacks steal most of their best players, not surprising, even the waiters look like Flankers. It is also home to the best Rugby Sevens player the world has ever seen, Waisale Serevi. He was to Sevens what Pele was to football. His international career started in 1989 and this exquisitely skilled sportsman played on until 2005. I had the privilege to see him in his last game when he captained Fiji to win the Rugby World Cup Sevens.

Excuse the rugby digression, any excuse, but to be fair there was a Sevens

Tournament in our village on the island opposite Tokoriki. Fiji is an archipelago of three hundred and thirty islands spread over 250,000 kilometres of beautiful crystal clear South Pacific Ocean. Tokoriki is one of the most remote. It is situated within the Mamanuca Islands and remained unknown to the outside world until the 1840's when a US exploring expedition completed the first chart of the Fiji Islands. The island covers only 160 acres and is fringed by a protective barrier reef about 150 metres offshore creating an emerald and aquamarine lagoon surrounding the island.

Tokoriki was uninhabited until the resort opened in 1990, it was later bought and developed by Andrew Turnbull the guy who brought Chupa Chups lollies to the rest of the world, the ones Kojak made famous in the 1970's. He leases the island from the Paramount Chief or Tui Lawa who used it for farming crops and his family spend a week or so each month at the resort in his villa; it has been named Top Hotel in Fiji by Facebook for 3 years running.

In Fijian, Tokoriki means "stay here", the same as Arequipa in Peru, the "white city" we liked so much, and given the welcome we received we thought we would enjoy our stay there enormously. The staff greeted us warmly with a "welcome home!", hung garlands and beads around our necks and gathered to sing a rousing Fijian song full of hand clapping and shouts of 'Bula!' Fijian for hello. Or hola or lorana or aloha. We seemed to have acquired quite a collection.

As we had learned over the preceding 3 months, the locals really appreciate it when you greet them in their own language, and we were always respectful of their traditions, beliefs and culture no matter how obscure. Fijians do not point at one another with their hands, fingers or feet and it is offensive to be touched on the head. In the villages where a visit is by invitation only one should never wear a hat because it is considered an insult to the chief. This sort of thing reminded us just how far we were from home, well over 10,000 miles, and how different our cosmopolitan culture is.

Maybe it's the laid-back vibe on the island but as soon as I introduced myself to the manager I was rechristened Dave. I let them get away with it though, as I think it's part of the homeliness of the place. And impressively, within 24 hours every member of staff from bar to beach referred to us by our Christian names and seemed to know which wine and beer we drank, Fiji Gold – *Refreshingly Gold!* was mine.

They are good-natured and warm-hearted people, friendly, open, hospitable and hugely proud of their islands. They had also recently been voted the happiest people in the world, not surprising at all, this was about as close to paradise as you can get. I never thought we'd beat our honeymoon in Bora Bora Nui but... well we would see.

The thirty-five elegant thatched beach bungalows, known as Bures, each had their own garden leading onto the palm tree adorned seashore and were stylishly designed with vaulted ceilings, a wooden four-poster bed and contemporary art and sculptures. But what I really adored were the two showers, one indoor and one out. I wondered if there was anything better than showering under a blue sky and sunshine creating your own rainbows.

The main restaurant and bar overlooked the infinity pool, soft sand beach and out across the lagoon to a cluster of desert islands not far in the distance, one of them is actually called Treasure Island, yo ho ho and all that and another Modriki was used in the Tom Hanks film Cast Away.

Although there was snorkelling, paddle boarding, sailing and glass bottomed kayaks for us to take out, most of our time was spent lounging, looking out to sea and listening to the couple of resident singers. They would start to strum and sing at any opportunity: hellos, goodbyes, birthdays, honeymoons, even a retirement and during lunch, over dinner or just for fun. They were often joined by other members of staff and occasionally guests on ukuleles, a skiffle box oddly, or just harmonising and clapping along, all great fun. There seemed to be guitars everywhere, propped up on a palm tree or leaning on a lounger just waiting for an excuse to be played.

One such occasion was after an excellent Teppanyaki meal in Oishii, meaning delicious, the onsite restaurant for eight. The meal was full of theatre and drama as the chef used his iron griddle like a sorcerer would his cauldron, conjuring up all sorts of mouthwatering locally caught fish and prawn dishes, all under the watchful eye of Mumma, a large happy woman dressed in layers of floral material and a matching turban headdress. While the chef weaved his magic Mumma provided a running commentary and flowing wine. We all laughed our way through an extravagant meal and left to continue the party on the terrace overlooking a moonlit sea.

Perhaps it was the unique aura of Tokoriki or the amusing ambience of an Oishii evening shared with new friends, but the atmosphere was clearly intoxicating and Helene was ready for a sing-song. The two boys were still strumming their melodic Fijian love songs on the terrace when one of them, Paulo, asked in his slow and deep gruff voice,

'Does anybody wanna a song?'

'I'll sing with you,' offered Helene, looking as surprised as the rest of us.

'I think Paulo may have meant any requests,' I suggested, but this was not going to put her off. Helene interpreted it as an invitation to take the vacant stool between the two of them and join in.

'Whataya gonna sing?' Paulo asked in a voice that now seemed to have risen an octave or two.

'Imagine, but I don't know all the lyrics,' Helene said, making herself comfortable between the two guitarists who now looked like her support band.

'That s'alright,' said Paulo, 'I dunno all the chords.'

As the bar emptied onto the terrace to watch and John turned in his grave, Helene turned on the charm and accompanied by the two boys she serenaded our fellow guests with a pretty damn good Fijian interpretation of the song.

The food on the island was without doubt the finest we had been served so far, their matching of fruit with either fish or meat was improbably excellent. Crispy chicken breast with green papaya, mango, toasted peanuts, lime and chilli was marvellous and the rack of lamb with watermelon, French beans, feta and mint was excellent. They also have a great dessert called Tokoriki sandy ice-cream with nut praline, brandy snap and Fiji coconut rum cream, what a treat.

After dinner we would often meet up with Paulo, the older of the two band members, with an impressive yet brave fifteen children. We were about to find out why and how!

'We take kava tonight,' he drawled, as the few guests willing to give-it-a-go sat on floor cushions in a circle around him and his kava paraphernalia, a large rusty bowl and ladle, a jug of who knew what and something in what looked like an old woollen sock.

As Paulo entertained us with fascinating stories about the islanders' culture and his ever increasing family he held up the woollen ball.

'This is our legal drug,' he announced.

The island's "legal drug" is a mild narcotic made from the root of the pepper plant.

'Now we know why they're the happiest people in the world,' whispered Helene.

'And, probably why he has so many children,' I added.

Paulo had earlier pounded the root into a pulp and put it in his old spare sock. He mixed it with water in the central large bowl and halved coconut shells were handed to the gathered and rather bewildered guests. I have to say the preparation looked more like Paulo was actually washing his soiled socks as he kneaded it in the bowl turning the water an unappealing milky grey. It was ladled into our coconut shells for us to drink, clap twice and bow to the kava bowl. It tasted like clay and liquorice, and made your lips go numb; it also made me sleep like a baby.

The kava ceremony is integral to the culture and customs of the Fijian communities where the island chiefs are still as powerful as the local and national governments. Without the chief's approval simply nothing gets done. So, any individual or corporate entity seeking planning rights for example or even permission to visit another group of islands has to sit with the chief concerned and "take kava". I guess enough kava until the chief has completely forgotten what the issue was and with a smile on his face will agree to just about anything.

Paulo also introduced us to a favourite Fijian song *"Don't you touch my Papaya"* sung with tongue-in-cheek, if that's possible, and much to the amusement of all the guests. He milked it for all it was worth and as the week went by we joined in the chorus.

Please don't touch my papaya
Everybody on the island will know
Please don't touch my papaya
Gonna save it from my good friend Jo

I suppose I should have guessed that the original song was from the wonderfully named Kavaholics.

Following another excellent dinner under the stars we were invited to participate in Crab Racing. Now this was not the fun my brother and I had as children on our annual 2 week holiday in Margate, this was far more sophisticated and just to make it interesting involved a shilling on the side.

The pitch was a circular board of about 2 metres in diameter, the players were ten carefully selected hermit crabs and the winner was the first one from the centre to fall off the edge of the pitch. But we started with the auction. Each crab was allocated a country and a name: Federer for Switzerland, Trump for America, oddly Johnson for the UK and so on. We then bid for each player starting at F$10.

Enter Big Joe. Big Joe was well, big; he was also from New York and had that loud drawl of a Manhattan accent where each word is given far too many vowels. To say he put the oik in Noo Yoik may be a little unfair but you get the picture.

'I voited for Trump and I'm sure as hell gonna win with Trump,' screamed Big Joe, as his bidding for Trump passed F$100.

'Goodness, Helene,' I said, 'your F$12 for Johnson looks like a bargain.'

Bidding over and Trump secured by Big Joe, the race began. This was not the Grand National or the Melbourne Cup but the cheering, shouting and vociferous encouragement was just as passionate. Big Joe "loist", due to his crab being a lazy SoB but Helene had an F$89 triumph she felt was better deserved in the staff Christmas box. A fine evening.

No animals were harmed in the making of this game.

Our last night on this sublimely beautiful island, enriched by its warm warm-hearted and affectionate people, was a Fijian version of fruit de mer under a smiling moon – the crescent is at the bottom there not the sides, so even the moon is happy – served on a candlelit table for two on the beach. The boys from the band, Tom and Paulo, serenaded the two of us with our favourite songs from the past few days as we fell hopelessly in love with the paradise we had found.

CHAPTER 14

Day 88 to 99: FIJI
Fiji Island Cruise

Who puts the Ah! in Relaxation?

It was a Magic Kingdom Moment goodbye to Tokoriki for Helene, perhaps only farewell, as the band and staff sung their final song about how the island will miss us as much as we would miss the island. The resort speed boat bounced us back to Port Denarau on a beautiful Fijian day of blue skies and emerald seas.

But our love affair with Fiji was set to continue with a 7 day cruise around the Yasawa Islands on the Reef Endeavour – they missed a trick there, really should have called it Reef Encounter, Cook reference accepted – a ship of around fifty cabins, or Double Staterooms as they are termed.

There was a rumour that when she was built 22 years ago in Fiji she began to sink on her maiden voyage, so was dragged to Australia to have her bottom re-bored, or hull settled to use the nautical term. I don't believe a word of it.

Our cabin was located in the centre of the middle deck so very stable, with two large windows and a comfortable bed, all okay for us on our first real maiden voyage. As soon as we had unpacked and explored the ship – five levels including a great sun deck with Jacuzzi and bar – snorkelling gear was allocated for the week and we were off on our first excursion, to Tigua Island. It was all palm trees and golden sand around its 800 metre circumference with of course the manicured essentials to ensure a tropical paradise island.

At dinner that evening we met Captain Ken the Aussie skipper of Reef Endeavour, immaculately turned out in gold braided white shirt and long white shorts meeting long white socks. He introduced his team of thirty or more as we introduced ourselves to some of our companions for the next week. An eclectic mix including a fun bunch of teenagers who had the cruise gifted to them as thanks for building a local school, an Australian who found a stool at the bar and had no intention of moving and a mum with four young kids, the strain of which you could see etched on her face in-between the Botox.

The following morning, we woke to a new view and a new island, perhaps to discover new marine wildlife during our "off the boat" snorkelling. It was very odd though, despite the abundance of sea life there was absolutely nothing in the air, no birds at all. On Tokoriki we were often surrounded by dozens of beautiful green birds about the size and shape of a sparrow but with a bright red head, called appropriately a Parrotfinch and a variety of sea birds. But around these islands, there was nothing.

Great snorkelling though, the colours on the reefs are spectacular, with 333 species of hard and soft coral including huge balloons of greenish brown Brain Corals and the striking Blue Coral, only discovered there in 2004 but now in abundance. And the 1,500 species of fish found around these reefs were equally colourful. It's thrilling to swim through shoals of them that make Finding Nemo look like our garden pond.

Another great day was spent on another great desert island called Brothers Beach where I attempted paddle boarding. The wind was too strong, the current went in the wrong direction, it was too shallow / deep and the board was the wrong shape. I fell off a lot. But the highlight was a visit to an island village called Gunu for a Lovo Feast and kava ceremony with the chief, or two chiefs in this village; don't know why but very democratic we were told.

Lovo is the traditional form of Fijian cooking where the whole feast is cooked buried in the sand. They heat rocks for a couple of hours then throw them into a pit dug in the beach. The fish, chicken and pork are tightly wrapped in banana leaves and placed on the rocks, on top go various root crops including dalo a sort of potato, cassava and uvi a wild yam, then the whole lot is concealed in palm leaves, covered with sand and left to "cook" for 3 hours.

It's then ceremoniously unearthed and unwrapped ready for the feast to begin. It tasted like very smoky barbecue food, not unpleasant and great fun to share as we all sat around the embers of the glowing fire.

'Are you going to take kava again?' Helene asked.

'Not if it sends me to sleep like last time,' I replied.

'I wonder if the chief has as many children as Paulo has,' she asked.

'No, he only has six,' came the answer from behind us. It was Herman, our boatman who ferried us to and from the ship. A giant of a man with hands the size of boxing gloves and bearing the scars of too many difficult dockings in rough seas.

To our surprise Herman knew Paulo from Tokoriki very well; they had taken kava together on many occasions when both back at port.

'Don't take kava here,' he whispered behind one of his big hands, 'they make it weak, for the tourists. Join us later, back on the boat.' Invitation delivered, we left the other tourists to the watered down version, rather hoping we hadn't got ourselves into deep water with Herman.

At the end of the island's festivities Herman managed to somehow navigate us back safely to the ship in the pitch black, picking up another scar or two when mooring against the ship. Most guests retired to their cabins but we retreated to the bar with another cruising couple for late, late sundowners. As Herman had promised, we were joined by the staff with the kava they had smuggled back from the Lovo and they began to concoct their own stronger version.

With our party in full Fiji swing the crew who had demonstrated the serious evacuation procedure a few days before, set the putting-on-of-life-jackets to music. As the music soared four of them bounced to the rhythm and in a Take That style of synchronised dance the performance began.

'Unfold the jacket,' they sang together and reached for the sky.

'Place over the head and pull down,' they sung with a shake of the hips.

'Wrap the straps around your waist and tie in a neat bow,' they chanted in unison while executing a sexy twirl.

'Then use the whistle and activate the light,' they chorused together. It was hysterical and brought the house down as we all cheered and clapped the surreal performance.

Dance over we had the serious ritual of the kava ceremony to contend with, but not there. Bizarrely, their tradition is to cover each other's faces with white talcum powder while they sit cross-legged around the kava bowl; apparently it expresses their happiness. We went to bed happy too.

We were unsure what to expect during the morning visit to an island school for the three villages on Ratu Namasi, perhaps humble, poorly dressed children in ramshackle huts for classrooms and desperately in need of resources. How wrong we were.

The thirty or so kids were immaculately turned out in school uniform, with the usual collection of bandaged arms and bruised knees, but with cheeky grins on their faces and a twinkle in their eyes. They couldn't wait to take us by the hand and show off what were indeed ramshackle huts for classrooms they were so proud of. First, was the matter of a few songs for their visitors that they giggled their way through nudging each other if they began a verse too early or forgot their lines.

They then descended on us like our own children did when they were at junior school, the girls took rather moist eyed mums to praise their pinned-up artwork on the walls and the boys took the dads onto the rugby pitch. It was surrounded by a running track that someone had painstakingly marked out with lines of loose sand, because there was no paint, ready for the athletics competition later in the day.

That someone turned out to be Joe, the English teacher, Sports Master and Mr. Fixit in the school. He described the set up for the enthusiastic children.

'The school is governed more by Yes, Miss than Yes, Sir,' he explained. 'The village men don't see teaching as a male role and the kids tend to pay more attention to female teachers anyway.'

'Would you like to help the boys practice their rugby?' he asked.

We spent a delightful hour or so with the kids who play mostly in barefoot so they can save their school shoes for best, inside. Joe told me that Sevens continues to be the most dominant code of rugby and the great Serevi had visited the school earlier in the week to conduct a training session with the boys, still going at 49, amazing guy.

I have watched and played rugby in some wonderful stadiums but nothing compares to this stage. The pitch was lined with palm trees and ended at the beach overlooking the shimmering Pacific. My goodness what a wonderful place for kids to learn, play and grow up. They were happy, proud, confident and full of brazen fun, it was sad when the bell went but we had to go in, we had a paddle boarding lesson to attend.

The afternoon was more falling off the paddle board, dazzling snorkelling on the reef and what Herman called "dry snorkelling" in the glass bottom boat. We were lucky enough to spot a huge Manta Ray, black on top and bright white underneath, just off Manta Ray Island appropriately enough.

During a swim in the lagoon I began chatting with one of the other guests, a delightful lady with mischievous eyes and a cheeky smile who seemed to know quite a lot about our ship, the Reef Endeavour. It was while we were sitting in the clear shallow water drinking a cold Fiji Gold together and encouraging fish to eat bread from our hands that I found out why.

'Well, it's my ship,' she said, as I almost gifted the contents of my Fiji Gold to the fish. 'In fact, I own the whole fleet, it's my company.'

'Goodness, does that make you an admiral? No probably not,' I said.

I didn't ask her about the dodgy first voyage of our ship but did suggest she changed the name to Reef Encounter; the idea sank without trace.

We had dinner with my new friend Allison, the owner, her husband Mike, and a couple they were cruising with, Sarah and James. The evening became somewhat chaotic as we drank the ship dry of Pinot Noir and the other guests retired to the top deck bar or bed. Sarah introduced us to an Australian game Cards Against Humanity *a party game for horrible people* which warns you should only play with the closest of friends due to its X-Rated content. The slight inebriation overcame the small inhibitions and we finished the evening the closest of friends as the game suggested, agreeing to meet again in Japan for the Rugby World Cup – must have been the sea air.

Allison had her own paddle board the crew prepared each morning so often reached whichever island we were visiting before the rest of us taken by Herman's boats. She was clearly quite accomplished at this form of boarding and offered to teach me the rudimentary principles or put another way how to stay on the blooming thing. After 10 minutes of being told when to stand, how to stand and where to stand I was given a hefty shove into the ocean. Success.

Sadly, lesson one did not include the technique for changing hands with the paddle, a necessity for straight line paddle boarding apparently, so I executed a wide circle to the applause and encouragement from my fellow cruisers on the beach. I am delighted to report that I remained not only upright but on the board, how much of that was due to Allison's training and how much to the small reef shark that swam alongside me for some 10 metres or so I'm not sure.

Later that day I met a fine, elderly gentleman named Charles who, like me, was a keen angler. He had brought two rods and his sea fishing tackle all the way from Sydney, where he often fishes in the harbour off his dayboat; he was looking for a little encouragement to try his luck. Using a variety of borrowed bait from the galley we fished from the shore without success so persuaded one of the crew to take us out beyond the reef for some deep-sea fishing with lures.

Helene often says my fishing should be called "ing" due to the lack of fish, but I was not dismayed this time. Surrounded by five volcanic islands in the middle of the deep blue Pacific, gently floating with the tide is a great way to fish, whether it actually involves any fish or not.

That day was curry day, well lunch actually, a spicy fish curry out on the foredeck with Tom Hank's Castaway Island, real name Monuriki Island, for a backdrop. As we enjoyed our Fijian curry with the ship's quartet tenderly singing a lilting love song and the clear blue waters lapping onto the beach of the island we were anchored off our thoughts turned to home. It was my son Elliot's birthday, and I wished I could package it all up, put a bow on it and send it home, but he would have to make do with a Skype call around midnight our time, if the ship's wifi held up.

That night we anchored off Tokoriki, our Paradise Island discovered the week before. We were sorely tempted to ask Cap'n Ken to arrange a speed boat for us to visit Paulo and our "old friends" for the evening but we talked ourselves out of it with the promise that we will return one day. I do hope so.

Our cabin view the following morning promised to be the most dramatic bay we'd visited so far, a full 270 degree horseshoe lagoon surrounded by golden sands and high rocky outcrops, one of which was Sacred Island where the crew presented the kava gift to the chief before mooring.

Fiji had no written language before contact with the Europeans so its history is largely based on legends passed down from one generation to the next. Why these particular islands are sacred no one really knows; I'm sure it has nothing to do with the fact that the huge outcrop of rock is exactly the shape of a Storm Trooper's helmet.

Scientists believe the islands were settled over 3,500 years ago by the people of South East Asia, that maybe true but I'm glad there is little written evidence of the history, it gives their traditions, culture and legends room to breathe and evolve organically. It was a delight to see that each village still has a chief who is respected across the islands, probably more so than the modern day politicians.

Apparently, sharks eat early. So, it was up at 7:00 AM for a quick bowl of universal flakes and local fruits before we prepared breakfast for the sharks, big sharks, the Blacktip Reef Shark to give them their correct name.

As we leaned over the starboard side of the ship peering into the clear deep blue waters of the lagoon a single grey shark, with black tips of course, gracefully cruised by, clearly with one eye on the ship's open galley below us, what elegant creatures they are. Shark feeding was obviously a regular occurrence because this reconnaissance shark seemed to know exactly where and when their reef feast was to start. It was joined by others circling off the side of the boat clearly in expectation of an early morning feed. The galley crew threw out the previous night's leftover fish with the morning's untouched bacon and the water began to boil as the breakfast battle began. A dozen or so sharks, each probably 2 metres in length broke the surface and fought furiously for their fare share of breakfast.

Bing Bong, announced the tannoy.

'Will those people snorkelling today please make their way to the lower deck for boarding?' We gave it a miss that day.

It was a strange place for a birthday, just about as far away from friends, family and home as we could be and sailing past exotic islands without another vessel in sight as usual. But distance does not prevent Helene's thoughtfulness or the kids' ingenuity to make a special fuss over me. So, after a gift and card in bed that morning and a beautiful Fiji day, the evening was a lantern lit champagne dinner for two on the sun deck under a full moon. Our strumming ship's minstrels and some staff joined us for a few songs under the stars and we laughed at the happy birthday video sent over from our friends back home. How lucky was I?

That was to be our last night on board Reef Endeavour and so as we swapped E-mail addresses and mobile numbers promising to meet up again in Sydney, Auckland or wherever our journey took us, it was with mixed feelings that we prepared to disembark.

We had visited some stunningly beautiful islands straight out of a Bounty commercial; we had both learned a new skill in paddle boarding and made some interesting and entertaining new friends. But, and there is a but, cruising is by its very nature an intimate experience shared with a hundred or so complete strangers, so it's impossible to set your own pace. Perhaps we have been spoiled by the one-to-one guides we have had. Would we do it again? Oh yes, the panorama from the ship as we made our way around these remarkable and spectacular islands more than made up for the necessary shepherding.

Our final few days in the glorious Fiji Islands couldn't have been more different. Our driver Moses, who insisted on calling me King David – not sure who is the more senior here – ambled us south for an hour along the main island's coast towards Maui Bay searching for an unimpressive address of "Lot 5, near the petrol station".

Lot 5 turned out to be a small complex of four adult only holiday villas set around a raised communal kitchen dining room and an infinity pool looking out to the thundering waves on the reef. The villas are owned by a South African who also owns the aforementioned petrol station, local grocery store, restaurant and just about every other commercial enterprise in the bay.

The individual villas seemed to be inspired by Shakespeare's Globe Theatre: tall, round and white with black beams and a thatched roof. We had apparently booked the Honeymoon Lodge complete with private pool and sun deck, outside shower for two, four-poster bed and simply the largest bath I have ever had the pleasure of swimming a couple of lengths in.

The gardens were Japanese in style, I'm not sure if Shakespeare ventured that far, and were laid out in four tiers down to the coral bay. Each level provided private dining, so the first night for us was a torch lit dinner for two on the beach enjoying fresh Mahi Mahi and Reef Fish Fillets. The House Speciality was Mud Crab, doesn't sound great, but cooked in a blend of aromatic Fijian spices, fresh coconut milk, a touch of coriander and served with rice and salad we could overcome the mud issue. This was followed by Soft Island Kisses: Cointreau, rosewater, soda water and lime. Wonderful.

This certainly restored the equilibrium from any cabin claustrophobia we had. There seemed to be only one other couple on site and they spent most of the time in their villa. He a bald large guy in his 60's and she a shapely Singapore girl in her 30's who really didn't want to talk to us, can't think why. The quick-to-laugh staff outnumbered the guests and often invited the two of us in for a shared lunch of curried eggplant or kimchi stew on the huge carved table in the kitchen. This definitely put the ah! back in relaxing.

Our last lunch in Fiji required a 10 minute stroll in the surf around the coral bay to a small shack perched just above the beach with a suspended wooden terrace and views out over the reef. As we had discovered, the best restaurants are not always the big glam affairs with sophisticated menus and ingratiating waiters. The He-Ni-Uwa catered for no more than twenty on a few long wooden benches, it provided a single handwritten menu depending on the day's catch and was not licensed. The food was glorious.

We shared Kokoda, a sort of fish ceviche in coconut milk and lime, and prawns in coconut curry. The bottle of wine we brought was taken away and served in an ice bucket made from a rugby ball signed by the great John Eales, the former Wallabies captain. We talked with the chef about rugby, our families, the islands and its food, and loved every minute of our F$45 lunch, about £19.

The following morning our driver Moses collected us for the trip back to the airport and the end of our Fiji experience which in reality were three diverse experiences: the paradise of Tokoriki, cruising on the Reef Endeavour and the indulgence of Maui Bay. The contrast had been terrific but it's the similarities that had absorbed us. The scenery of the sea and the exquisite islands, the music and song, the colour and culture of the traditions and of course the people. No wonder they are the happiest people on Earth, we were sad to leave.

CHAPTER 15

Day 100 to 112: NEW ZEALAND
North Island

Rolling Back the Years

Moses parted the traffic for us back from Maui Bay to Nadi International Airport just in time for the flight to New Zealand, home of the All Blacks, and Auckland home of the America's Cup.

If I thought Fiji was rugby mad that's nothing compared to the Kiwis, the TV broadcasts games back to back but most appear to be poorly attended college games, the waiters are still talking about the Lions Tour and comically most of the toilet symbols are rugby balls for men and footballs for ladies.

We arrived at the stylish Stamford Plaza to be greeted by the perplexing sound of piped Christmas music (it was mid-October for goodness sake), but fortunately it was mostly drowned out by the hilarity coming from the Teppanyaki restaurant. A glass or two of the local wine, Sauvignon from the

Square Mile Vineyard – there are over a hundred wineries around Auckland alone – and much discussion about bestest bits from Fiji and it was time for a restful night's sleep.

New Zealand is known as "the land of the long white cloud" by the Maori and we certainly appeared to have swapped blue skies and sunshine for thick clouds and drizzle. So, swapping our summer zippy-uppy bags for the winter ones again, we wrapped up and ventured out to investigate the best Auckland had to offer. Knot Touch was tempting – *a tactile exhibition celebrating the versatility and traditions of knots, with activities and demonstrations for all ages and abilities.* Not for us. Zip, Wine & Dine seemed closer to the mark; at least the order seemed right. Or America's Cup Match Racing – *go head-to-head in a thrilling America's Cup 3 hour match race – no experience required".* Really? Luckily only available from November.

'Let's do the harbour for lunch,' suggested Helene, and why not, there were plenty to choose from, although White & Wongs – *east meets west cuisine,* won the prize for the most imaginative name we went for The HQ at the end of the harbour. And what an inventive menu. Wood-oven Oysters, Soft Shell Crab Taco or Pork Steamed Buns just for starters. The cheese on toast was a deconstructed affair where melted cheese was served in a red hot skillet with walnuts, accompanied by rosemary flavoured honey and slices of hot ciabatta all served on a bed of smoky hay in a large wooden platter. A long way from our own Welsh Rarebit and what a time to start our overdue get-fit-again programme.

But first a spot of shopping prompted by Helene's gentle hint.

'I'm not dragging this bloody thing any further.' Our friendly crew at LATAM, the airline where running flights 9 hours late is commonplace you may remember, had in their haste to load all luggage on time sheared off one of the wheels from Helene's carefully selected suitcase.

I thought she became quite adept at three wheel baggage balancing around most of South America, Hawaii and Fiji, although some of the hotel porters struggled a bit. When a second wheel disintegrated just outside Port Denarau it may have become a bit too much of a challenge. Had the missing wheels been on the same side I thought I may have a fair chance of putting together a good case for carrying on, so to speak, but diagonally opposite was beyond even Helene's luggage dexterity.

'I've found the perfect case,' Helene informed me.

'Is it expensive?' I queried.

'No, it's value for money.' Not quite sure how this was to be interpreted, I attempted to interrogate the transaction further.

'Roughly, how much is it?' I asked.

Helene closed down the conversation with her unquestionable logic that meant we moved on.

'Price is not important,' she said, 'it's the cost per journey that makes it value for money.' Fair enough.

A bright blue shiny case featuring a full complement of secure wheels was secured, so we made the crossing to Waiheke on the wonderfully named Korora Ferry which means "Fairy Penguin" in Maori. How on earth they arrived at that I have no idea, I don't think they've even heard of kava there. It reminded me of my daughter Charlotte when she was young and in the world of Disney, obsessed with fairies, still is, judging by the arrival of a rather delicate tattoo.

'Charlotte, we're going to France across the sea,' I explained some years ago when she was around four years old and our travels were limited to a French beach and steak-frites.

'But how are we going to get there?' she quite rightly asked.

'By ferry, sweetheart, a ferry will get us there.' That seemed to satisfy the young inquisitive mind, at least until we arrived at Dover and I pointed out the port. She was then inconsolable.

'But that's not a fairy it's a ship!' she cried.

Waiheke is an island of no more than 20 km in length and 10 km wide at its broadest point, but what it lacks in quantity it more than makes up for in quality with over thirty vineyards, half of which are open for tastings, now there's a challenge. Waiheke contributes just 1% of New Zealand's wine which in itself provides just 1% of global production, so it's small, but it's very good. Stonyridge Estate make Fallen Angel Larose a Malbec and the greatest wine ever to be made in New Zealand, at NZ$550 a bottle it is still only available on the island and rarely exported unless bought pre-growth.

Our wine tour began after the newly introduced early morning brisk walk on the cold sands of Oneroa's vast crescent shaped bay below our cottage, part of our get-fit-again regime. It was full of dog walkers with their pets chasing balls bobbing in the ocean and retrieving washed up sticks thrown into the surf while we dodged dogs fetching their favourite toy at full speed down the beach.

'It's simple,' Helene suggested, 'we can visit the vineyards with what they call a hop-on hop-off wine bus, that way we can see all the island and visit the wineries.' This wine bus double whammy sounded like a terrific idea to me, I mean, how many must-see attractions can a small island possibly have and we'd done the exercise for the day. Degustation de vins here we come.

'Geat, I'll bring a case for the wine we're bound to buy from all these vineyards,' I offered with enthusiasm.

'I wouldn't bother we're going to walk to the port to pick up the bus, should only take 45 minutes and it'll do us good,' she said, opening zippy-uppy bags more appropriate to the hiking I thought we left behind in Peru than the wine tasting I was expecting in New Zealand.

Of course, the walk was exceptional; Helene had found an art and sculpture route through the town and parks down to the port and awaiting wine bus. We were warmly greeted by the first of our guides for the day, Royce, a happy chap who had lived on the island for 30 years and considered himself a local. Not sure what he had been doing for 30 years but it wasn't learning about the sights and scenes of Waiheke, he knew even less about the local wine producers. We hopped off.

We met some great wine makers and drank some of their equally great wines. We occasionally hopped off to see a must-see attraction, although I can't quite remember what we saw and we caught the last hop-on hop-off wine bus home. I may have dozed a little on the return journey across the island because Helene subtly renamed it the hop-on drop-off bus. In fact, we misjudged it slightly, the wine bus completed its circuit some way short of home by which time there was just us, the driver and an extremely knowledgeable guide called Jen who more than made up for Royce's lack of wine wisdom and appeared to have tasted as much as we had. We were having so much fun, Jen instructed the driver to drop us off home in the bus after his shift had finished. A fine wine day.

We were back in the Audley bubble, as we had begun to name this comfortable intangible place they create for us, so a car was ready and waiting for the next segment of our adventure, a self-drive experience on the north and south islands of this fascinating country.

Our first destination was a 3 hour up-and-over drive to the east coast the pretty way to the Coromandel Peninsula jutting out into the Pacific Ocean with a spectacular coastline that we hugged for the last hour overlooking the greenest sea you can imagine.

But first was the tricky issue of getting used to the 4x4 the two of us now owned for the next 9 days. I began driving on the right hand side of the road.

'David, what are you doing, we're in New Zealand?' screamed Helene as a stream of traffic entered the airport on what I thought was the wrong side of the road. Never adhering to the only-one-in-step theory I gave way to the oncoming cars flashing lights, beeping horns and helpful hand signals.

'Sorry, but if I'm abroad I think I should be driving on the right.' Lame excuse but actually the truth.

'It's just like home,' said Helene, clearly not understanding the issue here.

'I know, but it's not,' I replied.

'Well, just pretend it's Scotland then.' I was not entirely sure how this pretence would help. Unless we'd missed another referendum since we left I assumed Scotland was still part of Britain and continued to drive on the left.

'Right oh then, Scotland it is.' Only another 3 hours to go.

Hahei was our destination on the Coromandel Peninsula and a charming boutique hotel come guesthouse owned by Peter and Kay, with an agreeable pub restaurant close by wittily called The Pour House and serving gluten treated beer brewed on site that Helene could drink. I really don't understand the whole gluten debate but she seemed to enjoy it as if it was her first pint for 3 years, which she said it was. I ignored her pint of Longboard Lager in Hawaii that turned out to be full of the stuff.

Our early morning walk was of course along the beach, some 100 metres below the cliff car park. The cove we aimed for was Cathedral Beach and although I was already anxious about the return hike back up I have to admit it was worth the anticipated endeavour. It had icing sugar sand supporting white outcrops of rock towering above the clear seas with a soaring waterfall cascading onto the beach and a cave with entrances at both ends that delivered the beach's name. Wonderful.

We were planning our route to Hot Water Beach when the ever-enthusiastic Peter made what I considered to be an unusual offer.

'You'll need a shovel, you can borrow mine,' he said. I'm a bit past sand castles but not wishing to offend our hosts agreed to take it along.

'And, don't arrive until the tide's out because only then can the digging start,' Peter advised, 'have fun! But don't get burned.'

This was not a sunburn issue, at low tide tourists and locals gather to dig shallow pits in the sand that fill with hot water from the thermal springs running under the beach, just a few metres away from the freezing Pacific.

What a peculiar sight this was. Hundreds of visitors with shovels, spades, trowels, or garden hoes for the regulars – something about sand slippage – excavating their own hot baths on the beach and lying prone in the warm mineral laden soup. Of course, we joined in, but cuckoo style I commandeered a recently abandoned hollow and quickly refashioned it as Helene found some dry sand to leave our clothes on. At less than 6 inches down the warm water bubbled up to provide a bath-like temperature, but at only a foot down the water was unbearably hot. However, once regulated with a hastily dug channel to the cold sea water we could lie back and relax to watch the surreal scene around us. What a ridiculously eccentric way of watching the sun go down.

We were on the road again the following morning with a delightful 2 hour drive around the coast and then inland to Rotorua situated on the southern shore of the huge lake bearing the town's name. This was the heartland of New Zealand's geothermal activity and centre for Maori culture. In fact, the lake is a vast water-filled crater with stunning scenery, enhanced by New Zealand's vivid and lush green rolling hills which appear more like a well-kept golf course. Must be the quantity of sheep and cattle keeping those greens manicured. The only disagreeable element to Rotorua is S, the whole town smells of sulphur from the leaking volcanoes and steam emitting from dozens of fissures in the area.

Carol was our guide at Te Puia – *the centre of Maori culture and natural thermal activity – you enter entirely at your own risk*, whether this was due to the Maori people or the volcanic activity we were unsure.

'Kia Ora and welcome my family,' was the slightly overfamiliar greeting from Auntie Carol, as she insisted we call her. Now I know where the branding originated for that revolting artificial fruit drink served in cinemas when we had intermissions back in the 1970's.

Dressed in black from head to toe with her hair dyed to match and scraped back into a long pony tail, with the obligatory lost front tooth all the Maori's seem to have, she threatened to show us her ancestral tattoo across her back; luckily, she had a wooden carving of it. We learned how her ancestors lived in the Polynesian homeland of Hawaiki – sounding like a cross between Hawaii and our recently vacated island of Waiheke so must have been good – but left due to battles over resources. How many times have we heard that on our journey?

The Maori arrived some time at the end of the 13th century so are the indigenous population of New Zealand, some 500 years later Captain James Cook landed at Poverty Bay having anchored off the Bay of Plenty – odd decision but I'm sure he had his reasons. He has however, left a permanent imprint on the consciousness of New Zealanders with restaurants, hotels, schools, retail brands and even whole districts and suburbs bearing his name. He also renamed some of the villages and bays, a practice which continued during the 18th and 19th centuries so there is a quaint mix of both Maori and British names which makes for great fun when Helene is map reading. Blackpool sits only 2 minutes from Oneroa, Whangarei is a mile from Bream Head and Marsden Bay – I wonder who he was back in the day – and Kaukapakapa is just up the road from Helensville oddly enough.

Auntie Carol introduced us to some Maori carvers who honour their ancestors with the intricate totem poles we often associate with the area and explained the UNDRIP (United Nations Declaration on the Rights of Indigenous Peoples). As we had seen from many of the cultures experienced in our travels the indigenous populations do not always get on with the visiting, or put another way, invading Europeans: Easter Island, the Incas, Hawaii and Fiji all had a troubled time in trying to maintain their society and cultures in the face of European dominance.

New Zealand tackled it in a far better way, albeit not until 2010 after an extraordinary 22 years of negotiation. The UNDRIP was drafted by representatives of the indigenous Maori people in conjunction with the Government acknowledging that the Maori tribes of New Zealand hold a special status as "people of the land". To quote the constitution "it provides a standard of achievement to be pursued for the realisation of human rights in a spirit of partnership and mutual respect". Sounds a bit heavy and bureaucratic but it's about mutuality and really seems to be working.

The highlight of the excursion and star of the show was to see the Pohutu Geyser, the largest active geyser in the Southern Hemisphere often reaching 30 metres in height. Translated from the Maori as "constant splashing", it is the most reliable geyser on Earth, but not when we visited it wasn't. Auntie Carol was beside herself.

'This is all very odd, it should have gone off by now,' she said, peering into the bubbling waters. Essentially, this is what we had paid our NZ$138 for and I was wondering if the "it's very odd" routine was a normal response to inactivity.

'Can you tell when it's about to blow?' asked Helene.

'Well no, not accurately,' replied Auntie Carol, 'but let's go and sit on the thermal heated seats and wait, I've got 20 minutes until I'm off.' Thermal heated seats? As we walked up to what appeared to be half a small amphitheatre of stone seats there was an unusual warning sign that perhaps Helene missed: "DANGER! Hot Rocks – be careful when sitting".

I actually found it quite comfortable, possibly enjoyable. We sat patiently warming our cockles waiting for Pohutu to perform.

'What the... Jesus... Ow!' screamed Helene jumping up and rubbing her derrière.

'Oh! Sorry, my dears,' said Auntie Carol, 'I should have warned you, don't sit on the cracks, the volcanic steam can burst through.' Unsure whether to cover my stifled laughter or caress her burning bottom I opted for the rather lame question.

'Is there anything I can do to help?' There wasn't.

We were then ushered into the Kiwi Sanctuary, a building not dissimilar to Lonesome George's back in the Galápagos, and an experience that shared some of its comedy. We didn't actually go into the heated and dark preserve containing just two extremely shy kiwis, somewhere. Auntie Carol pointed to the two video screens showing the residents hidden in their respective boxes.

'There's really no point in entering, my dears, you won't see anything, you see they're nocturnal and sleep in their boxes all day while we're open.' I was about to ask the obvious question when Helene, who has a sixth sense about these things, gave me a nudge and asked about the nation's favourite animal's welfare.

Apparently, there were over 5 million only 75 years ago but their habitat has been destroyed and they've been hunted by new species introduced to the country, so there are now less than 100,000.

Auntie Carol bade us farewell with a rather touching ceremony, well very touching actually. "Hongi" is a traditional greeting, the equivalent of a handshake, which involves the touching of noses, not the rubbing of noses as she was quick to point out, that's the Eskimos.

'It's because of you we can hold on to what we have and share it with you,' was her poignant note for us to part on.

Noses touched, we returned to the reluctant Pohutu, its spring still bubbling insipidly and stubbornly refusing to spurt or spout or whatever a geyser is supposed to do when it spews into the air. As we waited staring at the steaming soup of volcanic minerals that simmered in front of us the security guys started to clear the park and we were joined by a Scottish couple. I guess waiting is a quintessentially British trait similar to queuing, but as the venue emptied the four of us were not moving until the obstinate thing did its stuff.

Whoosh! All good springs come to those who wait. And, Pohutu turned into a spurting geyser spraying steam high into the darkening sky just as Auntie Carol had promised, a fine end to the day.

As we woke the following morning at Leigh and Angie's great boutique guesthouse perched on the rim of the crater above Rotorua, we saw steam rising from other thermal activity across the valley, what a view. So, Angie served us a quick breakfast and we served their alpacas a quick breakfast – Helene had made her peace with them after her Luchito experience.

Leigh and Angie were originally from Lancashire but decided to move to New Zealand before actually setting foot in the country, they just packed up their lives and went for it, brave some would say. On arrival they visited a guesthouse and made an offer to the owners the following day. That was 12 years ago and they were now our hosts.

It was a beautiful warm day with blue skies and sunshine so it was back to the shorts and sunblock for our visit to Waimangu Volcanic Valley – *a unique hydrothermal environment showing how the world began* – they do seem to set themselves up for a fall.

To be fair, although I am none the wiser about the story of creation, it was an informative and delightful walk around a lush volcanic landscape that was once home to the world's largest geyser until a massive eruption in 1917. The rocks, streams and terrain reminded us that Mother Nature was in control there, not us. Steam rises and vents hiss while springs bubble alongside plopping mud pools and crater lakes with a warm mist drifting across their surface, it really was quite eerie. Particularly since we were the only ones there. Audley are particularly good at steering us clear of the crowds and queuing.

Our next visit was definitely a must-see, at least from its billing it appeared so. Wai-O-Tapu meaning Sacred Waters – *A Thermal Wonderland. Where unique volcanic wonders meet nature's surprises.* There were well over a dozen steaming and gurgling craters in the reserve but what astonished us most were the colours found in the volcanic pools, lakes and in the steam they generated that wafted across the park. The Creative Department had worked hard to characterise the natural attractions, we had Rainbow Crater, The Devil's Ink Pots, The Artist's Palette, The Opal Lake – they were beginning to flag now, but redeemed themselves with – The Champagne Pool and The Devils Bath.

To be fair the colours, which I assume were all natural, that's the cynic in me, were quite spectacular. We stood on a boardwalk in the middle of a sea of colour: yellow-primrose to pastel blues and vivid oranges all in one volcanic lake, The Artist's Palette, due to the different mineral elements reacting with the steamy water. Quite beautiful.

It's not surprising that the area is favoured by Hollywood for the backdrop to some blockbuster films, The Hobbit being one of them, and an interesting story about an enterprising and now hugely wealthy sheep farmer. When the director Sir Peter Jackson flew over the area scouting for locations he spied a holding just 30 minutes from Tauranga which he believed provided the ideal set for Middle-earth and so sent his location team to acquire filming rights "at any cost".

It was a normal Saturday afternoon in 1998 on the sheep farm when there was a knock on the door that was to change farmer Russell Alexander's life forever. He drove a hard bargain but finally agreed to vacate his twelve acres for 6 months to allow the production team to take over the farm and develop the Village, Hobbit Holes, the Mill and Green Dragon Inn. His 13,500 sheep were shipped out to be replaced by four hundred film crew and construction began. Farmer Russell was a clever man and demanded that the location be left exactly as it had been constructed for filming when the crew departed. He put up a sign "Hobbiton Movie Set" offered tours from nearby Matamata and Tauranga and the tourists flocked in to make it one of New Zealand's most visited attractions.

Our final visit that day was to relax in the thermal hot pools rich in minerals – *providing a feel back in time sensation*. Not quite sure what this meant but my experience wasn't quite the sensation I expected. We made our way to the appropriate changing rooms to slip into what the locals call "cosies" – they seem to shorten everything, even at the bar it's two glasses of Cab Sav or Serv Blanc. I always find these communal areas a little unsettling but this was positively unnerving. I changed and exited quickly.

'Helene, don't look now but that guy has bottomless pants on,' I whispered, from hot thermal pool number one.

'What? He had a hole in them?' she asked.

'No, well yes, but more like a designer hole right across his nethers,' I replied as tactfully as possible, 'and it had orange piping around it.'

'What did?'

'The large hole in his bottomless pants did, right across his bottom. Why would you do that, and more importantly why would you wear them to a public place?' I asked expecting some guidance.

'Oh! Don't worry, he's probably German,' she said, inferring that this clearly answered all questions, satisfied all curiosity and put an end to the discussion. We moved on to hot thermal pool number two.

That evening we took the cable car to the top of Mount Ngongotaha towering over Rotorua to visit the finely named Stratosfare Restaurant – *home to some of New Zealand's best award winning cuisine.* This was the country's version of Friday Brunch in Dubai, just about every dish imaginable, from the tidal mussel tank to the flame rotisserie of slow cooked beef and delicate sweet crepes served from a handsomely presented buffet.

As we watched the mountain's shadow draw a curtain slowly across the town below allowing lights to flicker into life in its wake, we began to discuss home again. Sure, we missed the kids, close family and our lovely friends, but social media is a wonderful thing and it's a delight to wake up in the morning to tea in bed and gossipy E-mails, WhatsApp messages that make us howl with laughter and witty Instagram observations on the photos we posted the day before. They keep us close despite the distance and 12 hours' time lapse and perhaps, with the help of Audley, we are charting a path across the world that some may follow in the future, what a privilege.

It was time for us to leave Rotorua and head for Tongariro National Park, a remote wilderness high in the mountains that promised some of the most beautiful and unusual scenery in New Zealand with ski fields and walking trails for us to enjoy and augment our get-fit-again programme.

During our 3 hour drive south we stopped off at the Huka Falls, a torrent of emerald water gushing out of what appeared to be a serene lake. As we crossed the narrow wooden bridge to peer down into the cascading waters below I became aware of a young couple taking selfies and trying to control the three high-spirited dogs they had on long red leads. The young man in trendy turned-up jeans, hoodie and dark glasses asked a stranger to take a picture of the two of them leaning against the bridge railings.

We stopped to allow the shot to be composed without interruption, at which point our hoodie friend went down on bended knee and flamboyantly removed the lid from a small pink box to reveal the ring inside. His fiancée to be, if she said yes, burst into tears, as did Helene. The photographer maintained his composure and kept clicking as the unofficial witnesses on the bridge gasped, clapped and cheered while the dogs tied the couple up in a lover's knot with their leads. She was inconsolable, and so was the fiancée, who had by now untangled herself and said yes. What a wonderful interlude to our journey.

We returned to the car hand in hand.

'That was lovely,' Helene simpered as she dried her eyes.

'Well, it was lucky he didn't drop the ring, they'd never have found it,' I thoughtfully agreed.

'You're such a romantic!' Helene scolded. 'Do you remember when you proposed to me?'

'Of course, now that was romantic.'

'It was in a fishmonger's,' she reminded me.

'No, it was a fish restaurant, it may have had a fishmongers attached but it was definitely in the restaurant.' Our memories of the occasion were somewhat clouded by the Spanish "champagne" the owner insisted on supplying.

'Well, it was the same as them, with all the other people looking on,' she said, which was a fair point and I felt I was going backwards on this one.

'It was on a table surrounded by all our friends,' I said, as a last attempt to salvage some honour.

'Yes, and that's why I love you.' As always Helene left me lost for words.

Funny thing about driving in foreign parts, although I had overcome my left and right side of the road issue, I was mystified by some of the traffic signs, and my goodness they have a lot of them in New Zealand. Large roadside displays of helpful advice like "Slow down, other people make mistakes" and "Drive your own drive" can be seen at regular intervals. But, it was the other more instructional signs that baffled me. What on Earth is a "No Engine Brake Zone", perhaps that's down to my lack of technical gumption, but when we entered a "No Cruising Zone" I was completely baffled.

I was just pondering what the sign "Join Like a Zip" meant when we arrived at Lake Taupo. With a surface area of 616 sq. km it is the largest in New Zealand and is the only lake I've seen with surfable waves hitting its shores. It also has a driving range straight out into the lake with a green size pontoon about 100 metres offshore to drive your lost balls onto. Our destination was Chateau Tongariro located in the diminutive alpine village of Whakapapa, the heart of the national park, so it was time to climb the winding roads into the volcanic mountains.

The elegant Chateau was built in the roaring twenties – *providing visitors with a timeless elegance, preserving history and tradition* – when size really mattered. It sits grandly in front of the volcanic slopes of snow covered mountains and provides accommodation from a long-forgotten era. It has huge rooms that would probably be converted into three if the likes of Hilton acquired it, heavy velvet drapes framing ornate picture windows overlooking its once manicured lawns, and broad square pillars with delicate glass chandeliers suspended from high ceilings in oak panelled rooms.

We were met by a couple of uniformed porters, or what may have been called bellhops in this "timeless elegance"and entered a cavernous lounge large enough to host an indoor tennis match. Astonishingly, it was actually hosting a dozen or so Flappers, all in their 60's or 70's, to be polite and dressed in short skirts, extravagant silk scarves and bright red feathers with flowers and beads in their bobbed hair, all enjoying a champagne High Tea.

Behind the grand piano was a Neil Diamond look-a-like playing soft jazz next to the full sized grand old snooker table, both surrounded by acres of burgundy red sofas and comfy chairs. Although I couldn't help but think of Hotel California – *you can check out anytime you like, but you can never leave* – somehow it just worked.

I guess space was everything in the 1920's and the Chateau just went on and on. We discovered the Chateau Cinema in the bowels of the hotel showing back-to-back Harry Potter films to thirty empty reclining seats and fitness rooms, a spa, guests' laundry and drying rooms, private function rooms and offices of every size and a separate wedding planning office; they seemed to have exhausted their ideas for the space they have.

Our accommodation continued in the same manner with a bathroom bigger than some of the rooms we have stayed in and a seating area and study desk to fill the bedroom space. But we were in an active volcanic region so our attention was brought to the lava flow warning map and alarm procedure on the back of our door. That's a first.

One of the mountainous active volcanoes is Ngauruhoe, impossible to say but easy to see because the Chateau overlooks it, or perhaps the other way around, seemed pretty threatening to me. Imagine Mount Fuji in Japan, cone shaped and streaked with snow or alternatively Mount Doom in Lord of the Rings for that is where it was filmed. Disconcertingly, there's a local guy called John Archer who dresses up as Gandalf and wanders the mountain paths to entertain walkers and visitors; that must be fun.

The climate in the national park was some 20 degrees lower than our previous day so a new prioritisation to our zippy-uppy bags was called for. Out came the scarves, hats, gloves and hiking paraphernalia we had not seen since Atacama Desert and it was off up the mountains into the snow slopes and skiing area. Could it really be only a day since we enjoyed hot sunshine and beer outside? We drove up to the ski lifts and enjoyed hot gluhwein and cold snowballs outside. The powder snow and volcanic steam streamed off the summit of the mountains in bright sunshine and blue sky, how wonderful.

We left the delightful 1920's Chateau in wind and rain heading for the famous Hawkes Bay, renowned for great wines, particularly Pinot Noir, which we were looking forward to. We passed through the Scottish Highlands, Mashpi Rainforest, Switzerland, Canada and the Cotswolds during our 3 hour drive south, to arrive 10 years later in the 1930's at the Art Deco town of Napier.

A devastating earthquake in 1931 killed over two hundred and fifty, injured thousands and in two and a half minutes demolished the town, a fire then wiped out what had survived. It was, and remains New Zealand's deadliest natural disaster, so the government of the time was quick to react dispatching architects, engineers and builders from all over the country to recreate the town. The rebuilding of the town in the 1930's when Art Deco was fashionable has created an incredibly ornate and colourful environment that often gave us the impression of being in a film set or on Disney's Main Street. It is without doubt one of the finest collections of Art Deco architecture in the world.

We moved on to the 1950's. We were staying at Cobden Garden "Home Stay", not a bed & breakfast or guesthouse we were clearly informed by our hosts Phillip and Rayma the owners of this huge house on the hill, and what great company they were. It was a very traditional property with equally traditional hosts. A comprehensive breakfast to rival any of the big hotel groups was served in their formal dining room, and at the end of the day we were invited to dress for cocktails and canapés, offered promptly at 6:30 PM in the wood panelled drawing room. Later a crystal decanter of local red dessert wine was thoughtfully provided on the bed side table as a nightcap. Nice, all we had to do was switch on the electric blanket.

But first we were required to read and understand the "Earthquake Evacuation Procedure" helpfully provided in our chintzy room, which starts *"Stay as safe as possible during an earthquake"* – good advice I thought. It goes on to suggest *"Drop to the ground, take cover by getting under a sturdy table or other piece of furniture, cover your mouth with a handkerchief or clothing and HOLD ON"*. Not sure what the covering your mouth bit meant but the instructions went on for a page or so, luckily, we didn't have to "hold on" during our stay.

Following a great fish supper at the creatively named Hunger Monger, the following day was a wine tour with a difference.

'Is the difference the fact that it's raining,' asked Helene, 'or that most of the wineries are closed? Why are we doing this?'

In the absence of a hop-on hop-off wine bus I had opted for bikes to visit seven of the Hawkes Bay wineries and thoughtfully, I thought, contribute to our get-fit-again campaign.

'They're not all closed, it'll be fun. Let's get a few miles under our belt and then visit the vineyards.'

'Is there any room under your belt?' she asked.

We moved on, by bike.

We managed only three wineries in the pouring rain so were forced to spend more time tasting than cycling, but we both succeeded in remaining on the bikes when required. As we completed our tour at Elephant Hills Vineyard and our back up vehicle arrived to collect the muddy bikes, sodden riders and a couple of bottles of rather elegant Pinot Noir from the Black Barn Vineyard, the skies cleared and the sun came out for the afternoon.

On the subject of alcoholic beverages, the Kiwis may do wine extremely well but their beer! Goodness me it's dreadful. There are usually ten draught beers to select from including The Barber Lager, Beacon Pilsner and something just called Black. They are all from Monteith's Brewing Co. 1868, who may have been practicing their art for over 150 years but they should be ashamed of themselves. Although their beers all sound different brews they all taste the same: too cold, too fizzy, too watery and too tasteless. Only my opinion and maybe the locals love it but it's one of the few things I miss from home, a well poured pint of Rebellion IPA.

We said our thank yous and goodbyes to Rayma as Phillip kindly cleaned the windscreen of our 4x4 and we set off for Wellington, our last destination on the north island. We sung along to our favourite songs on the way and wound our way up the mountains to then descend into the nation's capital and home to New Zealand's parliament. It was just about to have a new prime minister, Jacinda Arden the youngest PM for 150 years and former adviser to Tony Blair.

Wellington is compact but squeezes in much for us to see over a short two night stay in the QT Museum Hotel, a building that quite cleverly combines a modern art exhibition with comfortable and equally surrealist accommodation. The magnificent harbour like many coastal cities, lost its primary function many years ago with the warehouses and sheds converted into contemporary apartment living surrounded by bars, restaurants and cafes. Our favourites were Shed 5 a splendid wooden beamed building located on the waterfront and specialising in local seafood dishes, and the Crab Shack with the dubious and I guess predictable Ad line above its door claiming *We've got Crabs.* You can guess at the personal motif on the staff tee-shirts.

We took the vintage cable car up to the top of the hill overlooking the city, an interesting experience, halfway up it enters a disco tunnel with strips of colourful lights oscillating and pulsating to some unknown music. The walk down was far more sedate through the Botanic Gardens on a glorious day of sunshine and blue sky with of course the occasional long white cloud.

The following morning Audley had booked us Kaitaki Plus tickets on the InterIslander Ferry; apparently you can turn left on a boat too. We cruised through the open waters of the Cook Strait and through the stunning Marlborough Sounds passing pine tree covered islands with high cliffs plummeting into the sea below. The second half of our New Zealand adventure looked to be as promising as the first when we docked at Picton the gateway to the South Island.

CHAPTER 16

Day 113 to 127: NEW ZEALAND
South Island

Wails, Whales, Wales

A place to truly indulge, we were advised by Audley. So, with our first destination on the South Island being Blenheim in the Marlborough region, probably the best of New Zealand's wine industry, I took the advice as a clear directive.

The area is a vast plain surrounded by a horseshoe of mountains with snowcapped peaks towering into a sky of deepest cobalt. There are literally thousands of acres of vineyards; in fact, any flat space seemed to be covered with regimented rows of vines producing excellent Sauvignon. Oz Clarke wrote "they are arguably the best in the world" and include Pinot Gris and Pinot Noir from world famous vineyards such as Cloudy Bay and Hunters. There are over eighty wineries in the region most with an open cellar-door policy so plenty of opportunities to sample what makes this such a renowned area for great wines.

Our accommodation was in the Marlborough Vintners Hotel with a suite amongst the vines providing vineyard views up to the snowy mountains on the horizon. This area used to be known as the "fruit basket of New Zealand" when pretty much anything was grown in the fertile soil. The government then introduced a tax on land so farmers started to cultivate the crop with the greatest margin potential, grapes. Despite almost all the land in the Marlborough region now growing vines and some hops the oldest independent winery, Allan Scott's was only established in 1990.

'So, how are we going wine tasting this time, by boat?' was Helene's quip and quite unfair question.

'No,' I replied, feeling somewhat indignant that my efforts were going unrecognised. 'I accept the hop-on fall-off or whatever, didn't quite deliver and the bike option may have been a little wet...'

'A little wet!' Helene shrieked. 'It poured more on the bikes than it did in the wineries, should have been called Cote du Rain.' I ignored that.

We found a newly formed company specialising in the area and promising seven great wineries and a brewery that I might be able to squeeze in given there is a specialist chocolate company nearby to compensate.

'We've opted for a private guided tour by car,' I said.

'Have *we*?' she rhetorically questioned.

'Yes, so I've taken the weather out of the equation just in case it pours again.'

It was a gloriously warm and sunny day. Our driver Charles, a retired grower who clearly loved his new role, arrived promptly at 9:30 AM. Perhaps a little too early to taste wine, but the first stop was Allan Scott's, the oldest and arguably the best in the region we were advised by Charles. The wines were great but his son was more interested in beers than wines so created the Gooseberry Bomb. Sauvignon Blanc fermented with beer yeast and green hopped with Sauvin hops, then put in a can. Traditional wine making theory and brewery techniques combined to create an 11.5% vol. drink which is neither beer nor wine and really shouldn't be either.

We didn't quite make all seven vineyards but managed to fit in Moa Brewery – *enjoy* our *international award winning range of handcrafted beer*, most of which were extremely strong. It turned out to be owned by Josh Scott, son of Allan and maker of the dubious Gooseberry Bomb. In his attempt to establish a working partnership with their neighbours at the chocolate plant, he also produced a rather sweet and underwhelming chocolate beer. If two ingredients were ever supposed to be kept well apart it's these two. Chocolate and red wine fine, but chocolate and beer? No. Josh is obviously a pioneer in combining ingredients but perhaps his skill is yet to be fully discovered. It appeared the New Zealand beer quest was still to find an acceptable brew.

We enjoyed an excellent day in the sunshine visiting the vineyards and the wineries, with lunch at Highfield TerraVin Vineyard as the highlight, a table on the terrace overlooking the vines ripening in the sun with an informative wine tasting and excellent food to match. A long, lazy lunch put paid to the rest of the afternoon.

'That was wonderful,' said Helene, sipping a Sauvignon from grapes grown within yards of the hot tub we languished in on our return home. 'I do love a day's wine tasting.'

'We both do,' I said, making a mental note to retell the story before our next vino excursion.

We left the wine region and travelled from east coast to west coast taking the pretty way over the hills hugging the northern seashore, quite spectacular. We arrived at the charming colonial town of Nelson on Labour Day, and consequently it was shut. But the next day was to be a real highlight, the stunning Abel Tasman National Park on the sea shuttle – *hugging 40 miles of magnificent coastline and exciting maritime environment.*

What an extraordinary cruise it was. We sailed in exquisite clear blue and green water passing dozens of secluded coves and beaches, their sand sparkling with gold. Above them the mountains were covered in trees so dense it looked like vast hills of oversized broccoli.

We arranged to be dropped off on Apple Tree Bay, just the two of us, to hike for a couple of hours or so to Anchorage Bay where the boat would collect us later in the day. After a steep climb we found the narrow path cut into the hillside 100 metres or so above the bays below. It was not unlike some of the hikes at Mashpi with rainforest vegetation added to by New Zealand Ferns and the occasional teasing glimpse of the green waters below and the blue sea in the distance.

The terrific trek dropped us down to the bay to rest on the beach.

'Look what I've brought you,' I said, and with a flourish, pulled out a half bottle of local Sauvignon and glasses secreted in my backpack. Helene laughed as she pulled out a small selection of cold meats and salad secreted in hers.

'I'm beginning to think we may know each other too well,' she said, as we laid out our perfect picnic on the golden sands, and the gulls gathered.

That evening I met with our host Wayne, an amiable and unassuming man in his late fifties who spent his life cultivating his garden, supporting his wife and rescuing his casualties. I think that was the order. While we had been searching the coast for Anchorage Bay that afternoon he had been scouring the ocean for a father and son whose boat had gone down.

As the boat sank Dad used his mobile to call the coastguard and give an estimate of their position. Volunteer Wayne and his New Zealand equivalent of the RNLI finally found the two of them suffering from hypothermia 3 km away from the given location and returned both casualties home to safety. As Wayne, the reluctant hero told the story over a glass of his fine port that evening I realised how lucky we were spending our time travelling the world but also how easy it is to get into difficulty on such an adventure. It really put everything into perspective for us and we slept a little closer together that night.

We drove south through the mountainous Tasman region winding our way from Nelson to Hanmer Springs a beautiful alpine village in a high country basin surrounded by 170 km of indigenous and exotic forests. With roadworks almost all the way repairing damage from the massive earthquake the previous year our progress was slow, but as we descended the final mountain following a trailer playing skittles with the orange traffic cones we entered the Alpine Pacific Triangle.

No sooner had we checked in at Cheltenham House, unpacked in our Garden Suite and prepared for the hotel's own thermal pool than the earthquake siren wailed into extremely loud life. Our hosts had already drawn our attention to the evacuation procedure because aftershocks were still being felt nearly a year later, so we knew the drill, or at least Helene did.

'David, grab what you can and run!' she screamed. I slurped the dregs of my wine and put on my best earthquake shoes.

'David, come on,' she re-screamed, grabbing at various belongings to carry, as the instructions specify. The siren continued to wail, as did Helene, so I did my grabbing and we ran out into the car park muster area.

My grabbing had rescued a mobile phone, the car keys and my wallet, all very sensible and pragmatic I felt. Helene had salvaged her toiletry bag, her favourite top and the Audley Tour book. Thank goodness.

No one joined us in the car park; a few locals ambled by wondering what we were doing clutching our carefully selected worldly possessions as we looked at the ground waiting for shudders and shakes. Nothing.

The owner of the Cheltenham House wandered over grinning from ear to ear and not really looking as if his life, or indeed his guests' lives, were in danger.

'What are you doing out here?' he asked, as we stood sheepishly under the Earthquake Muster sign.

'Waiting for the earthquake?' said Helene, without conviction, clearly unsure whether earthquake waiting was a leisure activity in these parts.

'No, that's the call for the mountain rescue guys,' he laughed. And my, how we joined in. It frightened the blooming life out of us.

I had arranged a surprise for Helene the next morning; mountain biking – *to experience the beauty of the spectacular Hanmer Springs Forest Park.* What fun this would be for us.

'We're doing what?' Helene questioned, not quite as calmly as I'd expected.

'I knew you'd like it, and the sun's shining,' I said, 'we are going to experience, and I quote, "an awesome alpine environment with the most beautiful scenery, sights and sounds that nature can offer".'

'How far?' she asked.

'It'll only be an hour, or so...'

'How far?' she asked again.

'It has a beautiful lake,' I said. We moved on to be measured up for our mountain bikes.

I opted for the gentle ride, 7 km of undulating paths in the pine forest. They were a little narrow and a tad muddy due to the excessive rain the area had experienced before we arrived, and perhaps somewhat steep in parts, but that allowed us to use all of our twenty-seven gears!

It was splendid in the dark forest full of tall Douglas Firs; we cycled on a carpet of pine needles where the tyres made no sound.

'I'm not a mountain biker!' screeched Helene, breaking the silence from some way behind me. 'I'd rather be cycling in wet vineyards,' she added, pushing her bike up a slight incline.

I cycled on the next 50 metres to wait.

'And I've got the wrong bra on for this!' she announced, as she bounced over the next mound.

That went well then.

From Hanmer Springs we were due to head south along the Waiau Valley tracing the river but the recent earthquake had demolished the road so we were forced up and over the rolling hills and snowcapped mountains, in fact, a beautiful drive. We dropped down into Kaikoura a small coastal town bordered by the towering Kaikoura mountain ranges and the Pacific Ocean. It is an unusual, if not unique scenery of stunning contrast with sea, surf, sand and snow.

The town is also extraordinary as it still bears the scars of the 7.8 magnitude earthquake that hit at midnight on 14th November 2016 and shook the area for a full 2 minutes raising parts of the coast by an astonishing 6 metres. Restaurants, shops, the cinema and church remain closed a year later after Kaikoura was isolated by all routes except sea and air. But the locals remain resolute and the community is determined to re-establish the town as a holiday destination. I hope it does not fade through lack of support, I think perhaps not, as one local said to us "it is astonishing how through adversity, the town has rallied as one to rebuild our businesses".

We wished them luck, but it will be tough. Kaikoura is difficult to access at the best of times but the main road around the mountain is still being repaired so tourist numbers have declined dramatically. Many of the restaurants and bars are still in ruins and even the locals have left to rent out their accommodation to the labourers the government are funding to repair the damage. In fact, in the two or three eating and drinking establishments that remain there are more men in high vis jackets than tourists or residents. But the community spirit is strong; I think they'll make it.

The town is located on a rocky peninsula protruding from lush farmland beneath the snowy mountains so is an ideal environment for us to spot the final No.15 of the Galápagos Big 15, the Albatross. It is also a perfect location for whale watching, our Audley instructions were to make our way to the end of the disused rail track on the coast where we will start our 3 hour excursion at the "Whaleway Station". Nice.

Conditions: Rough – High chance of seasickness was the not so welcoming notice on the welcome screens at check-in.

'Seems fine to me,' I said, half to Helene and half to the ponytailed and bearded whale watching crew member I was looking to for some reassurance.

'No, mate, that's just in the big bay, outside of that it's blowing a howler,' he replied, in that happy disposition the antipodeans always seem to have when facing disaster.

'The whales are usually about 5 miles out but we'll need to motor out fifteen to get a glimpse of them,' he continued, without recognising the need for support I was hoping for.

'Fifteen? Glimpse of? Are we sure this is a good idea?' asked Helene, which in the circumstances was a fair question. Luckily before I could find an appropriate answer our hirsute head of check-in bent down to Helene to offer some advice.

'Just see Jen at the counter over there,' he said, pointing at a cheerful, waving Jen, 'she'll provide At Ease Tablets, Sea Legs and Acustraps.'

'There we are, Helene, seasickness pills and Acustraps,' I said understandingly, without really understanding where you strap them or indeed what to.

The purpose built large catamaran bounced over some impressively large waves as we peered through the spray to spot fur seals off our bows and dolphins playing in our wake. The grey skies soon parted allowing the sun to transform the grey sea into clear royal blue with a silver surf topping; even the ocean swell began to ease. Helene held her palm in the air inviting a high five.

'I think we've just completed the Galápagos Big 15,' she cried, pointing enthusiastically. Sure enough a beautiful white Albatross glided at speed across the wake of the boat inches from the surface showing off its spectacular 4 metre wingspan. What an awesome sight and what a special moment it was for us.

Our on board marine biologist, a young man with long tousled blond hair - seemed very popular with the whale watchers – a deep tan and Kiwi accent to match advised us that the whale watching plane – didn't know there was such a thing, but it provoked the obvious question from Helene – had spotted a large Sperm whale on the surface.

'They usually surface for 20 minutes and we are about 15 minutes away,' he said across the tannoy, 'if we really step on it we might just make it, so hold on!'

'Off the starboard side!' shouted our official whale spotter from the bridge. Most of us rushed to the right side of the boat just in time to see the tail disappear into the depths. Was that it? I wondered. There was an 80% refund if we didn't spot a whale, but a brief glimpse of part of a brown tail disappearing into the swell hardly constituted a "spot" in my book.

Bing Bong.

'If anyone has a plane or train to catch would they please come to the bridge immediately,' was the next intriguing announcement from our blond biologist, what could this mean? After a couple of minutes of us bobbing on the spot he returned to the tannoy.

'Whales usually dive for about 45 minutes, so we will track it until it resurfaces and will return to port later than scheduled.'

'Excellent,' said Helene, 'how exactly do you track a whale?' Good point, I went to find out.

After some discussion with the crew I met the specialist whale tracker and reported back.

'We have a highly sophisticated listening device which, when submerged, monitors the whale's sound waves, or sonar clicks,' I advised Helene and fellow watchers, who, convinced I was some sort of expert on the subject, were eager to hear more.

I was about to elucidate when Helene interrupted.

'Do you mean that broomstick he's just launched over the side?' she asked, peering over my shoulder and taking the wind from my sails. Everyone looked and seemed to lose interest in my expertise. To be fair it did indeed look like a kid's beach bucket had been nailed through its base onto the end of a metre or so of painted four-by-two. But he did have some headphones on.

Never underestimate a blond marine biologist and his listening device. After half an hour of very pleasant cruising in circles the sonar clicks stopped which apparently meant our mark was on his way up from 1200 feet.

'Everyone keep an eye out for the blow,' blondie broadcast. We waited, silently scanning the surface, and then,

'Thar she blows!' as a whaling ship lookout would shout, and sure enough the surface was broken with a soaring spurt of spray followed by the world's largest carnivore, all 20 metres and 50 tons of it. Quite extraordinary.

Of course, just 10% of this incredible creature was above the surface so we could only imagine and marvel at what lay below. It has the largest brain of any living mammal and inside its head is the spermaceti melon containing a massive 2.5 tons of oil, which when exposed to the cold air on the surface forms a solid wax denser than water to help it dive. This oil was once thought to be sperm, hence the name Sperm whale – although who thought it would be in the whale's head some 15 metres from where the action may be with a lady whale, I have no idea.

After 20 minutes the big beast prepared to dive and we were left with that iconic image of the broad tail held vertically in the air for a second or two as it plunged back into the depths.

'That,' Helene exclaimed, as she flung her arms around my neck, 'was amazing! Let's do it again in Australia.'

Maybe we would.

Christchurch was our next destination, a bittersweet experience. At 12:51 PM on Tuesday 22nd February 2011 a 6.3 magnitude earthquake killed 185, injured thousands and demolished a large part of the city, particularly the older buildings, churches, the cathedral and red brick structures due to their rigid stone construction. Seven years later they are still planning, rebuilding and reopening but are only 50% through the redevelopment of the city, with of course no guarantee that it won't all happen again tomorrow. It must be extremely difficult to live with this constant threat but they just seem to get on with it without too much tectonic worry, they even have a museum of earthquakes.

Like Kaikoura the community courage and determination are strong. Opposite what was a twenty-one storey hotel and is now just a dozen concrete pillars standing erect like tombstones in the rubble reminiscent of the twin towers is the city's art gallery, it has 3 metre rainbow coloured letters lit up on its high façade spelling out Bob Marley's sanguine advice "Everything's Gonna Be Alright". And, it probably will.

The red brick and stone structures are being replaced by steel and glass, a whole street of demolished shops has been replaced by The Shipping Container Mall allowing retailers to maintain their businesses in unconventional new premises, and the new High Street is busy and vibrant.

Roads are still closed, there are massive holes in the ground and weak propped up properties are still to be replaced or renovated. But the city has started smiling again; perhaps with a few teeth missing but there is an air of optimism and cheerfulness. We were, I believe, witnessing the rebirth of a vibrant, young, happy city that will laugh again.

'It's either left or right,' Helene directed, as we made our way out of Christchurch. She's never been great at differentiating between the two so a support question is always helpful I find.

'Is that over the river or not?' I asked.

'How should I know, I do roads not rivers?' she answered.

'Does the straight red line go over a squiggly blue line?' I encouraged.

Silence.

Together we found the SH1 a direct route to the Southern Alps and Mount Cook Village named after the highest mountain in New Zealand that seemed to suspend itself above the clouds watching those below.

In fact, the village is at the end of a single road that winds across a vast flat plain that enters a collar of soaring snowy mountains; 19 ragged peaks above 1,000 metres high with glaciers over 40% of the National Park. The road stops at the Sir Edmund Hilary Alpine Centre giving a 350 degree view of mountains with a narrow valley pass to allow an access route to the stunning retreat. This was where Sir Edmund and his team trained for their ascent on Everest, specifically on Mount Cook a truly foreboding peak that has claimed many lives. There is now a law forbidding climbers to follow in Sir Edmund's footsteps up the mountain.

Our first hike had to be to the glacier at the base of Mount Cook up Hooker Valley, so named because of all the scantily clad women in immodest walking gear leaning against mountain corners. We crossed three swing bridges – somewhat different to the scary affairs in the jungle – as we trekked up out of the valley. It was a glorious morning despite the Alpine Centre's forecast, so as we progressed more and more layers were removed adding to the weight in our backpacks, but the snow covered mountains lightened our spirits.

We were encircled by black craggy mountains topped with sparkling snow fields creating a blue hue, but when we rounded a bend in the path we were to be rewarded with one of the most spectacular sights we had seen on this adventure. A bright blue sky framed the regal Mount Cook smoking white clouds and snow from its peak. At its base was the imposing black glacier with sheer white cliffs plunging into a mint green lake. Across the vast lake were dozens of sculptured icebergs in greys, black and white floating their way across to the far end beach of ashen sand. It was magnificent, impressive and breathtakingly spectacular.

How a view can be so sublimely beautiful to move you to tears – a Magic Kingdom Moment – I've never really understood but this was about as emotional as it gets. We sat on a rock together to admire and appreciate what lay before us; I went to the shore of the lake.

'Look, I've got something for you,' I said, holding a crystal of clear ice in my hand retrieved from the icy waters, 'it's your very own iceberg.' She took it in her hand and melted.

'Thank you for being here,' she said. We held each other tight and I swallowed hard.

From glorious Mount Cook we travelled farther south to Queenstown, the greatest distance we would be from home at 11,835 miles, literally the other side of the world, and 13 hours ahead of those we regularly wake up with a call. Very strange.

Queenstown is a relatively young town, it was named after Queen Victoria because it was proclaimed to be "fit for a Queen" when discovered, oddly enough, by a Welshman William Gilbert Rees in 1861 who may have said 'Duw there's lovely Blodwin, let's settle here,' and so he built the first property by the lake. A year later gold was discovered in them there hills and the lucky young Welshman was given £10,000 for the part of his farm that included the Queenstown area. Taking his £1.1m in today's money he left for Kawarau Falls and spent his time fishing. Who could blame him?

Queenstown – *The Adventure Capital of the World* is set on the shore at the end of the longest lake in New Zealand, Lake Wakatipu nestled in the mighty Southern Alps and embracing the spectacular and rightfully named Remarkables mountain range with their vicious looking jagged peaks.

Our hotel overlooked the lake and someone – probably our friends from Audley – had mentioned we were celebrating our wedding anniversary, so an upgrade to the top floor master suite was a wonderful welcome.

'Right,' I said, picking up a selection of leaflets thoughtfully left by housekeeping, 'what sort of adventure do you fancy, Helene? Jet boating, bungee jumping, white water rafting, off roading, there's even skydiving and a zip wire…'

'It's our wedding anniversary,' she interrupted. 'And I'd like to see another one.'

'I haven't bought you anything,' I said, hoping this was going to be reciprocated.

'Nor have I,' she replied, 'but I have organised a flight to Milford Sound, a nature cruise up the fiord to the Tasman Sea and dinner at the best restaurant in town the Botswana Butchery. Happy anniversary.'

I had some ground to make up here.

The 45 minute flight over the mountains in a Cessna 12 seater was as thrilling as it was spectacular, with a low cloud base and strong winds throwing us around, or as Captain Blair described it as "jiggling us about a bit – just enjoy it".

During the Ice Age a 2,000 metre deep glacier ground its way to the sea creating a sheer-sided valley and leaving behind some of the world's highest sea cliffs. When the glacier melted the Tasman Sea flooded into the canyon it had formed creating the Milford Sound. Interestingly, New Zealand was the last place to be populated on Earth, but we know the Maori were fishing and hunting in the Sound over 1,000 years ago. It was only discovered by Europeans in 1823 – Cook managed to miss the entrance to the fiord twice – by a sealer, another Welshman John Gruno, he named it after his birthplace Milford Haven.

Kipling described Milford Sound as the "eighth wonder of the world". Its dramatic scenery of 800 metre sheer cliffs covered in rainforest vegetation with waterfalls cascading into the fiord below certainly put it in our top ten.

We were invited on board the Milford Mariner, which had been built in Scotland so the beautiful three masted traditional coastal trading scow seemed a long way from home, and met our nature guide. He was a ponytailed Kiwi with a roving mic and a wicked sense of humour who interpreted what we experienced through the gale that was howling down the Sound, drowning out the sound of his microphone. It is in fact the second wettest place on Earth, although our roving guide informed us that it hadn't rained for 7 days which constitutes a severe drought.

He identified fur seals sunning themselves on rocks after 3 or 4 months at sea. Apparently there were once over a million in the area but thanks to Mr. Gruno and his fellow sealers who literally bludgeoned them to death, their numbers were down to only a few thousand, and they are now a protected species. The Government is doing all it can to conserve indigenous species and rid the islands of foreign evasive animals and plants, such as the pine trees they are systematically poisoning across the country leaving large swathes of dead conifers.

All birds are protected in New Zealand, so the colourful wood pigeons may look beautiful but it will never be found on a menu. We also heard the magnificent Tui that sounds wonderful as it mimics other birds with its two voice boxes.

We were also lucky enough to witness a family of Crested penguins; they're the ones with huge yellow eyebrows that make them look so fierce. There are only around seven thousand of these still in existence so it was a privilege to watch them preen and groom themselves in the shallows. Welsh reference number three; penguin is a Welsh word. Odd I know, but if the Welsh virtually discovered New Zealand's South Island, as it appears they did, then perhaps not improbable. It comes from the Welsh pen gwyn meaning white head.

That evening we celebrated at the outstanding Botswana Butchery, so with only a couple of days remaining in New Zealand, mostly travel until we departed for Australia, we compared bestest bits from the past month in this glorious country.

The icebergs at Mount Cook and the whale spotting were right up there as were the volcanic lakes, particularly the Artist's Palette, and the variety of wonderful wine tasting tours we sometimes enjoyed. We both remembered enjoying the ridiculous Hot Water Beach experience and the incredible walk around the Abel Tasman Bay.

Helene summed it up really well.

'It's a country of generosity,' she said, 'it has so much to give.' She's right of course, the land of the long white cloud has a huge amount of diverse natural beauty to intrigue, fascinate and charm us. However, there's a catch.

The Maori and Kiwi people are immensely proud and respectful of their country, quite rightly so, but their relationship with this stunning land must be perplexing. We have seen both outstanding beauty and ugly devastation. It is a difficult place to live with the unpredictable nature of seismic activity continuing to threaten and often destroy communities. Does its natural beauty compensate for the natural disasters? I'm not sure, but as visitors we were enchanted by it.

Helene giving the weather forecast in Hawaii, looks like the beach again.

The statue of Duke Kahanamoku on Waikiki beach. The 1930's five times Olympic medallist, law enforcement officer, actor, beach volleyball player and a businessman who also popularised surfing.

Allison, the owner of our boat in the distance, teaching me to paddle board in Fiji with mixed success – oddly I kept turning left!

Blacktip Reef Sharks waiting for their breakfast served from the ships galley.

On Tokoriki Island with Paulo making the kava, Fiji's 'legal drug'. It tasted like clay and liquorice, made my lips go numb and sleep like a baby.

Another wonderful meal waiting to be served on a barmy night in Tokoriki.

Probably the best rugby pitch in the world – Sports Master Joe and me training the boys at Ratu Namasi Memorial School, Fiji.

Herman and the crew at the party on Allison's boat the Reef Endeavour on a cruise around the Yasawa Islands.

All good springs come to those who wait. The Pohutu Geyser in Whakarewarewa, New Zealand finally does its stuff.

Joining in the fun at Hot Water Beach on the Coromandel Peninsula, New Zealand and trying not to get burned.

Helene at the Wai-O-Tapu Thermal Wonderland of volcanic pools – 'how does that work then?'

The Artist's Palette at Wai-O-Tapu, aptly named we thought.

Helene getting soaked under the 162 metre Bowen Falls on our Milford Sound cruise.

CHAPTER 17

Day 128 to 140: AUSTRALIA
Cairns and the Great Barrier Reef

Friends shaking hands, 'How do you do?'

One of the most delightful aspects of travelling around the world is making new friends and where possible visiting old friends who have made their home in some far off foreign land. So, it was with great anticipation, as our flight approached Sydney granting us the iconic view of its magnificent harbour and bridge that we were to meet Helene's oldest school friend Tara, and her family. They now reside in the delightfully named town of Coogee, an Aboriginal word meaning "smelly place" a reference to when the drying kelp was washed up on the beach. It is now one of the most fashionable suburbs in Sydney.

Tara and Gordon took a similar adventure to us for their honeymoon some years ago and "got stuck in Sydney" as they like to say. After a year touring the world as young backpackers they decided to return to their favourite city and put down roots. They now have two delightful children and busy lives trying to keep up with the demands of school and the many out-of-school activities young children embrace, but they made time and room for us to use their home as our base.

We all know Australia for its beaches, barbies, blue skies and budgie smugglers but we arrived at Sydney airport in chaos, cold, cloudbursts and cagoules. It was the coldest November weekend for three decades but a warm welcome raised our spirits and we all wrapped up for the 21st annual 'Sculptures by the Sea' exhibition on the coastal walk to Bondi Beach. It is a spectacular 2 km walk featuring a hundred sculptures by artists from around the world, it is in fact, the world's largest free-to-view sculpture exhibition.

The grey skies and crashing waves provided a dramatic framework to the flamboyant and fanciful pieces sited on cliffs tops, in the sand and around green parks backing onto the beaches. The theme *Coming of Age* was interpreted widely and creatively using a variety of materials from Dinky Toy cars to colossal pieces of iron and steel work. A great way to spend catch-up time with the family.

It was Melbourne Cup week – *the race that stops a nation*. Offices close, shops shut and factories stop to allow the whole of Australia to enjoy one of the world's oldest races, held on the first Tuesday of November each year since 1861. "Going to the cup" doesn't actually mean *going* to the cup, to an Australian. It means going to the local restaurant, pub or club to watch the race, the boys suited and booted and the girls dressed in fancy frocks and hats. Or at least it means drink, eat and try and remember to watch the race. We had tickets for the terrace party at The Coogee Pavilion; this was going to be a posh do.

'I have absolutely nothing to wear,' complained Helene, 'and don't even ask about a fascinator.' I didn't, we went shopping. No zippy-uppy bag for posh frocks, I guess.

'You'll be fine in that little blue number,' I said, trying not to let my boredom show, 'and you could borrow some heels from Tara,' I offered helpfully. Apparently not.

Some dollars and half an hour later Helene had "cobbled something together". She looked stunning.

What a great day out. The sun shone, the champagne flowed and the canapés were hugely enjoyed on the terrace overlooking the beach. And to top it all Helene backed the winner at an extremely comfortable 16/1 that very nearly paid for her dress.

We said our goodbyes to the family the following day and took a slightly hazy flight from Sydney to Cairns, just up the road. It took 3 hours and the time zone went back an hour, my goodness that country's big. So big you can put the whole of Europe in it and still have enough space left over for Tasmania.

Our hotel was the Paradise on the Beach, quite a big claim for a small, or as they are now known, boutique hotel, but on the beach it was. So were a few other more unwelcome guests.

"WARNING! ACHTUNG! **Crocodiles inhabit this area – attacks may cause injury or death.** *Keep away from the water's edge. Take extreme care when launching boats"* read one sign.

"DANGER! Marine Stingers. No Swimming" announced another alongside a glass box containing industrial strength vinegar and instructions on how to apply for various Stingers:

"Box Jellyfish – Pour on vinegar, do not rub, seek medical attention.

Portuguese Man O' War – Soak with vinegar and apply shaving cream, seek medical attention".

Shaving cream?

But the flawless beach looked inviting and other couples were walking hand-in-hand. So, armed with sun block, Incognito insect repellent, not sure that will work with crocodiles, and Gillette GII Foam for Sensitive Skin, the best this man could get at short notice, we went for a careful walk up Palm Cove beach, named after the thousands of palm trees that line the immaculate shoreline.

'Oh my goodness! Look at that,' I shouted to Helene, no more than 10 minutes into our stroll.

'What? Where?' she answered, peering into the ocean and at my pointing finger.

'That! There!' I said, wagging a finger at a dark object no more than 20 metres off the shore.

'What? That stick?' she asked.

'That's not a stick, it's a croc.'

'It's a stick being carried by the current,' she argued.

'It's a croc, look at the shape of its head,' I pointed some more, firmly wagging my finger as if it would confirm my spotting.

'Okay, Crocodile Dundee,' she taunted, 'what's it doing in saltwater then?' The stick then flipped its tail and disappeared under the waves.

'Oh my goodness! Look at that,' shouted Helene, 'it's a croc!'

We walked back slightly faster than our stroll had begun, keeping an eye out for any movement on the seashore and overtaking the other hand-in-hand couples.

In the 1950's saltwater crocodiles (crocodylus porosus, if you're interested) were shot, skinned and turned into shoes or handbags for export all over the world. By the 1970's they were in danger of extinction so hunting was banned and their numbers climbed. They can grow up to 6 metres long and are one of the deadliest predators on the planet, so getting humans and these giant reptiles to coexist isn't easy. But coexist they do in Australia.

The Government launched a campaign into schools called "Be Crocwise" and still reserves the right to kill a crocodile it deems a menace. Quite right too, as our guide Lance told us their numbers are increasing so fast they are moving up the saltwater creeks they inhabit towards kids' swimming areas.

We arrived back into Palm Cove to a croc commotion and another sign hastily erected *"WARNING! Recent crocodile sighting in this area"*. The floating net used along these coasts to protect swimmers from the Stingers was being hauled in by various uniformed officials, biologists and croc specialists all peering into the surf. Apparently our croc had continued its journey and been caught up in the netting attempting to feed on the equally snared fish. He was a great deal bigger closer to. As he thrashed around in the netting being reeled in – goodness knows what they were planning to do when net and croc hit the beach – he looked to be a good couple of metres in length.

With a bit more writhing and wriggling, twisting and turning he disentangled himself from the netting and, amid cheers from the now sizeable crowd, made his bid for freedom and headed out to sea. Phew! We didn't expect that on a tranquil beach looking like another Bounty Ad. But it seems everything in Australia wants to kill you: spiders, snakes, sharks, bees, jellyfish, crocodiles, even a frightful octopus. Oh well, into the rainforest tomorrow.

Later that day "croc gate" appeared on the TV news; it seemed to be quite a political issue for the elections due in a week or so. "Dile it up" as one local paper wittily headlined it.

We were booked on the historic train to Kuranda in the rainforest – *one of the most unique rail journeys in Australia* – winding its way through World

Heritage Rainforest to the traditional home of the Djabugay people and first settled by the Europeans in 1885. I really resent that phrase "settled by Europeans" I'm sure the indigenous Aborigines were quite settled until we arrived.

A railway connection from Kuranda to Cairns was completed in 1891 by 1,500 men after 5 years back breaking pick-and-shovel hard work, to service the timber felling, gold and coffee industries. So, our train journey was spectacular with the old 19th century train clinging to the edge of the mountain and sides of deep ravines and gorges as we leaned out of the windows and watched the wonderful old carriages behind us snake their way up the pass.

Kuranda soon became known as a tourist destination – *the health resort of North Queensland.* By the late 1960's it was the place to be and hippy communes flourished until the 1970's when musicians and artists created a bohemian village of handmade crafts, it remains as such today. So, if you are in to healing crystals, knitted bags, painted bandanas or handmade ukuleles then this is the place for you.

I'm in to didgeridoos. As we wandered around the village Helene found the Aboriginal Art Centre & Didgeridoo Specialist.

'C'mon,' she said, 'let's get you on a didgeridoo.' I'm not sure one "gets on" a didgeridoo, but I'm always up for a go on a musical instrument so we entered to be met by the owner Alkina, an elegant and witty lady in her seventies, apparently named after the moon, who knows all there is to know about the didgeridoo. She puckers up and plays pretty good as well.

'If the Earth had a voice it would sound like a didgeridoo,' she said.

She told us that it is probably the world's oldest musical instrument, originating in the Northern Territory 40,000 years ago and is still used today in all forms of music from rock and pop to rap and hip hop. They are not bored by hand or with any tool but hollowed out by termites, so it is they that determine the depth of the note it delivers, I quite like that.

'Would either of you like a go?' she asked, pulling a brightly decorated two metre long version from the extensive collection.

'Stand aside, Helene, this is a man's role.' She rolled her eyes. 'To quote Lauren Bacall,' I said, 'you just put your lips together and blow.'

'It's not that easy,' Alkina said, 'you need to have really loose lips and blow a raspberry.'

'You know how to blow a raspberry, don't you, David?' Helene drawled, in her sexiest Lauren Bacall impression.

I limbered up my limp lips and let loose the best raspberry I could muster. To the astonishment of all gathered – quite an audience had now joined us – a deep didgeridoo din reverberated around the Arts Centre.

'That's very good,' said Alkina, clapping her hands.

'That's very surprising,' said Helene, folding her arms.

Despite the encouragement to play some more we thanked Alkina and left.

'Always leave them wanting more, that's my motto,' I said to Helene.

'You're going to be unbearable now.'

'Did I ever tell you about the time I played the didgeridoo with Aborigines in the rainforest?' I asked in a story teller's drone, as we walked back through the village.

'Oh! Good grief,' she said.

We took the walk into the rainforest – *the amazing jungle trek.* Leaving the village, the track descended to the river and the old rail bridge which was so reminiscent of Alec Guinness's *Bridge over the River Kwai, we were due to visit in a couple of month's time.* As we walked we talked about the amazing experience we had at Mashpi Lodge Rainforest, this was a slightly more refined and tamed version more suitable for us as tourists than intrepid explorers, but nevertheless it reminded us of our wonderful adventure in Ecuador.

Our return journey from Kuranda was up and over the mountain on the Skyrail. It's a delightful 40 minute cable car trip suspended above the tropical rainforest canopy with a guided boardwalk tour at the Red Peak station, the halfway point. It was very reminiscent of our trips over the Mashpi rainforest and those wonderful discovery walks with our guides.

That evening we were invited to dinner by Sarah and James, the couple we had so much fun with on the Reef Endeavour Cruise around the Fiji Islands. Gladly, she didn't get out **that** game again and we spent a highly entertaining evening and late night at their home in Cairns. How wonderful to make new friends across the other side of the world, we vowed to keep in touch and if there was ever a chance or even half they might be our way they promised to stay. What a great way to finish our day and our visit to Palm Cove.

We moved 30 km south hugging the coast on the Captain Cook Highway to arrive at the Thala Beach Nature Reserve just outside Port Douglas – *where the World Heritage Rainforest meets the Great Barrier Reef.* The Nature Reserve Hotel is located high on a private peninsula jutting out into the Coral Sea overlooking two glorious deserted beaches and a rocky "fringing reef" as they call it. The Eco accommodation located in the 145 acre estate are beautifully presented individual lodges perched on the side of the headland providing us with stunning views over the broad bays. We went to bed that night without drawing the curtains across the huge wall to wall windows, allowing us to wake up to the view of the rainforest, just as we did in Mashpi and Fiji.

The following morning, we discovered the rock pools for swimming, constructed on four levels in what looks like a natural waterfall, until you find the buttons to turn them into a Jacuzzi. Breakfast was in the circular open sided Ospreys Restaurant looking out over the canopy of the rainforest allowing us to enjoy our muesli of nuts and berries watching a dozen or so brightly coloured parrots, quite accurately called Rainbow Lorikeet, enjoying their breakfast of, well, nuts and berries.

We decided to attempt the Marine Walk along the fringing reef and around the headland towards what we were promised would be the isolated Oak Beach. We were warned it should only be attempted at low tide and to be prepared for the terrain.

'It's a bit rocky,' said Ranger Dave, the head warden, 'well, very rocky really, but it's low tide in half an hour so I'd go now.'

We made our way down the rainforest path to the cove and stared at the challenge ahead.

'Is this a good idea?' asked Helene, just a few hundred feet into the already very rocky terrain. This usually means it's not a good idea.

'It'll be fine,' I reassured her, 'nothing an intrepid explorer like you can't handle.' This was bound to boost her confidence.

'I can't do this,' she replied, 'let's go back.' She obviously saw the disappointment on my face. 'Okay,' she agreed, 'we'll go on a little further.' We clambered over huge rocks forced to the surface by past eruptions and climbed around black petrified lava with holes bored into it doing a reasonable impression of Munch's "The Scream". We found impressive crystals of quartz too large to bring home and boulders eroded by the crashing waves close by, creating our own natural *Sculptures by the Sea* exhibition.

An hour later some bruised legs and grazed shins rounded the last vast rocks, looking as if they had been tossed there like a handful of pebbles, to reveal an immense expanse of deep empty beach stretching as far as I could see or walk.

We "high fived" each other, hugged and compared cuts and bruises as we surveyed the miles of deserted sand in front of us.

'Let's create our Christmas card,' said Helene, racing down the pristine beach.

Christmas card? The exertion may have been too much for her I thought or perhaps the sun's playing tricks on her, a sort of yuletide mirage.

As I caught up with her she had already completed the large M, E and R in the sand, carved with a piece of drift wood. I joined in with the X of Xmas and with much festive merriment we completed our message to be photographed, photo shopped and forwarded to our friends and family from home. What fun.

We enjoyed a remarkably good dinner of crispy skinned Daintree Barramundi, red curry broth, coconut rice cake and young coconut sambal, gluten free for Helene of course. And seared Yellowfin Tuna, tomato kasundi, turmeric cauliflower purée, sweet potato and caramelised onion bhaji with roasted cashews for me. Afterwards we retired to our lodge to sleep until the rainforest dawn woke us.

The following morning it was up early for breakfast with the parrots and a guided walk through the rainforest with Ranger Dave. Ranger Dave looked like Tommy Cooper if he had been in *Carry on up the Khyber*, a huge man in khaki shirt and shorts revealing calves like shoulders of beef with half a lifetime of bites, stings, cuts and scars above his size 12 boots. Three or four pairs of binoculars were slung around his neck and various hunting knives hung from his belt. He has worked with the owner of the Nature Reserve for 30 years helping clear the area when it was mostly sugar cane and he planted most of the palm trees that now tower above him.

Ranger Dave handed out binoculars to the men and umbrellas to the women in our small party.

'It is after all, a rainforest, ladies.' He was of that generation, but my goodness he knew his stuff, as you would do after 30 years of it I guess. It was a 2 hour masterclass of fascinating minutiae about our environment and its birds, insects and other creatures that make it their home.

But Ranger Dave became the most animated when he spotted the rare Tawny Frogmouth bird. After much pointing, gesticulating and shushing, all binoculars were trained on the owl-looking bird sitting on its nest with its rear in the air displaying its tail feathers to us.

'It may not look much, but it's a spot,' he whispered, and focussed his super photographic binocs-with-tripod on its tiny tawny derrière.

Some of the wildlife in the Nature Reserve was a little more unexpected. Ranger Dave fed the wallabies every morning, sweet potato is their favourite.

Helene had a fine spot with an extremely rare Blue Tongued lizard, and a tree climbing iguana about a metre long walked into breakfast one morning. But while we were relaxing at one of the rock pools…

'I hope that's not what I think it is,' said Helene, curling her legs up to her chin on the sun lounger.

'Well, what do you think it is?' I asked, peering through the trees in front of us.

'Can you see those two big butterflies caught in a web?'

'Oh yes, what a shame, I'll release them,' I said, lifting myself up from the lounger next to her.

'NO!' she yelled, grabbing at any body part available to stop me. She knows how I feel about spiders and snakes and this one was just coming into focus.

I would normally dispense with a spider at home with a large beer mug and a sheet of paper, both to be shaken ferociously outside until absolutely sure it's not resolutely hanging on to either. If I had used the technique on this particular arachnid I would have left at least half of it outside the glass. It was huge. We've seen tarantulas in their dozens in the jungle carefully pointed out by a guide but this was bigger, well wider, longer legged if that's a term. It had a body the size of a toe and a yellow head, but it was also sharing our pool space hanging in an eight legged crucifix between two trees.

'It's attacking the first one,' she said, as it did indeed start to munch its way through the body of a despairingly flapping butterfly. The last thing I needed was a running commentary on the spider's progress through appetiser and entrée.

'You need a drink, I'll go to the bar,' I generously offered.

'You're scared,' she laughed, above her tightly curled knees.

'No, I'm not, Sav or sparkling?' It turned out to be a large version of a common non-toxic spider and not the killer I had assumed, not the man killer anyway.

I appeared to have developed the rather odd habit of placing tomorrow's underwear in my bedside table drawer as I went to bed, not completely sure why I'd adopted this routine but it's comforting both at night and especially in the morning. I spoke to Helene about it, and she mentioned something about an OCD condition I didn't know I had and frankly I'm not sure I understand. I'll check it's on the list and the spreadsheet, again.

During our adventure so far, we had established that man was finally moving on from "the demolisher" to "the conserver" and for some species it's just in time. As the transient guests to sites like Thala Nature Reserve, Mashpi Lodge and Amazonica we had been privileged to encounter the permanent guests in feathers, fur or scales – they are the owners not us, we are just visiting. It may be a little scary at times, but we have a duty of care to respect the creatures we meet and their environment we visit, to add to it however we can, never to detract from it.

What better way to live this ideal than an Eco Tour on the Great Barrier Reef. Our destination on board "Lagoon" – *a state of the art luxury catamaran all the way from France* – was Coral Cay and Heritage Island inhabited only by extremely tame terns, white-breasted swallows, mangrove kingfishers, a pair of magnificent ospreys nesting on top of the old lighthouse and Steve and Katrina. The couple moved on to the beautiful island 6 years ago to collect weather data and continue the first detailed scientific survey of a coral reef in the world.

Sadly, coral bleaching started here 3 years ago meaning the reef is dying. Twenty percent of it has already been lost and so the hundred and fifty species of hard corals and fifteen species of soft corals we snorkeled over are under severe threat. The reason for this destruction? Man.

Visitor numbers to the island and its reef are carefully controlled during the day, much as we experienced on the Galápagos Islands. There were no more than thirty of us for the excursion, and from 6:00 PM to 6:00 AM Steve and Katrina have it to themselves, an idyllic life perhaps, but somewhat tarnished by the deterioration of the very thing they are researching to try and protect.

As we sailed in glorious sunshine and a good breeze to speed us on our way, we were issued with snorkelling gear: goggles, mask and fins plus a stinger suit. A blue one-piece Lycra affair covering all exposed skin and extremities which included a stretch tight hood. This was a welcome addition to the gear, but no mention of vinegar or shaving foam.

We struggled, strained and squeezed our body parts into the tight fit Lycra suits that clung to every curve, bulge, lump and bump, so the only place for most of us was out of sight in the water. We looked like drowning Smurfs sitting in the shallows fumbling with our fins but were soon off across the Great Barrier Reef itself.

Our skipper Richard and the two marine biologists led us on the guided snorkel tour across the shallow reef. It was swarming with life including parrotfish sharing shades with their namesakes, turtles, reef sharks and shoals of vibrant fish set against a kaleidoscope of coloured corals. As we ventured deeper into the reef the water became a little cloudy due to the annual mass coral spawning at this time of year, or as Richard liked to call it "coral sex". Entire colonies and species of coral simultaneously release their tiny eggs and sperm into the ocean for external fertilisation. The phenomenon – which only happens after a full moon, at a certain temperature and at night – resembles an underwater snowstorm and we were, said Richard, privileged and fortunate enough to be swimming through the aftermath. Not entirely sure I agree but nevertheless it was wonderful to be able to visit the Great Barrier Reef while still in most of its glory.

The reef snorkelling was followed by a nature walk around the island. It was a perfect location, a circular island of no more than 400 metres of sandy circumference with a red topped white lighthouse standing proud of the lush rainforest. The island was crowded with nesting birds most of which didn't bother building a nest, there are no predators so they just lay eggs wherever they seemed to be at the time, and if that meant on the lighthouse doorstep, then so be it.

On our return we set sail into a glorious sunset with a glass or two of Australian Sav and delicious canapés served on the deck by Richard and his crew. Once again we felt privileged to have experienced nature and its wildlife at such close quarters but somehow a little awkward and ashamed that the beauty we had marvelled at we were killing simply by living our everyday lives. We resolved to do more.

We arrived back to Thala Beach late and began the laborious task of repacking; zippy-uppy bags can only make it so easy. Our time on the Nature Reserve was over and we were sad to leave. The following morning it was a transfer back to Cairns, a flight to Brisbane and a couple of hours' drive down to the Sunshine Coast and the lakeside town of Noosa.

CHAPTER 18

Day 141 to 155: AUSTRALIA
The Sunshine Coast

In the Rain

The Sunshine Coast boasts over 300 days of sunshine a year – *a warm temperate climate all year round. Rainfall is a relative rarity, with concentrated bursts happening over the brief rainy season in January without having a major impact on tourist activities as the rainfall usually occurs at night.*

It rained incessantly for 3 days.

The modern apartment we had rented for the week had wall-to-wall windows overlooking the lake; apparently; we hadn't yet seen it through the rain. There was also a barbecue, lounging and outside dining area on the veranda wrapped around two sides of the building which we couldn't use because of the flooding.

We hadn't seen Breakfast TV for a few months but being an ex-Ad man I find the commercial channels highly entertaining across the cultures. Australia advertising is, to say the least, direct. Not aggressive or pushy like the US but just lacking any subtlety. As we were watching the presenters discuss some inconsequential trivia about an insignificant celebrity we would cut to two others in the studio extolling the virtues of a demisting lens cloth, vegetable spiralizer or click pedestal fan, whatever that is. Why it took 2 minutes to demo a lens cloth I had no idea, although I had to admit it would have been helpful on our travels. What was that number again? I wonder if they would take a UK debit card?

The lack of advertising subtlety was best showcased in a 30 second piece to camera for Funeral Insurance. The bubbly young blonde (interesting casting) offers "a unique money back guarantee".

"If you're not dead by the age of 85, we'll give you your money back". There may be a reason it's unique, but at least the script refrained from using "a once in a lifetime offer".

Finally, the weather broke and we could stop watching TV. The view slowly materialising from the glass fronted apartment was indeed impressive. We were perched on the bank of a broad lake with views across to the mangrove on the other side. I could have sat on the now only damp veranda for hours watching the pelicans fish and drift on the water towards the mouth of the river.

In a moment of rain induced boredom I discovered that the pelican is both the highest and lowest flyer in the animal kingdom. I had watched them skim the surface with their wings rigidly horizontal gliding just an inch or so above the surface but what I didn't know is that they use thermals to soar to heights over 3,000 metres as they commute to their feeding grounds often more than 30 km away. Extraordinary. But the rain had stopped, it was time to go.

'We need air and exercise,' said Helene, 'and you need a haircut.'

She was right; it was more than over the collar. When Tara and Gordon went on their around the world adventure he let his hair grow down to his shoulders, but I had attempted to keep it in some sort of shape, or at least Helene had. Difficult in South America with the language barrier though, in Cusco after lots of scissor hand signals I came out looking like a cross between Chris Waddle and one of the Chuckle Brothers.

'A haircut can wait, let's discover Noosa,' I said, grabbing the local map and optimistically the shorts and tee-shirts zippy-uppy bag. 'Which Noosa do you fancy?'

Noosa is a collection of villages: Noosaville, Noosa Heads, Noosa Junction, Noosa Hill and more, all situated on the Noosa River of course, which drains the nearby Doonella and Weyba lakes into the Pacific Ocean. There's a lot of water here, we had watched it fall out of the skies for a couple of days, now we wanted to see what it offers when it's where it should be, in the rivers, lakes, creeks, coves and sandy bays of this delightful community.

We walked to the Noosa Marina to catch the Noosa Ferry up the Noosa River to the Noosa Sound. And my goodness it really was a discovery. Noosa, all of them, is definitely for us: cycle tracks, hiking paths, boating, beaches, fishing, great bars and restaurants, independently owned shops and art galleries, markets and craft bazaars all with ferry access. Now, we were beginning to understand why thousands of Brits a year emigrate to Australia.

We visited the information centre to be met by Grace who pointed us in the right direction for the 50 km beach where we could drive its length in a 4x4. She had been in Noosa for 30 years but was born and brought up in our home town in the UK and had recently visited the village in which we live. Halfway across the world and she knew the schools, pubs, restaurants and National Trust walks we were so familiar with, in fact Grace had been there more recently than us.

She also happened to be the host on the Eco Sunset Cruise down the Noosa River to the Doonella Lake and invited us on board as her guests for the evening. This was a Party Boat, but for visitors of a certain age. A glass of sparkling as we boarded, music, mainly Elton John and Queen but not too loud, and plenty of canapés and comfortable seating. We saw kangaroos on the banks, Grey Goshawk in the air and extraordinarily the White-bellied Sea Eagles that Grace fed by hand as they swooped towards the boat and snatched pieces of chicken she held. They grasped the morsel with their talons and either ate it on the wing or took it back to the young in their nest we could see in the high trees above the water's edge. An excellent evening.

The more we explored and discovered the Noosas the more we loved what they had to offer, particularly as we investigated mainly by boat up the river to its mouth with the ocean. What a stunningly beautiful place. We sat on a beach of caster sugar sand and watched Humpback dolphins play with paddle boarders, pelicans with long bright pink bills fish just behind the breaking waves, and enjoyed our day on the Sunshine Coast, finally in the sunshine.

On our way home from Noosa Beach we were alone on the small wooden river ferry skippered by Captain Col, an Aussie who spoke as if he was always halfway through the best joke you would ever hear.

'Come aboard, friends and let's pump up the music with ELO,' he announced over the boat's tannoy. Mr. Blue Sky reverberated across the river as we watched the blue sky turn pink. Other tourists on the bank and in assorted leisure craft waved and sung along with us.

I don't know where "we went wrong" and why "we had to wait for so long" to find the hidden joys of Noosa. But as we danced together on the top deck and crooned our way through the lyrics they seemed to echo our thoughts entirely. It may have rained a lot but never mind Noosa, "I'll remember you this way". So, we promised each other and the colourful Captain Col we would return some day.

Next was the fascinating city of Brisbane waiting for us, with a few surprises.

'Great news, Helene,' I announced, 'I've secured tickets for the Ashes.'

'That's cricket isn't it?' This could have started better.

'Yup, and best tickets in the house for Saturday's Test in Brisbane.'

'Saturday? I thought we were going to the gallery. What time is kick off?'

'Well it doesn't really kick off… But anyway, the lads will be on at ten,' I said.

'Fine, we can do galleries in the afternoon.' I needed to handle this delicately.

'Have you ever been to a cricket match? They tend to go on some while?'

'Yes, I went to a twenty something; it rained so we went home,' she said. 'What do you mean some while?'

'I'll explain on the way, it'll be fun.' I hoped.

It was a pleasant 45 minute walk along Brisbane River in the heart of the city to the stadium, the Gabba as it's known, nicknamed after its suburb of Woolloongabba. It turned out that 45 minutes was not long enough for me to fully explain the laws and strategies of the game to Helene, it's a far more complex game to describe than I thought.

The walk included passing by a beach in the city. It's a wonderful city full of ornate parks and green spaces with smoking barbecues, relaxing sunbathers and soft jazz bands. But to find a sparkling lagoon surrounded by white, sandy beaches and sub-tropical plants overlooking the towering city business centres was a surprise. To see lifeguards in their red and yellow budgie smugglers supervising the beach with suited businessmen and women walking by was surreal.

No sooner had we found our seats at the Gabba than England took their first wicket of the day to give us a commanding lead. That was to be the highlight of the day, as the Aussie skipper Steve Smith went on to score an unbeaten 141 and England lost two quick wickets before the close of play.

'That was a great day,' said Helene, 'although I think England need to be more aggressive in defending the Aussie bowling if they continue to play two slips and a gully.' Thank you Richie Benaud. As always, Helene had picked it up quickly, and had been discussing tactics with the Brits and Aussies around us most of the day.

'I think I could get addicted to cricket,' she went on, 'where's the next Test?'

'Adelaide's a long way; let's discuss it over a beer.' Which in my world means no.

It was not only the Ashes in Brisbane that weekend; it was also home to the Rugby League World Cup Finals with the England team doing rather better than their cricketing colleagues. The bars and pubs were full of Poms – shortened version of pomegranate, Australian rhyming slang for immigrant apparently, because their fair skin turned the colour of a pomegranate – cricket's "barmy army" were attempting to out drink the rugby Northerners. We went for dinner.

I appeared to have had my haircut too early. I'm not one for girly bars and whatever it is they actually do with poles and laps, but as we made our way to the restaurant I noticed an extraordinary poster plastered to the shabby wall of a rather dubious looking building. *"World Famous Barber Babes"* was the headline. Unsure what Barber Babes were and why they were indeed world famous I read on: *"Topless Hairdressers. Wed – Sat 12 PM to 8 PM"*. Pity they couldn't do the morning, I could have squeezed them in before the river cruise. It continued: *"Brisbane's ONLY Qualified Topless Barbers"*, does this suggest there are some unqualified topless barbers in Brisbane I wondered, that could be nasty. The poster finished with the important instruction: *"No appointment necessary"*.

Dinner was Turkish.

Our city centre apartment was a 13th floor modern penthouse which may be described as deceptively spacious. At the front was a large and extremely open *breakfast terrace* – that's a new one – and a glass box known as the bedroom. It had wall-to-wall, floor-to-ceiling windows overlooking the city which looked stunning lit up at night. We adopted the same approach as we did at Mashpi and left the blinds up to allow the soft morning light to gently wake us. At 4:30

AM the sun was blazing into the room and had turned the glass box into a microwave; blinds down tomorrow.

Our last day in the fanciful city that is Brisbane was spent touring the parks now in full bloom, visiting the West End – a bohemian area not unlike London's Camden Town – Christmas shopping in 27 degree heat and a long lazy lunch overlooking the river and listening to the live bands in the park.

'This evening we're going to find a prohibition bar,' said Helene.

'Didn't they finish in the 1930's? Or are you taking me somewhere illegal?'

'No, these are speakeasies. No one knows where they are, why they're there, or what they're like.'

'Then why are we going?' I asked.

'Because I have the password.'

I may have missed something here but apparently cities are now harbouring hidden, ultra-exclusive bars that aren't meant for regular punters. As a former marketer I found this very confusing, I spent my entire career raising the profile of brands to encourage customers to visit or buy, these bars were doing the complete opposite; keeping their profile low and making it difficult for customers to find them – how does that work then?

'What's the password?' I asked.

'I can't tell you, we are told not to share it.'

'But I'm going with you.'

'Yes, but you don't know where.' I was clearly not going to make any headway here. 'I was given the map coordinates online,' said Helene, 'and the password...' she had now adopted a hushed tone, 'is Betty Grable's year of birth.'

'Can't we just have a beer at the local?' Apparently not.

Helene coordinated the coordinates, or whatever you're supposed do with the odd set of numbers she was given and after some searching we found the hidden door and keypad. Helene entered Betty's DOB on the keypad and with a sharp click the door released. It was dark inside but we found our way up some stone steps, pushed hard on another anonymous door and entered a shabby chic bar with silver chandeliers and black sofas.

'Welcome! You are the first to find us,' said the young trendy owner.

'What, ever? No one's ever been here before? Can't say I'm surprised, if you don't advertise you won't bring in the customers,' I said, giving the owner the benefit of my years in Adland. There was a famous book on advertising I read when I first started my career, called *The Hidden Persuaders* but this was taking it too literally.

'No,' young trendy owner laughed, 'first tonight. We change the password on our Facebook page every week so customers can't easily return.'

'Is that wise?' I suggested. 'Surely you want regulars? You'll never get a strong clientele if you make it hard for them to return.' With that the door creaked open and a dozen businessmen and women walked in, followed by two couples who were obviously regulars and a group of Chinese students. The bar was now packed. I adopted a low profile and left as discreetly as we had arrived.

Two hours' drive south we arrived at the Gold Coast, it's not a coast it's a city. But wonderfully named, it looks exactly like the golden city of Dubai, with towering modern apartment blocks and hotels, and more contemporary shopping centres than we could possibly walk around in our 4 days. It was also Queensland "Schoolies Week", a concept I was not familiar with. The centre of town was teeming with what I would know as post A-Level students who arrive in their hundreds to celebrate the end of school each year, good fun to watch but we left them to it.

It also has the most beautiful beach I have ever seen; a 100 metres of powder sand stretched down to the clearest sea and disappeared in both directions as far as we could see. The biggest question of the day was left or right for our early morning walks – we were still on the get-fit-again campaign, but we thought we were winning. Helene said her walking trousers, with detachable legs, were looser fitting than ever.

The city is not only built on 30 km of golden beach but also around the Gold Coast's 860 km of navigable tidal waterways, in fact it has nine times more canals than Venice. Not surprising then that it attracts over 12 million visitors a year although strangely it only has half a million permanent residents – judging by the price of some of the water residences the owners are probably renting them out to the visitors all year.

Being in Australia we had a barbie. We had a barbie on the 41st floor of our hotel. It's what you do over 100 metres above the beach apparently. What fun it was with a group of young Chinese, an ex-international Hungarian footballer and his family and a couple from Lancashire who moved there 10 years ago. We took it in turns to play our favourite music to each other off our iPhones and offer our favourite foods to each other off our barbecues. Great evening.

The following day we indulged ourselves in a three tier afternoon tea of pastries, gateaux and what my dad would have called tea fancies at the Palazzo Versace. The forecourt was full of stretched Hummers in silver, white, black and pink, very Versace, very over the top. The hotel seemed to be full of big blondes – all boobs and Botox – wearing designer fashion matching the furnishings. We appeared to have joined the filming of a celebrity reality programme held in the nearby rainforest, or as they call it, jungle. We got out of there, but not before we enjoyed a very pleasant afternoon of tea and cakes.

Our final drive south in Queensland was a short 1 hour trip down the coast to Byron Bay just over the state line of New South Wales, which helpfully advised us to put our clocks forward by an hour; different state, different time.

Speaking of time, we were at Day 153, halfway through our adventure and time to take stock: zippy-uppy bags still in good shape, travel plans going to plan, and we were still talking to each other. All good then.

Byron Bay was a must-see we were advised by those who we felt were in the know. A bohemian surfing village with musicians playing on street corners, sounded perfect to me although Helene suggested I was confused between bohemian and eccentric.

Despite roads such as Tennyson Avenue, Keats Way and De La Mare Drive, along with The Lord Byron Hotel in the centre of town, Captain Cook originally named Byron Bay after Admiral Byron, not after his nephew the poet Lord Byron – bit of a cock up by the Byron Shire Council I believe.

But there was lots to do during our short stay, also shared with Schoolies, from NSW this time. A visit to the lighthouse with a tough hike to the most easterly point of the Australian mainland tested our fitness, but there was not much to see, just sea. A must-see as far as Helene was concerned was the Crystal Castle; it had Magic Kingdom Moment written all over it, but was pretty impressive. We walked around the Buddhist inspired grounds decorated with huge crystals and took heed of the notices to be cautious of the venomous whip snakes that also reside there. A must-see as far as I was concerned was the personal invitation from Alistair the Master Brewer at the Byron Bay Brewery to visit and sample his brews.

Ali, as he introduced himself, was a tanned and fit Aussie with long wavy hair bleached from the sun. He looked as if his surfboard would always be within arm's reach and addressed the answers to my questions exclusively to Helene, but she didn't appear to mind. The brewery specialises in craft beers, of which there are hundreds of different brands in Australia, Ali's is known as Little Creatures – *Born out of a Love Affair.*

Ali is very proud of the beers he brews; in fact he is so much of a brand ambassador that he tends to talk in advertising strap-lines:

'So, Ali, what varieties of beer do you brew here?' I asked.

To Helene: 'From our Pale Ale to our Pilsner, we've got you covered.'

'I see, and are they all new, like other craft beers?'

'No,' he smiled to Helene, 'we've reached into the vaults to share some of our past glories.'

What I did learn is that beer in Australia is rarely served as a pint; they prefer schooners, about two-thirds of a pint. I thought schooners were the glasses my parents served sherry in before Sunday roast or a trip to the Berni Inn. Ali also surprised us about pubs in Australia, they don't have any. Confusingly, they are known as hotels not pubs, yet hotels are also called hotels. And, despite Fosters being a hugely popular brand in the UK, the Australians hate it; in fact it's difficult to find any "hotel" serving it.

We thanked Ali for his informative and entertaining tour, which Helene seemed to enjoy just as much as me and retired to the brewery bar to discuss the last day or so in beautiful Byron Bay.

'Tomorrow I'm going surfing, Helene,' I mentioned casually.

'Don't be ridiculous.'

I was hoping for a little more encouragement here. 'The only surfing you've done is with a keyboard not a surfboard.' I wasn't going to get it.

'I surfed in Cornwall a few years ago, I'm sure it's just like riding a bike,' I argued.

'Thirty years ago you did, probably taught by The Duke on a wooden board.'

'The Duke was in Hawaii, and in the 1930's and... Oh! Never mind, I'll surf, you look and learn.'

'I'll look and laugh, Duke!' she said.

My hired '"rashie" – dreadful Australian term for a surfer's top preventing sunburn – was in black and blue, Helen thought this very appropriate, and matched my hired board. I certainly looked the part but may have spoiled the effect somewhat as it took the two of us to heave my 3 metre board onto the beach. I don't remember my borrowed Malibu board weighing that much back in the 1980's.

As luck would have it there was a Schoolies Surf Class in full swing so I found somewhere to hide in the melee, tagged along with the students and eavesdropped on the instructor's advice. Meanwhile, Helene raised the stakes by filming my efforts for "a good social media giggle", as she put it.

Perhaps it was my timing, but as the waves crashed in I crashed out, spending more time clinging on than standing on the board. After an hour or so I disappointingly dragged the board out of the surf with the realisation that the young man on the Cornish Coast may have been better equipped than the old boy in Byron Bay.

'I'm very proud of you!' said Helene, as she helped me haul the board across the sand.

'I didn't really do very well.'

'You stood up just as I was filming you, everyone will be impressed,' she added. 'You gave it a go and that's what matters. That's what we promised each other on this adventure, and you did it.'

She was right of course and with a hug and a kiss on the beach she made me feel 30 years younger. How wonderful.

CHAPTER 19

Day 156 to 172: AUSTRALIA

Ayers Rock

A Black Bridge, a Red Rock and a Blue Mountain

No trip to Australia would be complete without a visit to its most famous natural landmark, the world's largest monolith, Uluru, or as we know it Ayers Rock. The same can be said about its most famous manufactured landmarks, the iconic Sydney Harbour Bridge and Opera House, we were to visit them all. So, it was a flight from Ballina back to our friends Tara and Gordon for a guided tour around their home city.

But first a piss up in a brewery – well organised.

Gordon is "something" in the Australian brewery business, his best mate, Dylan, obviously is "something" in the Australian music scene and plays a mean electric guitar in a pretty heavy rock band. So, it was Dylan's gig in Gordon's brewery, a marriage made in good-time heaven. *Highway to Hell* was far too loud, there was nowhere to sit down and the floor was horribly sticky with spilt beer. It was a terrific evening.

In May 1787 the "First Fleet" of eleven ships commanded by Captain Arthur Phillip left Portsmouth with more than 1,300 people on board, consisting of 778 convicts and their children, plus the mariners and their families. Two hundred and fifty days later they arrived at Botany Bay on 18 January 1788 after a journey of 20,000 km but Captain Phillip perceived it to be unsuitable for a settlement because the area had poor soil, no safe anchorage and no reliable fresh water.

He explored an area to the north of Botany Bay and found a natural harbour that he described in his reports as one of the finest harbours in the world. He named this site Sydney Cove in honour of Lord Sydney the British Home Secretary. This was the first non-indigenous landing in what was to be renamed Sydney Harbour. Two hundred and thirty years later we arrived.

And so to Sydney Harbour Bridge, The Coathanger as it's known locally. Sydney is built on a series of bays and inlets that befuddles any sense of direction you may have, but you can always spot the landmark of the bridge to help navigate the city. It is the world's tallest steel arch bridge at 1,149 metres long and 49 metres wide accommodating eight lanes of traffic, dozens of trains travelling across the city and thousands of cyclists and pedestrians each day. It's big.

It's also British. The contract was awarded to Dorman Long Ltd of Middlesbrough who built the similar Tyne Bridge in Newcastle. They may have won the pitch for their attention to budgeting detail, their quote was a precise £4,217,721 11s 10d. Okay it actually cost more than £6.25M and was not paid off in full until 1988, but Dorman Long – *technology for modular construction,* is still building bridges all over the world including the arch over the new Wembley Stadium.

When the bridge first opened it cost a car six pence to cross and a horse and rider three pence. It now costs AU$3.30 for a car and you can't take a horse across it. But the best anecdote about the bridge – one rarely discussed by the fiercely proud Australians – is its inauguration on Saturday 19th March 1932.

It was estimated that one million people turned out to watch NSW Premier the Hon. John T. Lang cut the ceremonial ribbon in the opening festivities, a phenomenal number given that the entire population of Sydney at the time was about 1,256,000. This was going to be a big do, posh frocks for the ladies and frock coats for the gentlemen I reckon. After months of planning and organising, the celebrations included an armada of decorated floats in the harbour, a procession of passenger ships sailing below the bridge, a twenty-one-gun salute and to the amazement of the onlooking cheering crowds, a RAAF flypast.

A proud John T. Lang, with golden shears in hand, solemnly approached the red, white and blue ribbon as the crowds hushed and stared up at the historic moment. He was just about to execute the ceremonial cut when a uniformed man on horseback, sabre whirling above his head, charged out of the crowd on the bridge and galloped towards the bewildered VIP. He slashed the ceremonial ribbon with his sword so opening the bridge and becoming the first to cross it before being promptly arrested. The ribbon was hurriedly retied and amongst howls of laughter from the crowd below and stifled giggles from the dignitaries on the bridge John T performed the official opening ceremony, again. Priceless.

As an equally comical footnote, the intruder, identified as Captain Francis de Groot from Dublin, was convicted of offensive behaviour and fined £5 after a psychiatric test proved he was sane. I guess most convicted Australians have the same test. He then successfully sued the Commissioner of Police for wrongful arrest and was awarded an undisclosed out of court settlement. He died back in Dublin in 1969, his sword remains in Sydney and all **three** sections of the ceremonial ribbon are owned by different museums.

This may be a bit contentious and probably shouldn't be mentioned to an Australian but here goes. They say big is beautiful and the Sydney Harbour Bridge is most definitely monumentally big, but beautiful it is not. It is impressive but sits like a dark black ogre abreast the harbour presiding threateningly over the city's inhabitants below. It dominates the city and peers at you over the top of buildings and from behind trees; in fact it's difficult to take a picture in Sydney without being photobombed by the bridge. For an odd sum of AU$227.88 you can chain yourself to the balustrade and walk over the steel arch of the bridge, providing you pass the breathalyser test first. We gave it a miss.

Remember our new Fiji friends Mike and Allison, she who owns the ship on which we cruised the Fiji Islands? It turned out they have a house somewhere around Bondi Beach and were throwing a Christmas drinks party for a few acquaintances. Invitation extended, we investigated the posh clothes zippy-uppy bag for something to iron and went along on a barmy Aussie evening to meet some of their closest friends.

I was chatting with Australia's leading paediatrician and an artist who had taken the Christmas jumper concept to a new level with matching festive jacket and waistcoat, when Allison rushed over. She is a tall, gangly and beautiful woman with an abundance of blonde hair and it seemed too many limbs as they all flail in the air when she's excited.

'Darling, I have someone you absolutely must meet,' she gushed, guiding me across the manicured lawn, 'he wants to hear all about your adventure and you'll love him.' Fine by me, we are always prepared with the answers to the favourite three questions: packing, planning and the state of our marriage.

'David, this is Malcolm,' she said, introducing me to a gentleman of about my age who looked both tired but full of energy and ready for a laugh. We shook hands; maybe it was my quizzical look that encouraged Allison.

'Malcolm Turnbull?' she prompted me. 'Our Prime Minister.'

'So, David I hear you're travelling the world, how do you find my country?' This could have started better, no mention of zippy-uppy bags, spreadsheets or our married state.

He was indeed quick to laugh and clearly in relaxed out-of-office mode and ready for a gossip and a giggle. We quickly moved on from the recent same-sex marriage bill he famously made legislation 3 weeks after the Australian vote, and the Brexit referendum Theresa May is famously making legislation 3 years after the UK vote, when I saw a twinkle in his eye and a barely concealed smirk at the mention of our PM. What's this I wondered.

'Theresa May is our MP, we often see her at local openings and ceremonies,' I encouraged.

'Ah! Lovely Theresa,' he said, 'we go back a long way. Had it not been for me, well...'

'Oh! Really,' I said not needing to feign interest in this small talk. 'How did you meet?' I coaxed.

This was the story he told.

'I was at Oxford with her then boyfriend Phil,' he started, 'we bumped into each other at the G20 Summit a few weeks back, she came over to me and said "Malcolm!".' At this point he adopted a frightfully posh post-war BBC voice and a high-pitched tone extending the vowels more like a camp comedian.

'"We can never thank you enough for the advice you gave us, especially Him".'

I had to mentally pinch myself at this point, was I really watching the Australian Prime Minister give a fairly poor impression of the British Prime

Minister? It appeared so.

He went on, 'I had no idea what advice she was referring to or indeed who He was. Perhaps it was on cross border trade strategies with David Davis or international diplomacy in the Far East with Boris, so I just waved it away with a "no problem, any time" in case the cameras were on us.'

'Did you ever find out?' I asked.

'Oh! Yes.' He leaned closer as if sharing some state secret. 'I caught up with her over drinks after the G20 and while we were alone asked her who He was and why the gratitude. She told me it was not state business at all, but apparently I sat Phil down while we were at Oxford and told him to get his finger out and propose to her, and he did!' At this he roared with laughter, 'So if it wasn't for me there would be no Mrs. May.'

Maybe it was true, maybe not, but he's a good story teller and seemed to enjoy telling it as much as I did hearing it. He was whisked away by all sorts of dark suited security people before the party became too raucous but we continued on until the small hours with wonderful Allison and her eclectic friends. Great fun.

Nippers is a Sunday morning institution in Australia. Over 30,000 young Surf Lifesavers aged 5 – 14 years get together on the beaches of NSW alone each Sunday to learn lifesaving skills and compete in their own mini triathlon: swimming, running and boarding. So, it was with a slightly fuddled head and not enough sleep that we joined the four hundred kids on Coogee Beach to watch the weekly competition and clear our senses with a strong coffee, cold swim and hot bacon roll.

It was terrific entertainment cheering on the kids in their pink high-vis costumes and colourful Nipper Lifesaving caps – like a skull cap but in four quarters of red and yellow, and tied under the chin. My goodness they put in some effort and seemed exhausted at the end of their events but loved every minute of it whether they were first or trailed in last a lap behind the rest. Funny how everyone cheers loudest for the one who comes last, but quite right.

It was a great morning and reminded me of watching my son play rugby every weekend from Minis up to Colts, the only difference being the 24 degrees of bright blue skies and sunshine. I was already looking forward to Nippers the next week, especially as apparently Santa was arriving on a surfboard.

I'm not entirely sure the Australians quite get Christmas, at least not the way the British do. There are very few decorations in the towns. No lights wound around lampposts, draped over trees or suspended across streets. No Christmas Markets where busy villages are pedestrianised for late night shopping, sweet mince pies and hot mulled wine. Perhaps that's the clue; it's just too darned hot. The Australian humour is always there though, poking fun at the establishment as contentiously and provocatively as possible. The best example, or worst depending on your view, religious persuasion and nationality, is a popular Christmas card featuring Santa Claus crucified on the cross. Odd bunch.

They know it though and happily ridicule themselves. One comedian we saw typified it superbly:

'Have you heard? The Australian Government has just raised the terrorist threat level from "Aw, what the f***" to "Now hold on a minute". Apparently, that's the highest level Australia has.'

Back to reality. We left the kids to enjoy their well-deserved barbecue following their triathlon and went to explore more of Sydney, particularly the Sydney Opera House that coincidently hosted the triathlon for the 2,000 Olympics.

'I think we should see something at the Opera House,' I announced.

'You don't like opera; you fell asleep at Madame Butterfly.'

'Well, it was too long. And too hot.'

'You snored when she died.'

'Okay. But this is the famous Sydney Opera House,' I said, trying a different approach. 'We agreed to give everything a go.'

'Alright. But if you drop off, we leave.'

That was good enough for me, so I went in search of the box office and a calendar of events. Paradoxically, the Opera House is not just opera; maybe you know this I didn't. The diverse options included Nigella Lawson's talk on Home Cooking, Stairway to Heaven by the LED Zeppelin Masters, The Nutcracker and The Unbelievables' Circus & Magic Show.

And, Handel's Messiah for 3 nights only, Helene's absolute favourite oratorio. Tickets started at AU$49 up to a whopping AU$1,009 and were selling fast, mostly at the cheaper end. But I was committed now. Clutching the precious tickets, I hurried down the wide steps to find Helene staring up at the magnificent white sails of the Opera House.

'So, what are you falling asleep to?' she asked.

'I don't think they'll be any snoozing at this one,' I said handing her the tickets. The Magic Kingdom Moment wasn't far away.

'I haven't seen this since the Albert Hall,' she shrieked and threw her arms around me, 'you'll love this.' Yup, I probably will.

The Sydney Opera House is surely one of the world's most recognisable buildings, it's like bumping into a well-known celebrity, I know you but you don't know me. Like the bridge, it was put out to pitch in 1956 attracting two hundred and thirty-three designs submitted from around the world. But there the similarity ends; the story of its building is quite an unhappy one.

Jørn Utzon from Denmark was announced the winner, receiving £5,000 for his design. Unlike Dorman Long for the bridge his quote was more of a guesstimate, well more of a guess really, a poor one, very poor. The original cost was AU$7M, the final cost was AU$102M, that's a hell of a guess.

But he didn't just get that wrong, the estimation for construction of his *expressionist modernism* architectural style was 4 years, it took 14. By 1966 the breakdown between the Australian Government and Utzon was beyond repair, he resigned as chief architect and left Australia, never to return to see his design take shape into the completed Opera House. It was finally opened by Queen Elizabeth II on 20th October 1973 but Utzon was absent from the ceremony. How very sad.

The other unquestionable contrast with the bridge is that it is stunningly beautiful. From every angle and every viewpoint, near and far it is a delight to the eye. Utzon may not have been much of a Project Manager but he was definitely an adventurous and innovative architect. He has said that the inspiration was nature; its forms, functions and colours, and his designs were influenced by bird wings, the shape and form of clouds, shells, walnuts and palm trees. Although legend has it that his eureka moment for the design was while he was peeling an orange. But whatever inspired him, he created an exceptional structure far ahead of its time.

The American modernist architect Louis Sullivan coined the phrase "form follows function" agree or not, we couldn't wait to see the Messiah, a performance for which I'm sure Utzon designed the Opera House.

A final novel anecdote from the building is that it claims rather grandly that the first performance was Sergei Prokofiev's *War and Peace*, in September 1973. Not true, Paul Robeson was the first person to perform there. In 1960, he climbed the scaffolding and sang *Ol' Man River* to the construction workers as they ate lunch. I like to think Utzon had a hand in arranging it.

From one iconic Australian landmark to another, Ayers Rock and Uluru, it has two names. In 1993, a dual naming policy was adopted that allowed official place names to consist of both the traditional Aboriginal name and the English name. "Ayers Rock / Uluru" became the first official dual-named site in the Northern Territory.

Our flight from Sydney to Uluru, for simplicity and respect we will use the traditional name, took over 3 hours and moved our time zone back by an hour and a half – I always thought time zones were in full hours, apparently not, there are even some that move by 15 minutes, seems a lot of trouble for quarter of an hour.

Uluru is almost at the geographical midpoint of the country in the Red Centre – the colloquial name given to the southern desert region of the Northern Territory – flying over it we saw why. It is a barren, desolate and fiery red landscape, quite spectacular in its isolation. It really is the outback.

Our hotel, The Sails in the Desert – *an oasis of luxury,* celebrates the local Anangu people's culture in its design, furnishings, sculptures and artwork so I hoped we would have the opportunity to embrace the Aboriginal philosophy here. Unlike New Zealand where they are proud of the indigenous Maori life, so protect and celebrate their traditions, it seems as though the Australians at best tend to ignore the Aboriginals, some would say suppress them, perhaps this is changing, we'll see.

Our hotel is one of four on Ayers Rock Resort – *Touch the Silence,* and has a terrace tantalisingly overlooking the rock, which never seems to stay the same colour. So, it was with great anticipation that we set the alarms for 4:00 AM; one is never enough, to join our guide Toby on our first excursion, Desert Awakenings – *Experience Uluru in the tranquillity of the pre-dawn under a canopy of stars.*

Six of us bleary early birds were collected from Sails by a vehicle resembling a Disney ride simulator, or Starship Enterprise as guide Toby called his beloved machine. We arrived at our "private dune" to enjoy a traditional Aussie breakfast of homemade damper and syrup, a wheat flour based soda bread baked in the coals of a campfire that Helene couldn't eat. Bacon and egg rolls were available for the traditionalists.

We watched the dawn ignite a fire in the sky as the sun rose over the desert turning the rock purple, pink, orange and finally red. It is often called the spiritual centre of the Earth, I'm not sure, but I defy even the staunchest sceptic not to be moved by something here as Mother Nature unveils her spectacular light show.

There was silence in the small group as we made our way off the dune towards the rock itself and a wonderfully poignant moment when guide Toby recited *My Country* a 1904 poem by Australian Dorothea Mackellar written in England when homesick for her country.

The love of field and coppice
Of green and shaded lanes,
Of ordered woods and gardens
Is running in your veins.
Strong love of grey-blue distance,
Brown streams and soft, dim skies
I know, but cannot share it,
My love is otherwise.
I love a sunburnt country,
A land of sweeping plains,
Of ragged mountain ranges,
Of droughts and flooding rains.
I love her far horizons,
I love her jewel-sea,
Her beauty and her terror
The wide brown land for me!
An opal-hearted country,
A wilful, lavish land
All you who have not loved her,
You will not understand
though Earth holds many splendours,
Wherever I may die,
I know to what brown country
My homing thoughts will fly.

Indulgent, yes, but absolutely fitting for the time and place, particularly for the two of us with its references to home, maybe we all understood *Touch the Silence* at that moment.

Ayers Rock itself rises abruptly out of the desert like a cathedral from a graveyard. It is 348 metres high, some 200 metres higher than the Sydney Harbour Bridge, nearly 10 kilometres around its base and is located just about in the middle of Australia's vast barren and arid zone. It's also extremely hot, rarely dropping below 30 degrees and mostly above 40 while we were there.

Perhaps it is not surprising that a place of such natural beauty has been the subject of much dispute and conflict over its ownership. The story is one of resilience and courage in the face of extreme adversity.

The Aboriginal civilisation is the oldest in the world with a culture that goes back an astonishing 60,000 years or more. So, to the Anangu people who lived at the rock and cared for the land for thousands of years it is a spiritually sacred place. Yet the first white person to see the rock, William Gosse in 1873, promptly renamed it after the Chief Secretary of South Australia Sir Henry Ayer. In 1959 after generations of the Aboriginal Anangu population had made it their home they were thrown off their land to allow tourism and mining to flourish. Unbelievable.

I have a deep resentment and frustration for this repetitive story of white man disregarding the indigenous people. We have seen the same appalling behaviour on Easter Island, with the wonderful Pachacutec and his Incas in Peru, the Maori in New Zealand, even Fiji and now Australia.

As recent as 1911 with the NSW Aborigines Protection Act, the Aboriginal children were removed from their parents to be "educated" in farm labouring and domestic work, grooming them as servants for the wealthy Sydney residents.

Incredibly, during my lifetime, in the 1960's they were still denied their basic rights. The "assimilation policy" stopped them from raising their own children, stopped freedom of movement, having access to education, receiving wages, marrying without permission, eating in restaurants, entering a pub, swimming in a public pool or having the right to vote. It is only in recent years that modern society has begun to recognise, acknowledge and share with the traditional owners of the land, a long way to go yet and long overdue.

Meanwhile, back at Uluru in the early 1960's the Aboriginal people submitted a petition to the Australian Government requesting recognition of their rights as traditional owners, but it was ignored. In 1967 the indigenous people were formally recognised as Australians and entitled to vote, yet in 1971 the petition was finally rejected. Unbelievably, the reason given was that before white man arrived, Australia was 'terra nullius', an empty land, effectively denying the very existence of the Aboriginal people.

A year later protestors set up an Aboriginal Tent Embassy on the lawn outside Parliament in Canberra. It is still there today highlighting the dispossession of the Aboriginal people and the continued lack of equality.

In 1973 a Commonwealth Parliamentary Committee stepped in and called for the protection of traditional Aboriginal rights, recommending they were given a role in the management of the proposed Uluru National Park. It was this political struggle that finally led to the *Aboriginal Land Rights Act 1976* but in a devious political sidestep the newly formed Uluru-Kata Tjutu National Park was excluded from the Act.

Of course, there was lobbying against this exclusion with offers and counter offers made but the stalemate continued for 10 years until 1983 when the Bob Hawke government announced it would amend the Act and return the title deeds of Uluru to its traditional owners.

But the story did not finish there. In consideration for returning the ownership to the Anangu people they had to agree to lease the land back to the government via the Australian National Parks and Wildlife Service for 99 years. Clever; crafty, but clever.

More meetings, debate and argument continued until a further compromise was reached to the mutual benefit of both parties. The ownership was to be returned to the Anangu people, they agreed to lease it back to the Parks and Wildlife Service providing it was run under a joint system with a Board of Management including representatives from the Anangu people.

At a ceremony on the 26th October 1985 the title deeds of Uluru were symbolically handed back by the Governor-General to the Aboriginal people, who had been forced off their land 25 years before. They in turn signed the agreement to lease it back to the government under joint management. And so, it remains today.

It was a colossal fight of determination against impossible odds at a time when the Aboriginals were barely recognised as people with any rights. One of our Aboriginal guides Leroy explained their perseverance. He said, 'We got our land back so we can look after the sacred site properly, only the Anangu can do this because only we understand it. We look after the beautiful things on our land the same way as our ancestors did hundreds of years ago so that the beauty remains for all in hundreds of years' time.'

'This must stop!' said Helene, pointing at the steady stream of tourists hauling themselves onto the rock. 'Don't they realise this is a sacred place?'

There are indeed signs reading "Please Don't Climb", but Uluru has been promoted as a place to do just that since the 1940's when people didn't know about its sanctity, or didn't care. Chains have been hammered into its surface to help with the steep ascent but it has claimed many lives of ill equipped or reckless tourists.

'The energy here is so sad,' she said, clearly disappointed. 'I didn't expect so many people to be violating the rock.'

Our guide Toby explained that the Anangu consider it disrespectful and after years of discussion the Board of Management agreed to close the climb on October 26th 2019. Unfortunately, this has just encouraged more visitors to attempt it before time runs out. He went on to say that it is currently up to the individual. 'Is this a place to conquer or to connect with?' was his rhetorical response.

Having witnessed Uluru's stunning beauty at sunrise we returned for sunset and the *Field of Light Show*. British artist Bruce Munro created his largest installation of 50,000 lights across 50 acres of desert plains with the rock providing the perfect setting on the horizon. It was a memorable evening watching the sun paint the sky orange and pink before finally disappearing allowing the soft glow of the lights to materialise below us.

'I've booked us on the bush tucker experience tonight,' I announced to Helene.

'Is that before or after dinner?'

'Well, instead of really. It'll be fun foraging in the outback for local bush fruits and witchetty grubs,' I encouraged.

'I'm not eating anything with the word "grub" in it. In fact, you go, I'm rather looking forward to Executive Chef Sara Rezguis's cuisine at the Ilkari Restaurant.'

I seemed to be committed to the desert delicacies.

'Okay, you fine dine; I will be foraging and feeding off the land like a true Aboriginal.'

Perhaps not the best decision I had made on this adventure.

I met up with Leroy, a giant of a man dressed from head to toe in khaki. Somewhere in the dust coloured folds was a desert utility belt holding all manner of weapons and digging implements. He smiled a toothless smile, but what he lacked in the dental department he more than made up for up-top with masses of black unruly hair barely controlled by a ragged bun on the back of his head.

We stepped out of five star luxury into a star lit desert that seemed to have lost some of its romance, appearing a little more menacing and sinister in the moonlight. Leroy didn't help.

'We call the poisonous snakes Liru in the Anangu language.'

'What poisonous snakes?'

He grinned his gappy grin.

'Just watch out for the Mulga, when it bites it hangs on injecting lots of toxic venom. And the Ngiyari, it's a thorny little lizard, drinks through its feet actually, but be careful of its spines.'

Spines? Venom? This was not the charm and glamour of desert survival I was anticipating.

We went in search of tjanmata, a bush onion and native pigweed; it has a taste to match its name. We nibbled on seeds called wakalpuka translated as "dead finish", wangunu and wollybutt grass washed down by kaliny-kalinypa a desert honey plant dipped in water. Leroy's signature dish was a sweet treat known as tjala that turned out to be honey ants. I wondered how much tjala was in Helene's culinary creation from Executive Chef Sara.

'We should eat kuka in the desert,' said Leroy, selecting a broad serrated knife from the collection hanging from his waist and approaching a covered table strategically placed earlier in the day judging by the number of flies attempting to access the secrets beneath.

The kuka was meat, what sort of meat was a mystery and should have remained as such.

'It's Sand Goanna,a Monitor lizard,' he said.

Pass.

'And so is the Perentie, but it's tougher.' The rabbit seemed okay but Leroy was very keen for us to try the especially brought in crocodile, in a bun. I returned to the hotel restaurant and left my appetite in the desert.

'Well,' said Helene, 'how was it?'

'I had a croc dog,' I sheepishly replied.

'A croc dog, what's that? It sounds awful.'

'It was awful, what's the dish Sara created for you?' I asked.

'It's like croc dog without the croc, and possibly without the dog. Would you like some?'

'No, Leroy's about to come in and I don't want to upset him.'

'Oh dear! Well there's always breakfast, and I hear witchetty grubs are on the menu tomorrow, darling.' I guessed I deserved that.

We left the red rock and headed for the Blue Mountains; 5,000 square miles of dense eucalyptus trees encompassing a canyon twice the size of the Grand Canyon. We checked in at the famous Carrington Hotel in Katoomba on a fiercely hot day with the thermometer reaching out for the 40 mark. Undeterred, we sweated our way to the Jamison Valley and peered towards the Three Sisters peaks through the blue haze created by the evaporating eucalyptus oil.

We crossed the valley by foot on the elevated boardwalk, by glass bottomed Skyway suspended 270 metres above the ground (our guide delighted in telling us that if we fell it would take 6 seconds to hit the ground), by Cableway, Australia's largest and steepest cable car, and oddly by train.

No ordinary train. When mining became uneconomic in the late 1890's an enterprising young ex-miner recognised that bushwalkers and tourists would pay well for transportation up and down the mountain. The 310 metre rail track used for the miners was obsolete so he refurbished the coal skip (secured a couple of benches to its floor) and charged customers to shuttle up and down the steep incline. Business boomed so he replaced the coal skip with what must have been one of the first white knuckle rides: *The Mountain Devil.* Today it is a modern Disney style ride traversing the 52 degree incline, the steepest passenger railway in the world, with the additional option for passengers to adjust their seated position by a further 20 degrees. Why you would do that I have no idea, but the younger passengers clearly enjoyed being suspended above the drop.

We returned to the wonderful Carrington Hotel where I had the good fortune to meet General Manager Mark. He was a tall and elegant gentleman who, despite being dressed in a dark formal suit, complete with waistcoat, seemed to be handling the heat better than all of us. His natural gait was standing to attention but with a soft and welcoming smile, so I introduced myself by enquiring about the history and legends of the beautiful building.

'It once housed the Dali Lama, was the setting of an horrific murder and it's haunted,' he said. 'Oh, and we celebrate Christmas in July!'

'Can I buy you afternoon tea?' I offered.

It was built in 1883 to cater for wealthy tourists to the mountains and attracted aristocracy from around the world soon becoming the most popular hotel in the Southern Hemisphere, rivalling Raffles in Singapore. The murder turned out to be the hotel's chef who was killed by his own filleting knife when his wife discovered him in one of the hotel bedrooms serving up more than an entrée to a guest.

The oddest anecdote from Mark concerned a group of Irish visitors 40 years ago who were so struck by the clear crisp winter of the Blue Mountains in July that they persuaded the hotel's manager to host a traditional Christmas dinner. Decorations were hung, a Christmas tree found from somewhere and a full feast of turkey, hams, mince pies and steaming plum pudding was served accompanied by choristers singing the joys of the festive season. Like all good Christmas events the "Yulefest" as it is now known, became tradition, not only at the Carrington but across the Blue Mountains' towns, villages and hotels. So, if you want to celebrate a traditional Christmas in July you know where to head for.

We were heading for Melbourne, boasting the largest number of cafes, bars and restaurants per capita than any other city in the world – should be fun for our Christmas. It looked like being a hot Christmas as well; the forecast was a clear and sunny 35 degrees, how odd. But first we had a stopover in Sydney to rework zippy-uppy bags and enjoy the pre-Christmas festivities.

CHAPTER 20

Day 173 to 185: AUSTRALIA
Sydney & Melbourne

A Wonderful Christmas Time

Jingle bells, jingle bells
Jingle all the way
Oh, what fun it is to ride
When Santa catches a wave, hey

It was Nippers day at Coogee Beach and Santa was due to arrive on a surfboard. I was not missing this.

'Is that Santa on a RIB?' asked Helene. 'I thought he was supposed to surf in?'

The broad channel from the sea onto the beach was very choppy; the kids were finding it particularly difficult in their Christmas Triathlon so Santa had decided to come down the channel by boat. Easier than coming down a chimney by sleigh I suppose.

Red robes and white beard billowing in the wind Santa rang his bell and Ho Ho Ho'd through the waves as children cheered and chanted his name. Then it all stopped.

'Where's he off to now?' asked Helene to no one in particular. The RIB turned only metres from the beach and set off back to sea, this was odd. The chanting stopped and the younger Nippers began to blubber. 'Where's Father Christmas going? We haven't had our presents yet,' snivelled one child wiping his nose on his rashie.

'I think Santa may have forgotten his sack,' answered Mum, obviously a regular at Coogee Christmas for Nippers, although how Santa usually surfs in with a bag of gifts I have no idea.

Sure enough Santa disappeared around the headland only to reappear a minute or so later, sack in one hand and bell in the other.

'Here we go again then,' said Helene. More Ho Ho Ho's, more bell ringing and this time Santa reached the beach, almost. The RIB was 10 metres off the beach as the kids ran and swam towards their Christmas hero.

'Why hasn't he reached the beach?' Helene asked.

'That elf at the back shut the engine off for safety reasons,' I explained.

'Don't say it, David.' I didn't.

The elves eased him over the side of the boat and the stout Santa started to slowly slip under the surface, bell still ringing and sack held above the water.

'Blimey, Santa's drowning!' said Coogee mum next to me, as snivelling son looked on in horror.

'No! It's okay, Santa's surfacing,' said Helene, as a soggy Santa lifted himself from the surf and the children cheered, 'but I think Santa may have a wardrobe malfunction.'

His big black knee high boots were now full of water and seemed to have rooted him to the spot. With little option, the boots were cast aside and a bare footed Santa waded up to the beach to sit exhausted on the sand surrounded by excited and slightly bemused children hoping for a delve into the big brown, and surprisingly dry Christmas sack.

Bizarrely, the Nippers all meet up again on Christmas Day morning to hunt for eggs in a bright green sea. This odd tradition – that seems to me more appropriate for Easter than Christmas – has been performed for so many years no one can really remember why they do it. The adults use gallons of colouring agent to turn the inlet from the open sea bright green, they then throw in eggs by the hundred for the children to try and retrieve unbroken. Why not use hard boiled eggs you may ask, as I did. They'll sink.

We left them to their bizarre traditions; Christmas for the two of us was to be in Melbourne, a short hour or so flight south from Sydney to the wrong airport. Like London, Melbourne has more than one airport to choose from and we chose the wrong one; the Melbourne equivalent of London's Gatwick. It was a pleasant enough bus, train, walk and taxi journey, arriving at our Richmond cottage fairly late in the evening, but it still left us with enough time to discover a wonderful local restaurant and its owner, both called Frankie. There we planned our few days in the city and particularly what on Earth we would do on Christmas Day. I still couldn't believe everyone had beach barbies and I was intrigued to find out.

Melbourne, or "Melburn" as the locals pronounce it, – *the world's most liveable city*, whatever that means, but it has been ranked as such every year, since 2011. Back in 1837 the Australian Government was unsure what to call the settlement and very nearly named it after the pioneer J. Batman, wouldn't it have been fun if they had? They opted for the boring alternative of honouring a long forgotten UK Prime Minister.

Our driver said Melbourne is how Australians see Australia, while Sydney is how visitors see Australia, maybe he's right, it does have a very different feel to it, or vibe as the over 60's and under 20's might say. My view is that whilst Sydney is about commerce and enterprise, Melbourne is about leisure and pleasure, it has a personality, and the residents don't just work in the city they enjoy their city, and there's plenty to enjoy.

Our house for the week or so was in Richmond, a suburb much like London's Richmond but only a 20 minute walk from the city. We took the city tram or the "Rattler" as it's called locally, the slowest tram in the world, officially, at an average of 16 km per hour, but it is also the largest network and has the only travelling tram restaurant. Can't have everything I suppose.

The city wraps itself around the Yarra, known as the river that runs upside down because of its muddy brown surface created by the eroded clay in the area. Melbourne also has a huge fox problem. They were introduced to reduce the rabbit population; the rabbits, twenty-four of them, were introduced in 1859 as sport for the settlers and to make them feel more at home. They really should have known.

In 1851 Melbourne had a population of 75,000, but then they discovered gold so the Europeans invaded to seek their fortune and the population exploded to half a million. It became the richest city in the world for a time and exported enough gold to the UK to pay off all its foreign debts and amplify the industrial revolution.

Today, Melbourne is centred on festivals; there are fifty a year from art and music to literacy and beer. And sport, all sorts of sport. We watched the Melbourne Cup of course and the Boxing Day Ashes at the 100,000 seater MCG which is an institution doing its best to have the same effect on the country. The locals claim the first Australia v England Test was played in Melbourne in 1877, long before the famous satirical obituary in The Times dubbed it the Ashes.

Australian rules football, known as AFL, is the most popular attendance sport in the state originating in Melbourne in 1858, although the Brits here believe it was only invented to keep the cricketers fit.

Basketball has the highest participation rate in Victoria, then there are stadiums for soccer, rugby league and rugby union. Australia's F1 is held here as is the Australian Open, not surprising then that the city has thirty sporting venues.

The city was fun, frenetic and festive, at last an Australian town celebrating Christmas, so we hopped on one of those open top buses to soak up the celebrations and visit some of its attractions, the best of which was The Lanes.

Once the delivery access alleys to the large retail stores The Lanes now challenge the big retailers for the tourist buck. Just an aerosol's throw from the vibrant Federation Square The Lanes are now full of street art, buskers, cafes and small restaurants sharing the pedestrianised narrow streets full of tables and chairs. We ordered a coffee to watch the bustling world go by and really weren't sure which establishment we were served by.

We've always liked street art, the legal and illegal, it's colourful, surreal and often witty so we went in search of the wonderfully named AC/DC Lane.

'A must-see if you're into street art,' our city tour guide Miriam said, who clearly wasn't. It seems Melbourne has never forgotten the day in 1976 when the band AC/DC rode along Swanson Street on the back of a truck recording a video for *"It's a long way to the top"*. The lane we were searching for was renamed to commemorate the occasion.

It was full of the most bizarre musical art from the curious to the ludicrous, celebrating not only the band itself but what appeared to be their influences and creative inspiration, absolutely fascinating. We returned to our new friend Frankie for a Christmas Eve drink; tomorrow was the big day but neither of us really knew what to expect.

'Merry Christmas, darling,' said Helene, with beautifully wrapped gift in hand.

'Merry Christmas to you too,' I replied, with loosely wrapped gift bound in cling film – I couldn't find any Sellotape in the house so improvised.

We were up early to co-ordinate the various calls to friends and family still enjoying Christmas Eve at home and it was already well over 20 degrees with not a cloud in the sky. We maintained some Christmas traditions: scrambled eggs, smoked salmon and champagne for breakfast and dispensed with others: Santa stockings, log fire and mulled wine for the morning.

'Secret Santa bought you this while we were at Uluru,' said Helene, handing me her perfectly wrapped present. A beautifully hand painted glasses case appeared from the festive paper with an artist's authenticity card:

Artist:	*Janelle Allunga*
Date of Birth:	*c. 1980*
Language:	*Aranda*
Country:	*Mount Denison*

A few interesting points from our Aboriginal artist here. Her family name Allunga means the sun. She's not sure when she was born but has taken a guess at 1980, her language is not English or even Australian, but Aranda from the Aboriginal people who lived around Alice Springs. And for her, her country is not Australia but Mount Denison, a region in the North West territory, around 250 km north of Uluru. What a great gift to remember all we saw and learned at Uluru.

My gift of clothes from Oscar & Wild didn't really hit the mark.

We had booked a wonderful restaurant for lunch called the Water Front which, as you would expect, was on the quay in the city. So, we caught the Rattler into town and walked along the embankment, feeling entirely overdressed. It may have been pushing 30 degrees by now but shorts and tee-shirts seemed inappropriate so we dressed up for our celebratory lunch.

The Water Front produced a traditional Christmas lunch of turkey with all the trimmings, crackers with the customary poor riddles and a quite passable Christmas pud. We arrived home late, but in time to wish festive greetings to our family just starting their day, and then dozed in the evening heat in front of a film we had seen many times before. A strange but splendid Christmas.

A funny thing happened on the way to the barbers. Yes, it was time to catch the hair just before I took on the appearance of a 1970's musician.

Before we left on our journey I was given some beads by a Spanish friend who said they would help us on our way. Despite the vaguely bohemian appearance I wore them on my wrist from the start of our travels, but the previous night they broke.

As we wandered the streets in search of what Helene calls a "rustic breakfast" we were approached by a one legged monk.

'Look,' I said, 'I think he wants to give me those beads.' What he waved in the air looked identical to the ones gifted by my Spanish friend. This was divine intervention surely.

'I'm not sure he's **giving** anything,' Helene replied as he hopped over, orange robes billowing behind him and gesticulating wildly with the string of beads and a holy book of some kind. Not only was our bald monk short of one vital limb, but he also appeared to be dumb.

'He's not dumb, David, he's taken a vow of silence,' Helene rebuked.

Waving beads and bible in his crutched hand he raised his other palm with fingers spread. Not quite sure what this meant I gave him a "high five".

'What on Earth are you doing, David?' screamed Helene. 'You don't high five a Buddhist monk!' As his holy book slapped the floor I bent to retrieve it for him, but he took this as another gesture entirely and placed his hand on my head and wailed something unintelligible. This really wasn't going well.

'I think he wants five dollars for the beads,' Helene said, interpreting the high five gesture.

Having replaced the book in the old man's hand, he shuffled through the first few pages and showed me the inscription within. Far from being a life enhancing Buddhist proverb or reflective Confucianism adage it read *"Special Today. Beads + Blessing $50"*.

Fifty dollars! For fifty dollars I would expect at least a divine benediction.

I mimed a polite yet firm refusal, still confused over the vow of silence, and walked briskly away. He didn't seem to take no for an answer but I wasn't negotiating over the price of a prayer.

A minute or so later we were continuing our rustic breakfast research when Helene looked over her shoulder.

'David, we're being chased by a one legged monk, do something.'

Where's a hop-on hop-off bus when you need one? sprang to mind.

To celebrate New Year's Eve in Australia there was only one place we could be. So, it was a short flight back to Sydney to prepare for the iconic big night out on a boat in Sydney Harbour. Billed as the biggest New Year's Eve party in the world, the numbers are pretty impressive: 8 tons of pyrotechnics costing AU$7 million, deliver 80,000 fireworks to the Oohs! and Aahs! of 1.6 million people on the banks of the harbour, 5,000 boats on the water and a TV audience of 1.1 billion watching from around the world.

The theme that year was "Wonder" in recognition of the same-sex marriage bill that Malcolm (I think we're on first name terms now) pushed through parliament just before Christmas. It certainly was a wonder to watch. The ugly old bridge exploded into a beautiful kaleidoscope of colour reflected in the majestic sails of the Opera House and illuminating those on board. Tears were in Helene's eyes as a Magic Kingdom Moment overwhelmed her.

'Darling, this is wonderful,' she whispered holding me tight, 'it's all been wonderful.' True, it had and we were 6 months to the day since we left on our adventure of wonder. How appropriate.

Our sighting caused a bit of a croc commotion at Palm Cove in Cairns, Australia.

Helene at Crystal Castle the Buddhist inspired grounds in Byron Bay, Australia. Quite impressive but watch out for the whip snakes.

My guide Leroy and some of his bush tucker from our frightening foraging evening in the desert around Uluru.

Our guide Toby explains why the rock is sacred. 'Is this a place to conquer or connect with?'

Me in a "rashie" with matching surfboard about to realise the young man on the Cornish Coast may have been better equipped than the old boy in Byron Bay.

With the guidance of Alkina, owner of the Kuranda Aboriginal Art and Didgeridoo Centre, I limbered up my limp lips and let loose the best raspberry I could muster.

Tickets in hand for Handel's Messiah at the Sydney Opera House, Helene's favourite.

It's not just huge steaks and shrimp on the barbie in Australia, Moreton Bay Bugs for tea anyone?

Helene creating our Christmas card at Thala Beach Nature Reserve to be photographed and forwarded to friends and family back home.

Too rough for Santa's surfboard on Nippers day at Coogee Beach, but where's his sack?

CHAPTER 21

Day 186 to 192: MALAYSIA
Kuala Lumpur and Singapore

Entry to the Orient

W e gave our thanks and said our goodbyes to Tara and Gordon – what generous hosts they were – turned left on Malaysian Airlines and enjoyed the 8 hour flight to Kuala Lumpur, back over the equator and three time zones closer to home. Should make the calls to friends and family easier I hoped.

The flight gave us the opportunity to reflect on our time in Australia and why up to 50,000 Brits emigrate there each year. Certainly, the climate plays a significant role, it provides for an outdoor life based around a huge variety of sports and leisure activities. And, with 80% of the population living on the coast around the big cities the infrastructure is designed for a healthy alfresco lifestyle. But the rest of this vast country – it is the only continent to be a single nation – is a barren wilderness, virtually uninhabitable by Western terms.

Like any country it has its pros and cons. Great barbies, beaches and blue skies but awful spiders 'n' snakes, supermarkets (they don't even sell alcohol) and Saturday night TV – well any time TV really. It's been said that Australia is like Britain in the 1970's without the strikes, punk and power cuts, which sounds pretty good to me, but would I have my time again as an Aussie? On balance, probably not.

As Sydney sweltered in a record breaking 47.5 degrees, we arrived at the correct airport this time, but still some way outside Kuala Lumpur- *the city of contrasts and diversity.* Our taxi to the centre cost 74.80 ringgit, about £15, sounds more like a tip than a fare for an hour but this is Malaysia, an entirely different economic kettle of fiscal fish.

Given that KL, as it is referred to all over the city by its inhabitants the KLites, is the capital of Malaysia, it is a relatively young metropolis, founded in 1857 by eighty-seven Chinese prospectors in search of tin. They set up camp and named it Kuala Lumpur meaning "muddy confluence" after the meeting point of its two rivers, the wonderfully named Klang and Gombak. Sixty-nine of the explorers died in the poor conditions but a thriving mine was established and the town flourished.

In 1874 Sultan Abdul Samad allowed the British to rule provided he remained "head" of the Selangor district. What this entailed is unclear given British sovereignty, but KL became the capital in 1880 and completely burned down the following year. Just as the new owners were rebuilding the city it flooded and the rebuilding programme commenced again, taking 5 years.

The development of the rubber industry, fuelled by the demand for car tyres, led to a boom during the early 20th century attracting huge foreign investment and new companies to the city. However, in 1942 KL was occupied by the Japanese for a period still known colloquially as the "3 years and 8 months", which virtually halted its economy.

On the 6th and 9th August 1945, atomic bombs were dropped on the two Japanese cities of Hiroshima and Nagasaki resulting in General Seishirō Itagaki surrendering to the British in Kuala Lumpur. It gained historical significance again in 1957 when the Union Jack was lowered for the last time and the first Malaysian flag was raised on the cricket field to mark the country's independence from British rule. The 100 metre flag pole, the tallest in the world, is still there proudly flying the Malaysian flag as an acknowledgment of the event.

KL is now a classic centre of British colonialism; Anglo Asian in its architectural style with both a Moorish and Gothic influence. There is a bit of Dubai in its sixty-five designer shopping malls, ironically the largest is only minutes from the street market where you can buy "the same" brands at a fraction of the price. They have a Chinatown, a Little India and a Moroccan Souk. It was time to shop.

'These silk dressing gowns are just what we need,' I said, as we ignored the bargain Rolex watches, Armani shirts and Mont Blanc pens offered to us by enthusiastic market traders.

'Why?' asked Helene.

'They're only asking 65 ringgits and I think I can get them down.'

'Bartering is ridiculous, they're only £13, how much do you want to save?'

'That's not the point. Step aside and let me handle the negotiation.' Bartering is of course all part of the fun in street markets like these all over the world, with ridiculously high prices initiated by the seller and equally ridiculously low prices countered by the buyer, I've always enjoyed the charade.

'Sixty-five! You must be joking,' I laughed. The owner of the market stall smiled and nodded but was pushed aside by his diminutive and intimidating wife who had sniffed a deal and the scent of her next prey, me.

'No no no,' she said, 'real silk, real silk. I give you best price, special price.'

'Two for 80,' I offered, using the multi-buy strategy I learned from years in retail marketing, this always worked.

'You choose two for 120,' she retaliated. We were making headway but there was a long way to go yet.

'Done!' said Helene.

What? And with that the two women shook hands and the deal was sealed, negotiations completed.

'I could have got her down another twenty at least. Why did you do that?'

'Because it's getting late and we don't want to miss the Reflexology Fish Spa Therapy I've booked.'

'The what?'

Helene explained what sounds like a bizarre fish pedicure where unsuspecting clients dip their feet into a tub of water filled with minute fish called Garra rufa or "doctor fish". Although they are actually toothless they eat away dead skin on the client's feet, leaving newer fresher skin exposed. Okay, we'd give it a go.

Minute they were not. And I'm not convinced they didn't have teeth either. A small tented area behind a heavy curtain in the market revealed a shallow square pool surrounded by seating. Helene checked in as I checked out the pool's inhabitants, hundreds of black and silver fish between 2 and 3 inches long, piranha sprang to mind.

'You first then, Helene,' I said. She also looked a little dubious but slowly lowered a foot into the warm water. A few fish showed some interest, sniffing around her toes, if fish can sniff, I doubt it. So, in I plunged, feet first, so to speak.

'Good grief!' I yelped. To say the water boiled may be a slight exaggeration, but if dead skin is their food of choice I seem to have served up the dish of the day. The water turned black and silver around my feet with the Garra rufa climbing over each other to get at the pied du jour.

'Why did you find that so funny?' I asked Helene as we patted our feet dry.

'I'm sorry, are your feet okay, have you counted your toes?' she laughed.

Food is an incredibly important facet of Kuala Lumpur, and it's also incredibly cheap. We brunched in the spotlessly clean food court below our hotel, the Doubletree in the heart of the city, where it seemed most of the businessmen and women in the city start their day. There were a dozen or so food stations creating all sorts of pleasing aromas, we both opted for rice, a vegetable mixed dish and ginger chicken. Total cost was 5.15 ringgits about £2.85. Not sure if you tip in these circumstances but 15% didn't seem appropriate for two complete meals.

There are food stalls on just about every corner cooking up spicy fruit, vegetable soups, grilled fish, chicken and pork dumplings, satays and of course noodles, all sorts of noodles. One stall specialised entirely in porridge, their menu was like Goldilocks meets Monty Python:

Fish Porridge

Raw Fish Porridge

Fish Head Porridge

Mixed Seafood Porridge

Seafood Porridge

Frog Porridge

Frog porridge? But my favourite was Mixed Special Porridge, not sure what this may contain, I'd guessed at fish, but it was 2 ringgits more expensive than the others.

We decided on an authentic Malaysian restaurant for the evening and asked the owner manager to talk us through some of the specialities and more unusual dishes on the menu. He recommended the KL speciality of fish head soup, which was probably better than it sounded, although Cold Jellyfish Salad probably wasn't. The jellyfish is mixed with cucumber pickle and is a popular appetiser because of its texture. Maybe, but I'd had my fill of "stingers".

Ginger Phoenix Claws sounded promising until he explained that they were boneless chicken feet with minced celery in ginger sauce.

'Braised duck wings might be of interest,' he suggested. 'It's a traditional aromatic dish of duck wing stew that's sure to whet your appetite.' Maybe not.

We bravely left the final decision to the owner manager and chef. Chicken noodles, unidentifiable fish in ginger, pak choi and what looked like raw chicken was served up, a tremendous meal to discuss the plans for exploring the city.

Kuala Lumpur's transportation system is excellent, there are trains, a monorail, an underground system, a hop-on hop-off bus of course and free city buses that run a circuit around the city. They may be free but they're not for the faint-hearted, my goodness they go at speed, the drivers must be paid per circuit, although the marketing leaflet suggests differently – *Visit Kuala Lumpur at your own leisure and interest, and no tour itinerary that will hectic your holiday in KL to make it a more enjoyable holidays.* That's good then.

There is a lot of traffic in KL despite the transport infrastructure, and most of it is motorbikes, hundreds of motorbikes, buzzing everywhere like mosquitoes around the city and interpreting traffic lights and signs as suggestions rather than regulations. An odd idiosyncrasy of the bikers is that they wear their jackets back to front, arms through the sleeves with the buttons on their backs. Although it makes them all look like vicars, not Hells Angels, I'm not sure whether this is a bike rider's fashion statement or that it has a more functional purpose, but it does look strange.

'I've been looking forward to this since we were planning,' said Helene, clutching her ticket to the Petronas Towers – *towering above the rest.*

It certainly is one of the most iconic buildings in the world and completely dominates the city. It is a beautiful construction of steel and green glass built in 1998 in a distinctive postmodernism style, and it cleverly blends the Eastern and Western design aesthetics found throughout the city. The straight lines of the right angles and curves of the columns in the crowns of the two towers are an obvious reference to Islamic design and create a dramatic and magnificent gateway to the city.

The green of the glass seemed to spread itself across the whole city reflecting from one tall skyscraper to another and the silver steel shone like a beacon from the two towers during the day and lit up the city at night like a candelabra. It is a stunning building, magnificent in its design and beautiful at day and night, no wonder the Malaysians are so proud of it.

When it was built it was the tallest building in the world, it is now the highest twin towers in the world. But despite its claims of being the highest building in Malaysia, it is not. Just over a mile away across the city is The Exchange 106, still under construction, but its height passed the Towers in December 2017 and when complete will be 40 metres higher and clearly visible from Petronas.

It reminded me of the 1930's "race for the sky" in New York between the Chrysler Building, 40 Wall Street and The Empire State Building. The architect for the Chrysler, William Van Alen hid a 125 foot needle in the frame of his building and waited for the opening of 40 Wall Street that became the world's highest building. Ninety minutes later Van Alen raised the spire and claimed the accolade. My goodness he must have laughed as the needle was cranked up through the roof depriving 40 Wall Street of its record after only an hour and a half. But not for long. The Empire State's developer John J. Raskob reviewed his plans and added five more floors and a spire of his own to his 80-storey building so claiming the tallest in the world. Boys and their toys.

The Petronas was designed by Argentinian Cesar Pelli who is also responsible for Torre de Cristal in Madrid the tallest building in Spain, the UniCredit Tower in Milan the tallest building in Italy, Canary Wharf Tower the second tallest building in the UK and the Gran Torre, the tallest building in Latin America. This guy does big. But interestingly the two Petronas Towers were built by two different companies; Samsung produced a beautifully vertical tower, but the other, built by the Japanese Hazama Corporation, has a tilt of nearly 10 inches. Oops!

'You will be allowed just 10 minutes on the Skybridge connecting the two towers on the 41st floor,' our uniformed guide strictly informed us. The glass bridge is 170 metres above the ground and is the only link between the two towers, it's about 100 metres long and you could probably just about drive a double decker bus across it. No one has.

Twenty minutes later we were still waiting to be ushered off the bridge.

'We have a technical problem, please do not panic,' said our young guide looking quite alarmed. 'Our lifts have stopped. The engineer has been called. Please wait.'

'Silly question,' I said, 'but how does the engineer get to the 41st floor?'

'By lift.'

'But the lifts have stopped,' (dear Liza, dear Liza).

It appeared we were stuck. Stranded halfway up the Petronas Towers, no way down, no way up. *Your mission, should you decide to accept it* seemed appropriate at this point.

A further 20 minutes or so and a sweaty helmeted engineer gave us the thumbs up to proceed to the 86th floor, by lift.

From our lofty position we could now clearly see the old and the new of KL existing quite comfortably next to each other. The sky rise apartments and single storey homes, the designer shopping malls and the open air markets, the old city hall and new parliament buildings, St Mary's cathedral and the Jamek mosque. Sure enough a city of contrasts and diversity.

This was accentuated the following day when we visited the Sri Mahamariamman Temple. It is the oldest in KL, built in 1873 and is situated on the edge of Chinatown and the street markets just off what was once known in colonial times as the High Street. Now sandwiched between two office buildings the Hindu temple is still a place of worship, the oldest still functioning in Malaysia and very busy when we visited. The bare chested monks presided over a ritual with a lot of prayers, wailing and anointing going on, each visitor was blessed over incense and gifted an offering of small bananas wrapped in pink tissue.

But most impressive was the entrance tower or gopuram as it's known. Five tiers of 228 brightly painted Hindu gods sculpted by artisans from southern India, create a pyramid shaped gateway into the temple. The main Prayer Hall is ornately decorated and contains the inner sanctum where the chief deity Sri Maha Mariamman is located guarded by two large and richly painted gods. Mariamman is often worshipped by those travelling overseas because she is looked upon as their protector during a trip to foreign lands. Seemed appropriate.

Almost opposite, across the busy road we found the Khan Ti Temple, a colourful and even more elaborate affair altogether, dedicated to Guandi the Taoist God of War and Literature – seemed to me an odd combination. The building has a bright orange façade with huge threatening golden dragons coiled around its columns, larger than life stone Chinese lions to ward off negative energy and two brightly painted Men Shen, the fierce Door Gods. A pretty impressive family to greet the visitor and protect the gods within.

Inside, the open courtyard was thick with the blue smoke of incense and joss sticks from the hundreds planted in polished brass cauldrons filled with sand. More brightly painted dragons in green, blue and red wrapped themselves around the pillars in front of three elaborate golden altars. Guandi was at the centre with a long black beard and inscrutable stare, his gold face representing his elevated status, and his two attendants either side looking equally menacing.

We bought joss sticks and chatted to a local who invited me to ring the large black bell suspended in its own tall frame, it must have weighed well over a ton. This was no delicate chiming bell. He handed me a large red length of timber also suspended by chains and encouraged me to pull the heavy beam away from the bell and let go. The deep boom resonated through the temple and hung in the air as it echoed around the building, I did not expect that, nor did the other hushed guests in the temple.

We enjoyed our final evening in KL at another superb restaurant overlooking the Petronas Towers lit in gold against the dark blue sky, it was magnificent. We could have spent a great deal more time in the city investigating its cultural diversity but we had a flight to catch, a quick hour west to Singapore.

Not so quick. A 3 hour delay caused by "aircraft rotation due to a technical problem" before we landed in the cosmopolitan hub of the country. The evening was spent planning how we "do" Singapore in a day. This challenge was made a little easier by the complimentary mobile phone provided by the hotel, with free international calls and an App to guide us around the city. Very thoughtful.

Singapore is a city, capital and state all in one, one of only three City States in the world, Monaco and the Vatican City if you're wondering. But as we saw when we flew in, it's one big island and a whole load of small mostly uninhabited surrounding islands, sixty-three at the last count, that make up this small country of less than 700 square kilometres.

I knew little about Singapore apart from Raffles – closed for renovation – and its role as a global financial centre. Or more specifically where Nick Leeson's spectacular £827m speculative trading caused the equally spectacular collapse of Barings Bank, the oldest merchant bank in the UK. Heck of a 28th birthday present for him, he served 6 years in the local Singapore jail.

The hotel concierge seemed a little reluctant to discuss the "Leeson Affair" as he called it, even 20 years later the city shares some guilt for the financial disaster. Far more interesting than Leeson's record breaking crash, he suggested, is the record breaking duck race. In 2011 Singapore hosted the biggest duck race in the world, 123,000 plastic ducks raced for the line on the city's river at Clarke Quay, where our hotel was located. Not sure it quite stacks up against a major financial catastrophe but our concierge seemed proud of his hotel's part in breaking the duck race record.

A must-see in Singapore according to our concierge and the App on our new mobile was the "Gardens by the Bay" – *where wonder blooms.* So, we set off early and were the first to arrive at what appeared to be a setting from the film Avatar. Dominated by the Supertrees, tree-like structures of steel that tower up to 50 metres above the 100 hectares of gardens below. The gardens are a surreal spectacle and part of the government's strategy to transform Singapore from a "Garden City" to a "City in a Garden". The Supertrees are covered in ferns, vines and exotic orchids clinging to the infrastructure and are linked by a suspended walkway, vaguely reminiscent of the footbridges at Mashpi connecting the vast Capoc trees.

From the Supertrees we could see the equally impressive Marina Bay Sands Hotel – they really know how to design spectacular buildings in this part of Asia.

'That's where we need to go for something long, cool and refreshing,' I said to Helene, pointing at the huge slab perched across the three tower blocks, like the base of a house of cards. The five star hotel has the highest and longest infinity pool in the world on its one hectare roof terrace and I was betting there'd be an equally impressive bar alongside the pool.

The public lifts only took us up thirty floors where we bumped into a German couple in fluffy white gowns and hotel slippers to match, waiting outside the lifts opposite. I knew where they were off to.

'We're stuck,' said Helene.

'Guten morgen, wie geht es dir?' I said, using the only German I know

'Danke, gut,' our German bathers replied and held the lift door for us tapping their key card against the guest pad. The 55th floor was as impressive as it had promised to be from the gardens below and we were lucky enough to be shown to the only unoccupied table for two on the edge of the terrace. What a view. We spent an idyllic hour picking out the sights we were planning to visit later that day and looking up the ones we weren't on the new mobile. Perhaps the strangest of which was the full sized football pitch floating on the large lake directly below us with a single bridge the only connecting point to the overlooking stand.

With tired feet and what Helene calls "rugby back" from hours on the touchline watching our local team, we completed our long day and short stay in Singapore at an authentic local restaurant on Clarke Quay. Curried lobster or crab seemed to be the speciality but was obviously a messy process. Those who ordered it, mostly Chinese, were dressed for the occasion – dressed by the restaurant staff. Cellophane bibs were fastened around the guest's neck and matching gloves were dispensed along with the various tools needed to tackle the shelly crustaceans. And hand to hand combat commenced. Not for me.

KL and Singapore were entertaining, often spectacular and such a departure from our weeks in Australia. They also felt like the entrée before the main course of Bangkok, our next destination.

CHAPTER 22

Day 193 to 211: THAILAND
Bangkok and Ko Phra Thong

Remember us?

Sometimes you just can't turn left. When city hopping around Australia and country hopping around South East Asia the internal flights are short, inexpensive and frustratingly restrictive in their luggage allowance. This is fine if you're on a weekend visit to the in-laws or an overnight business trip to a client, but if you're carrying 10 months' of baggage it is exasperating.

So, we arrive at airports to play the charade of luggage shuffling. In fact, the whole of the check-in area is littered with open cases and their owners kneeling over them adding or removing clothing, toiletries and assorted gifts to make the weight. It's quite a spectator sport, surreptitiously inspecting the contents of other people's baggage, apparently.

There's usually a scrum around the scales thoughtfully provided by the airport to assist in the fun, while specially trained airline staff prowl the concourse looking for offenders who may have slipped a gram or so over the 7kg limit for carry-on luggage or have a bag that struggles to fit in the frame they drag around. Don't leave your luggage unattended or the baggage police will be measuring and weighing it when your back is turned, then insist you pay an exorbitant fee to put it in the hold.

Some passengers just put on as many clothes as they can until their case hits the targeted weight; we saw one lady wearing three jackets and two scarves. Helene seemed to have cracked the system though. She worked out that in addition to the 7kg limit we could also carry a handbag each. What constitutes a handbag I'm not completely sure, but ours were huge, particularly my over the shoulder flowery orange number.

In three days, with three countries and three capital cities under our belt, we arrived in Bangkok.

Bangkok, officially the hottest city in the world and the only city on our travels we had visited in the past. Why? Because we were meeting the kids and couldn't wait. They may be well into their twenties with their own successful careers but they'll always be "the kids" and when asked where in the world they would like to meet us, brother and sister unanimously agreed, Thailand.

We arrived in the colourful city of Bangkok or to give it its full name; Krungthep mahanakhon amon rattanakosin mahintara ayuthaya mahadilok popnopparat ratchathani burirom udomratchaniwet mahasathan amonpiman avatansathit sakkathattiya visnukamprasit as our driver delighted in showing off. Not surprisingly the locals refer to it as Krung Thep – City of Angels.

With a couple of days before the reunion we decided to explore the city by foot and tuk tuk, those remarkably colourful machines that are no more than a highly decorated frame over a very loud motorbike. There are over 20,000 registered in Thailand as taxis and probably a whole load more that are not. They appear to have two foot pedals either side of the steering column and handlebars with twist grips and bike brake levers; goodness knows how they drive them, but they're fast and scary.

The drivers never seem to take us anywhere direct.

'You wanna go to shrine? I take you to buy tee-shirt first.'

'You wanna go to shopping centre? I take you to buy lunch first.'

The shop and the restaurant are invariably owned by the driver's brother or uncle out to make a fast Baht from an unsuspecting tourist. But the most entrepreneurial one was an absolute gem, as it turned out.

'You wanna go to Buddha temple? It shut! I take you to good one and you buy nice jewellery.' We were whizzed through the city to a garage, his brother's presumably. At the back of the working garage full of worn tyres and spares from long dead cars our "guide" slid back the door of the ramshackle office and there between the Pirelli calendars and Michelin Ads was a life-sized gold Buddha.

'Good Lord, it's a life-sized gold Buddha,' I said to Helene, accurately.

'Let's get out of here,' she replied. 'I'd like to go to the hotel,' she instructed tuk tuk man. But not before we had been taken to a working jewellers round the corner, his other brother's presumably.

'This really is quite inexpensive,' Helene whispered as the brother hovered close by, 'and I haven't even started bartering yet.'

'I thought you said bartering was ridiculous.'

'That was different, this is more expensive,' said Helene. Somewhere in there was some Helene logic. We landed an absolute bargain apparently. It also turned out to be the most expensive tuk tuk ride I've ever taken.

Every major city has its park and Bangkok is no different, bang in its middle is Lumpini Park the equivalent of London's Hyde Park, and with a small lake the equivalent of the Serpentine. As it turned out a very apt analogy. As we walked along the towpath of the lake there was some movement in the water.

'Is that an otter?' Helene asked, pointing to a head slowly emerging from the surface about 10 feet from us.

'I'm not sure that it is,' I said, as a forked tongue protruded from what was now clearly a scaled purple head. The remainder of its thick upper body materialised followed by a long prehistoric tail swaying from side to side just below the surface.

'Good grief it's a croc. Run!' screamed Helene. As luck would have it we ran into the arms of a Park Warden. He explained that although it looked like a low budget horror movie in the park they were harmless to humans and only eat fish, turtles, birds and the occasional stray cat. They were Monitor Lizards and were causing a huge problem in the area, all four hundred of them.

'Four hundred of them,' said Helene, 'are they all that big? That's got to be 2 metres long.'

'Oh no,' laughed the warden, 'some of them are over 3 metres in length.'

Our friendly warden went on to explain that he was part of the operation to remove a hundred of the scary serpents and relocate them to a sanctuary outside the city. It didn't seem nearly enough to me but I guess they know what they're doing.

If food was a high priority in Kuala Lumpur it is off the scale in Bangkok. It is of course known for its Street Food, but every street? There were woks sizzling, barbecues smoking and pans spitting on every corner, before we even made it to the food markets. Add these to the plethora of international, fusion and themed restaurants and you wonder how on Earth there can be enough people in the city to consume anywhere near the amount of food being prepared.

It makes for a city that constantly smells of cooking, everywhere, all the time, which is not unpleasant until you come across the Durian, a huge spiky fruit of yellow green in colour about the size of a football. Frankly it looks like a medieval war club; indeed it is against the law to use one as an offensive weapon in Bangkok, the punishment for which is determined by the number of spikes impaled in the victim.

The Durian smells, it smells really awful, like something has died eating blue cheese. But the Thais love it, it's available on street stalls, from barrow vendors, in markets, out the back of pickup trucks or just piled up on street corners, but never in hotels or shopping malls – it's banned because of the odour. They eat it as a dessert with sticky rice, in ice cream, as a fruit roll or pastry, there are even Durian crisps, but most just devour the mushy pungent mess straight from the shell.

Our driver told me that they eat it by the truck load in Bangkok because it helps to manage the heat, but it actually warms up the body and should never be consumed with alcohol or bizarrely Cola, as the combination will raise the blood pressure to a dangerous level. I'm not a fan.

It was time to meet up with the kids. We waited at Bangkok International Arrivals with a sign displaying their names and held aloft chauffeur style, in case they didn't recognise us after 6 months away.

'Remember us?' What a great reunion it was.

We had moved from our hotel into an executive apartment for the four of us, ready for a couple of days' sightseeing with the now obligatory hop-on hop-off tickets – on a boat this time – and guidebooks in hand. We visited temples, shrines, street markets, the largest Chinatown in the world, the Grand Palace and a variety of impressive Buddha including the small emerald Buddha, the most sacred in Thailand, but barely visible perched high on a pyramid of gold in a hugely ornate building. And we marvelled at the vast reclining Buddha 150 feet long. Not stretched out lounging due to tiredness or laziness as its expression may suggest, but representing the historical Buddha during his last illness.

They were all spectacular and awe inspiring as were the temples that housed them, but the one that entertained me the most was the story of the Golden Buddha, virtually hidden away between Chinatown and Little India, like his secret.

He is a big fella, probably three times life-size, sitting sedately on a fairly plain white plinth staring down at his subjects with an enigmatic smile suggesting he knows something we don't. And so he did, for many years.

His origins are uncertain but estimates suggest he was made in the 13th century probably in India and transported to Ayutthaya, later known as Siam. In the 1760's the Golden Buddha was plastered over and painted to protect it from being stolen by the invading Burmese. He was considered of little importance to them, just another insignificant Buddha I guess, and was left in the rubble and ruins of the city to rot.

By the 1800's the secret of the Golden Buddha had been lost, but he was brought to Bangkok along with other bygone Buddha images of insignificance and located in an old disused building with a tin roof that eventually fell into disrepair and was closed in 1935. His true identity had simply been forgotten.

On the 25th May 1955 he had to be moved from the collapsing building, so a simple winch was made to lift the "plaster" statue. "Shouldn't weigh much, it's only plaster" I guess they thought. They thought wrong; it actually weighed in at 5.5 tons of solid gold. The winch broke, the Golden Buddha crashed to the concrete floor cracking its covering and after 200 years his secret was revealed.

He now sits serenely cross-legged in a temple befitting his status that was built around him, he looks a bit smug but I suppose you would if you've just been valued at US$250 million in gold weight alone.

We continued through Chinatown, Elliot found coconut ice cream served with nuts and honey in its own coconut, Charlotte found Mango Sticky Rice.

'Best one pound thirty I've ever spent,' she said.And I found skewered scorpions; about eight blackened crispy whole scorpions that looked less appetising than a bowl of Durian. Helene lost her appetite.

What a fun afternoon we had, trying to identify the fruit and vegetables in the market, sampling the street food and bartering with the eager stall holders for bargains the kids could take home to friends. Over dinner we caught up with the news and gossip that social media and long distance phone calls just can't do and we strolled home through the frenetic city dodging the tuk tuks, traders, food carts and masseurs overwhelming the streets.

On reflection Bangkok was fun and lively, full of a wonderful heritage with traditions and customs we all wanted to learn more about, but it is a city in transition. Local market traders share the same brands with global designer retailers, multistorey glossy hotels tower over single room gloomy homes and street food vendors cook outside executive chef kitchens. One doesn't have to scratch too hard at the five star veneer to discover the Third World reality beneath.

Perhaps this is typified by the story of a soft drink called Krating Daeng, first produced in 1975 by a Thai worker called Chaleo Yoovidhya for his labourers. An Austrian chemist found that it also helped with jet lag for the Westerners flying into the country and so began to mass produce it. Its name translates as Red Bull and when Chaleo died in 2012 he was worth over US$5 billion.

It is this competing clash of contrasting cultures that makes Bangkok a fascinating destination for the traveller, a great choice by Charlotte and Elliot. But it was time to experience another side of Thailand completely; we were off to the jungle again.

The 3 hour drive west took us into a more mountainous and lush terrain so familiar from our time in South America, the vegetation becoming larger and more dense as the jungle attempts to reclaim its land from the ever increasing tarmac.

'Are we nearly there yet?' Elliot said, mimicking his voice from 20 years ago.

'You don't even know where we're going,' I replied, having wisely decided to keep this part of our adventure a secret. 'Well, we're taking you to stay for 3 days at a Prisoner of War camp, won't that be marvellous?'

'A what?' chorused the two of them.

'Like a POW camp in the old black and white war movies? You must be joking!' Elliot seemed unconvinced.

'It'll be great, we'll have our own hut and everything,' I said.

'But you don't **do** camping,' Charlotte argued, with more than a little surprise in her voice.

To be fair the Hintok River Camp is a five star version of glamping rather than a two star version of camping. But from July to September 1943 it was a

British POW camp for three hundred men forced by the Japanese to work on the Thai-Burma Rail Link, *"The Death Railway"*, running from Nong Pladuk in Thailand to Thanbyuzayat in Burma. Most famously known for the nearby bridge over the River Kwai.

Today the camp pays homage to those men and specifically the seventy-nine who, working in horrendous conditions, died from malnutrition, disease or physical exhaustion. The wooden lodges are reminiscent of the POWs' tents in shape and design, although the air con and en suites are a welcome addition. Motifs of railway ties are found in the restaurant and bars and the guard tower is still in place. It is a unique and remarkable setting.

Our two guides Lam and Ise, pronounced ice, were like a Thai double act, humorous, highly entertaining and informative. In fact, it turned out they weren't from Thailand at all, they were from the Mon people, a Burmese society of five million that doesn't actually have a country to call home. Many of them move across the border from Burma, now Myanmar, when they leave school at 14 to work at hotels and tourist attractions, saving money or sending it home until they can afford to return and buy a small parcel of land for their family. Myanmar is a poor country, but to put it into context Lam said that although Mons are not allowed to own vehicles, the cost of a medium sized car in Thailand would buy a substantial farm in his homeland.

Lam and Ise invited us to their village just downstream from our Hintok Camp, their houses were about the proportions of a good size lounge at home and made of bamboo with reed roofs. They slept eight. There were a hundred and sixty Mon people in the village, most working in nearby hotels as waiters, cooks, cleaners and so on, and after a full day's work they start their English lesson at 9:30 PM finishing at midnight.

The children were eager to meet us and practice what little English they had, mostly hello, my name is, or my age is. Sadly, their open air school we visited had been closed for 4 months because the teacher had left the village. Had we not been on a schedule I would quite happily have called the kids together and taught basic English, maths or geography, anything I could communicate without the use of their language.

The basics were all there in the village: fresh water, rudimentary shelter during the rainy season, an ample supply of rice and vegetables and strangely a single TV for the village to watch their favourite team play football. Who did they all support? Manchester United of course.

Lam took us to the disused railway built by the past residents of Hintok

Camp over 70 years ago. As we trekked through the undergrowth to find the old wooden sleepers and the railway cuttings carved by hand out of the granite, the story began to unfold.

In 1942 Singapore fell to the Japanese and plans were hastily drawn up to create a railway for transporting troops and equipment to support Japan's increasing invasion of Asia and their access into India. Feasibility studies had been made before by both the Thais and the British, but it was considered too difficult, too costly and fraught with danger.

The Japanese, however, believed they had an almost inexhaustible supply of unpaid and disposable labour. In March 1942 64,000 British and Australian POW's were transported to Thailand and Burma to start laying the tracks from either end. A further 36,000 Asians were forced to work on the 415 km railway. By early 1943 they were behind schedule so a further 200,000 Asians were brought in and the work day increased to 18 hours. In October 1943 the two tracks met and Japan held the "golden spike ceremony" to celebrate the opening of the line. A hundred thousand men had died in the process – *a life for every sleeper.*

Only 18,000 bodies were found and were either repatriated or buried in the nearby war graves. Lam is convinced the remaining bodies were just thrown down the hillside where the track had been built.

Lam told the story of one such individual who, assumed dead by the Japanese soldiers, was disposed of down the steep slope towards the river. He was found by local monks and cared for until fit to return home. How did Lam know the story? Because it was told first-hand when the now elderly former POW returned to the site the previous year. Unable to walk, he was wheeled to the cutting known as the Hellfire Pass where he had worked in his early twenties. As he began to tell his story a few tourists gathered to listen. By the end of his account a hundred people surrounded the veteran, most in tears, as he relived his remarkable survival at the very spot where he was discarded like a worn out tool.

That evening we enjoyed a delightful silver service buffet around a campfire under the stars. The spectacular menu, contributed to by the four of us following our Thai cooking lesson, accompanied by the fine wines belied how awful the conditions must have been during that summer of 1943.

A long-tailed boat awaited us next morning. These river vessels are uniquely Thai and follow their tuk tuk road cousins as being completely unstable, too fast and a little scary. The principle of construction is also the same; find a huge engine and strap it on to a colourful frame. The boats are around 15 metres long accommodating ten passengers seated in pairs just above the water line. They have an open car engine perched on the back where a long steel pole with a prop on the end had been shoved up the drive shaft. Ours was a Nissan TD 2.7 Turbo – they proudly display their engine type in red painted letters on the side of the boat as an alternative to naming it.

Our destination down the Khwae Noi River (mispronounced by non-Thai speakers as Kwai) was to be a delightful National Park for bathing in the waterfalls although our enthusiasm was somewhat checked by the sighting of what we were sure was a large crocodile in the margins of the river. Ise reassured us that it could only have been a 2 metre lizard, similar to the one we saw in Bangkok's park, but as Charlotte said, 'I don't care what they call it, I'm not swimming with it.' Fair enough.

We were also advised not to enter the caves in the area. There was a sign at the entrance that read *"check your body because low oxygen in cave"*. Not quite sure which bit to check or indeed how to check it, but this was not the reason for Lam's warning. The caves are home to the world's smallest bat – the rare and vulnerable Kitti's hog-nosed bat, still nothing to put us off here. But they are also home to the poisonous Bat-eating snake. Neither Ise nor Lam could enlighten me on how the Bat-eating snake actually eats a bat, I guess it either climbs and surprises its upside down prey from above or waits for one of the sleeping bats to drop off, so to speak. We decided not to find out.

The river did, however, have two wonderful residents: dozens of magnificent kingfishers showing off their electric blue and vivid orange as they darted from one branch to another down the river bank and a floating bar. A 20 foot square travelling pub made of bamboo and reeds complete with thatched roof was being towed gently up and down the jungle river by a surprisingly quiet and slow long-tailed boat. There were tables and chairs in the bar and an outside seating area to watch the world slip by as you sipped a cool Chang Beer – *let the world's entire worries float away on the River Kwai as this tranquil jungle raft bar allows you to enjoy the thrilling yet peaceful surroundings.* Okay then.

'What do monks actually eat?' asked Helene.

'Good question. Loaves and fishes?' suggested Charlotte.

'Rice and fish?' I offered.

'Monk fish?' laughed Elliot, to a series of groans. I don't know where he gets it from.

We had been invited to visit the temple down river and feed the monks, well serve them breakfast. They seem to breakfast extremely early because it was up at 6:00 AM for a cycle ride led by Lam to a small temple with five huge Buddha outside, well over 10 metres tall and each a different colour: red, gold, white, green and purple, each one symbolising the five generations of Buddha.

A single bald monk with bare feet and robed in orange was waiting for us at the entrance guarded by fierce golden dragons. I'm not sure which was more intimidating, the monk or the dragons. We abandoned our bikes and climbed the steps.

'Behave yourself this time,' hissed Helene, clearly remembering our encounter with his one legged colleague in Melbourne.

'It'll be fine,' I said, hoping they don't have a WhatsApp group.

He bowed, we bowed, he put his hands together in prayer and we did the same. As the game of Simple Simon went on he pulled out of his robes what looked like a round paint brush, mumbled some mantra and used it to throw water over our heads. As I wiped the holy water from my eyes he grabbed our offering and I just caught a glimpse of him returning into the temple.

'Was that it?' I asked.

'Yes, that was it,' said Lam, 'congratulations.'

'Congratulations?'

'He liked your offering; usually you have to pay for a blessing.'

'Yes, we know,' we said.

That afternoon we visited Bridge 277, the infamous bridge immortalised by Pierre Boulle in his book and the 1957 film based on it, *"The Bridge over the River Kwai"* winning three Oscars and officially the 11th greatest British film of the 20th century. We visited underneath it by boat and then by old locomotive train on top of it, using some of the track built in 1943.

Or then again, we didn't. The truth is there never was a bridge over the River Kwai. The "Death Railway" ran parallel to the Kwai River but never crossed it. The bridge people flock to see is really over the Mae Klong River. After the movie came out and people began coming to Kanchanaburi in search of "the bridge", the local authorities renamed a section of the Mae Klong to Kwai Yai.

The bridge over the Mae Klong, or Kwai Yai, or whatever, really was one of those built with POW and Asian slave labour by the Japanese during World War II. The bridge now has steel plates over the ties to make it easy to walk across the span. There are also viewing platforms between the bridge "trestles" giving a view of the river as well as providing refuge when a train travels across.

It is an impressive structure nevertheless and a fitting tribute to the 1,700 men who worked in dreadful conditions to construct the original bridge, many of whom died in the process.

We left the wonderful Hintok River Camp by long-tailed boat to meet our driver for the return journey to Bangkok and an hour's flight south to Phuket. From here we travelled north to be met by speedboat and taken to the remote island of Ko Phra Thong in the Andaman Sea and our home for the next few days, the Golden Buddha Beach Resort – *providing a stress free vacation, far away from the troubles of the modern world.*

Alone on its 12 km beach fringed with coconut trees, the resort has thirty wooden lodges and tree houses, built on stilts and beautifully designed on a 20 hectares spit of land with coastline either side. One bay looks out towards two small islands and the other into the vast emptiness of the ocean.

Our lodge, named Tamarind, looked onto an empty beach, it had an outdoor lounge and dining area and we were able to introduce the kids to the delights of outside showers. We had resident frogs in most rooms who barped and grunted from dusk to dawn but were mostly drowned out by the cicadas and crashing surf. It was wonderful.

The resort is the biggest employer on the island with thirty full time staff, about 20% of the island's population, all of whom seem to be related in some way. The children spend weekends with their parents working on the resort where all food is free for family members.

The inhabitants also included a troupe of monkeys who apparently visit the lodges in search of food, toothpaste, and any small trinket that takes their fancy. Why toothpaste no one is really sure, perhaps it has something to do with that odd lip curling, nose wrinkling smile they often seem to have. There are also the most wonderful toucans, or at least I thought they were toucans, they actually turned out to be the Great Hornbill. A prehistoric-looking bird with a toucan-like long bill and a further extension on top like a horn making it look quite comical but fitting its name.

One encounter with the local wildlife I didn't anticipate culminated in what Helene referred to as "shoe-gate". We had removed our shoes, as everyone does when entering a building there and left them at the foot of the steps leading up to the open sided raised restaurant.

The four of us were enjoying our dinner when Charlotte asked, 'Isn't that one of your shoes?'

'Where?'

'In that animal's mouth,' she replied, beginning to laugh.

'What animal?'

'There,' she pointed, 'the one with your shoe in its mouth. I'm not sure what it is, it's too dark,' by this time the giggles were taking over.

'It could be a monkey on all fours,' suggested Elliot, joining in the fun.

'Hey! That's my shoe, come back,' I shouted at the animal now scampering off into the undergrowth. I tried to give chase but that simply encouraged more speed from the perpetrator. By this time the restaurant had come to a standstill as all diners stared at me gesticulating at a long gone thief and shoe.

The manager appeared, a delightful French lady by the name of Maddy, to find out what all the commotion was about.

'Merde,' she said, in her lovely Parisian accent, 'I am so sorry, that is Bernadette, she loves shoes.'

'Clearly. Who or what is Bernadette?' I asked.

'She is our old dog, she loves shoes.'

'Yes, you said. Where does she take them?'

'We will find it!' And with that Maddy recruited the waiters, chefs and hotel staff to start what looked like a well-rehearsed search. They disappeared into the darkness until all we could see were ten torch lights in a wide formation heading towards the beach. Nothing.

I hopped home and hoped that it would re-emerge in the daylight. Two days later it was found, slightly chewed, in the vegetable garden near the kitchen along with three other long forgotten sandals of varying designs. Bernadette was nowhere to be seen, she'd gone to ground after the robbery.

Apart from shoe searching there was plenty to do: showing off our new paddle boarding skills to the kids, snorkelling, kayaks, swimming, yoga and cooking classes, but lying on the beach near the small rustic beach bar and catching up on family plans seemed to be the favoured pastime. And why not, we hadn't seen each other for six months and wouldn't meet again for another four.

The food was a real highlight. There are no freezers on the island so everything is fresh; fish is all line caught, shrimps come straight from the sea to the table and vegetables, grown in the organic orchard, include mangos, papayas, passion fruit, longans, dragon fruit, tamarind, cashew nuts and coconuts – there are hand painted warnings across the island; *Beware of Falling Coconuts.*

'Fishing today, Elliot,' I said, 'I've booked a boat, a skipper and a gillie, all we have to do is haul them in.'

'Can I come?' asked Charlotte, who had never fished in her life, either at sea or on a river bank. Helene also thought it might be fun, so the four of us met Mas our local guide and today's gillie, who knew all the best spots he assured us. How you can have a "best spot" on a vast ocean I have no idea, but apparently Mas did.

Our transport to these special spots was a very old and very brightly painted long-tail boat of green, blue and red that chugged its way out of our bay heading for the open sea, as Mas started to "bait up" from a foul smelling bucket.

'I'll sit at the front,' Helene suggested, 'I think the open air may be better,' as the colour began to disappear from her face. We sat at spot one with lines hanging over the colourful sides and then, nothing happened.

'So, when does the "hauling" start?' asked Helene, with more than a suggestion of boredom in her voice.

'It takes patience and finesse; gently hold the line and wait for a tug.'

'I thought we were on it.' I ignored that. Spot two had a similar outcome and it was beginning to look like our 4 hours would be more like the "ing" as Helene likes to call it when I return home with an absence of fish.

But Mas came up trumps with spot three as all four rods bowed towards the sea. Charlotte roared with laughter as she dragged in a sizeable grouper of purple and pink, and we followed with a collection of brightly coloured and, Mas assured us, extremely tasty fish.

That evening the restaurant feasted on our catch as we embellished our fisherman's tales to our fellow guests. All in all a pretty good haul.

We departed the island with a little sadness, as Helene said, 'Whenever we leave an island we always seem to leave a little bit of us behind.' Very true. But we were on our way back to the mainland and a 3 hour drive to Phuket for some rest and relaxation.

Rest and relaxation? My goodness this was a shock to the system. A full on holiday resort with the shops, restaurants, bars and inevitable street food markets open all night and some of the early morning. It certainly showed us yet another side of this extraordinary country.

'Let's take a walk into Patong market after dinner,' suggested Helene, 'I hear it's really entertaining.' And so it was. We were encouraged into restaurants, masseuse establishments and bars along the way with the promise of all sorts of special offers.

'Those ladies were really friendly,' I said to Elliot, as we left a lively bar we had been persuaded into with free wine.

'Yes, and really broad shouldered.'

'I wish I could do my make-up as well as that,' Charlotte added.

'Really? I thought it was a bit overdone.'

'Darling, they're having fun with you,' Helene interjected, 'those ladies are not all they appear to be.' I finally got it. But I should have guessed, along with the usual male and female toilets, Thailand is now one of the first countries to introduce a third option for transgender men, or more commonly known as ladyboys.

But it's not just the boys. Lam told us that many of the Thai girls visit cheap cosmetic surgeons in South Korea clutching photographs of a pop idol, actress or favourite model saying 'make me look like her.' But then they can't get back into the country because they no longer look like their passport photo. Sad, but highly amusing.

Our next trip was to meet the elephants of Thailand, but the venue had to be selected very carefully. Despite them being protected and their use allegedly highly regulated many are still torn from their jungle homes and forced to perform in shows or carry four people on treks in those awful wooden cradles they strap across the elephant's back. And of course, it wasn't long ago when they were being treated appallingly by the logging companies who used them to haul mostly illegal timber.

Ignoring the many leaflets and posters of happy tourists and sad elephants offering treks, our research found an eco-sanctuary about an hour out of Phuket. Run and owned by a small family, where Lia the mum is clearly the boss, it is an open 20 acre tropical forest which is as close to the natural home as possible for the five elephants in her protection. Her elephants had either been rescued as orphans or saved from further beatings in the name of entertainment or business. They cannot be returned to the wild, so as Lia said, 'Someone has to look after them, so that's what I do.'

One 30-year-old elephant, the friendliest of the lot who we really took a liking to, was given a 50/50 chance of survival by the vet when Lia rescued her from a tourist show. Apparently, she had been hit so many times her skull had fractured. Lia nursed her for 6 months spending all her savings on drugs and medical fees. She is now a fit, healthy and beautiful animal and has a relationship with Lia similar to that of the soppiest dog and its equally soppy master. Oddly, it is petrified of dogs, spiders and snakes so Lia built her a shelter for the evenings and the wet season.

The elephants are never chained, tethered or shackled so are free to roam the natural beauty of the forest or wash, bathe and play in the large muddy pond. Remarkably they also love people, especially if those people have bananas or sugar beet with them. That was us.

What a glorious afternoon we spent as a family with Lia and her two families. There was no structure to it, no performance or tricks, we wandered around, the elephants wandered around and Lia stood in the middle of it all with the widest, brightest beaming smile that lit up her whole face.

We fed the elephants, petted them and enjoyed their company, as they did ours I believe. When they had their fill of fruit they simply wandered off across a bamboo bridge to the pond for a soak and a play in the muddy soup. But first they had a good hose down which they seemed to love and joined in spraying themselves and us with their trunks. Once in the pond they waited patiently for us to join them, brush in hand, to give their broad backs and vast shoulders a good old scrubbing. I'm not sure who enjoyed it the most, the elephants or us but it is a memory we will treasure and I hope, like it is said of them, never forget.

'You ride elephant, yes?' asked Lia.

'We agreed not to do that,' advised Charlotte, 'we said it was cruel.'

She was right of course, so I explained our views to Lia. She gave us one of her special beaming smiles and an infectious giggle.

'How much you weigh?' she asked me.

'Around 12 stone,' I said. At this the giggle turned into a near hysterical laugh.

'Elephant weigh 3 tons! You think you hurt her?' she screamed. 'Look, no cradle, no chain, no rope, no stick. If they don't like, they go.' Fair enough.

I was first up, so to speak, and first down, having fallen off the elephant's bended knee. Elliot went next and did a pretty good impression of Mowgli with his legs tucked behind her ears as she plodded around seemingly enjoying the game immensely. He was soon joined by Charlotte on an elephant she seemed to have created an attachment to. And there I was watching the children parade bareback on elephants in a Thai jungle and loving every second, it almost moved me to tears. Soppy old sod.

Lia funds her elephant sanctuary from the rubber trees all over the 20 acre site – she sells the latex to the local condom factory – and the craft trinkets made by her family and presented for sale in a small wicker basket. We just about cleared her out of the lot.

Our last night together in Thailand was to be a celebration of the wonderful time we had spent together, a farewell for 4 months and of course the family tradition of deciding on our personal bestest bits. Befitting the occasion, we booked a table at the best restaurant in Phuket the Kampong Kata Hill. Perched, as the name suggests, above the town and filled with the most ornate Thai artefacts which wouldn't look out of place at Bangkok's Grand Palace we had visited at the start of our adventure together, only 2 weeks ago.

We had a problem. None of us could get our bestest bits down to one single experience, so we agreed at three, with Charlotte being allowed a first reserve. As Helene said later, 'What's really rewarding is that they were all different.' True, we all seemed to enjoy different things, but one we did all agree on was that it was a wonderful adventure.

We flew together from Phuket to Bangkok the following morning and said our goodbyes. The kids were on a long haul 13 hour flight back to London, leaving us to continue our tour of South East Asia. There was the inevitable Magic Kingdom Moment for Helene as we waved off Charlotte and Elliot but as we boarded our flight to Phnom Penh the capital of Cambodia the next leg felt like a real step into the unknown.

CHAPTER 23

Day 212 to 233: CAMBODIA
Otres and Phnom Penh

A Remarkable Encounter

Cambodia. If you are of a certain age this one word will remind you of *News at Ten* reports, usually from the journalist John Pilger, concerning the Khmer Rouge, Pol Pot, Kampuchea and the Killing Fields where an estimated 2 million died in 3 years, 25% of the population.

It is almost impossible to reconcile the brutality of that regime with the beauty of this country. But still it goes on. It had only been 10 years since the Khmer Rouge trials began, 5 years since the conflict with Thailand and a few months since the shadow opposition leader was charged with treason.

Since winning its independence from France in 1953 this stunning country, sandwiched between Thailand and Vietnam on the Gulf of Siam, has had more than its fair share of political and social turmoil. It is only relatively recently, the late 1990's, that the country has been "open for business" as the politicians like to say, and tourism has flourished, now accounting for nearly 30% of employment and 40% of GDP.

We were met by our guide at Phnom Penh airport who told us that the 70 km journey on National Highway 4 – Cambodia's equivalent to the M4 I guessed – to Otres Beach would take about 5 hours, maybe more.

'Good grief,' said Helene, 'my elephant was faster than that. Is there a problem?'

'No, just the usual rush hour,' he replied.

National Highway 4 turned out to be a dusty road of orange sand about six lanes wide, but without any lanes. If a vehicle didn't like following a smoky old truck it just made a new lane, either on the inside beeping pedestrians to get out of the way or on the outside on the opposite side of the road, flashing at oncoming traffic. This was going to be an alarming journey.

I asked our driver about the traffic. 'Don't you have a Highway Code or any road regulations?'

'Oh yes! The traffic police will stop and fine us,' he replied.

'For what? This is just a free-for-all,' I said pointing at a battered car overtaking a speeding lorry overtaking three young girls on a moped.

'We can get fined for not having side mirrors…' I looked, he had one. 'Running red lights or not having a number plate.' I made a mental note to check. But these hardly seemed to address the chaos on National Highway 4.

'Well that's good, at least there are some rules, I suppose. How much is the penalty?'

'The fines are one to two dollars. But it's all negotiable.' I bet it is.

Rush hour was the emptying of workers from the Sabrina Garment Manufacturing plant, otherwise known as Nike. Hundreds and hundreds of women leaving the factory, like the emptying of a Take That concert, and climbing on board the back of open trucks. Heads and faces covered in scarves in an attempt to filter the dust and standing shoulder to shoulder on the back of the vehicle holding the hoops above their heads where the canvas roof had once been.

There were scarred cars, the models of which were barely recognisable, being overtaken by largely broken bikes and scooters with three passengers, all competing for space with the trucks full of standing women. Our driver adopted the create-your-own-lane approach and drove with his hand on the horn and a foot on both accelerator and brake. It was a hairy ride.

We arrived late; our driver was right, and in the dark. The Tamu Beach Hotel was apparently on the beach, we couldn't see it, as there was a power cut. And so we went to bed, deciding to worry about it in the morning.

It was indeed on the beach, a beautiful beach with palm trees in the sand to provide shelter from the sun, but beware of falling coconuts, again. Breakfast was served looking out to sea with the multicoloured fishing boats bobbing on its glistening surface. It also happened to be the warmest sea I have ever had the pleasure of splashing about in.

'This'll do us,' I said to Helene, as we walked off breakfast down the beach of gloriously fine sand.

'The most difficult decision will be where to have lunch,' she said, as we walked past beach bars, restaurants and cafes, all of which seemed to have Happy Hour virtually all day with the local draft beer, aptly named Cambodia and oddly sponsors of Manchester City FC, at US$0.50 a glass and a comprehensive wine list due to the past French influence.

'Oh yes! This'll do, time for some good old fashioned R & R,' I said, as Helene prepared to investigate trips and excursions.

'Yes, but we've a whole new country to discover.'

'We have a whole new beach to discover! The beach is calling and I must go.'

We had a week to try out all the side by side restaurants in the bay, each with its own strip of sand with every conceivable type of lounger and soft cushion recliner. It was going to be a challenge but I was up for it.

The Dumpling Soup with what they call "Chinese raviolis" in a spicy chicken broth and lemon grass was a particular favourite at any time of day, they serve it at breakfast and lunch, and as a starter at dinner. Amok de Poisson is a famous Cambodian delight of fish cooked in coconut milk and spices, served with steamed rice. But my favourite was Loc Lac au Boeuf, a stir-fried dish of beef in oyster, tomato and soy sauce with cauliflower, carrots, broccoli and green beans. It was usually accompanied by Le Poussin Rose from Sacha Lichine a fine winemaker from Provence who makes some of the most acclaimed Rose wines in the world. He appeared to have cornered the market in at least this part of Cambodia.

'We've been invited to an evening of music and merriment at the market,' said Helene.

'Will we be back for dinner?' I asked. With four restaurants still to try time was running out.

'No, we'll eat there; they have street food and bars around the open air stage. It'll be fun.'

Tuk tuk fee negotiated off we set, bouncing our way into town.

'I don't know why you bother negotiating, David, $3 or $4, it's all the same, especially when you insist on tipping them,' said Helene.

We avoided young kids on mopeds twice their age, small packs of large dogs play fighting on the main sandy-track road and bizarrely a white ox with its head seemingly stuck deep in a green wheelie bin, and arrived at the floating musical market.

'We appear to have found a lost civilisation,' I said, looking around at a bohemian mix of aged hippies with long grey pony tails and those odd woven bags they carry slung over one shoulder, and young tanned backpacker couples in matching silk trousers Aladdin might wear.

'You are so far out of your comfort zone,' laughed Helene, 'let's get a beer and watch the band.'

The "band" appeared to be a young lad looking lost in the middle of the stage clearly set up for a large group later. He was strumming a painted guitar repeating the same two lines over and over. Something about his girl not understanding him, I think his dog was dying or lost as well. It was dreadful.

'Isn't this great?' Helene said. 'It takes me back to my student days.'

'You were never a hippy and as I remember it the reason we're on this journey now is because you thought a backpacking gap year was too rough.'

'Be quiet, the next band's coming on.'

'Good.'

A Frank Zappa lookalike joined the misunderstood singer on stage; he appeared to be the compere.

'Ladies and gentlemen give up some love for Vincent.' I might have guessed. There was a murmur and a rustle of applause as Vincent shuffled off stage.

'You're in for a real treat tonight,' said compere.

'I bet we are.'

'Shush, this is fun.' Helene nudged me.

'Tonight we have Guthrie on his 7 foot ukulele,' continued compere.

'Good grief that will be fun, I'd pay to see that.'

'Sorry, did I say ukulele? I meant unicycle,' corrected compere.

'Shit!'

'David!'

'Sorry.'

'Unicycle,' he said again, just in case anyone was in doubt. They weren't. 'I meant unicycle but said ukulele.' Yes, we got it.

'It must be something in the water,' compere laughed embarrassingly.

'Must be something in the tobacco,' I corrected.

After the hilarity of Vincent, compere and the once eagerly anticipated Guthrie, I was quite looking forward to the rest of the evening. Sadly, the next "turn" made Vincent look like a convincing contender for X-Factor so we visited the market part of the musical market.

It was as bohemian as the music, with stalls manned by the avant-garde makers of the equally exotic merchandise which we could barely see through the joss stick smoke. If we were in the market for far-too-large-to-wear jewellery, handmade smocks or carved rustic mobile covers, then this was the place to be. We bought another beer.

A few beers, a homemade quiche and a gluten free frangipani tart Helene could eat hardly compared with the delights of Chez Paou on Otres Beach but a good evening was had by all, including Guthrie playing his 7 foot unicycle and Vincent who came back on for a quite passable encore.

It was time for another island. A 40 minute boat trip out into the Gulf of Siam to Saracen Bay on Koh Rong Samloem Island took us back to the jungle and back to paradise. My goodness we'd stayed on some beautiful islands and this one was right up there with the best of them. The island is 9 km north to south, 4 km at its widest point and 1 km at its narrowest, so an effortless 20 minute walk from one sandy beach through the jungle to the other.

The back packers head for sunset beach on the west of the island while those turning left favour the 2 km horseshoe cove of Saracen Bay, a white sandy beach accommodating excellent wooden lodges in front of the thick jungle. Ours had a veranda with steps down to our own sandy, picket fenced garden and then twenty-two steps to the sea. I know; Helene caught me pacing it out.

We were introduced to our resident gecko, a chunky chap of about a foot long who lives in the lodge and takes care of any unwelcome flies for us. Piggy, as we named him, lorded it over the property, often making an appearance just to keep an eye on us and always said good morning with that loud kissing noise that large geckos make, like a greeting from a rarely seen great aunt. At night we left the blinds open to be woken by the sunrise, as we did in Mashpi, but this time the sounds of the jungle were joined by the waves gently rolling on to our beach. Idyllic.

The Saracen Bay is full of restaurants, bars and lodges similar to ours dotted along its length. It was on the way back from dinner at a particularly good beach restaurant called The One that we had our close encounter of the herd kind.

It was a starry night as we paddled our way in the surf – footwear is not needed on the island – when a rather distressed French girl stopped us.

'Pleeze be careful,' she advised, holding my arm, 'big bungalows on ze shores.'

'Yes, I know we're staying in one, they're not dangerous,' I replied, quite unsure why she was still gripping my arm.

'No! Bungalows. Very dangerous.'

'What on Earth is she saying, Helene?'

'Well, I don't think dangerous bungalows can be right,' she suggested.

'Yez. Pleeze careful,' she said, looking over her shoulder back down the beach towards our lodge. We thanked her and continued on our way.

'What was all that about?' I asked Helene.

'No idea but turn on the torch from your mobile.'

'Okay. What does a dangerous bungalow look li... bloody hell!' The small beam immediately picked up one of four huge buffalo shin deep in the shallows staring straight at us, no more than 15 feet away.

'Turn it off,' screamed Helene. I hit some buttons and Madonna's "Like a Virgin" broke the silence. This seemed to arouse the curiosity of the other three. Eight blinking eyes and eight fearsome horns were now fixed on us as the heavyweight animals stood their ground.

'Back up,' said Helene. Fortunately, as we began withdrawing they continued wallowing and we made it to the safety of our flimsy lodge. Later that night Helene nudged me in bed.

'The buffalo are behind us,' she whispered.

'Sounds like a coded message, but what on earth do you want me to do about it?'

Sure enough there were munching and lolloping sounds just a few feet behind our heads the other side of the flimsy reed and bamboo built lodge wall. It was a restless night and the following morning we discovered that the buffalo, although disappeared, had left us a large smelly gift in our sandy front garden.

Most of our time on the island was spent walking the white beach of the bay, occasionally stopping to enjoy the wooden swings for two, or the hammocks the bars had obligingly sited in the shallows of the crystal clear water. This was relaxation at a completely different level. Probably just as well as we readied ourselves for what was inevitably going to be a harrowing and emotional visit to Phnom Penh.

But perhaps nothing could have prepared us for the horror and savagery we found during our visits to the security prison and the killings fields, that day in Phnom Penh. To get anywhere near fathoming the level of atrocities we saw we have to understand some of the background and the motivation of one man, Pol Pot, the Cambodian politician, revolutionary and leader of the Khmer Rouge from 1963 to 1997, responsible for the deaths of over two million of his own people or 1 in 4 of the population.

Born in 1925 to a wealthy farming family he was sent to Phnom Penh at the age of 9 to be educated at some of Cambodia's best schools. At 24 years of age he went to France, joined the French Communist Party and adopted Marxism. It was here that he started to develop his radical blend of communism and nationalism. He began to plot a revolution to re-establish his country based on the ancient civilisation of 800 years ago, with the intention of creating the perfect race he believed would save Cambodia.

Tensions were high between the French owners and the corrupt Cambodian puppet monarchy which gave Pol Pot the opportunity to provide an alternative to the working farmers and labourers. He returned to Phnom Penh as a teacher, but by night he was anonymously recruiting for his newly formed Communist Party, he was simply known as "brother number one". In 1962 he gave a mesmerising speech encouraging his new followers to overthrow the royal family. Not surprisingly the monarchy responded with force and Pol Pot fled into the jungle where he began recruiting the local tribe leaders into his party with the promise of revolution.

In 1965 France gave up its control of the South East Asian countries it owned and the Americans effectively took over. By 1969 Nixon was bombing the Vietnamese troops in Cambodia and Pol Pot's communist rebels had become the Khmer Rouge offering the Cambodian monarchy a deal he never intended to honour – promising to return them to power after the revolution in return for support of his new party.

Cambodia was in chaos, a million sought refuge in Phnom Penh from the American B52 bombers but there was little food, no medical resources and a failing economy and infrastructure. When Nixon pulled the Americans out in 1973 the world had effectively abandoned Cambodia and Pol Pot took his chance. On 17th April 1975, 2 weeks before the fall of Saigon and the end of the Vietnam War, the Khmer Rouge defeated the American backed army of Cambodian President Lon Nol and marched into the capital Phnom Penh. There were celebrations and partying, the streets were lined with grateful families and the rebels were applauded and congratulated as heroes.

Three hours later it all changed. The egotism and paranoia of the new dictator became evident when he arrested the king and announced that he was closing the city so all two million inhabitants must leave for the country immediately. His excuse was that the Americans were on their way to bomb the city – another lie – in reality he believed the cities and anything modern was impure, he wanted to return to the ideology of the ancient civilisation, a pure communist society. Within 3 days every city was empty. It was not a rebirth of Cambodia it was suicide.

It was at this point that Pol Pot established Kampuchea, the Khmer Rouge controlled state, and took over the Tuol Svay Prey High School in the capital, Phnom Penh. He transformed it into Tuol Sleng the notorious security prison called S.21 a torture and interrogation centre run by the Khmer Rouge. This was our first visit of the day.

My first impression was surprise that this torture centre, or Genocide Museum as it is now known, was right in the middle of the city. It looked like any other high school from a distance; five, three storey buildings, about the size of a UK junior school, face on to a play area with gym apparatus, courtyard and green lawns. We were to find out later that this play area and apparatus was adapted to torture prisoners.

Surprisingly, it is not in ruins, far from it, it is in near perfect condition having been built in 1962. But then we forget it was converted to a torture centre only 40 years ago, in the mid 1970's.

Twenty thousand prisoners at Tuol Sleng were tortured, interrogated and "processed" before transportation to the killing fields; seven survived. Seven survived, out of twenty thousand.

Our guide was Socmail a quietly spoken lady in her mid-fifties. As she led our small party into the classrooms converted to torture chambers she recounted how the monks, artists, professionals, doctors, teachers, the educated and intellectuals were all arrested on suspicion of being traitors to the new state. Bizarrely this included anyone with glasses or soft hands and those who could speak a foreign language. Pol Pot believed the peasants were to be the heroes of the revolution while those living in cities should be wiped out or sent to the country to work on the land. Pol Pot's radical aim was to eliminate all traces of the previous culture and modern way of life.

The decaying 15ft square rooms, had the original rusting beds in place with their chains and shackles attached, alongside the instruments of torture. Every inmate was interrogated each day until they confessed to something, anything to stop the pain. The rooms would have included a typewriter so when the prisoner admitted to an act of treason the interrogator would stop the punishment and record the confession. Once completed it was given to the victim for an X to be scrawled onto the paper. They had in effect signed their own death warrant; the Khmer Rouge believed they now had the justification to send the prisoner to the killing fields.

Prisoners were also forced to give the names of their family and friends, who would then be rounded up and arrested. Whole families were imprisoned, tortured and dispatched for death at the killing fields: men, women, children and most distressing of all, their babies.

Unbelievably brutal and barbaric torture at Tuol Sleng included electric shock, water boarding with boiling water, nail extraction with alcohol poured over the wounds, drowning, hanging and snake bites and scorpion stings for the women. This was torture on an industrial scale, vicious, inhumane and excessively cruel.

The Security of Regulation sign remains in the school courtyard, new inmates were forced to recite it when they arrived. It reads as follows, with the poor English:

1.   *You must answer accordingly to my questions – don't turn them away.*

2.   *Don't try to hide facts by making pretexts this and that. You are strictly prohibited to contest me.*

3.   *Don't be fool for you are a chap who dare to thwart the revolution.*

4.   *You must immediately answer my questions without wasting time to reflect.*

5.   *Don't tell me either about your immoralities or the essence of revolution.*

6.   *While getting lashes or electrification you must not cry at all.*

7.   *Do nothing, sit still and wait for my orders. If there is no order, keep quiet. When I ask you do something you must do it right away without protesting.*

8.   *Don't make pretext about Kampuchea Kromin order to hide your secret or traitor.*

9.   If you don't follow all the above rules, you shall get many lashes of electric wire.

10.   If you disobey any point of my regulations you shall get either ten lashes or five shocks of electric discharge.

Each inmate was photographed on arrival and if they died during torture they were photographed again so the image could be sent to the Khmer Rouge officials. It was during this explanation that Socmail quietly told us that her brother and her father, a teacher, had both been taken to Tuol Sleng, never to return. Our little group fell silent, what can you say?

At the age of 13 she was expelled from Phnom Penh and forced to walk the 183 miles to Bat Tambang to work in the rice fields for the Kampuchea Democratic Regime; it took 3 months. Socmail said she worked 12 hours a day for 3 years, 8 months and 20 days, that was 43 years ago; she counted each day.

We were shown classrooms on the second floor where up to fifty prisoners were shackled together to sleep on the hard stone floors. The rusted rods and manacles were piled in a corner and the steel hooks in the floor were still in place. Greying black and white photos on the walls showed what was found in the torture rooms when Phnom Penh was liberated; fourteen tortured bodies, bloodied, bare and broken were left on their beds. Further rooms were lined with thousands of mug shots of prisoners, some alive some dead, all were tortured. Barbed wire was still strung across the exterior landings to prevent suicide; death was a better alternative than life in the prison. Socmail's tour was remorseless in its brutal reality.

Of the seven survivors, two are still alive today; one of them is Chum Mey. We visited his cell, number 022, a clumsily built brick space of about 2 metres in length and no more than a metre wide, his chains, shackles and latrine box remain. He survived gunfights with the Khmer Rouge, rocket attacks during the civil war and having been dragged blindfolded to Tuol Sleng, endured 12 days and nights of repeated beatings, torture and electrocution. He lost his wife and four children during the brutal Khmer Rouge regime and saw friends and family chained, tortured and processed in the assembly line of death.

He confessed to counter revolutionary work for the CIA, an organisation he had never heard of before the torture began, but anything to stop the pain. He was a mechanic by trade and his life was spared when he offered to fix his own interrogator's typewriter. He was given food and put to work mending all the prison typewriters until the liberation troops arrived.

I asked Socmail about his life after the liberation in 1979.

'You can ask him yourself,' she said, 'he's visiting today, would you like to meet him?' This took me completely by surprise, but what an honour, what a rare privilege.

Chum Mey is now a charming, cheerful and contented 86-year-old. Perhaps surprisingly, he is happy to talk about his time in Tuol Sleng, maybe it's part of the healing process, but his physical scars are still apparent.

We met for a few minutes; I have to say I was overwhelmed by this guy. I had just heard his tragic story and stood where he was tortured yet he greeted me like an old friend. The lump in my throat made my voice falter and tears stung my eyes as he took my hand and posed for a photograph; he was far more in control than me. How do you react in such circumstances? Frown, glare, grimace? I turned to him to see a broad smile and genuine happiness on his face. How Helene managed to take the shot with tears streaming down her face I don't know but that picture and the signed book I have from him are extremely special and treasured gifts from this increasingly amazing adventure.

We talked for a few minutes through an interpreter about his time spent 40 years ago in the very place he was now visiting as a guest. He was keen to explain the torture and showed me his broken bent fingers where he tried to defend himself from the clubbing he received all those years ago, and the deformed toes where his nails had been viciously pulled from their sockets with pliers. His body may not have healed but his mind was alert and quick, answering my questions explicitly and with clarity.

'Why are you here today?' I asked. 'Surely you would prefer to forget the past and lead your own life without being reminded of the atrocities you experienced?'

'No, David,' he was quick to correct me. 'I am one of a handful to survive and most of them are now gone. I believe it is my duty to tell my story; I want the world to know what really happened. I don't want those thousands who died horrible deaths to be forgotten. Then perhaps we won't see this terrible time repeated again, not just here, but anywhere in the world.' What a courageous man.

I thanked him, wished him well and we shook hands. As I stood to leave, he pulled on my sleeve and looked expectantly at me; I had forgotten to pay him for the signed book. Slightly overwhelmed I think, but it was a remarkable encounter, an honour and a privilege to meet this awe inspiring man.

While Pol Pot's utopian vision was becoming a reality his cleansing programme grew to staggering levels. When an interrogation extracted a name, the whole family would be wiped out at the killing fields. This was our next visit.

Choeung Ek is about 10 miles southeast of the city in the lush landscape of rural Cambodia, it is also the most well-known of the three hundred killing fields found all over the country. It is here that the inmates from Tuol Sleng were transported in their thousands for execution.

Between 1976 and '78 Tuol Sleng would send up to three hundred people a day to Choeung Ek. Tortured, terrified and traumatised victims the Khmer Rouge believed had committed crimes against the state. Trucks loaded with men, women, children and babies to be slaughtered the night they arrived.

The area had hardly been touched since the end of the Khmer Rouge regime in 1979. Although there are paths and some boardwalks over the hundred and twenty-nine mass grave pits, when it rains there is still the odour of rotting corpses, while bones, teeth and pieces of clothing rise to the surface.

Each visitor is provided with headphones and an audio commentary so the memorial site is eerily quiet as groups and couples split up for each individual to try and understand this astonishingly sad environment at their own pace. There are visitors in silent contemplation sitting under trees, others unashamedly sobbing as the narrative plays out and some clearly unable to take in what they are seeing and hearing. It is tough.

Likewise, Helene and I separated rather than share the experience; I think one has to manage this in one's own way. I was tempted not to describe what I saw and heard, but my conversation with Chum Mey persuaded me otherwise, perhaps we too have a duty to tell the story of what really happened.

Victims were told they were being taken to a safer environment but were blindfolded and murdered on the side of the mass graves in the most efficient, expedient and inexpensive way possible. Few bullets were used, they were too costly, so they were hacked and bludgeoned to death with what they called "killing tools", nothing more than farm implements. Scythes, axes, bayonets, cleaning rods, chisels, knives, hammers and clubs were displayed alongside the skulls they had beaten and broken.

One mass grave of about 5 x 10 metres contained four hundred and fifty victims, another hundred and sixty-six without heads. The Magic Tree was in the centre of the mass graves, it was used to hang speakers playing loud music during the executions to drown out the screams of the dying. The brutality here was almost palpable.

The most harrowing by far was The Killing Tree alongside a 4 x 4 metres mass grave of a hundred naked women, young children and babies. Unbelievably, the bullets were reserved for the babies, not out of any sense of morality, compassion or sympathy, but grotesquely for fun. One executioner would throw the baby in the air for another to shoot at it.

The obscenity of the executioner's actions continued with The Killing Tree, it has a large well established trunk perhaps a metre in its diameter, it is covered with thousands of donated colourful wristbands, and beside it is a hand painted sign, which reads:

THE KILLING TREE – AGAINST WHICH EXECUTIONERS BEAT CHILDREN TO DEATH.

A 62 metre tall Memorial Stupa was built in 1988. It is a Buddhist construction of seventeen shallow levels with acrylic sides, the first ten of which displays nine thousand skulls. The remaining levels carry some of the victims' bones but there was just not enough space to display them all so most are left in the earth.

The day's experience was of course shocking and distressing, I believe we were both somewhat traumatised by what we encountered. Then there was anger. I asked Socmail about justice for the Cambodian people who were victims of the Khmer Rouge regime.

'Only five were prosecuted,' she said, 'two of whom died during their trials. The other three including "Duch" who ran Tuol Sleng are serving life sentences for genocide, crimes against humanity and war crimes.'

They were finally jailed between 2010 and 2014, 30 years after committing their crimes. Two others remain free despite the issuance of arrest warrants.

'Why do these two remain free?' I asked her. She pulled me to one side and dropped her voice to a whisper.

'Their arrests are being opposed by the Prime Minister Hun Sen,' she said quietly.

'Why would he do that?' I asked; she looked reluctant to add any more.

An American lady intervened.

'I believe it may have something to do with the fact that Hun Sen used to be a Khmer Rouge commander.'

Unbelievable.

Anger gave way to disbelief that these barbaric atrocities could occur during our lifetime. In fact, disbelief that we even share the same world. But the obvious question remained. Where was Pol Pot? Why wasn't he prosecuted?

The violent dictator's rule over Cambodia was in fact fairly short mainly due to his egotistical approach to the neighbouring countries, particularly Vietnam. During a recruitment drive in May 1978 Radio Phnom Penh declared that if each Cambodian soldier killed twenty-five Vietnamese, only 2 million troops would be needed to eliminate the entire Vietnam population of 50 million.

This pushed Hanoi's threshold of tolerance simply too far and the Vietnamese understandably opted for a military solution. On December 22nd 1978 Vietnam launched its offensive with the intention of overthrowing Democratic Kampuchea with a force of 120,000 troops. After a seventeen-day campaign, Phnom Penh fell to the advancing Vietnamese on January 7, 1979. Pol Pot and the main Khmer Rouge leaders fled and took refuge again in the jungle, while the Vietnamese discovered the torture centres and the killing fields.

However, peace continued to elude Cambodia as the Khmer Rouge fought back in an attempt to topple the Vietnamese controlled regime in the capital. Unbelievably, the UK still recognised Pol Pot as the legitimate leader of the country in the early 1980's and the UN provided the Khmer Rouge with a seat at the General Assembly under the name Democratic Kampuchea. The truth was yet to out.

In 1992 the UN effectively took over the country to end the violence and provide a democratic system of government with new elections. The monarchy eventually took back its power and in 1997 Pol Pot ordered the execution of his right-hand man Son Sen for attempting peace negotiations with the Cambodian Government. In 1998, Pol Pot himself died, still an active communist, he was never captured or made to pay for his atrocities.

Other key Khmer Rouge leaders surrendered to the government of Hun Sen – the former Khmer Rouge officer – in exchange for immunity from prosecution, leaving Ta Mok as the sole commander of the Khmer Rouge forces. He was detained in 1999 for crimes against humanity and the brutal organisation essentially ceased to exist. It took another 10 years for the trials to come to court.

There has been a great deal of controversy over the commercialism of the sites we visited and schools no longer include the atrocities as part of the curriculum, government influence here perhaps, which sounds to me like trying to rewrite history. Some will argue it has to be preserved, like Chum Mey, others that by creating tourist sites it dehumanises and victimises the Cambodian people.

They argue that Cambodia has a very young population due to the barbaric actions of the Pol Pot regime in the mid 1970's, indeed by 2005 three quarters of Cambodians were simply too young to remember the Khmer Rouge years. Is that a reason to tear the chapter out of the history books? I'm not sure that works. It has been said that Cambodia will take 100 years to recover from Pol Pot's ruthless revolution, and that may be true, but would it be any quicker if the lesson is ignored?

The two sites we visited were not commercialised, in fact they are relatively untouched from 40 years ago. But tourists are encouraged to visit, fees are charged and there are companies providing trips, guides and all that go with it. As we left the Killing Field of Choeung Ek the audio narrative finished with a poignant message. "What happened here was tragic but not unique. It's happened across the globe in the past, in China, Russia, Chile, Argentina and may well happen again. It is a lesson we must all learn from, so as you return home remember our past when you look towards your future".

CHAPTER 24

Day 234 to 240: CAMBODIA
Siem Reap

A Look Back in Anger

'What on earth is that dreadful smell?' cried Helene, 2 minutes into the 4 hour drive to Siem Reap.

'Sorry, Madame,' replied our driver, 'you want go back to hotel?'

'No, I want to get rid of that awful smell. It's coming from the boot, what is it?'

'That, my dear,' I said, 'is the wonderful aroma of Durian, if I'm not mistaken.'

'Yes, Durians,' said our driver, 'I bring them for my brother.'

'Not in here you're not,' argued Helene, 'it goes on the roof, or I get out!' I leaned over to our driver.

'Probably best if you pull over, I'll help you strap it to the roof.'

'Madame not like?'

'No, Madame doesn't and the next 4 hours will be a bloody nightmare if we can't get rid of the smell.'

'I strap it on roof.'

'Good thinking, Columbo.'

With a large black bin liner full of stinking Durian precariously bound across the roof, the journey 320 km north to Siem Reap was, in Cambodia terms, uneventful. In UK terms it was unforgettable. We were on National Highway 6 this time, like the terrifying National Highway 4 but with lanes, three lanes. This may seem a good idea at first, designed to stop drivers creating new lanes presumably, but it merely encouraged both directions of traffic to use the middle lane and play a vehicular game of chicken. This often resulted in another lane being created on the inside to allow the middle lane users to dodge the oncoming traffic by forcing lane one users off the road. So, we're back to National Highway 4 driving etiquette. I decided to read.

Siem Reap literally translates to "Siam Defeated", Siam being the former name of Thailand. It is the gateway to the Angkor region, itself a mega city in the 12th century. Supporting 0.1% of the world's population it was the largest pre-industrial urban centre in the world. It is now famous for two things: the wonderful temples and Angkor Beer – *Our Country, Our Beer* – the most widely consumed beer in Cambodia; I can vouch for its quality and refreshment capabilities.

Angkor was the capital of the Khmer Empire which flourished from the 9th century to the 15th century covering most of what is now Cambodia, Thailand, Laos and southern Vietnam. Angkor Wat, Wat meaning temple, is claimed to be the world's oldest religious monument and one of the ancient Seven Wonders of the World – although that seems to be an ever changing list.

Clearly, the Cambodians are proud of their most iconic symbol, it is the main feature on their flag; we were to find out why early on our second day with an excursion to see the sunrise over the temple. We were collected at 4:30 AM by our guide who arrived in full uniform and greeted us in the traditional way, clasping his hands together as if in prayer and bowing his head.

'Choum reap sor,' he said, 'I am Mr. Samsung.'

'Hi, I've got one of your TV's.'

'David!'

'Sorry, good morning to you too, Mr. Samsung,' I greeted him in the traditional way of clasping his hand in mine and smiling.

'My name is David and this is my wife Helene,' I said, hoping he would reciprocate with a first name. He didn't.

Mr. Samsung advised us that before we visit Angkor Wat for the sunrise we must first visit the Exchange to have our photo taken for the 3 day pass to the temples. Seemed a bit excessive, but we queued up at what seemed like some airport customs, showed our ID, had our photo taken, paid our US$62, signed a form, read the rules and were finally given a printed ticket with more security graphics on it than a passport. But we were in.

A long tree-lined tarmac boulevard, by far the best road we had travelled on for weeks and resembling The Mall, led us, and thousands of tuk tuks – everyone wanted a good spot for the sunrise – to the Rainbow Bridge crossing the moat. A 350 metres wide rectangular moat was excavated around the perimeter of Angkor Wat requiring the removal of 53 million cubic feet of sand and silt. This was an astonishing feat for the early 12th century before we even consider the construction of the vast temple.

Mr. Samsung like all good guides, directed us away from the crowds.

'Come, come follow me,' he instructed as we took a shortcut in the dark over a low wall towards the bridge.

'He's going at a heck of a pace,' said Helene, 'I'm not sure I can keep this up for long.'

'Just follow his torch light, I'll tell him to slow down, if I can catch up with him.'

Mr. Samsung had beaten the crowds and we arrived at a long derelict stone built building, apparently a library built in 1113.

'We climb steps and sit here,' instructed Mr. Samsung, 'it has best view of temple.'

'Really? Where?' I asked; it was still some time before sunrise. He pointed towards a dark silhouetted shape which did indeed look like the Cambodian flag insignia.

'Sit please, best place for sunrise.' Fair enough.

At 5:00 AM in the morning as the light began to appear we realised that Angkor Wat was full of activity. Locals selling guide books, coffee and sticky buns Helene couldn't eat, polystyrene packs of hot breakfast were being prepared next to the tuk tuk park and charcoal drawings of what we were going to see in an hour or so were peddled from group to group of bleary tourists.

Angkor Wat is a complex rather than a single monument, built between 1113 and 1150 for King Suryavarman II as his state temple and capital city, and dedicated to the Hindu god Vishnu. It was later converted to a Buddhist temple in the 14th century so statues of Buddha were added to the already elaborate stone artwork. It makes for quite a confusing religious chronicle.

As the dark shadows became lighter silhouettes I asked Mr. Samsung how on Earth they were able to construct this huge edifice with the limited technology of the 12th century.

'People,' he said, 'thousands and thousands of people.' They also had the wheel; it had been invented there hundreds of years before the South American empires were given the idea by the Spanish.

Mr. Samsung explained that the sandstone blocks from which Angkor Wat was built were excavated from a quarry at the holy mountain Phnom Kulen 50 km away and floated down the river to Siem Reap on rafts. From there it was the might of 300,000 men and 6,000 elephants to push, drag and lift the blocks into place. No wonder it took nearly 40 years and was never actually completed.

As the sunrise lit the famous central tower and its four smaller supporting towers, the layout of this remarkable palace became clear so we made our way, at a slower pace, past the stone lions guarding the route, to the main entrance of the 500 acre site. It is not only the oldest but also the largest religious monument in the world, and at its peak Angkor Wat was home to over a million people.

Considering the temple is around 900 years old it is in remarkably good condition, thanks largely to the moat preventing the jungle from reclaiming the area. There are over three thousand heavenly dancing nymphs (Apsaras) ornately carved into the walls, and extraordinarily each is unique. It was good to see the artists and sculptures had a sense of humour; there are thirty-seven different hairstyles, one nymph bearing her teeth and another smiling as she clasps a biting snake to her breast.

Mr. Samsung led us to the walls around the outside of the central temple hall. With his help we spent a fascinating hour or so interpreting the 800 metre long series of intricate and astonishing carvings (bas-reliefs) depicting historical events and stories from Hindu mythology.

'I would like a blessing from the monks,' Helene announced, as we watched the shaven headed young men in orange robes and matching umbrellas file by.

'Okay, I think I'll leave you to it, monks and I don't seem to get on,' I said. 'Mr. Samsung, where do we find the blessing shop?'

'I don't think it's a shop, David,' Helene corrected.

'I take you to monks, remove shoes please,' instructed Mr. Samsung.

A young monk, probably not yet in his twenties, sat cross-legged on a mat surrounded by various blessing objects. A brass dish containing coloured woven bracelets, an ornately designed bowl with an equally embellished paint brush resting across its top and the inevitable and sizeable metal box with a strong lock and the word "Donation" hand painted on the lid in English and Khmer, sat next to him.

Helene knelt on the mat, bowed her head and said in a theatrical whisper, 'David, I need money.'

I counted out some local notes and passed them to her.

'That not enough,' said Mr. Samsung.

'Oh! Let's not start this again.'

'David, this is not Sydney, just keep passing me notes until he does something,' instructed Helene.

After a few more handfuls the monk started humming, I took this as a good sign and ceased the offerings, I had obviously hit the required donation level.

He changed his humming to a whirring drone and selected a red braided bracelet to secure to Helene's wrist. She held out her right hand but this was immediately waved away.

'Try the other one,' I suggested.

'Yes, I know. That's the only alternative,' replied Helene. This one seemed to hit the spot and as the whirring turned into a melodic buzz, the young monk tied the band, dipped the paintbrush deep into the metal vessel and stirred it around a bit in the holy water.

Helene bowed her head and held her hands in prayer as he started to flick the holy water at her. She flinched a little, he upped the buzzing and flicking a bit and water was flying everywhere. We've had hotel showers with less water than this, I thought.

It was then that I spotted Helene's shoulders begin to bounce as she lowered her head even further to hide the giggles and avoid more of the shower now soaking her hair, face and shirt. Our young monk had worked himself up into quite a buzzing whirring frenzy with the wet paintbrush flying around like a conductor's baton when Helene and monk both collapsed into laughter.

He wished her health and happiness, she wished she hadn't laughed and wasn't so wet, and with that the blessing ended to the merriment of both of them, the onlookers and I even caught the serious Mr. Samsung having a chuckle.

As we toured our second temple of the day Mr. Samsung explained that over the 300 years between 900 and 1200 the Khmer Empire built some of the world's most magnificent architectural masterpieces. In fact, the temples in the Angkor area alone number over one thousand, ranging in scale from nondescript piles of brick rubble scattered through the landscape of rice fields to minor temples and the magnificent Angkor Wat, and Angkor Thom with the huge smiling faces and Ta Prohm, both of which we were due to visit. An equally astonishing three thousand were built within the whole Khmer Region.

A day of rest and recovery was definitely welcome before we took on the "Big Circuit" as it's known locally, a visit to seven temples culminating with sunset over Phnom Bakheng. But first we were going to a temple of an entirely different kind, Siem Reap's famous Pub Street.

Officially titled Street 8, they number all their streets in the cities but they're not built in blocks like New York so there's little point. But it is the culinary hub of Siem Reap, so we were told. We should have known. It's actually a long road teeming with bars and restaurants most of which offer insanely cheap and dreadful beer and "a turn" playing equally bad music. Consequently, the pedestrianised road is busy with backpackers and full of restaurant staff with menus in hand almost forcing one to take a seat with the promise of great beer and equally marvellous music.

Before we left there was a slight altercation with a street vendor outside the gloriously named bar "Angkor What?" – *promoting irresponsible drinking since 1997.*

'Look, Helene, that reminds me of my bush tucker experience in Uluru,' I said, pointing to the tray hanging in a cinema usherette style from the neck of a fierce looking local lady. Instead of ice creams, confectionery, popcorn and Kia Ora drinks her tray displayed coiled snake on a stick, brochettes of scorpion, barbecued tarantula, big black bugs that could have been cockroaches and an assortment of plump white grubs, possibly witchetty.

'I have to photo this and send it back home,' I said.

'No photo, no photo,' screeched the bush tucker usherette. 'Only if you eat. One dollar, one dollar each,' she said picking up a skewered brown snake.

'Oops, I've just taken it, but no thanks.'

'One dollar, one dollar,' she repeated brandishing the speared serpent in my face.

'You'll have to pay her now, David,' said Helene, 'go on, enjoy your snake,' she laughed.

I lost the dollar and gained the snake as a small crowd gathered to watch me dine on the viper. Not a chance. I pushed it into the hand of a laughing backpacker and wished him Bon Appetite.

The following day Mr. Samsung afforded us a lie-in and leisurely breakfast before the monument marathon began at 9:30 AM. It was 35 degrees with 75% humidity; thank goodness we opted for an air-conditioned car rather than an open tuk tuk. On our way to the start of the Big Circuit, Angkor Wat was alive with the hustle and bustle of the locals making their living either on the roadside or taking things to market.

We saw a pig on a bike, slaughtered perhaps the night before; it rested on the lap of the rider and the handlebars of his motorbike, very odd. Breakfasts of all sorts were being cooked and served to hungry men either returning from hunting in the jungle or on their way to the day job. A small team were digging or filling a roadside hole we had to queue to navigate around, all the labourers were women.

Many of the kerbside stalls had a rack of bottles on display that used to contain water, wine or an unknown spirit but were now filled with petrol at one dollar, for the tuk tuks. I often wondered where they filled up; there are hardly any petrol stations.

As Mr. Samsung guided us around the spectacular temples the story of the empire started to emerge. It was immensely powerful and wealthy with both Hindu and Buddhist religions; in fact they shared some of the temples evidenced by the remaining carvings and architecture. Despite internal conflict between kingdoms and wars with neighbouring countries the Khmers thrived for 500 years.

The scale of the empire was best seen at Angkor Thom (Big Angkor) a 9 km square walled and moated city built in the 1180's. This is the one with the huge stone smiling faces carved into the 23 metre towers at the city gates and the wonderful central temple of Prasat Bayon, in my view the most impressive of all we visited.

'Why are they smiling?' I asked Mr. Samsung.

'Who knows?' he replied. 'Maybe it is the king himself, wouldn't you be happy?' Fair point.

In front of the Royal Palace area is the Terrace of Elephants, a 350 metre viewing platform built for the king and his subjects to view the victorious army returning from war. It reminded me of the military parades we see in Red Square and Pyongyang. The landscape clearly shows where the armies marched in front of the twelve towers of the zodiac across the shallow valley from the king's position. It must have been quite a spectacle.

Another temple named Ta Som was constructed in the middle of a man-made square reservoir. This was actually the hospital, where those suffering from malaria, dysentery or any other common ailment in the 12th century would be taken by their family to be treated. There are stone built quarantine rooms in each corner to house the sick, once capable of movement patients were treated in the island temple, usually with a blessing and copious amounts of holy water.

The demise of the Khmer Empire is a subject of much debate and still remains a mystery. Undoubtedly, the two religions would have been in conflict, the wealth would have created internal power struggles within the kingdoms, there may have been civil revolt from the poor, or foreign invasion, drought, monsoon rains, plague, no one is really sure.

But it is largely accepted that in 1431 the Khmer kings abandoned Angkor when the now weak capital city was invaded by the Siamese kingdom of Ayutthaya. They then led the population south to the coast setting up a new city, Phnom Penh, now the capital of Cambodia.

Similar to Machu Picchu that had been abandoned signifying the end of the Inca Empire and lay undiscovered for many years, so it was with the abandonment of Angkor Wat signifying the end of the Khmer Empire. The discovery or re-discovery has been somewhat controversially accredited to a young French naturalist and explorer in 1860 by the name of Henri Mouhot. But it had not ever really been lost, it was always known by the local Khmers and visited by missionaries but Mouhot promoted it and with the help of his sponsor The Royal Geographical Society, claimed it as his discovery.

By the 1970's Khmer antiquities were one of the most popular and in-demand collectables, their value in the West was recognised by the Khmer Rouge who orchestrated a strategy of looting and plunder to fund their civil war. Banteay Srei, a temple built in 950 we visited in the north of the Big Circuit had been decimated from systemised looting by a highly organised criminal ring. The villagers had been "invited" to loot the temple at night or face violence, possibly death if they refused. They were paid US$12 a day to hack the heads off statues, cleave off wall sculptures and chisel away the dancing Apsaras.

Soldiers from the US backed Lon Nol side of the conflict were just as bad. They would close a temple and seal off the area, the raid was made at night and their spoils carried off by helicopter to be smuggled to dealers across the Thailand border and eventually grace the covers of UK and US auction house catalogues.

Mr. Samsung was desperately sad as he pointed out the empty platforms where 1000-year-old statues once stood, wall carvings with bodies prized out of the relief and empty shapes of half-human half-animal figurines, all long gone. It is outrageous that such a poor country should be raped and ransacked of its wealth by egotistical politicians and greedy speculators.

But still it goes on. In 1998 soldiers surrounded a temple at dawn blockading it from the local community without any explanation. For two weeks they used heavy machinery to break up the monument and load an estimated 30 tons of stone onto six trucks, including 30 metres of wall prized for its bas-reliefs, and fled for the border. One truck was stopped and its contents returned to Cambodia, the rest vanished, presumably to collectors and dealers in Europe and the US.

Mr. Samsung said the looting and trafficking of antiquities had abated, mainly because all the good pieces had gone, but he had heard that at the Thai border there are still "receivers" who, if given a picture of a piece still in situ, would deliver it within a month, at a price of course. In the past 6 months the head of a statue had been hacked from its shoulders leaving a forlorn headless torso.

Commendably, Sotheby's, Christie's, New York's Metropolitan Museum and California's Norton Simon Museum have started returning 1000-year-old statues that have been illegally cut from their bases and trafficked out of Cambodia. Let's hope the government addresses the problem within the country, but from what I have seen I somehow doubt it. I asked Mr. Samsung who was responsible for the protection of the sites now, after all we had paid US$62 each for our visit, prices have doubled in a year, so presumably the two million visitors were generating enough revenue to maintain and protect the temples.

Apparently, the Cambodian Government had given a 99 year lease to a Vietnamese hotel group who now effectively own Angkor. There was very little evidence of restoration or even preservation from the elements and encroaching jungle as far as I could see, but a vast hotel from the group had appeared in the city.

We continued our journey of temples crossing a bridge of fifty beautifully carved but headless torsos until we reached the temple everyone wants to see. It seemed a little more poignant now, the temple was Ta Prohm made famous in the film "Tomb Raider". It is an astonishingly atmospheric place, and it was difficult not to believe we were standing in a film set. The crumbling towers appear to be in a slow wrestling match with the jungle as the vast roots have locked the temple walls in an embrace which can realistically only have one outcome. It is a stunning place; every view was awe inspiring wherever we looked.

Our last venue was Bakheng Hill and a towering temple from which we watched the sun go down on a glorious day of adventure and discovery, and our time in Cambodia. It was time to reflect on our visit to this country, a country of extremes.

We had seen its beauty and its brutality, it had made us laugh out loud and cry unashamedly. We had been amazed by its history yet horrified by its recent past. It is a poor country, and seeing the children and the land mine victims beg is to say the least, uncomfortable, but tourism is bringing investment and a level of prosperity to the citizens they could only have dreamt of 20 years ago. Cambodia touched us like no other country had on this adventure, so we wished them well that night and promised to follow their fortunes over the coming years.

CHAPTER 25

Day 241 to 244: VIETNAM
Hanoi and Ho Chi Minh City

A Long, Long Legacy

Flight forty, Siem Reap in Cambodia to Hanoi in Vietnam, our twelfth country in the last seven months. Hanoi was the closest we had been to a modern Westernised city for a while: no tuk tuks, few street traders, brands I actually recognised on poster sites and, as Helene pointed out, a contemporary dress sense that wouldn't look out of place in any European cosmopolitan city.

Just as many motorbikes though, there are 45 million in a country of 90 million people, and the government wants to ban them, starting in the capital Hanoi, by 2030. No chance. Despite the two hundred and fifty deaths on the roads each week, cars are simply too expensive, largely due to the 300% tax the government currently imposes on imported vehicles.

So, the bikes buzz around with two or three passengers on the back, perhaps a young child wedged between Mum and Dad, or a pretty girl riding side saddle behind her man. At least they were all wearing crash helmets unlike Cambodia and Thailand where they seem to be as rare as zebra crossings.

The currency is also rather unconventional; it takes a little getting used to walking around with millions of Dong in your pocket, even buying a beer and a wine set us back three hundred thousand or so. But not to worry it's only about £10. Most retailers tend to ignore the thousands, so a thirty pound bottle of wine costing a million Dong is price marked as one thousand, all very confusing. It meant no coins rattling around in your pocket though, and as credit card swiping hadn't yet really caught on I was left carrying a wad of notes in my back pocket making me look like I was wearing a nappy.

While on a lavatorial theme I had the most extraordinary toiletry experience in the airport lounge high-tech loos. It sensed me walking into the trap so the toilet lid rose automatically in a welcoming kind of look up from a bow, and bizarrely a rather comforting blue light came on in the bowl itself. This was not the only comfort, the seat was heated, nice touch, so to speak, although when it's over 30 degrees outside I'm not sure it's entirely necessary. But we were not finished yet, upon sitting the personal piped music began to play, mine was Grieg's "*Morning Mood*" from the Peer Gynt suite. Nice. There was a digital display just above the auto loo roll dispenser offering a variety of flashing buttons and symbols including; spray, +/- spray strength, nozzle position, cleansing, wide/narrow, bidet, blow and massage. Massage? Well, we promised to try everything.

Hanoi was only ever intended to be a stopover to sort through our zippy-uppy bags and leave our large cases at the wonderful Silk Path Hotel, as we travelled the length and breadth of the country before returning to the city 3 weeks later. We arrived on a Sunday and after checking in spent a delightful afternoon walking around the Hoan Kiem Lake in the historical centre close by. It is, or was, home of the Hoan Kiem turtle, which may, or may not, be extinct.

In 1967 what the locals thought was the last of the soft shell turtles, a whopper at 440lbs and well over 3 metres in length, was killed by an abusive and very hungry fisherman with a crowbar. Its body was preserved and put on display in the city temple, reminiscent of Lonesome George in the Galápagos.

In 1998 an amateur cameraman caught another on video, but by 2011 there appeared to be no sign of him, or her. So, the city authorities commissioned a local turtle farm operator to search for the elusive creature. They caught it in their net but it escaped. The operator said, 'It's very hard to catch a very large soft-shell turtle.' I guess it is, that's why the specialists were brought in. Finally, the turtle went ashore to bask in the summer sun and the city authorities sent in the Vietnamese military to capture it.

She, it turned out, was returned to the lake and survived on her own for 5 years and was found dead on 19th January 2016. Although some witnesses believe there are at least two still living in Hoan Kiem Lake, officially they are considered to be extinct. We sat in one of the many bars around the lake and watched intently to try and rediscover the *Rafetus leloii* species. No luck, but their excellent local beer from the Hanoi Brewery may have been a distraction.

As we promenaded with the elegantly dressed locals we came across a game of Jenga.

'Look at the size of that tower,' said Helene, peering over the small crowd that had gathered. This would not normally be possible but the Vietnamese are indeed a short race.

'I need an assistant,' cried the Jenga man holding a bamboo ladder next to the Jenga tower, the top of which was already beyond the reach of his outstretched arm.

'I'm your man,' I shouted over the melee and squeezed past a mother desperately trying to hold back her 4-year-old son, who seemed to think he was better qualified than me.

'Thank you, sir,' Jenga man said. 'Hold this tight, while I climb to the top,' he instructed, thrusting the ladder into my hands.

'You climb to the top? I thought that was my job? Are you sure?' My enthusiasm was now slightly tempered by the task in hand, but as the increasingly large crowd clapped I had little option.

They may be small, but they're not light. I attempted to keep the ladder still as my Jenga friend started his ascent. If this was not difficult enough, the 4-year-old boy had broken free from his mum's grasp and was now trying to help by clutching the other side of the bamboo ladder and pulling it towards him.

'Helene, help! He's making it wobble. It's NOT funny!' There were gasps from the now sizeable crowd as the Jenga man placed more bricks on the equally sizeable tower and the bamboo ladder began to sway.

It was then that the 4-year-old decided the Jenga man needed more help than me and started to climb. This was not good. I looked up at the swaying Jenga man who had now given up building the tower and was more concerned with hanging on. He looked down at me and tried to ease the scaling boy off the bamboo ladder with his foot.

It was then that his mother intervened grabbing him from the ladder, the consequence of which was that I now overcompensated for his weight. Jenga man jumped, the child kicked the tower and my ladder fell.

'That went well then,' said Helene, as we walked away from thousands of bricks scattered on the ground around Jenga man, a crying 4-year-old and a silent crowd. 'Hanoi beer, darling?'

Our flight to Ho Chi Minh City in the south was full of expectation; we were meeting some old friends from Spain who were also spending a couple of months exploring South East Asia. Coincidentally, we were in the same country at the same time, although Gary and I eventually found out the two ladies had been planning the coincidence for months.

Known as Saigon until the end of the Vietnam War in 1975 and renamed after the communist government's first leader, it is a sizeable modern city with high-rise hotels offering sky-bar cocktails, ideal for a sundowner catch up with Jacki and Gary.

Being boaty people they had already booked what we thought was a gentle cruise up the Saigon River to the Cu Chi tunnels. Far from meandering up this beautiful river, not dissimilar to the Thames in Berkshire, our crew took it at speed in a far too powerful motor boat dodging the green clusters of floating lilies and assorted debris making its way to the South China Sea close to the Mekong Delta.

After an hour or so of loud bone-shaking fun flying past local fishermen trying to keep their balance in their shallow wooden kayaks and the occasional industrial barge carrying tons of gravel, bricks or timber, we arrived at the tunnels themselves. Our guide for the day was Eshie a beautiful local girl, quick to smile and with a have-a-go attitude that encouraged us to venture into the tunnels and down the man traps.

Eshie explained that we were investigating just part of the immense 250 km of tunnels built in Cu Chi by the Viet Cong from the north who engaged in guerrilla warfare against the anti-communists and the US in the south. They were not just used as hiding places or as quick access for combat, they served as communication and supply routes. There were underground rooms for dining, meeting and general living, including kitchens and even a hospital.

'Who would like to come into the tunnels with me?' asked Eshie, as we peered down steep steps carved into the soil that disappeared into blackness.

'It's a bit narrow and quite low, us Vietnamese are small people but it's only a 100 metres long. Anyone?'

'Go on, boys,' encouraged Helene, pushing us forward to the delight of Eshie.

Male bravado is a dangerous thing in the hands of adventurous females, so it was with a swagger and some trepidation that Gary and I ventured into the black hole, if it's possible to swagger when you're bent double.

'Mind your head,' said Eshie as she led the way crouched low in the cramped underground passage.

'Never mind my head, what about my knees, I'm going to pay for this later,' I shouted up the tunnel.

'Sod your knees,' replied Gary, 'my back's bad enough already. I think it's going into spasm.'

'Is there a shorter route, Eshie?' I asked.

'There's a link further on that will take us out earlier if you like?'

'Yes, we like,' we both agreed.

It was dark, dirty and hot, there was very little air and we were still on all fours as we emerged into the bright sunlight beyond the escape hatch. We stretched our stiff limbs and dusted off our hands and knees, quite impressed that we had survived the 20 metres and a little less than 5 minutes in the tortuous tunnels. Until Eshie told us that the Viet Cong lived like that for 12 years, from 1963 to 1975.

At one point the tunnels were home to twelve thousand people but the lack of oxygen could not sustain the level of occupancy.

'Despite the hidden air holes bored through the surface only 3,000 people could live underground,' she said, adding with a sympathetic smile, 'one of those was my mother.'

It's at moments like these that we feel humbled and full of admiration for those who have suffered huge hardship for the cause they believed in or have endured dreadful conditions simply to survive. My knees and Gary's back no longer seemed to be as painful.

Life in the tunnels for Eshie's mum and her colleagues must have been dreadful. As we had experienced in a few short minutes the heat was stifling and the air stuffy, add to this the lack of food and water, the infestation of ants, venomous centipedes, scorpions, spiders and snakes, how they survived is a miracle. Of course, many didn't, without the necessary medication malaria became the second largest cause of death after wounds from battle.

And it was a battleground, although the Americans knew the tunnels existed they were frustrated by their inability to destroy them. So, in January 1966 B52 bombers dropped a massive 30 tons of high explosives on the Cu Chi area, turning the dense jungle into a barren landscape of craters. When that failed to reveal the full extent of the tunnel network a closer combat strategy was adopted with a colossal 30,000 "Tunnel Rats", infantrymen employed to flush out the Viet Cong by flooding the tunnels with water, gas and hot tar. They even forced poisonous cobras down the entrances when they finally located one.

As Eshie showed us, the openings were very well camouflaged and the air vents of hollow bamboo were impossible to find, so the Americans brought in 3,000 sniffer dogs to identify the tunnels. That didn't work either; in fact three hundred of them were killed for food. Needs must at the time I guess, but it seems they acquired the taste for culinary canine, because prior to 2014 five million dogs were slaughtered for meat each year.

By 1969 the American forces had still not eradicated the tunnels so in a final attempt B52's carpet bombed the whole of the Cu Chi area, but by that time the Viet Cong had succeeded in controlling where and when battles were to take place. Ultimately, they had allowed the North Vietnamese to survive in South Vietnam and had prolonged the war until eventually the Americans pulled out in 1973 and South Vietnam was defeated in 1975.

I asked Eshie why the Viet Cong were so successful in their 12 years in the Cu Chi tunnels; she said that her mother was given simple instructions which saved her life: "cook without smoke, talk without sound and walk without tracks". We returned down the river at speed a little more educated, humble and, as had often been the case on the adventure, astonished by the perseverance, resilience and ingenuity of people around the world fighting for the cause they believe in.

It's great fun to catch up with friends in person and find out what's up rather than WhatsApp but we had to say our au revoirs to Jacki and Gary as they continued their exploits elsewhere in South East Asia, promising to catch up and compare experiences when we were all back in Spain. Helene and I decided to find out a little more about the war from the Vietnamese perspective. Ironically, we seemed to have only scratched the surface with the Cu Chi tunnels.

The War Remnants Museum in Ho Chi Minh City studies – *war crimes inflicted on the Vietnamese people by foreign aggressive forces*; it may have been a little partisan. The museum's concourse is a military hardware graveyard of tanks, planes, helicopters and various rocket launchers and bomb cases. As tourists of many nationalities wander around they broadcast a loud soundtrack of planes dropping whistling bombs hitting the ground with almighty explosions, very uncomfortable.

What I didn't appreciate was the extent of French control and cultural influence over the country for 100 years until Ho Chi Minh proclaimed Vietnam's independence in 1945. The city even has its own Notre Dame Cathedral. France continued to besiege the country to recover its sovereignty and by 1953 America waded in with $400M of financial aid to support the French, believing it would protect the US trade channels and halt the spread of communism.

Despite continued investment and support, France surrendered in May 1954 ending their effort to retain Indochina and leaving the US to take up the fight against Communism. The subsequent elections attempting to unify Vietnam actually created a country that was further divided. The north sought reunification of the two countries under Communism, led by Ho Chi Minh. The south, led by anti-communist Ngo Dinh Diem was supported by the US in line with their policy of "Containment" – preventing the spread of Communism across the world. The museum argues that it was a civil war fuelled by US investment.

In 1962 the US Military Assistance Command was formed to support the south and pacify the north. The museum's point of view is that this was no more than formalising the US commitment to war and that the 16,300 "advisers" sent to set up "strategic hamlets" actually managed concentration camps.

When Ngo Dinh Diem was killed in an army coup the following year, the war escalated with the US sending in more troops, artillery, fighter jets, bombers and aircraft carriers. Over half a million young Americans were fighting on Vietnamese territory by 1969 with a directive to "burn all, destroy all, kill all". When Operation Rolling Thunder was launched there were 300,000 air attacks, 864,000 tons of bombs dropped and over 3,000 American planes shot down over 44 months.

Despite the high profile protests across the globe and the huge investment of $2 billion a month beginning to bankrupt the US, Nixon extended the war in 1970 to Laos and Cambodia. In perhaps a last effort 2.75M tons of bombs were dropped in 14 months, more than the total used by the allies in World War II, it created two million Cambodian refugees and destroyed 20% of the country's property. It failed.

On 27th January 1973 with huge US losses and intensifying political and social pressure from around the world America signed the Paris Peace Accord effectively ending the 20 year war and handing victory to the communists. But it wasn't until another US President, Gerald Ford, eventually pulled out the last troops in 1975 that 25 years of American intervention ended and unity for the Vietnam people began. Strangely, some Americans often argue that they did not lose the war at all, South Vietnam did. They argue that when US Congress pulled the funding and the troops from the conflict North Vietnam was still being funded by China and Russia so the south's surrender was inevitable.

However, it has a long, long legacy as the War Remnants Museum is determined to demonstrate. There are pictures, mock ups, descriptions and interviews detailing the dreadful torture from both the Americans and the French. It was as bad as anything we saw in Phnom Penh's sadistic detention centre and killing fields. Helene and I had a long debate over dinner that night about whether the means for dreadful abuse and mistreatment during the course of war lays dormant in our civilised society and is triggered by war. Or whether war desensitises people so much they start behaving in a way they would not normally imagine, a type of PTSD but out in the field during combat.

The longest legacy from the war is seen on the streets and in the towns of this still recovering country. The museum argues that the US utilised weapons prohibited by the international laws of war: napalm, phosphorus bombs, gases and toxic chemicals, the worst of which was known as Agent Orange. It was a highly toxic substance designed as part of their "defoliation tactics" to reveal the opposing forces. But in addition to killing vast areas of jungle over four million Vietnamese were also exposed to it.

From 1961 to 1971 around 80,000,000 litres of Agent Orange were indiscriminately sprayed over 25% of Vietnam's territory. Not only is it a primary carcinogen but it has now become evident that it had genotoxic effects, the evidence is seen not only in the first generation of birth defects, but the second and third generations. We have seen some dreadfully deformed people begging on the streets, some who spend their whole lives on all fours unable to stand, others with equally painful contorted and disfigured limbs.

After the war there were 600,000 tons of bombs left behind and 6.6 million hectares of land were contaminated with explosives. Not surprisingly then, that in addition to the 3 million who died in the conflict, during the 25 years after the war ended over 42,000 have been killed by undetected explosives and 62,000 have been left maimed and wounded. We often see a small group of land mine victims playing music at tourist attractions raising money to care for their colleagues with missing limbs.

These are dreadfully sad and shameful legacies of an appalling war that continues to have consequences on the people in this country. As a final note that reflects the injustice we see in so many poorer countries, the chemical companies that manufactured Agent Orange and the US Government have recognised their liability and compensated the American Vietnam veterans who were exposed to it. The Vietnamese, the actual victims, have filed lawsuits against the manufacturers for compensation but the US Supreme Court has dismissed them without admission of liability by the chemical companies. Unbelievable.

CHAPTER 26

Day 245 to 263: VIETNAM
Hoi An, Da Nang and Hue

Good Morning Glory

We flew north from Ho Chi Minh City to Da Nang – I must say VietJet offers an excellent service, probably the most on-time carrier we had been with – then travelled an hour or so south to the beautiful town of Hoi An on the east coast of Vietnam.

Hoi An, also known as the "city of lanterns" is a UNESCO World Heritage Site and was voted the sixth most beautiful town in the world by Business Insider. It reminded me of that quaint village in the Cotswold's, Bourton-on-the-Water, pretty rivers winding their way around the village, charming properties overlooking the streams and crammed full of Chinese. Hoi An is a well preserved graceful and delightful town from the 15th century when it was an Asian trading post. It is now a glorious hotchpotch of architectural styles with narrow streets of wooden Chinese shops and temples, French colonial buildings, ornate Vietnamese merchant houses and a beautiful Japanese pagoda bridge.

'Let's go to the Full Moon Party in town,' suggested Helene.

'I've heard of these,' I said, 'it's all loud music and dancing until dawn, I'm not sure it's really us.'

'No, not that sort of party, they float candle lit lanterns on the river as good luck for the family.'

We arrived before sundown so went for a sundowner on a terrace bar overlooking the golden pagoda bridge to watch the preparations. Small wooden punts lit by their own Chinese lanterns of assorted colours were drifting lazily on the river to the delight of tourists who had to virtually lie down to pass under the golden pagoda bridge. Beautifully dressed families were parading in their silk tunics and gold trousers, wearing those lovely straw cone shaped hats that look like lampshades. It was a delightful scene, and then the street lights went out.

From nowhere what seemed like hundreds of small and extremely elderly Vietnamese grandmothers appeared carrying dozens of red paper lanterns, some already throwing a flickering yellow candlelight over their deeply lined faces.

We finished our surprisingly good local Sauvignon to join in the fun on the river bank. It started as a trickle, with the odd one or two lanterns emerging from under the golden bridge, their flames fluttering in the breeze and illuminating the water. The trickle became a tide of glowing red as more lanterns appeared floating downstream turning the water into a sparkling river of candlelight.

We were inevitably accosted by a grandmother with a tray of glowing lanterns.

'How much?' I asked.

'We'll need two,' said Helene, one each for the kids.

'How much for two?' I asked again.

'Fifty thousand,' grandmother answered. I thought it churlish to barter, so handed over a note, took two lit lanterns from her tray and handed them to Helene.

'Fifty thousand, each,' grandmother corrected. She'd done this before. We peered through the dark into the diamanté river below glistening with candles.

'How on earth do we get the lanterns down there?' Helene asked. I started to climb and slide down the muddy bank.

'We've bought the things and they're going in.'

'No, no!' screamed grandmother, hobbling over with her lantern tray bouncing in front of her. She pulled me back up – surprisingly strong woman for her age – and pushed a long bamboo pole with a bowl on the end into my hand, this it turned out was the lantern dispenser.

We wielded the 8 foot bamboo branch and bowl, carefully placing Charlotte's and Elliot's lanterns in the river wishing them good luck and good health. We watched them glow and sparkle as they drifted towards the golden pagoda bridge.

'Poo Sticks!' shouted Helene. Blast, I had forgotten the family tradition whenever we see a bridge.

'I'm winning!' she cried, as she ran across the bridge. How she could tell which red lantern was hers within the identical thousands approaching the golden pagoda I don't know, but she may have been right.

Having launched our lanterns, we decided to push the boat out for dinner at the wonderfully named Morning Glory, named of course after the vegetable, the second most popular food after rice in Vietnam. It is owned and run by Trinh Diem Vy the accomplished food writer, chef, hotelier and restauranteur with eight establishments to her name in Vietnam and others in Australia. Busy lady.

In Morning Glory, she presents her signature dishes using local ingredients in new or reimagined traditional Vietnamese dishes like Pho the noodle soup available just about everywhere anytime. It is an absolute staple of the Vietnamese and everyone seems to have their own special recipe, including Ms. Vy. The Goi Cuon were particularly good, they are translucent cigar shaped rolls with prawn, greens and herbs to be dipped in nuoc cham a clear but fiery mixture of fish sauce with garlic, carrot and chilli. But my favourite was My Quang Hai San a combination of pork, shrimp, shredded banana flower, fresh herbs and yellow rice-flour noodles, absolutely delicious.

On the lower floor of the restaurant she has created a rather elegant street food court with open cooking stations around its perimeter where all the ingredients are on display. Dozens of steel pots were bubbling on gas rings as sous chefs cut, chopped, peeled and prepared on huge wooden boards. In amongst some of the traditional favourites like Prawn Wonton Noodle Soup, Rice Flour in Banana Leaf and Tapioca Flour Dumplings were some slightly unconventional salad dishes Ms. Vy had obviously thought worth experimenting with. These included Pig Ear Salad, Jelly Fish Salad that we were offered in Kuala Lumpur, and Silk

Worm Salad, but perhaps the most challenging was a tall pot with its lid rattling and bouncing on top containing Steamed Pig Brains with Black Pepper. We ate upstairs.

Hoi An was once a major port on the silk route so its continued reputation as a tailoring mecca is not surprising, there are literally hundreds of bespoke tailors in the old town. Helene had found Sewing Bee where you consult with Bee herself and jointly design your new outfit. But I knew better.

'You stay here, Helene, I'm going shopping,' I said, as we sat outside a bar watching the world go by.

'On your own? Is that wise? What are you hoping to buy?'

'A couple of shirts from one of those stalls,' I answered.

'That's definitely not wise,' she said. I thanked her for her confidence and went window shopping in the market, if you can window shop without windows.

In hindsight the silk may not have been silk and the patterns on the short-sleeved shirts may have been more at home in Hawaii, but I managed to negotiate the owner down to 300,000 VND for the two, what a bargain.

'They're dreadful!' said Helene. 'You look like an extra from Miami Vice. And the cut is awful.'

'Technically, you may be right; you're the one with the fashion degree. And okay the sleeves may not be exactly the same length and I can't do up the first two buttons but look at the colours.'

'I'm taking you to Bee, she'll sort you out.' Somewhat disheartened but keen to prove my point I accompanied Helene to Sewing Bee and wore my favourite of the two shirts. She laughed.

There was much measuring and a long discussion between Helene and Bee over my fabric, colour and cut. Apparently, I was not needed for this. After a couple of return visits for fittings and minor alterations I was the proud owner of three stylish shirts and an extremely comfortable and I'm told trendy, new jacket.

We left wonderful Hoi An having made new friends with Bee and her staff at Sewing Bee and the team at the Little Hoi An Beach Hotel; I hope we have an opportunity to meet them again. Our driver on the 3 hour journey to Hue asked us if we wanted to take the faster tunnel route or the slower but more dramatic route across the mountains. Up and over it was, on the Hai Van Pass.

It is without doubt the most scenic road in Vietnam, winding its way around the Annamite Mountains that jut out into the East Vietnam Sea, and it is probably the most famous. Apart from the presenters of BBC TV's Top Gear swooning over its beauty it is also marks the difference between the tropical south and subtropical north, the political boundary between ancient kingdoms and was a key strategic military post during times of more recent wars.

The Deo Hai Van – *Ocean Cloud Pass* – lived up to its romantic name on the day we passed through, it was wet, cold and blowing a gale, but that didn't stop our driver finding the best lookout spots. Including one where the café owners dare their customers to climb a huge boulder stuck in their back garden with an equally large drop below but a great view out to sea through the dark clouds and mist.

Hue is a far more industrialised and utilitarian city located in the centre of the country on the banks of the wonderfully named Perfume River, so called because of the flowers from the orchards up river falling into the water giving it a perfume-like aroma. It was the capital of the Nguyen Dynasty during the 17th century to 19th century and for 150 years was the capital of the whole of Vietnam. Given its strategic importance in the middle of the country it was also the battleground for one of the fiercest and bloodiest battles of the Vietnam War.

Its major attraction is the vast 19th century citadel encompassing the Imperial City and the Forbidden Purple City. It sounded intriguing so was on the list to visit along with a beautiful pagoda we were told not to miss. But, our zippy-uppy bags had let us down.

'I have nothing to wear,' complained Helene, 'it's blooming freezing and I've only packed strappy tops.' We had left the large cases in The Silk Path Hotel to collect on our return so our warm wardrobe was in hot Hanoi.

'Me too, I only have shorts,' I said. 'Let's go shopping.'

'We'll never be able to pack more jeans and sweatshirts, they'll just be too heavy,' Helene said.

'Okay, we need disposable jeans.'

'You may have just invented those.'

I had, but a quick visit to the market and a few hundred thousand Dong later and we were fully equipped for the excursion in the cold miserable grey days forecast for the next week.

We woke to bright blue skies, sunshine, 33 degrees and 90% humidity. I disposed of our disposable jeans and we set off in search of the Pagoda of the Celestial Lady, or Chua Thien Mu to give it its correct Vietnamese name. It lies on the bank of the Perfume River so it seemed to make sense, and more fun, to go by boat rather than car. We strolled down to the river where a couple of dozen Dragon Boats were moored. These are colourful, glass sided long barges with ornately painted dragon heads on the bow, not dissimilar to a Viking ship, but with a very powerful and loud long-tailed motor at the stern.

They looked as if they could accommodate twenty or so passengers but after some haggling and handing over wads of Dong I appeared to have hired a boat for just the two of us. And the skipper, his wife, and the two kids. We were ushered onto the boat and entered the low roofed central cabin of the barge; it was bare apart from some toys. Two flimsy red plastic chairs appeared from the engine end and were plonked in the middle of the carpeted cabin where we were invited to sit down.

'I think this is their house,' whispered Helene, as the children ran in with toy cars for him and shiny beads for her, it was playtime with the new guests. Mum shooed them away and with a flourish whipped off the table cloth from a side table to reveal a small collection of souvenirs. By this time, we were chugging up the river so she had her captive market.

'I think we better buy something,' I said, inspecting the offerings on what appeared to be the kitchen table. Mum handed me some greetings cards.

'Hand painted,' she said, 'I hand paint.'

'Very nice, we'll have four to send home. Yes, alright and a bookmark then.'

Having sat back on my wobbly plastic chair I noticed the cardboard box under the table packed with similar cards. "Made in China" was hand stamped on the outside.

The seven storey pagoda towered impressively above us although it seemed somewhat the worse for wear and was probably last climbed many years ago. Not surprising though, it was built in 1601. The temple behind it now houses the giant bell cast in 1710 for the pagoda, and it is said to be audible 10 km away, and perhaps it was, before the invasion of the thousands of motorbikes.

Bizarrely, attached to the temple is an open garage with an old blue restored 1950's Austin Westminster car behind an intricately carved low wooden fence. A quiet group were staring at the vehicle; what an odd place for an old car in this tranquil and serene garden behind the ancient religious monument. A small plaque revealed the story I had long forgotten.

On June 11th 1963 a Buddhist monk by the name of Thich Quang Duc drove himself in the car to the Cambodian Embassy in Saigon. He sat on a cushion in the lotus position in front of the vehicle, poured petrol over his body and sacrificed himself as a protest to the persecution of Buddhists by the South Vietnam Government. The horrific pictures were broadcast all over the world showing him gently rocking backward and forward reciting a prayer next to the car as the flames engulfed him. JFK said that "no news picture in history has generated so much emotion around the world as that one".

'I'll race you, Helene,' I said, as we each clambered aboard our cyclos, or Xich Lo as the locals know them, a three wheeled bike taxi where the driver cyclist sits at the back and the passenger is positioned comfortably but precariously in the front. They were introduced during the French Colonial period when the rickshaw was oddly rejected by the residents. My driver doing all the leg work was Thanh, he had been making his living this way for 40 years. He was small, well over 60 and had a permanent toothless grin as we fought to keep our lead ahead of Helene.

'That's not fair,' she shouted above the constant stream of blaring motorbikes, 'you had a head start.'

Once we were both over the bridge and on to an open road the distance seemed to take its toll and Thanh began to tire. Helene was still high fiving her driver when Thanh and I finally made it to the Citadel.

'I take you round the Citadel, only 500,000 Dong for 8 kilometres,' Thanh suggested.

'I think we've both had enough thanks, Thanh,' I said, already feeling guilty for the race I had put him through.

The Imperial City was built from 1804 by the self-proclaimed emperor, Gia Long who had succeeded in reuniting Vietnam in 1789. So, from 1802 Vietnam was ruled by the Nguyen Dynasty for nearly 150 years, a really powerful family. But, the last emperor, Bao Dai, who frankly preferred sports, hunting and dancing to politics, gave up the "seal and sword" the symbols of royal authority, in front of 50,000 pretty pissed off Hue residents thereby ending the monarchy in Vietnam in favour of the new communist government being set up by Ho Chi Minh.

The Citadel is not dissimilar to Angkor Wat in design, protected by a moat built around the square perimeter of the fortified ramparts, but once through the magnificent yet foreboding entrance gate it felt like we had stepped into ancient China. The restored exterior corridors are exquisitely decorated; deep red wooden walls, ceilings and bulky beams are adorned with gold carvings and calligraphy. And the buildings themselves have those quintessentially Chinese tiled roofs with carved dragons and serpents in each corner and mosaic tiled columns. If anything was to prepare us for China then this was it.

The 36 hectare site was the centre for political affairs and the daily activities of the Court and emperors until 1945. Here they held the royal ceremonies and rituals but it was also a place of entertainment for the emperor and his family. In the centre of the Imperial City is the wonderfully named Forbidden Purple City where access was restricted to the Imperial family, and even then, only by invitation from the emperor himself. It once had many buildings and hundreds of rooms but sadly most were destroyed by the French in 1947. One of the few remaining is the Emperor's Reading Room, a beautifully ornate building decorated with ceramic mosaics.

What did survive was then fought over in 1968 by the Viet Cong and US troops. Anti-aircraft guns were mounted on the Citadel's towers and were of course targeted by the warplanes. Out of a hundred and sixty buildings only ten remained after the Battle of Hue. Bullet holes can still be seen in some of the stone walls. It was a fascinating day out, although decimated by war it was easy to imagine how magnificent the Citadel must have been in its golden age, I am sure it would have rivalled Angkor Wat and Machu Picchu.

We left Hue to drive back south for a couple of hours to Da Nang, a huge city. We entered over the extraordinary Dragon Bridge, the longest in Vietnam at 666 metres and constructed in the shape of, well, a golden dragon. The dragon arches high above the six lanes three times before the fearsome head protrudes from the tarmac at the end of the span. Legend has it that the Dragon Bridge provides the city with the power, nobility and good fortune dragons symbolise. It spits water and breathes fire on weekends and during special festivities and every evening glows from gold to green as it straddles the Han River.

We checked into the impressive Muong Thanh Luxury De Nang Hotel overlooking the bay, but the view from our 25th floor room looked as if we had arrived back on the Gold Coast: beautiful beaches sweeping up the coast in both directions with waves breaking far out full of surfers. We walked in the sand to find a sea view restaurant for dinner; not sure why, it's always pitch black but the sound of the crashing waves is a good backdrop to a great seafood meal.

'Let's take a look at the menu here,' said Helene selecting an open fronted restaurant on the beach.

'No menu here, lady!' said the young maître d'. 'You choose there, we cook,' she continued, pointing at rows and rows of tanks and dozens of large blue bowls containing bubbling water. On closer inspection each of them was individually priced with a peeling sticker and crammed full with a species of fish thrashing around in the shallow water.

'Not a chance,' said Helene, 'I can't look one of these creatures in the eye and give it the thumbs down.'

'You choose, we cook,' repeated our now animated maître d', prodding a stick into a tank full of lobsters with blue bands around their claws. We ate in the hotel, quite an appalling meal of what was translated on the menu as stir-fried knuckles of chicken. Didn't know chickens had knuckles.

The Marble Mountains promised to be one of the must-see attractions in the area. Just 9 km south of the city centre these five small pitons protrude from an otherwise flat landscape as if they were man-made, somewhat similar to Uluru.

We ran the gauntlet of the over eager street sellers attempting to drag us to their stalls, all of which were offering the same merchandise of questionable marble ornaments, spheres and figurines, to arrive at the base of the Thuy Son mountain – The Mountain of Water – the highest of the five. Unexpectedly, we found a glass and silver tubed structure erected against the ancient site, which turned out to be a lift to the top. Convenient yes, but not quite in keeping with the spiritual sentiments of the setting.

The mountain's plateau, over 100 metres above the city, was surprisingly large and home to elegant Buddhist temples and shrines dating back to the 17th century and wooden arched bridges bowed across the small rivers and ponds. There were carvings everywhere: intricate and delicate dragons formed out of the rock face, stone panels with traditional Chinese symbols and larger than life-size figures appearing out of the landscape.

There were also caves of various sizes that had been remodelled by the monks to create holy shrines complete with giant Buddha sculptured in the green oxidised rock. It is a remarkable place and I'm informed by Helene, who knows about these things, it is full of spiritual energy. It may well have been but I just loved it.

'We're doing Korea and karaoke tonight,' I informed Helene, on the way back to the hotel.

'Korea possibly, karaoke doubtful,' she said.

Korean Barbecue restaurants are extremely popular in the larger cities of Vietnam, almost as popular as karaoke, but we entered not knowing entirely what to expect. We were shown to a table large enough for six with a hot plate barbecue at one end and opted for the fixed price menu of five different meats.

Ten minutes later the table was laden with meats, vegetables, salads, dips and sauces. There were dishes covering every surface and some balanced on others as the table for six was swamped with a mass of exciting but totally raw food. We must have looked overwhelmed or intimidated by the sheer scale of the task ahead so an extremely helpful and friendly waitress took pity on us and explained the format. The meats and vegetables were cooked on our barbecue; the salad leaves were covered in sauces and then wrapped around the sizzling meat and vegetables before we selected our dips.

What fun.

'What karaoke?' asked Helene, as the table began to emerge again from the thirty or so dishes.

'It'll be great; we love a night of music.'

'There's something you're not telling me, David.'

'You enjoy a "turn" and it's only booked for 2 hours.'

'What's booked for 2 hours? And, who's the "turn"?' Helene asked, in that way she does when she already knows the answer.

'We are.'

Karaoke is big in these parts, very big. Just about every other bar seems to advertise it in neon flashing lights, our hotel was no exception. On the seventh floor alongside the spa, sauna, pool, outdoor tennis court and indoor table tennis were the karaoke rooms, four of them, bookable by the hour.

The room I had chosen was like a miniature version of the set from a Saturday night TV singing contest, where you have to have a certain factor to win it. We were escorted to our room by Roy, who introduced himself as our technician for the evening, I meant to ask what that meant but the moment passed as he opened a thick deeply padded door and invited us in.

Our karaoke room featured a pink and purple reflective chequered floor, highly polished silver tables with glass tops, a flashing ceiling and sparkling gold friezes on the walls in amongst the obligatory flickering neon. There were burgundy sofas studded in glass diamonds around the central performance area where two gold mics stood in front of a screen inviting us to select our songs.

It had been a while since Helene's performance of "Imagine" with the band on Tokoriki but with a glass or two of bubbling Dutch courage and an insistence that I stood outside and checked the soundproofing we had a splendid evening belting out some of our favourite 70's and 80's songs. The time flew by and when the meter ran out after midnight, the room went dark and quiet as the door was opened by Roy grinning from ear to ear.

'Would you like a copy of your recording?' he asked.

'A copy! Of the recording?' Helene screamed. 'You didn't, tell me you didn't.'

'Happy birthday, darling,' I said.

The following morning we flew back to the capital of Vietnam, Hanoi. Despite Vietnam having some extremely wealthy residents it is largely a poor country without, it seems, a middle class as we would know it. There are few cars, simply because they are too expensive for the large proportion of the population, hence the millions of motorbikes. It is also one of the few remaining communist countries in the world, something that either the residents or the government are fiercely proud of, as almost every house and shop flies the national flag of bright red displaying a gold star. On the central reservations of major roads there are propaganda posters attached to lampposts and flags every 15 metres or so, the national flag and the communist red flag with gold hammer and sickle appearing one after the other. Ironically, the only other country I have seen demonstrating the same level of nationalist pride is the US.

I am a great fan of the propaganda art we associate with the communist countries, a red illustrative style of block colour usually featuring a happy family alongside equally smiling workers and contented military, as a symbol of collective unity. These posters could be seen in most towns and often included the fatherly smiling portrait of Ho Chi Minh. He is immortalised in Vietnam, and quite right too, he saved, unified and created the country, so like the thousands of pilgrims each day we walked to his Mausoleum in the northern part of uptown Hanoi.

It is a huge grey stone cube of a building perhaps 20 metres square and mounted on a plinth about 10 metres high. It's impressive; ugly, but impressive. It overlooks a parade ground and has banners either side stretching well over 30 metres proclaiming "Vietnam lives forevermore, Ho Chi Minh lives forevermore". Inside the Mausoleum is the man himself preserved for those who wish to pay their respects.

'Look, they've rolled out the red carpet for us,' said Helene. Sure enough, up the broad steps to the entrance guarded by two soldiers dressed from head to toe in crisp white uniforms adorned by gold braid and matching buttons, was a long pristine red carpet.

'That's rather good, let's go in before the crowds arrive,' I said, striding onto the bottom steps. A loud blast of not one but two whistles screamed out across the square, quickly followed by shouting from two white uniformed soldiers looking like they may unbutton their holsters at any moment.

'No, no, no!' screamed the more frightening looking one. 'It closed for you today.'

'Closed for me? Why me?' I said, as I was ushered off the carpet.

'I think he means it's closed to the public today,' Helene said, helping the ushering. With that a black limousine with a flag on each wing appeared and the ushering became a bit more forceful. I never did see the dignitary or Ho Chi Minh.

That evening we met Kelly, our local guide for a street food walking tour of the city, this called for a strong nerve and possibly a strong stomach, but as she explained everyone eats out for breakfast and lunch in Hanoi. Kelly was studying Business Administration at the local university and being born and bred in the city used her knowledge as a local guide to practice her already excellent English and help pay her way through the degree course.

We were taken through backstreets where we would never normally walk and served in the smallest of restaurants where we would never normally eat, nothing more than open kitchens really. Kelly introduced us to two ladies sitting on extremely low stools side by side surrounded by steaming pots with rattling lids, hot oil creating a smoky haze and a circular hot plate where one of them was making delicate pancakes with a single chopstick. They had formed a little production line of dishes each of which was snatched away as quickly as they were made by one of their sons, the street waiter.

We sat at a low plastic table in an alleyway with the occasional motorbike flying past our faces, and the son handed us some small white bowls of soup with unidentified meat, noodles, lemongrass and a handful of herbs.

'Mix it all up,' Kelly instructed, 'squeeze in this lime and then slurp the noodles.' It was delicious.

Spring rolls are served everywhere in Vietnam, from the best hotel restaurants to stalls in the market and Kelly promised to let us try the best in Hanoi, the creations of Ms. Pang. After a short walk down a dimly lit street we came across a small group of locals gathered around a seated Vietnamese lady dressed in red, this was the famous Ms. Pang. In front of her was a large steel wok of deep glistening boiling oil balanced precariously on a single gas ring.

'This is her,' announced Kelly in triumph, 'these will be the best you have ever tasted.'

The Michelin star of the street looked up but her hands continued to roll her secret ingredients in the delicate rice paper and sink them with dexterity into the fiery oil. She removed a couple of the crispy brown rolls, thankfully with a pair of old tongs, and wrapped the lower half of each in lettuce to enable us to hold them. My goodness they were good. The crispy rice paper cracked and crunched revealing a piping hot filling that tasted like cooked pate and al dente vegetables.

'They are amazing, Kelly,' I said, 'and Ms. Pang can prepare them blindfolded.'

'When you're producing well over a thousand a day, it becomes automatic,' Kelly replied.

Not bad at a dollar for two, and the only overhead your front porch.

Helene's favourite was the seventh and last stop for coffee, but a very special coffee, only available from Mr. Hoy whose father invented it. He was working at the famous Metropole Hotel in Saigon when milk became very scarce so he created a new method of making coffee and it became a great success. He opened his own coffee house in 1932 in Hanoi and it's still going today. It's tiny, just 3 metres wide and Young Mr. Hoy is now in his seventies but still sits behind the till keeping a watchful eye on another two generations of his family preparing this deliciously sweet coffee.

The Hoys serve it in a white teacup placed in a circular plastic bowl of boiling water, presumably to keep it warm. The actual measures are a family secret but what we do know is the ingredients of egg yolk, condensed milk, honey and sugar are whipped together and poured over strong hot coffee. Despite Helene doing her best English Rose impression to engage one of the sons in conversation, this was the only bit of the secret she could prise out of him. It was a tremendous evening of fun, food and fascinating facts from Kelly; we agreed we'd eat more with the locals on the streets of this great city.

The following day it was up early for our drive to Halong Bay and a cruise with Royal Wings – *the signature of luxury* – unsure how that was actually going to be delivered.

We travelled out of the city and towns into countryside of green rice fields neatly arranged into a chequerboard of small squares, oddly enough occasionally separated by graveyards, or even a single tombstone in the paddy fields themselves. In the fields were women in their lampshade hats bent double in what looked like backbreaking work doing whatever needs to be done to the green shoots of rice.

Each of the single road villages we passed through had a wedding marquee erected on the verge, often with a band playing loud local music; they seemed to have an awful lot of weddings early on a Sunday.

Our boat for the cruise had four decks including a stylish bar, lounge, restaurant and the obligatory karaoke bar on the sundeck; the two middle decks contained the twenty cabins. For some inexplicable reason we had been upgraded to the Royal Suite, a room designed with a large helping of decadence in mind. The five picture windows provided an incredible view of this extraordinary seascape, the bed was probably the largest we'd slept in and the silk pyjamas and bathrobes were a nice touch. The seating area included two wooden and tapestry sofa chairs and bizarrely a chaise long, but the highlight was undoubtedly the teak wood panelled en suite bathroom.

There was a squeal of delight from Helene. 'You will never believe this,' she called from the bathroom.

'Look,' she said, 'we've got a bath, a corner bath. And it has a Jacuzzi facility.'

Having been used to showers on our cruises around the Galápagos and Fiji Islands, this was indeed a welcome novelty, but it didn't stop there. Ludicrously it also had its own water feature, a five-tier waterfall cascading into the bubbling bath below. Oddly, the ceiling was mirrored and featured antique light fittings while the loo was one of those high-tech ones I had so much fun with in the airport lounge at Siem Reap.

Halon Bay is quite surreal, once out into the open waters it never really opens at all. Dotted across the seascape are thousands of sheer mountains or pitons that rise dramatically from the sea all to around 60 metres in height. The day was grey and misty at sea, making the view of layer upon layer of the coned pitons on the horizon most eerie yet spectacular.

We visited a floating fishing village of about thirty families living in bamboo and tin houses built on rafts. The men fished, the women rowed the tourists around their homes and the children went to the floating school. They didn't have much and lived a simple life but in one of the most stunningly beautiful settings I've ever seen.

Over a six course dinner that evening we met a couple who were taking a break from working at a scientific station in Antarctica to travel Asia for a few months. Stories were swapped, wine was shared and it wasn't long before the four of us were the only ones in the restaurant. Some of the crew came over and invited us to their party. I assumed this would be down below in the crew quarters so we wouldn't disturb the other guests; they had a far better solution.

We were taken down to the tender used to ferry guests to and from the ship, the crew had replaced the seats with a large carpet upon which snacks were cooking and bottles of beer, wine and an unknown local spirit were being served. We were welcomed by the rest of the crew, about fifteen of them and the rope tethering us to the ship was fed out to allow us to drift into the dark some 30 metres from our sleeping cruise colleagues. The music was turned up, the beer flowed and we swapped songs and mimed stories until retiring early the following day. I don't think we really made the most of our Royal Suite upgrade.

Over dinner on our last evening in Vietnam we discussed our bestest bits, it had been quite an adventure and not what either of us had expected. Like Cambodia it has had a difficult recent past but has a wonderful cultural history. It is clearly an emerging country as the tourism revenue and investment pour in and its people are embracing its relatively new role as a holiday destination. Would we return? Most definitely, Helene was already looking at a VietJet loyalty card.

CHAPTER 27

Day 264 to 273: MYANMAR
Yangon, Mandalay and Bagan

Where China meets India

'Never heard of it,' I said to Helene, as she put her pink pin in the map somewhere between China and India all those months ago.

'Yes, you have, it used to be called Burma and I've always wanted to visit the golden temples.'

Our rules of selection included one destination the other could not challenge, mine was the Galápagos Islands and Helene's turned out to be Burma or Myanmar as we are now calling it.

I decided to do a little research and very quickly regretted it. The Anglo-Burmese wars lasted over 60 years and eventually led to British colonial rule in 1885 when they made it a province of India. But not before creating a cricket club, building a golf course and launching a brewery still today producing

Mandalay beer – *Brimming with optimism.* They couldn't pronounce Myanmar so renamed it Burma after the largest ethnic population.

In 1948 Burma gained its independence and since then there has been ongoing internal fighting between government forces and various ethnic minority groups. The conflict has been labelled as the world's longest running civil war and the country has been under military rule off and on from 1962, in the process it became classified as one of the UN's "Least Developed Nations" in 1987.

The UK Foreign and Commonwealth Office travel advice was *"political tension and unrest could happen at short notice… the situation in some ethnic states is volatile, there is ongoing conflict and the possibility of violent clashes".* The FCO ended its advice with *"Most visits are trouble free".* We hoped we'd be one of those.

We were back in the Audley Bubble, with our wonderful tour operators, so were welcomed to The Golden Land by our guide for the next few days, Nin and our driver, the splendid Mr. G. As we left the airport to make our way into Yangon the roads seemed eerily quiet.

'Where are all the motorbikes, Mr. G.?' I asked. I had become perversely used to the constant buzzing of thousands of them in Vietnam.

'No bikes,' he said, 'all motorbikes banned in city.' So, maybe the Vietnam Government will succeed with their ban after all.

'That's good, but why are there as many right-hand drive as left-hand drive cars?' I asked Mr. G.

It turned out that on the 6th December 1970 Myanmar made the radical change to swap from driving on the left to driving on the right, overnight. This was a decision made by the then Prime Minister, former Military General and soon to become President, Mr. Ne Win. This guy was, to say the least, eccentric. He was also a great believer in astrology, which is huge in Myanmar. Apparently, his wife's astrologer told him that to win the election he needed to change the side of the road the country drives on, to the right, perhaps due to his party's right wing views, who knows.

This was the guy who led the military coup in 1962 and sent the troops into a peaceful protest at the university campus killing a hundred students. The following day his army blew up the Students' Union building. Ne Win was also the ruler who almost led the country to bankruptcy because his astrologer told him his lucky number was nine. He promptly cancelled all notes that were not divisible by nine thereby leaving only 45 and 90 kyat notes as valid currency; extraordinarily this was only in 1987.

But my favourite story of this maverick was when his astrologer told him that in his mystical readings the next president seemed to look female. So, Ne Win started cross-dressing. The Emperor's Clothes sprung to mind but my how the astrologer must have laughed.

Nin and Mr. G. took us into the city giving us our first glimpse of the Shwedagon Pagoda, a colossal golden building in the shape of a mountainous upturned gold funnel dominating the city; it was a Magic Kingdom Moment for Helene and our destination for dawn the next day.

But first, a visit to a large reclining Buddha at the Chauk-htat-gyi temple, actually more like an aircraft hangar, he was a whopper, stretching the measuring tape to over 70 metres from ornately painted head to intricately engraved toes. However, it is only the fourth largest in the country, add another 100 metres and we're getting towards the longest reclining Buddha in the world, where you can enter near its ear and walk around its body, which seems an odd thing to do.

'I'd like to visit an astrologer,' announced Helene, as we stood admiring the beautifully made up face of the reclining Buddha complete with bright red lipstick, blue eye shadow and shiny black emerald eyes that do that thing where their gaze follows you around the room.

'That will be Mr. Bong,' said Nin, 'his consulting room is around the back.'

The consulting room turned out to be a curtained area about 2 metres square wedged between two souvenir stalls and adorned with dozens of fading black and white photos of Mr. Bong in his prime, probably 50 years ago. It looked like a barber's wall from the 1960's.

'How old is Mr. Bong?' I whispered to Nin.

'I am 84!' he proclaimed, appearing from behind the far curtain like the compere to a musical show. Mr. Bong had a full head of jet black hair, sparkling eyes, and a strong voice and there was nothing wrong with his hearing. He moved some more pictures of himself from the low table and knelt gesturing for Helene to do the same.

'Is he any good, Nin? He's asking for a lot of money.'

'I have won the state lottery twenty-three times,' he declared, shaking a dusty book at me with incomprehensible symbols on the cover.

'It's all about ancient numerology,' said Nin. 'You need to give him your date of birth, Helene.'

She wrote down the numbers, he consulted the dusty book, and I asked why he still did this if he'd won the lottery twenty-three times.

Mr. Bong gave me what could have been one-of-his-looks and started to tap out some hieroglyphics with chalk onto a handheld slate he probably used in school many years ago. His sparkling eyes may be failing him slightly because he picked up a large thick magnifying glass Sherlock Holmes would have been proud of and consulted his dusty old book.

'You were born on the 22nd. Two and two make four, so does three and one. Three is good, so your lucky numbers are nine, eighteen and twenty-seven, you should carry coconut wood and wear dark colours.'

I was lost already.

After further discussion around Helene's health, wealth and happiness he decided that she would be married twice in this lifetime. I think this may have been directed at me, we hadn't really hit it off. He took Helene's left hand, sprayed it with some secret potion and moved a picture of himself in his twenties to provide room for a very tatty pack of tarot cards. Helene was instructed to cut the cards and Mr. Bong started to turn the top ones over, more discussion ensued around her career and family. I reached over and turned a card around to face me, this apparently was not the done thing and it was snatched back, but not before I read the logo featured on the back of the deck of cards: "*Lord of the Rings*".

'Time for tea I think,' said Nin.

Tea shops in Yangon are like British pubs in the 1950's, almost exclusively a male domain, where men sit in small groups discussing the key issues of the day: the role of the President – who resigned the day we arrived – the best astrologer in town and the price of rice. Occasionally a small but fierce woman enters and drags her husband off to fulfil some household chore or be forced back to work.

We sat around a low black lacquered table at the Lucky Seven Tea Shop, the best in town according to Nin. Tea comes in four styles: green tea, sweet tea, very sweet tea and barely drinkable sweet tea that hurts your teeth. Spring rolls and samosas, that Helene couldn't eat, are served with the tea as accompaniments along with lamont, the stodgiest cakes you could imagine, full of thick bean curd and practically impossible to swallow. The menu looked like a black leather bible from the outside and a photographer's contact sheet on the inside, a huge amount of dishes that may or may not look like the ones we were about to order.

Nin ordered for us and various dishes of soup, noodles, chopped chilli, sliced vegetables, breads and dips turned up in no particular order. We followed her in rolling, dipping and mixing; it was a very fine meal and cost a little under 6,000 Kyat, about £1 each.

We were up at 5:00 AM for the highlight of our visit to Yangon, sun rise over the Shwedagon Pagoda, the most sacred Buddhist monument in Myanmar. It is said to contain relics from four Buddha: the staff from one, a piece of clothing from another, a water pot and finally eight strands of hair from the fourth, all buried deep below the 99 metre high golden stupa.

Nin told us there was some debate over the age of the structure, archaeologists have dated it to somewhere between the 6th century and the 10th century, but legend has it from the locals that the first stupa was built there in 550 BC and over the following 2,600 years was added to, thereby creating the vast area of gold monuments today. This tradition continues with donations to maintain the gold plates and fund the never ending process of replacing the gold leaf.

Near the pointed top of the stupa is what appeared to be a cage. Nin told us this was the umbrella crown tipped with 5,448 diamonds and 2,317 rubies, and at the very top is the diamond bud containing a 76 carat diamond weighing 15 grams. Surrounding the towering main stupa are dozens of smaller ones, each one covered in gold leaf, the amount of gold here was simply overwhelming. When the sun rose to light the main stupa it glowed golden pink against a lightening deep blue sky, the effect was stunning.

We had visited some extraordinary places on our adventure witnessing some remarkable sights and the Atacama Desert, Machu Picchu, Uluru and Siem Reap temples took some beating but this was up there with the best, it was remarkable in its beauty. As we continued our walk around the pagoda the sunlight started to reflect off the hundreds of gold surfaces, the young nuns in their pink robes and saffron sashes appeared and initiation ceremonies began with families in traditional dress. It was a cacophony of colour, every direction we looked screamed for our attention. What a wonderful morning, one that neither of us will ever forget.

It was time to move on from Yangon, we took a short flight in a small plane, met with Wyn our new guide and were soon on the road to Mandalay. A surprisingly good road, more like a UK dual carriageway, but as she explained Mandalay is the centre of the commercial world for Myanmar with a 175 km direct access into China, India and Thailand so the government has invested in the transport infrastructure for the city. Agricultural produce is exported and agricultural technology is imported, but that didn't prevent us from stopping every 10 minutes or so to let the working oxen and buffaloes cross the road from one field to another.

Part of that commercial world is the jade market in the middle of the city where the locals meet the international traders, many from China. Like any other trading market, Billingsgate or Smithfield for example, it starts early, is fast and frenetic and full of characters, but the jade market is huge, over 40,000 buyers and sellers attending every morning.

The market is actually a production line for the manufacture of jade jewellery, mainly bangles that bring good health and good luck to the wearer, their price depending on the quality of the stone but can vary from as little as $5 to as much as $200,000. For a bangle? I would expect to be fitter than Mr. Bong and win the lottery more often than he does for that price.

The jade is mined a hundred miles from Mandalay and brought to the market in its raw form, boulders of it, some as large as a small car. Helene was invited into an open fronted factory by some young inquisitive men to demonstrate how they cut the huge rocks.

I say inquisitive because we are somewhat of a novelty in Mandalay, particularly Helene. We are occasionally stopped by locals to join them in a selfie, or by parents to explain who we are to their young children pointing at us. Wyn explained that some, especially those from the country, will never have seen a white woman with blonde hair before.

As Helene watched the cutting and polishing process a buyer on behalf of a large Chinese importer invited me to help inspect the cut rocks he was purchasing. How much help I could be I'm not sure but I was given a small powerful torch to hold against the smooth sleek surface to examine the clarity of the rich green stone. The buyer held his mobile next to the rock giving a live video feed back to China, and he asked for my appraisal.

'Is the green a consistent colour across the stone?' he asked.

'Yes, it's all dark green.'

'What about flaws? Can you see any lines or cracks in the jade?' he asked, holding the camera closer to my torch. 'And what about the depth of colour?'

This was all getting a bit technical, the seller was eager to move my torch to the best parts of the stone, which I now noticed had red rings lightly drawn over its surface. These indicated how many bangles could be cut from it, about twenty from this particular loaf sized stone.

'It looks clear to me,' I said, 'and the colour is the same across the stone, quite deep.'

He translated my comments to his Chinese importer on the mobile, answered a few questions and shook the hand of the seller. It appeared the deal was done. Wads of notes wrapped in bands appeared and the stone was wrapped in some grease proof paper that made it look even more like a loaf of bread. Buyer and seller looked pleased with the transaction and I looked fairly bemused by it all. I do hope the importer was satisfied with my purchase.

'I would like a piece of jade,' said Helene.

'Well, we couldn't be in a better place,' I said, 'and as luck would have it you are now with an experienced buyer, I know what to look for. Let's start with colour.'

'As dark as possible,' she said.

'Oh! Are you sure?' asked Wyn, looking rather concerned.

'Don't you worry,' I said, 'we'll find it from one of these small traders and I'll drive a hard bargain.'

We had now arrived at the end of the production line, this part of the market was full of one-man-band sellers behind portable tables displaying their wares of beautifully cut and highly polished bangles, brooches and beads.

A small man wearing a long dusty longyi and a huge bright green emerald ring set in silver was shuffling a dozen or so jade stones around an old white mat on a plastic table that may have once been in his garden. In amongst them was a deep dark green stone about the size of a fingernail, perfect.

'Leave this to me, Helene,' I said, borrowing his pencil torch to inspect the quality of the jade.

'Clarity and consistency of colour good,' I reported. 'No blemishes or flaws. Depth of colour good. Yes, I think this will do. How much is this one?' I asked.

'$10,000,' he said.

Wyn looked expectantly at me, Helene just laughed.

The temple in Mandalay contains one of the most sacred Buddha in Myanmar, believed to have been cast during the lifetime of one of the four Buddha so probably resembling him more than any other. It is a place of pilgrimage and religious ceremonies and we were lucky enough to visit on a Saturday which also happened to be the Sabbath – it moves around a bit depending on the new moon. So there was a lot going on including dozens of families dressed in brightly coloured robes and traditional silk costumes accompanying their sons and daughters who were being initiated into the monasteries.

They can stay as long as they like, a minimum of 3 days or all their life, but the soon-to-be monks and nuns looked awfully young to me. Wyn explained that providing they can wash and clean themselves they will be accepted in, but the cost of the initiation ceremony, procession of family and party for the villagers can be as high as $20,000 plus $1,500 for the optional elephant. Most families will therefore have just one ceremony where all their children will have their heads shaved, have make-up applied and be dressed in the family's traditional silk and gold robes for a joint initiation.

After watching the formal photos, just like a wedding but far more colourful, we went in search of the look-a-like Buddha. So sure are they that he is in the image of a Buddha they seem to believe he is actually a living being. At 4:00 AM every morning a ceremony is performed where he has his face washed and his teeth brushed, just to make sure he's looking his best for the day's visitors.

He is a big Buddha and getting bigger by the day. The tradition in this men only shrine is to add gold leaf to the already bullioned Buddha; he was weighed in 2005 and tipped the scales at 7.5 tons of pure gold.

As we left and walked past the inevitable stalls and open shops where you can buy a life-sized shrink wrapped "gold" Buddha, there was the bizarre sight of a decorated elephant overtaking a hearse.

'That's for a wealthy family,' said Wyn.

'How do you know?' I asked.

'The hearse is expensive, it has air conditioning.'

'Air con?'

'Yes, to stop the body smelling.'

Nice. But it was 37 degrees.

Wyn hailed three cyclos, far better than the ones in Hue, here we sat next to the cyclist like a sidecar but in a half reclining position on an extremely comfortable padded armchair. The bikes seemed to be a little older than the monuments, pagodas and stupas we passed, but somehow very British, equipped with straight handlebars, a large loud jangling bell and oddly bright pink brake levers. My driver had a furled umbrella hanging from the front which he unfolded and held above my head as he cycled. I felt guiltily like a maharajah, but loved every minute of it.

We arrived at the Ghost Market. We've done markets trading in meat, fish, vegetables, clothes, flowers, coffee and jade, but surely you can't trade in ghosts? No, you can't, it is named as such because it disappears as quickly as it appears. The food market is packed with huge woven baskets of onions, garlic, peppers, tomatoes and assorted vegetables and is situated along the train tracks in town. But that's okay there's only one train a day and it's the end of the line. The problem is no one knows exactly when the train may arrive, who needs an accurate timetable for one train a day?

Large umbrellas, usually found outside street cafes and bars, shelter squatting farmers' wives from the baking sun as they ply their traditional trade on the train tracks. It's busy and as Wyn explained, the most popular market in town because it's so cheap, there are no market stall fees for the owners to pay. We were wandering around being shown herbs, spices and seasonings in small open cloth bags when there was a deep rumbling and all hell broke loose.

Umbrellas were yanked out of the sleepers, children were scooped up from playing on the tracks and dogs were running ahead of the train blaring its horn but not for a moment slowing down. Wyn pulled us out of the way of the speeding train as we watched the locomotive and five carriages enter the market and arrive at a disused shack that she assured me was the station. Comically, the baskets of vegetables and sacks of spices were just left between the tracks for the train to trundle over. Once the train had passed over the produce the umbrellas, children and dogs returned and trade began again as if nothing had happened. What a wonderful sight that was, we both thought that was how India might be.

We made our way across town to the Royal Palace or at least a 1994 reproduction of what it probably looked like before all one hundred and fourteen buildings were completely destroyed in WWII by the British bombing the Japanese who had occupied it in 1943.

To be honest, it was a bit disappointing, the original buildings were covered in gold leaf but this was just too expensive for the reproduction so most of the elegant timbered palace simply had flaking gold paint. The palace walls were the most impressive part of the construction, they escaped the bombing and had a moat around the four sides, each one of which is 2 kilometres long. There seems to be a theme going on here with Angkor Wat and the Imperial City at Hue, both of which were constructed in the same square design with a moat.

The last Myanmar king was exiled to India in 1885 so the British took over the palace; it is now a military base with five thousand soldiers and their families in barracks around the reproduction. I asked Wyn why there were so many buildings when it was a functioning palace; a hundred and fourteen seemed to be excessive even for the largest royal family.

Apparently, the king had his main wife who was the major queen, a few minor queens and a whole load of concubines including three sisters. The total of his female companions was an impressive forty-nine. Or put another way an unmanageable forty-nine, they didn't all get on so he tried to keep some of them apart in separate buildings. That didn't quite work so he hired a few eunuchs to keep the peace; must have been a nightmare on his birthday.

Our final visit was to Alabaster Alley where there are dozens of open workshops making alabaster Buddha, from statuettes of a few inches to figures standing well over 3 metres high. Each is carved by hand, so walking on the white dusty road we are watched by thousands of carved white Buddha, or rather we're not, they don't have their faces created until they find a customer.

They look extremely odd sitting in the lotus position with delicately carved hands in the enlightenment position and beautiful braided robes, but with a flat cube of stone on their shoulders. It was reminiscent of the Cybermen from Dr Who. The customer can therefore choose the shape of the Buddha head, the hairstyle, width of smile, eyes open or closed, length of earlobes etc. I think one could have a great deal of fun with that.

On our journey to pick up the boat at Pakokku taking us down the Irrawaddy River to Bagan, I asked Wyn about a couple of rather peculiar practices I had noticed with the locals. Every morning they paint their faces with a yellow substance, looking like very poorly applied make-up, some add a circle on each cheek, others two broad square brushstrokes and a few cover their whole face. And this is not limited to the women, male and female use the dye, young and old, even the toddlers have it smeared on them.

Apparently, the use of Thanaka is purely cosmetic and unique to the people of Myanmar. It is a paste made from ground bark and sold in shops and markets throughout the country in its raw form of a short, but thick branch from the Murraya tree. Of course, we stopped, ground the branch on a circular slate slab with water and applied the paste to each other's face, it creates a cooling sensation and dries to a powdery consistency. We looked pretty odd sitting in the back of the car in this war paint, but why not.

The other practice was exclusively male and quite revolting. They spat a lot, and it seemed customary to make the loudest spitting noise they could, leaving a red dollop of spittle in the dust. At first I thought they were spitting blood and put it down to the obviously poor dental care most middle-aged and elderly locals had. Wyn said that as cigarettes became more expensive the men started chewing pann, a leaf coated with some sticky yellow substance then wrapped around a betel nut, a mild narcotic. It is this that creates a mouthful of red dye they spit out. Horrible.

It was another early start on our first morning in Bagan, but the 4:00 AM wake-up call was a small inconvenience for what promised to be a highlight not only of Myanmar and South East Asia, but the whole adventure. This was ballooning at dawn over the 3,000 temples and monuments of Bagan.

Until the 6.8 magnitude earthquake struck in August 2016 the small town of Bagan had over four thousand monuments in its 42 sq. km region. Temples, stupas, libraries, monasteries and ordination halls mainly from the 11th and 12th centuries still litter the landscape and horizon of this magical place. So that day we were to see those that remained from the air and the ground. It was to be a day of firsts: neither of us had been ballooning before, it was my first time on a motorbike and first time riding with a pillion passenger, who made it quite clear when she thought I was going too fast. Although how I've reached sixty without driving a motorbike I'm not quite sure.

We met with Piers, our pilot for the morning, a frightfully British gentleman from Bristol, who gave up his job as an airline pilot to spend 6 months a year ballooning guests across Old Bagan. We were joined by couples from Spain, Korea and Russia for breakfast in the field where the balloon was inflated and there was a little nervous laughter around the table. But once we were in the basket with the flame roaring above our heads as we rose serenely into the brightening sky any apprehensiveness disappeared as quickly as the ground below us.

It was stunning. The morning mist draped itself around the hundreds of temples and across the parched land, as we rose higher the sun broke through to give the scenery below a golden hue and all was quiet. Apart from a snivel or two from someone having their second Magic Kingdom Moment of the week. Can't say I blamed her though.

A couple of hours later we landed softly on the sandbanks of the broad Irrawaddy River and after a celebratory glass or two of champagne, allegedly an acknowledgement to the French inventors of ballooning, we were collected by boat and taken back to the hotel to start the day with another breakfast. My goodness what fun.

We met Aung our guide for the day, a lawyer and it seemed to me part-time political activist who had campaigned hard for UNESCO protection of the area. I believed we were now to view the monuments from an entirely different perspective, in more ways than one. He was a charming man, keen to debate the difficult issues the country has to address with a joint military and democratic government, but with an infectious giggle and an encyclopaedic knowledge of the area and its monuments. I was keen for him to take us off the usual tourist route, as Audley often do, and he didn't disappoint.

'Can you drive motorbikes?' Aung asked.

'Yes.'

'No.'

We answered together.

'Helene, when have you ever been on a motorbike?' I asked.

'We used to sit on the back of the boys' bikes in Italy all the time,' she argued.

'That's not the same, this is driving! And anyway, that was 30 years ago, or more.'

'It'll be fine, I'll pick it up, I'm sure it's just like... well you know.'

We traded down a level on the advice of Aung and settled for electric scooters, which still seemed awfully fast and unstable. After 10 metres Helene decided her training in Italy "with the boys" had not equipped her with the necessary skills to tackle the dusty roads of Old Bagan and so became my first pillion rider.

Aung explained that in 1990 the military forced the whole population of Bagan to move to a new Bagan outside the old city walls. This was only ten thousand people but nevertheless if, like Aung, it's your home and family then it's going to be pretty traumatic so they refused to move. The military cut off the water supply, then the electricity, and when that failed they threatened to open fire. Aung, his family and the remaining villagers left to set up home in New Bagan.

Old Bagan where all the monuments are located was now deserted. The military demolished all the shops, homes and town buildings to allow the building of hotels and private residences for the generals. They had taken ownership of potentially one of the most popular tourist destinations in the world and were not going to let UNESCO interfere; they now charge overseas visitors 25,000 Kyat, about £13, to enter the Bagan Architectural Zone. It is rigidly policed – *show your prepaid card for the officer inspects in any time, the Culture Zone,* as it clearly stated on the pass.

This story is indicative of the difficult political situation in the country. There are a hundred and thirty-five ethnic groups some of which continue to fight with the military, hence "the world's longest civil war" tag. The military make up 25% of the government but are unable to vote. The remaining 75% is democratically elected, their leader is Aung San Suu Kyi, known by everyone as "The Lady"; she is a politician, diplomat, author and winner of the Nobel Peace Prize. She achieved a landslide victory in the 1990 elections with 81% of the seats but the military refused to hand over power. They argued she could not be Prime Minister because she was married to a foreigner, ironically British given the country's history. She was placed under house arrest for 15 of the 21 years from 1989 to 2010.

In 2015 her party the NLD swept to victory and although the military still prevented her becoming Prime Minister she was made State Councillor and effectively rules as PM. Although the military are in the minority and have no vote in government, they wrote the constitution and the balance of power is most definitely with them.

We managed to move Aung on from politics towards the first of three must-see monuments according to all the tourist information. They certainly were impressive, each in their own distinctive way. The first built in 1183 was a huge red brick affair with a strong Indian influence in its architecture, carvings and remaining wall drawings. The 2016 earthquake had shaken the spired top off the building that now lay as rubble in the temple's old gardens, and there was a solitary individual numbering the jigsaw of bricks but little sign that it will ever be rebuilt.

During our visit to Ananda, the most revered of the Bagan temples and totally restored, interestingly by the same team who worked on the Taj Mahal, Aung attempted to explain to me why Buddha sought to be free of any attachment.

'This should be interesting,' said Helene, 'I'm not sure you'll entirely get this.'

Aung recounted the story as we contemplated the towering gold Buddha standing on each of the four sides of the temple's core.

'You mean he gave up everything?' I asked. 'The Royal Palaces and all its riches?'

'Yes, he even gave up his family,' Aung said.

'Goodness, couldn't he find enlightenment without becoming poverty-stricken and turning his back on his family?' I asked.

'Told you,' said Helene.

'No, he believed that the fewer attachments you have, the less suffering you'll have.'

'I'm sorry to question one of the largest religions in the world,' I said, 'but that's not my experience.'

'It's not a religion,' said Helene.

'Well, it's certainly not easy,' said Aung, trying to keep the peace.

'Okay,' I argued, 'if it's about losing all our possessions and wealth, why on Earth are the stupa and Buddha covered in millions of dollars' worth of gold? Wouldn't that be better spent on education or health?'

'It is an interesting dilemma,' he replied, 'the 400,000 monks in Myanmar have nothing, even their robes are donated by the people, but the monuments they worship are priceless.'

More contemplation was required but given that Aung had just condensed the 20,000 pages of teachings into a sentence or two it was as impressive as it was difficult to comprehend.

Our third and final "tourist monument" seemed to underline the argument. It was the huge gold Shwezigon Pagoda built in the 11th century as the prototype for all the stupa in the region. The building needs new gold gilt every 6 years costing $900,000 each time. Below the gleaming structure we found a room around 5 metres square and ankle deep in money, the notes were being counted and bundled by three kneeling women who couldn't keep up with the bucket loads being thrown onto the floor by the men.

Maybe there's not that much difference to the tall hand painted donation thermometers we see at home outside churches that need a new roof but the opulence and poverty in Myanmar do not sit comfortably together for me.

We mounted our scooters and hit a dusty trail that Aung promised us was off the beaten track of tourists. After 20 minutes or so, with our eyes streaming and noses full of grime we arrived at what appeared to be a deserted orange brick temple about 30 feet square with the upturned bell like spire balanced on the roof. It looked neglected but in fairly good condition having escaped the effects of the earthquake.

Disappointingly the entrance was sealed by a wrought iron gate with a huge padlock; we peered through the bars into the darkness within.

'In here is my favourite Buddha,' said Aung.

'We can't see anything, Aung,' said Helene. 'Are there any lights?'

As the three of us squinted into the musty smelling entrance there was a sharp clanking sound making all three of us jump, it was quite eerie in that isolated spot. A small man appeared out of the darkness removing a large ring of keys from the waist of his longyi.

There were no lights inside the temple but as we found our way around the perimeter wall we entered a room with natural sunlight pouring in from three high openings in the walls above us. They were clearly strategically placed, for they shed a stream of light on the most beautiful seated Buddha we had seen. In the gloom and the shadow that surrounded him his pale face shone with red lips and dark eyes looking down on us with a small smile. The remainder of his terracotta coloured body was swathed in a painted vermilion robe leaving one arm bare and hands in the enlightenment mudra position. It was elegant, dignified and stunningly beautiful.

'You can keep all the gold stupas,' said Helene, 'this is by far the most exquisite of them all.'

Of course, she was right.

Our final destination in Myanmar was to be Inle Lake. A 30 minute flight east took us to He Hoe for a day with our guide Tata on a long, long-tailed boat. It was more like an extended punt – lengthy, narrow and flat bottomed with three armchairs one behind the other and a noisy engine at the back.

Our adventure on the lake included a visit to the floating farm, an extraordinary piece of basic agricultural technology where the farmers created rows of reed mounds a couple of feet thick layered with the fertile soil from the bottom of the lake. On this 4 km x 2.5 km vegetable garden they paddle up the narrow strips tending their crops from their boats, mainly tomatoes, cucumber and squash. How very British.

As we made our way up the lake, Tata recounted the story of the Buddha discovered there. During the 18th century in a steep field behind one of the river banks, five small Buddha were found and so the site became a sacred area and the first Buddhist stupa was built. Then another was erected, and another until the landscape was littered with them wedged together with little space to walk between. There are now over eight hundred. Sadly, the region was the centre of conflict for many years and became a no-go zone until the late 1990's by which time the monuments had begun to decay, the roots and plants overpowering the drying bricks.

We hiked our way up the hill and manoeuvred our way around the stupas realising that the recently renovated ones had small plaques inlaid into the ornate brickwork.

'Who is funding the restoration of all these?' I asked Tata.

'They are all privately funded, either by the family whose ancestors first built them or by private individuals who want to help rehabilitate the holy site.'

'You mean anyone?'

'Yes.'

'How much does it cost to sponsor a stupa?'

Helene caught up with us, 'I'm not sure it's "sponsor a stupa", David, these are sacred relics.'

'They are,' said Tata, 'but $500 should cover it.' Sounded like a bargain to me.

The story of the five Buddha was not yet finished. Every year they are transported by the villagers' boats to the Pagoda Festival. Unfortunately, one year in stormy conditions the boat capsized sending all five to the murky depths below. After hours of diving and searching only four were recovered and returned to the temple, but imagine their surprise when they found the fifth was already seated in its place on the shrine. The villagers now only take four, on rotation, to the annual Pagoda Festival.

Our path back to the boat took us through a bamboo forest where we entered a small clearing. To our surprise, in the clearing was a silver service dining table set for three under a bright orange canopy, and a waiter in full livery inviting us to take a seat.

'This is your picnic,' said Tata, uncorking a bottle from the local Red Mountain Estate Vineyard.

Over miniature potatoes, salads and a variety of kebabs on small cutlasses we discussed our time in Myanmar, inviting Tata to comment on our bestest bits.

From the six countries we visited in South East Asia, Myanmar was the one we knew least and the one we enjoyed the most. Perhaps because it is still a novice in competing for the tourist pound, dollar and yen. The infrastructure is there but its "political tension, unrest and ongoing conflict" as the FCO put it, clearly deters a lot of visitors; all our guides believed tourist numbers were down around 30%.

That's a great shame because the country has a wonderful history, some magnificent sights and a great culture. But it is the people that make the difference. They are gentle, friendly and kind who want nothing more than a smile, and maybe a photo with Helene. They are officially the most generous people in the world by share of income donated, an astounding fact given the level of poverty in the country. Then again, maybe not if you follow the example of Buddha.

The bridge over the river Kwai in Kanchanaburi, Thailand. Or is it?

Young monks enjoying the early evening view over the Mekong River in Cambodia.

The lovely Lia and one of her "family" she rescued from a Thai tourist show and nursed back to health.

On our way to the paradise island of Ko Phra Thong in the Andaman Sea I thought we might do a spot of fishing...

Rather overwhelmed at my meeting with Chum Mey, one of only seven survivors from Tuol Sleng prison in Phnom Penh, Cambodia.

In a Bounty Ad on Koh Rong Samloem Island, Cambodia. But beware of dangerous bungalows.

Helene face-to-face with one of the 1,000 year old giant towers at Angkor Thom, Cambodia.

The crumbling towers of the Preah Khan temple in a slow wrestling match with the jungle. Siem Reap, Cambodia

Helene's rather wet blessing at Angkor Wat, Cambodia ending with them both in laughter

I accidently bought a skewered snake at Cambodia's famous Pub Street in Siem Reap

Helene's victorious cyclo having beaten me with Thanh doing all the leg work in a race to the Imperial City at Hue, Vietnam

The hidden Buddha our guide Aung finally found for us in Bagan, Myanmar. Perhaps the most elegant, dignified and stunningly beautiful of them all

The young monks arriving for their blessing at the Shwedagon Pagoda in Yangon, Myanmar

Sunrise at the golden Shwedagon Pagoda in Yangon. I didn't realise my rather impressive Longyi was see-through.

Helene and Nin at the Lucky Seven Tea Shop in Yangon with cake that Helene can't eat and tea so sweet it hurts your teeth

With 84 year old Yangon astrologer Mr. Bong deciphering the numbers that meant Helene would marry again!

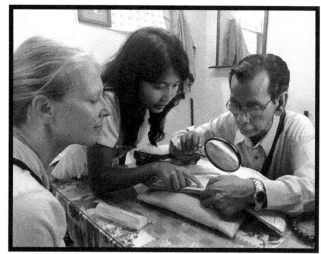

Ladies in traditional dress on market day in Shan, Myanmar

Being paddled around the floating farm village on Inle Lake, Myanmar

Me buying jade at the market in Mandalay, Myanmar on behalf of a large importer on the phone in China

The Ghost Market in Mandalay just before the train arrived and all hell broke loose

CHAPTER 28

Day 274 to 281: CHINA.
Hong Kong and Beijing

"We're gonna build a wall"

Our overnight flight from Yangon to Hong Kong allowed us a short sleep before arriving with bleary eyes and bags of anticipation in *Asia's World City*. Chris and Anita, two of our closest friends from home had flown in to meet us. A great opportunity to catch up on all the latest news and developments from home over dinner.

'Nothing's changed much,' said Chris.

'Not over 9 months?'

'No, not really, same old, same old.'

They were far more eager to hear from us of course, so we spent a splendid evening answering their many questions and discussing our experiences, both planned and unplanned. As late evening became early morning I realised just how much we had packed into the adventure so far and how life at home can easily become the same old, same old as Chris said. Until of course you decide to throw off the bowlines and sail away from the safe harbour.

Hong Kong is essentially two islands, Kowloon and Hong Kong Island itself, both offering high-rise living in the hundreds of tall, but very narrow towering apartments, alongside equally lofty hotels and office blocks littering the slopes, and not one of them with a 13th or 14th floor. The word for four in Cantonese sounds like the word for death so elevators and seat rows just skip from 12 to 15. Oddly, our hotel had a fourth floor.

Our hotel, the elegant InterContinental Grand Stamford, was on the Kowloon side, so to discover the two sites of the city we bought tickets to allow us to hop-on and hop-off all sorts of modes of transport: the tourist bus, the wonderful 100-year-old trams, the older funicular railway, the famous and even older Star Ferry and the granddaddy of them all, the sampans in the harbour.

It's not surprising there is so much hopping going on, you can barely walk anywhere. The overwhelming impression in the city is people, thousands of people. Even though we were a week too early for the Hong Kong Sevens there were crowds everywhere making a walking tour almost impossible. It was Sunday which is known as Manila Day in Hong Kong when all the domestic staff, mainly Filipino, have the day off to congregate in the pedestrianised roads. Oddly, they bring huge flattened boxes to make a temporary cardboard city where they sit and picnic, sing, give each other manicures or pedicures and hold fashion shows, mainly for shoes. Their compatriot Imelda Marcos would have been proud of them.

Hong Kong Island is built on three levels so rather than jam up the roads as much as the pavements the city has a chain of escalators connecting the tiers, known as the Hillside Escalator Link carrying eighty thousand people a day up and down the metropolis. Extremely clever thinking by the council I guess but with one slight flaw, there's only one of them so they only go one way. They are timed to take commuters downhill from 6:00 AM to 10:00 AM and then halt and reverse back up until midnight. A real pain for those working the late shift I guess.

We made our way up the first few connecting escalators, built as bridges over the old part of the city, and were nearing the last set to take us to the top when a whistle blew and they all stopped. Stranded mid escalate we were ushered down by some local authority gentlemen, judging by their official yellow dungarees, and pointed towards the steep steps running underneath the automated alternative.

We never made it to the top, but later that day watched the "Symphony of Lights" laser show across the water where the neon-clad skyscrapers flash with colourful lights and send Lightsabre beams across the city. Pretty spectacular.

It was tremendous fun to meet up with friends from home in a city that was clearly on the back nine for us, but Helene and I had an adventure to continue, next stop China's capital city, Beijing.

We arrived in snow. This would be a challenge for our zippy-uppy bags; we had sent most of our cold gear home while in Australia and had disposed of the disposable jeans in Hue, Vietnam. Wendy, our guide for the next few days, took us to our accommodation, the Double Happiness Courtyard Hotel, a 200-year-old house in the centre of the city. Our double happiness turned out to be an upgrade to their Wedding Room as they quaintly put it, a bedroom of red silks, ornately carved wood and a sizeable bed of more silk and tapestry walls covering three sides of the four-poster. Definitely had the feeling of a Parisian boudoir, apparently.

Beijing, known as Peking until the founding of the People's Republic of China in 1949, is a cosmopolitan modern city, immaculately clean and well cared for. There are no signs of poverty in the city, no begging, very few street traders apart from at the tourist spots and elaborate wealthy business premises throughout the city. There seems to be a free yellow bike for everyone, thousands of them line the roads and the transport infrastructure above and below ground is cheap and virtually free of congestion. So, we ignored our bikes in favour of public transport.

The stereotype image from the Cultural Revolution of a grim grey environment of communism, full of people in boiler suits queuing at poorly stocked shops is long gone; this is a thriving commercial city full of Michelin star restaurants, five star hotels and designer brands. We began to question exactly where we may find any evidence of communism.

Beijing has an astonishing 27 million citizens, a huge number, particularly given the one child per family ban, only lifted in 2017, so everything is supersized to cope with the masses of people. Main roads are twelve lane boulevards, pavements are four times the width of those in the UK and our first visit, Tiananmen Square, is a huge 44 hectares of paving stone and tarmac in the city centre.

My knowledge of the square is limited to the "Tank Man" as he is known who became a global phenomenon when he stood in front of the tanks after the student uprising in 1989, and the enormous painting of the father of the country Chairman Mao looking down benevolently on his subjects. His body lies in a crystal coffin, housed in an elaborate building on the square with a constant queue of people wishing to pay their respects.

Tiananmen Square is, however, dwarfed by its neighbour the Forbidden City, a colossal 72 hectares right in the heart of Beijing surrounded by the now obligatory square moat, but wider than the others of course at 52 metres. Built in 1407 this was the home of the emperors and the Imperial Palace of the Ming Dynasty (1168 – 1644) and the Qing Dynasty (1644 – 1911), it is also big. Hundreds of rooms account for 167,000 metres of buildings, twenty-six of which were one emperor's bedrooms. This had nothing to do with the hundred or so concubines he had but to keep his enemies guessing which room he was sleeping in thereby reducing the chance of an attack.

It was bitterly cold and full of people, but the architecture of the gold tiled buildings and elaborate painted carvings were worth the frozen nose and ears, Helene suffers with cold hands but was fine; she used socks as gloves.

'Let's warm up with some tea,' suggested Wendy.

As we entered the Quing Shan Ju Tea House I was invited to tea by an attractive young lady in a red and gold satin tunic and stunning black hair framing her porcelain face.

'I've been asked to take tea with my companion here,' I said.

'I bet you have, David,' replied Helene.

'I've always been interested in the ritual of tea making.'

'Of course you have. Is it the history, the method, or the blends used by the extremely pretty Chinese girl?'

It was quite absorbing, and what a ritual, involving two pots not just one. The lovely lady first served us peanuts, really not sure why, despite my questioning and encouragement she just smiled warmly and nodded at me.

'David, stop gawping!' Helene admonished with a nudge.

'It's fascinating,' I said.

'I'm sure she is.'

Our host poured hot water onto some tea leaves in pot one, swilled it around a bit, poured it into pot two, swilled that one around a bit and emptied it.

'Didn't she like that one?' I asked.

'That was just warming-the-pot, as you call it,' said Wendy. 'We warm the pot with tea.' Seemed to make sense. My pretty tea partner then poured hot water over the outside of the pot, more of the warming I think, before asking me to select a blend from the many she had displayed on the table.

'Please,' I said, 'you choose, or we can choose together.'

'Oh! Good grief, David. Just get on with it.'

We decided on Litchi, a lychee black tea apparently good for lowering blood pressure.

'Just as well,' said Helene.

She delicately poured the black tea brew from the steaming pot into tall narrow egg cup style vessels and placed the small tea cups upside down on the top. I followed her instruction to turn them the right way up, emptying the contents into the cups and we then rolled the empty egg cups in our hands inhaling the aroma. A warm and comforting lychee sweet fragrance with a slight bitterness from the tea emanated, only then could we taste the tea.

'My goodness, that was excellent,' I said. 'How was it for you, Helene?'

'It's tea, David.'

We left the Tea House much warmer, but not before I had said goodbye to my beautiful tea partner and £120 for assorted teas.

That evening we were invited to prepare a meal with the head chef from the Sheraton Hotel in the city. Dan, as he liked to be called, was an entertaining thirty something dressed in his whites with the tallest of chef's hats and not a word of English.

So we copied his demonstration using the only utensil Chinese chefs use, a lethal looking and incredibly sharp steel meat cleaver to carefully pierce, slit and half slice a cucumber. When finished, we had surprisingly created a flexible spiral of the vegetable to be used in a dish with garlic, dried chilli and soya sauce.

This was to accompany four other dishes requiring delicate knife skills to carve symbols into mushrooms, slice potatoes into noodles and chop pak choi. We finally stir-fried sweet and sour pork in the heaviest of woks with the hottest of oils. All terrific fun and with the full count of fingers still in place the three chefs sat down to share our meal.

We had been looking forward to visiting the Great Wall of China immensely, a highlight of the whole adventure, so were delighted to wake to a clear morning of blue skies and sunshine, still only a couple of degrees above freezing though. Wendy had warned us there was still snow on the wall so we wrapped up as warm as our zippy-uppy bags would allow and set off determined to walk the iconic monument.

One of the Seven Wonders of the World and allegedly the only man-made structure visible from space, parts of the wall are over 2000 years old. In 221BC the first emperor, Qin Shi Huang managed to unify the seven warring kingdoms of China and facing the threat of the invading Mongolians said, "we're gonna build a wall".

It took 20 years to build the 6,250 miles of magnificent wall including towers every 100 metres or so as beacons for communication, storage of weapons or accommodation for the armies who would spend a 2 week shift fighting the enemy and protecting the country.

Our visit to the Great Wall was at Jinshanling a couple of hours' drive from Beijing but one of the quieter parts not overrun by visitors, something Audley have the talent and experience to achieve for us regularly.

The gentle walk up became a tougher climb as we neared the entrance to one of the towers and the steep steps onto the wall itself. This was a Magic Kingdom Moment just waiting to happen.

'Are we really here?' sobbed Helene, as we traced the wall's route clinging to the ridge of the mountains and disappearing miles away over the bright horizon.

'We are and it's everything I expected,' I said, as we hugged in the sunshine. 'Come on; let's walk the Great Wall of China.'

All those months ago when we stuck our blue and pink pins in the map where we thought the wall may be it had still been a dream we hoped would become reality, but this was it. We were indeed there, we were living the dream and occasionally on this adventure we had to stop to pinch ourselves and acknowledge it.

We spent a glorious couple of hours or more hiking the steep steps of the wall as it meanders up and over the peaks of the mountains. The snow had kept to the hill slopes and the air was warm and crystal clear, it was simply perfect. What a wonderful experience, if you haven't, please go.

We were both asleep in the back of the car when we arrived back in Beijing.

'I have a surprise for you,' announced Wendy. 'I have bought you VIP tickets for tonight's Chinese Acrobatics Show; it's the best in the country.'

We looked at each other with that I'd-rather-have-a-quiet-glass-of-wine look, but said, 'Thank you, we'd love to go.'

We were packed off to the early evening show with all sorts of snacks and provisions provided by Wendy, including a bucket full of popcorn that looked like cornflakes, a bag of scorching hot chestnuts and a sugary fruit apparently from the Hawthorn tree.

There was the usual excited pre-show babble from the largely local audience, but extraordinarily the babble volume went up as the show began and the acrobats started their performance. This was a new type of audience participation perhaps but as the show continued everyone was talking and at the top of their voices to be heard above their neighbour's continuous chatter. Very odd.

It didn't seem to put the performers off though, in fact some of them actually encouraged it before executing another high tumble or speedy somersault. There was plate spinning eight at a time and parasol balancing from the girls, juggling of plates, bowls and various items of kitchen cutlery from the boys, a high wire act Helene couldn't watch and a finale involving seven motorbikes being driven far too fast in a large wire mesh ball. It was great fun and the hour or so whizzed by.

The following morning found us in Waiting Room 8 at Beijing Central Station to catch the 10:43 AM bullet train to X'ian, an adventure in its own right. We turned left and travelled the 600 miles or so south at 195mph in seats that convert to flat beds, at tables where lunch is served by staff in immaculate uniforms and bizarrely a floor cleaning crew that walk constantly up and down the ten carriages with large brooms. The tannoy announced that "crying children should be taken into the vestibules immediately and those leaving the train should do so in an orderly fashion". And, "mind the gap", some things don't change across continents I guess.

CHAPTER 29

Day 282 to 291: CHINA
X'ian, Guilin and Shanghai

The Emperor of Two Miracles

W e arrived in the immaculately clean city of X'ian coincidentally on "tomb sweeping day", a 3 day holiday when families meet at the graves of their ancestors to smarten up and decorate the tomb or headstone. Our guide Pan or Sally, they have both Chinese and English names, told us that time off from work doesn't really exist as we would know it. While we can select our dates for a 2 week holiday in the sun, the Chinese Government provides holiday dates that all workers take, like our Bank Holidays I guess.

Our introduction to the city was an evening tasting tour in a tuk tuk led by Rosemary, a young lady so passionate about her local cuisine she simply couldn't stop eulogising over her favourite noodle or best way to cook pork as we dashed from one restaurant to another. Her premise was simple; the best restaurant does not necessarily prepare all the best dishes, so we zipped around X'ian visiting a different restaurant for each of the six courses.

Mr. Clow had made the best kebabs in town until he retired 2 years ago, and such was the disappointment from his clientele that he was forced out of retirement to cook for just 3 hours each day with his reduced menu of just one option. We met Mr. Clow bending over a long steel barbecue in his kitchen and surrounded by colourful spices, seasonings and the family's secret recipe relish he was painting onto the beef. The Chinese eat very little beef, in fact 80% of their meat is pork, but what they do eat is soft, tender and succulent. Rosemary explained that their beef is marinated overnight, lightly boiled and then fried in a wok or in this case on Mr. Clow's famous barbecue. He handed out the kebabs and showed us how to fill the freshly cooked dough buns with the sizzling meat, it was delicious.

We had heard about the Bang Bang Noodles but had yet to find them on a menu. After tearing across town in our tuk tuk, Rosemary led us down a narrow street, and as we approached the open doors of a restaurant's kitchen there was a loud boom. Then another and another. Inside the kitchen was a young man in white apron and wonky hat whirling thick metre long strands of dough above his head, then thwack, he hit the dough ropes on to the wooden table in front of him. Bang, bang. It tasted a lot better than it literally sounds.

We joined a table of locals to try their Seven Treasure Porridge. Helene said she wanted to make it for friends, so after much miming by our fellow diners to explain the seven ingredients Rosemary gave us directions of when to add what and it was all written down to take home. A family restaurant in the Muslim quarter apparently made the best whole crispy chicken dish. It really is the whole bird including giblets, head and feet; they lightly boil it, then steam it before finally roasting. It's presented to the table in a huge bowl and was expertly dismembered and portioned with chopsticks and served with mushrooms, walnuts, pickled radish, tea and toxic rice wine. Helene and Rosemary loved it; I was rather put off by the staring head hanging over the side of the dish.

The Soup Dumpling was my favourite, not a soup with dumplings in it, but a dumpling with soup in it; that needs careful eating. The steamed dumplings are ferociously hot, so we were first shown how to nibble an air hole in the top, not easy with chopsticks and the hot soupy dough hovering over your lap. Having sucked and slurped the spicy soup from within, we ate half and were instructed to dunk the other half in a peppery aromatic sauce.

'That,' said Rosemary, 'is why they are known as three dish dumplings. Shall we go to a brewery?'

A fine evening ended at the X'ian Brewery and Bar sampling a selection of their local beers, the IPA was surprisingly good. A slow walk back to the hotel in the bright neon lit city cleared our heads ready for the main feature, a visit to meet the Terracotta Army.

In 1974 a poor farmer named Mr. Yang was digging a new well in his field when a head rolled out of the earth landing at his feet, followed by an arm, hand outstretched, as if trying to grasp him. He ran in terror believing his ancestors had returned from the afterlife to punish him. He returned later that day supported by two other farmers and they began to dig. What they found was the start of one of the most extraordinary archaeological finds in history, eight thousand Terracotta Warriors protecting the vast 2200-year-old tomb of the first emperor, our friend Qin Shi Huang . He of the Qing Dynasty who built the Great Wall.

He is known as the Emperor of Two Miracles: the wall and the warriors. But he also stopped the civil war, unified the country, created a single currency and a common language, invented chrome-plating technology, built high-speed roads and dug canals to connect the Yellow River to the Lijiang and West Rivers, linking the main cities via a 437 km waterway network. It sounded like he came from the same mould as Pachacutec.

He was 13 years of age when he became emperor and started planning his biggest initiative, his own mausoleum, the biggest in the world, out scaling even the pyramids. But his life was to end in tragedy 37 years later at only 50 years of age while his mausoleum was still under construction.

His principle was based on what seems to be an obsession during the China Dynasties, longevity in this life and a fulfilling afterlife. His coffin was to be floated on a river of mercury 100 metres below the surface, which he believed would protect his body, on top of which he instructed to have a 100 metre high hill built surrounded by the natural course of the Yellow River. Below ground he set traps using crossbows and spears – real Indiana Jones stuff – to protect against tomb raiders and looters. He then commissioned all the craftsmen in the newly unified country to construct life-size warriors to defend him, all eight thousand of them along with horses, animals, eunuchs and acrobats for entertainment in the afterlife. This guy had more than a healthy preoccupation about his own death.

Our terrific guide Pan dodged us through the queues and led us to the first of only three pits that have been excavated to date. A construction larger than an aircraft hangar covered the pit containing hundreds of warriors row after row all facing the same direction, their backs to their ruler's tomb ready to defend his honour. The pit was divided into rooms separated by thick walls and once covered with beamed roofs.

Pan explained that Qin Shi Huang had directed clay to be used from a nearby mountain, moulds were made for the life-sized bodies then arms and heads were made separately and attached. After firing they would last forever, protecting him for eternity. Every warrior they have found so far has a different face and the name of the craftsman engraved on the back of its neck. Legend has it that if the emperor didn't like the design the craftsman would be identified and executed.

'So, that's why they're called "The Terracotta Army", Pan?' I asked.

'No, not really,' she said.

Apparently, when excavation began they found brightly painted warriors, but as soon as they were exposed to the air the colours began to fade, and within 30 minutes they were the colour of terracotta, and the description stuck.

We visited all three of these remarkable pits containing around two thousand warriors standing to attention in line and in expectation of battle, bizarrely resembling a scene from the science fiction film "I, Robot". The detail and intricacy of carving was extraordinary, even after 2000 years the fingernails, facial wrinkles and strands of hair are easily identifiable, particularly on those of a senior military rank where more attention was paid to the carving.

'There are another six hundred pits yet to be discovered,' said Pan.

This piece of information seemed impossible, but another six thousand warriors have been detected by underground scanner and will not be excavated until the technology is available to protect their quickly vanishing colour. In other pits there are untold treasures still defended by the emperor's traps and his river of mercury. How exciting.

It was an incredible experience and another of the adventure's highlights China has presented us, both from Emperor Qin Shi Huang . So what of his dreadful demise? It seems his obsession with a long life was the cause of his short existence.

His scholars and advisors referred him to a written legend suggesting there was an elixir for long life that could only be discovered by monks.

'Off you go then, boys,' he may have said, 'and don't come back without it.'

Of course, it didn't exist but the monks, in fear of losing their lives if they returned empty handed, found mercury.

'This looks like it would make a good elixir for a long life,' they may have said erroneously and returned to present the emperor with the solution to immortality.

The daily potion of perpetuity inevitably took its toll and while the monks survived the emperor sadly went bonkers, executing swathes of the population. He eventually died of poisoning and brain damage and the peasants rebelled looting what they could from his Terracotta Army. A sad end for an emperor now held in the same esteem as Chairman Mao.

We returned to the city for a glorious afternoon cycling the top of the 50 metre wide, 13 km long city wall, built in 1370. I think it may have exhausted the very slightly built Pan who had only cycled the city limits once before.

Our China Southern Airline flight the following morning from X'ian to Guilin was the normal internal flight requiring the juggling of contents between suitcases, carry-ons and rucksacks to make the weight, but with one extremely odd, but very Chinese exception. As the plane was towed off the gantry and positioned for the aircraft's engines to take over, all the service and maintenance crew lined up on the tarmac and started to wave us goodbye. Of course, we waved back but it was not until the full length of the plane had been given this eccentric gesture that they retired to the safety of the airport buildings.

From Guilin we turned left on a river cruise boat for 3 hours of astonishing scenery as we meandered our way south on the Lijiang River to Yangshuo. The river looked too narrow and shallow to navigate a boat of a hundred and fifty passengers but despite running aground a couple of times that no one apart from us seemed concerned about, we managed a wonderful voyage.

Both banks were curtained by narrow cone shaped mountains of two or three hundred feet, dozens of them in view at any time. The early morning mist swirled between and around the lush covered peaks making the surrounding panorama seem like an unearthly experience as we drifted downstream. It was Milford Sound meets Halong Bay on a river the size of the Thames in Windsor.

On arrival at the small harbour of Yangshuo we met our new guide Melinda who immediately introduced us to Mr. Trin, a frail looking local of senior years, I wouldn't have been surprised if he had received his telegram from the President some years ago, if they do that sort of thing in China. His brown lined and wizened face displayed a long grey Ho Chi Minh style beard, he wore the blue dungarees we associate with a time long gone in China and balanced on his head was a wide and tall cone shaped bamboo hat. But, most surprisingly of all resting on one shoulder was a 2 metre length of bamboo with a large black cormorant balancing on each end.

Melinda explained that this was for a fishing skill unique to the area and passed down the generations for over 600 years. The birds are taught to catch the fish but not swallow, returning them to the boat while the old man puts his feet up. He waved us over and gestured for me to take the bamboo pole; my goodness the cormorants were heavy and there was certainly an art to balancing them on either end as they fluttered their wings. He may have been old and wizened but like his trained pets he was a tough old bird.

The following day we cycled the river valley with the extraordinary mountainous pitons jutting out of the otherwise flat landscape, oddly they reminded me of my mother's hairpins I hadn't seen for years. It was 3 hours of thoroughly enjoyable relaxing cycling watching people on bamboo rafts float gently downstream and waving to the locals working the fields with their buffalo.

'You must go to the show in town,' said Melinda, 'it's spectacular.'

'I'd rather have a quiet dinner, I'm exhausted,' said Helene.

'No, come on it'll be fun seeing some local culture, book us two of the best tickets, Melinda.'

A whopping £100 later for a show lasting less than 90 minutes seemed extravagant for a few dancers from the village and a singsong in Chinese, but we were promised by Melinda we would never forget the experience. I hoped it was for the right reasons.

The Liu Sanjie show turned out to be directed by Zhang Yimou who masterminded what is widely believed to be the most extravagant show ever, the 2008 Olympic Games Opening Ceremony in Beijing. He was not limited this time by the size of an Olympic stadium, this setting was vast, a 2 kilometre long lake, framed by beautifully lit towering pitons either side, the largest natural theatre in the world. An audience of three thousand took their seats in the open air arena at the end of the 300 metre wide lake that disappeared into the dark distance of the evening. The stage was set for six hundred performers to take to the water by boats streaming bands of red silk. It was as dramatic and spectacular as Melinda promised. Even Mr. Trin and his cormorants made an appearance at one point.

We left the remarkable landscape of Yangshuo and set off north for the mountains and the small village of Longji perched on the side of what looked like the Swiss Alps but glistening with terraced rice fields rather than snow. The landscape reminded us both of Pachacutec's laddered botanical laboratory and the Inca terraces in Peru.

'Are we sure this is a good idea?' Helene asked. The electric thunderstorm had kept us both awake that night; most of it spent watching nature's show across the valley. The morning was cold, misty and grey but Audley assured us the hike up and over the mountain to a neighbouring village was a highlight of this part of the China adventure.

'It'll be fine,' I said, 'we just need to dress appropriately.'

That was not going to be easy. The road had stopped some way from the village where passage is restricted on the narrow cobbled paths to horse, on foot or comically via sedan chair provided by some of the locals. I refused to watch two fellow men struggle to carry me up the steep alleys no matter how much I paid them, so we walked carrying our limited clothing in small rucksacks.

We dressed in the contents of the backpacks. Luckily, Helene had prepared us well with scarves, two pairs of socks each, hats, hiking trousers a couple of waterproofs and sturdy boots. Melinda arrived to guide us on the 16 km challenging hike in blue culottes, pink plimsolls and a flowery umbrella. Nice, I thought, entirely inappropriate, but nice.

No more than 10 minutes out of the village our roadway, built into the side of the mountain, was blocked by boulders, rocks and sand, there had been a landslide during the night's storm. But, more importantly, like an aftershock of an earthquake, there were still occasional rumblings from high above us as the odd rock came bounding down the mountain bringing with it a stream of small stones and debris.

'This really isn't a good idea,' said Helene, watching another rock bounce down the hillside, cross our path, disappear over the crash barrier of the road and continue its way into the valley.

'Keep looking and follow me,' said Melinda, showing a clean pair of pink heels as she jumped onto the newly deposited rubble on the road and traversed the obstruction.

We made our way up the tiered rice fields as the mist continued to swirl around the slopes below us. Rice has been a staple for the Chinese for hundreds of years and continues to be so. The government provides each household with their own patch of land to cultivate the crop, so the family will never go without food. Melinda argued that this was one of the reasons there is no begging in the streets. I'm not so sure, the government want Westerners to see and hear what they want us to, so would simply clear the streets of beggars.

Rice growing is labour intensive and extremely hard work, the small patchwork of fields are ploughed by buffalo or the family cow, the seeds are planted by hand, each shoot has to be replanted again by hand and harvesting is back breaking work. Little wonder that so many farmers have given up on the traditional way of life in the villages and now earn their living from tourism. The evidence of this surrounded us as we hiked the hills; there were acres of abandoned rice fields. Large terraced mounds once cultivated for rice were now covered in flowers to be made into floral headwear the Chinese tourists seem to love. The old rice fields had also been adopted as burial grounds. There is something rather ironic that the land provided by the government to sustain a family is now used as their graveyard, the hills are littered with ornately carved tombstones decorated with red ribbons and banknotes. But what a delightfully peaceful and serene place to be laid to rest.

Melinda explained that the traditional way of life in China will disappear in a generation or two, the young people want to live in the cities and the villages we were hiking through were being rebuilt for tourism. There is of course a dilemma here, the very reason tourists are visiting is slowly being lost as the rural population discards its traditions and adopts a more modern and commercial way of life. Can't say I blame them though.

I guess this is an inevitable consequence of China's tyrannical Cultural Revolution which only ended in 1976. During the 10 years of Mao's attempt to preserve communist ideology more people died than the total in World War II, the youth in the cities were displaced to the countryside and property was seized from its owners to accommodate multiple poorer families. It paralysed the country economically and socially and probably set China back 30 years or so.

China adopted a more open approach in the 1980's and started to encourage tourism, although you wouldn't think so given the difficulty in obtaining a visa. It began trading with the rest of the world and became the economic powerhouse it is today.

But some traditions are maintained, particularly by the older generations, and these can often be quite extraordinary. Such as the Yao people who live in Huangluo one of the small towns and villages we were visiting on our hike over the hills. As we approached an old covered wooden bridge we met Pin, a Yao lady in traditional dress who was keen to have her photograph taken with Helene. This had become a common occurrence, they, like those in Myanmar, seem to be fascinated by her blonde hair, but as Helene shook out her hair from a woolly hat Pin started to unravel her own hair. All 2 metres of it.

Melinda acted as our interpreter as Pin held up her hair, the end of which was touching the ground. Pin said that Yao women only cut their hair once in their life, on their 18th birthday, and then they just let it grow and grow. There was no practical reason for it, apart from her husband liking it; it's just what they have always done. It seemed the start of the tradition had been lost in time. But there was something odd here, as she held up her glossy black hair out of the wet grass, I asked if she wouldn't mind telling me her age. Sixty-five, and not a single strand of grey in her long locks. How could this be? The answer she said was clean air, hard work in the fields and boiled rice water.

Pin washes her hair every 3 days in the water she boils rice in, this she believes gives it the healthy shine and maintains the jet black colour.

I looked at Helene, more than 15 years her junior.

'Perhaps we should be eating more boiled rice, then you could…'

'Don't,' she interrupted.

'Well, you know about these things, is it dyed?'

Pin was quite happy for Helene to inspect the tresses and handed her an armful or two.

'It's in beautiful condition, far better than mine. No, this is natural, I'm sure of it.'

'Goodness, if we could bottle this rice water, we'd make a fortune at home.'

Pin curled up her 2 metre ponytail and somehow locked it into position on the top of her head without any pins; I wondered if that was her real name. A comb appeared from a pocket to ensure all the individual strands were in position and off she went to visit her sister in the village we had left 2 hours before. What an odd encounter, not my last on this eventful trek over the abandoned rice fields.

I suppose it was bound to happen, I just didn't expect it to happen in China. We were in single file on a narrow path built into the side of one of the steep terraced hills when I heard a squeal and a squeak from the undergrowth at about shoulder height. I stopped to investigate – that was a mistake – and heard it again, this time more of a screech and a scream. I parted the vegetation and saw a coiled snake as thick as your wrist with a large frog struggling and squawking in its mouth. The snake looked at me, I looked at the snake and the frog looked for a way out of the jaws tightening around it.

'Shit! It's a snake,' I said, stating the obvious but unable to move.

'Move quickly on,' said Melinda, giving me a gentle but firm nudge along the track. She explained that this was a Bamboo snake, one not to be messed with, although they rarely attack humans.

'Exactly what do you mean by rarely?' I asked.

Helene joined in with some sage advice, 'You just need to be more snake aware,' she said.

The remainder of the walk seemed to be a little quieter as I led the way watching out for any movement in the grass, listening for more squeals and generally being more snake aware. Arriving back in the village late in the afternoon we deserved something tall, long and refreshing so visited an Audley recommended bar called The Green Garden Café. The owner is a witty and captivating gentleman who juggles the tastes of the locals with the needs of the tourists so had a large selection of beers for me to select from and an extensive wine list for Helene.

'What are these under the heading Local Wines?' I asked him.

'Ah! We make our own wine here,' he said.

'That's odd,' I said, 'I haven't seen any vineyards locally.'

'We improvise,' he said, adding no more.

'How intriguing, I'm sure Helene would like an improvised wine,' I suggested.

As he disappeared to fetch a glass of chateau unconventional, I'm sure I saw a knowing smile flicker across his jolly face. He returned with a chilled glass of something that looked like an over honeyed Chardonnay.

'That looks okay,' said Helene, 'maybe a bit too, well, yellow for my taste though.'

'Would you like to try one of our others?' our host asked. 'We have ant wine, wasp wine or...'

'Ant and wasp!' shrieked Helene. 'What on earth is this then?' she asked, lifting her glass.

'That? Oh! That's snake wine,' he replied, lifting the napkin from around the bottle to reveal two sizeable snakes wound around the inside. Horror is an often overused word but seemed perfectly appropriate for the dread and revulsion on Helene's face.

I gave her a hug and a glass of French Sauvignon.

'You just need to be more snake aware, darling,' I said.

'Have you ever been in a motorbike sidecar?' I asked Helene.
'No, and I'm never going to be.'
'Ah!'
'You haven't? Oh, my goodness, you have, haven't you?'
'It's the only way to see Shanghai, apparently.'
'We'll look like Wallace and Gromit!'

We had arrived in the commercial metropolis of China where a third of the country's trade is handled, making it one of the busiest ports in the world. Shanghai was established over 2000 years ago, became a city in the 13th century, was a huge British Colonial trading post and is now Asia's financial centre.

Our hotel was on the famous Bund, the equivalent of London's Embankment, so overlooked a bend in the busy river similar to Canary Wharf, yet only 30 years ago it was farmland. The skyline is like a picture book of famous modern city buildings from around the world. There is the second tallest building in the world looking like London's Shard, a version of New York's Chrysler building, the Toronto Communication Tower, a tower clearly created by Cesar Pelli, the architect for the Petronas Towers and I believe we even walked past Liverpool's Liver Building.

The city is now home to 24 million inhabitants and thousands of tourists, but it is incredibly clean. There is a constant reminder of this spotless city because all the cleaning trucks play *"It's a Small World"* the Disney song my daughter loved when she was younger.

Our motorbike sidecar escapade was great fun and despite Helene's initial protest turned out to be more of a race than a tour as she encouraged her driver to overtake mine. We biked around the old part of the city in the British Colonial and French quarters that are protected buildings now. Shanghai was known as the Paris of the East before the big change in 1949 and some of the ballrooms and party venues still exist, although the homes of the wealthy were later seized and given to families brought in from the countryside.

It was a great way to finish our time in China, a country that surprised us both. I wasn't expecting the China of the Cultural Revolution but I certainly wasn't expecting such exciting vibrant commercial cities. I enjoyed its remarkable history, wonderful traditions and unique culture but it felt like an emerging new country, perhaps it is, given the changes since the mid 1970's.

It is of course one of the few communist countries in the world. However, this is not communism as we know it; this is overt and conspicuous capitalism. But, and there is a big but, the influence and control of the government is everywhere. There is no Google, no Facebook and much to our frustration and those at home, no Instagram, they are simply banned. What little social media there is available is monitored. One Frenchman we met used a regional French dialect on the phone to a friend in France and a voice came on asking them to use conventional French. Education is state controlled, and even at university level the students learn what the government wants them to learn. And Winnie the Pooh is banned in China. Why? Have you ever seen their President?

CHAPTER 30

Day 292 to 306: JAPAN
Tokyo, Kanazawa and Kyoto

A Final Hurrah

 It started at the airport. We were waiting patiently at the vacant check-in desks for the Japan Airlines flight to Tokyo when a dozen immaculately turned out uniformed airline staff marched in single file to the front of the counters and stood to attention facing us.

The queue, including at least two bemused customers, stared at them looking at us. On an unidentifiable signal they all bowed a deep bow from the hip, then in unison turned to take their positions behind the check-in counters. Now it was our turn. We approached the desk, they bowed, we bowed, they bowed again and with the formalities over we could check-in.

We had been alerted in the briefing notes from Audley that Japan is a very formal and ritualistic country, they are dignified people with many customs so we did our best to familiarise ourselves with as much as possible so as not to offend. These included not pouring a glass of wine for yourself, the necessity of wearing brightly coloured toilet shoes when the need arises and to never blow your nose in public.

For the next 2 weeks we were going to explore Japan by train, so we met our Tokyo guide Yoko and collected our Japan Rail Pass, the only ticket we would need for the twenty-five national trains, bullet trains, local trains and cable cars needed to discover the country. This was going to be a challenge trying to decipher the two thousand or so symbols in the Japanese language and find our way around the stations, let alone the country.

The capital Tokyo was to be our first introduction to Japanese culture. It is a diverse and exciting city, and like many of those where an ancient past meets a commercial present there are high-rise glass offices sandwiching ornate tiled temples, and Michelin star restaurants on the same street as noodle bars. So, our expeditions were equally diverse, the biggest fish market in the world and a glimpse into the future of IT and sci-fi at the Miraikan, The Museum of Emerging Science and Technology – *The Hall of the Future.*

Our city hotel was in the Shinjuku district, home to the busiest station in the world, where the equivalent of the entire population of Canada passes through each day. It's big, and easy to be overwhelmed by the sheer choice of subways, platforms, escalators and ticket barriers. But we soon learned that a bemused look while staring up at the hieroglyphics of the flashing train board will prompt a bow and the question "can I help you?"

So, it was up early for our first train, a short hop to Tsukiji fish market to trace the process and preparation of sushi. The market has been in business since the 1600's when Tokyo was known as Edo but was moved to its present site in 1923 after the Great Kanto Earthquake, which devastated much of the city.

The tuna wholesale buying and selling starts extremely early at 3:00 AM where these vast fish are sold in that mysterious and covert environment of a trade auction. They are then covered in a large damp white cloth and wheeled away on a steel gurney by gentlemen in white coats looking rather disconcertingly like porters in a morgue.

The filleter, if that is the correct expression, also treats the "body" with enormous respect as he and his assistants lift it onto the thick wooden operation table for surgery. It is carefully cleaned with more damp cloths in preparation and he selects his choice of instrument, what looks like a narrow Samurai sword, about a metre long and honed to a fine sharp edge that slices through the skin and flesh with ease.

Now in more manageable sized fillets, but still the size of a fishing boat's fender, the traders start selling to the retailers and sushi preparation specialists. The same Samurai sword is used to delicately slice a thin sliver for tasting, there is much muttering and discussion as both the wholesaler and sushi master compare tasting notes, a quick bow and the deal is done. The fleshy tuna is then wiped down again with the damp cloths and often assiduously cut into smaller pieces before careful wrapping for the customer.

Surrounding the market are dozens of small restaurants offering sushi and sashimi breakfasts, perhaps the freshest in the city. What a treat, somehow it tasted a whole lot better watching the sushi being prepared in front of us with just as much respect as the wholesalers and retailers had shown an hour or so before and knowing the short journey this wonderful food had been on.

'Meet Asimo,' our Honda representative said at the Miraikan Museum.

Asimo is a walking, talking and remarkably, thinking robot about 5 feet in height and made of shiny white plastic.

'Good day, I am Asimo,' said Asimo walking over in a rather bent fashion.

'Good grief,' said Helene, looking somewhat unsure of how to converse with the real-life version of I-robot.

'Say hello, Helene,' I encouraged, 'you don't want to hurt his feelings.'

Asimo bowed. Helene bowed.

'Er… Hi,' she said, holding out her hand and quickly withdrawing it.

'Shall I sing you a Japanese song?' Asimo asked. 'I can show you the hand actions as well.'

'Oh! Yes, do,' I said.

Asimo sang his song, now in a female voice and showed the small crowd the accompanying hand actions apparently explaining the song about the high green mountains and fresh pink blossom. When the song was over there was a sprinkling of applause; do you really applaud a robot? Who knows, if Honda have their way we will all probably find out very soon.

Our luggage was forwarded on to our next hotel with typical Japanese efficiency allowing us to take the bullet train and local trains to Magome for one of the highlights of our Japan leg, a hike on the Nakasendo Highway. But not before we had our first sight of the magnificent Mount Fuji as we hurtled out of suburbia into rolling lush hills and picturesque valleys. Like every National Geography image we have seen of Fuji it stood majestically in isolation , dominating the landscape with its summit in snow as if it had been dipped in a bucket of melted vanilla ice cream. It was a crisp clear day without a cloud in the blue sky, my goodness it was a wonderful sight.

The Nakasendo Highway was first established in the 8th century linking the areas around the then capital Nara, as the state grew. It continued to develop until the Edo period when the centre of power moved to what is now Tokyo and it became a communications route to send messages, goods and personnel across the empire. Its full length is an impressive 531 km between mountain ranges, on paved and cobbled paths. Villages were selected as Post Towns to provide food and lodgings for official travellers, our hike was from one of these, Magome to the most beautiful of them all, Tsumago the finest traditional Post Town in Japan. In the 1960's the locals banded together to protect the heritage of the town and preserve its old buildings and unique character, so there are no TV aerials, telephone pylons or electric cables. It looks just like it did hundreds of years ago.

We were just setting off to tackle our small part of the route when we met two elderly ladies a little red faced and puffing a bit, coming in the opposite direction.

'Goodness,' said Helene, 'you look exhausted, is it that tough?'

'Are you just setting off, dear?' one of them asked, in a broad North Country accent.

'Yes, how long has it taken you?' she asked.

'Four days,' replied the elderly lady.

The couple went on to explain they were hiking half of the whole Highway. We felt a little too ashamed to admit we were tackling only a few miles, so wished them luck and set off up the narrow cobbled path on a beautiful warm and clear day.

"*Ring bell hard against bears*" read the sign attached to the first bell post we came across. Without a bear to ring it against I gave the chain a long hard pull with the hope that the peels would scatter any bears on our path. The bell posts were dotted every half a mile or so along the track as it passed through the pine forest above the gushing river.

Coming out of the bears' home we arrived at the river bank and an absolutely stunning view of cherry blossom in whites, pinks and reds, some trees surprisingly displaying all three. The scene was thick with colour and an ideal place to stop for our picnic of sushi, Sapporo beer and a small bottle of sake on a low table under the cherry blossom. What could be more Japanese? Wonderful.

Our stay that night was at a traditional Japanese hotel known as a ryokan, where we were to really experience the best of Japan's hospitality and its exacting etiquette. It's the footwear that poses the biggest challenge. Shoes off and lots of mutual bowing on arrival, we were then provided with slippers and followed our host to our room where we were required to enter bare foot, apart from the colourful toilet sandals of course.

The room had a low table with still lower and quite demanding chairs, the floor was covered in tatami mats and the walls seemed to be made of paper. But there was something missing – no bed. Our non-English speaking host must have registered my confusion as I peered into wardrobes, the bathroom and even the balcony, well you never know.

'Futon, David,' said Helene, who knows about these things.

Our host mimed making a bed and not to touch the rolled up colourful duvet affair in another cupboard the maid would deal with.

'Fair enough, floor it is then,' I said, 'only one night I suppose.'

We were then handed our own yukatas, apparently. A dressing gown kimono type of affair that tied, importantly left side over the right (no idea why), with a huge double waist band around the middle, and fell to the floor. Helene looked terrific; I looked like I'd just got up.

We were now all prepared to tackle our first onsen bath, a long-standing tradition the Japanese are very proud of and which is riddled with ritual. We needed to be careful here, onsen bathing is enjoyed naked. These hot cypress springs are both indoor and out and can be communal, but fortunately our ryokan provided a segregated option so we set off in our colourful yukatas and a pair of open clogs to find a black flag for me and a red flag for Helene signifying the entry to our respective onsens.

The changing room had a multilingual notice with instructions for use.

1. Strip naked.

Now I'm as uninhibited as the next person, but it's difficult to maintain your dignity swanning around an onsen with nothing more than an insubstantial flannel generously provided in the bamboo basket where you deposit your yukata. Where do you hold it, for a start? There seemed to be two schools of thought here, those who gaily flounced around with flannel flung brazenly over their shoulder, and those who surreptitiously held it casually, but carefully in front of them.

Opting for the latter strategy I entered what at first looked like a cross between a beautician and a milking parlour. Three legged low stools were lined up in front of large wall mirrors and a selection of soaps, oils and other unidentifiable cleansing potions were presented on another low table.

2. Wash thoroughly before entering the onsen.

Each mirror had a shower attachment next to it, one of those on a coil that is intended to be pulled out of the wall. I glanced at my fellow onsen users for a clue, trying desperately for my glance not to be confused with a stare.

What an odd way to shower. Having eased my way down onto the low modesty stool I selected a couple of colourful liquids in Japanese bottles giving no indication which part of the body they specialised in and held the shower above me. I must say it was quite an enjoyable experience, I'm not convinced it will replace the more conventional alternative of standing up, but once I realised no one paid any attention to where all the hot steamy water was flying around it was fun.

3. Enter the onsen slowly, it is hot.

I made a quick dash to submerge myself in a vacant area of the open air onsen. By heck it was hot.

I watched the sun go down behind the blossom laden hills in the distance as the hot oily water soothed my aching limbs from hiking the Nakasendo Highway. And I got it. What a wonderful way to spend an early evening, no wonder the Japanese are so proud of the tradition.

Dinner was to be an equally traditional affair. Dressed back in our yukata and second set of slippers we were directed to our personal dining area in the partitioned restaurant and seated at a low table laid beautifully with small bowls and dishes, jugs of sake and glasses of a wonderfully sweet plumb wine.

The dishes kept coming from our waitress in her colourful kimono and the sake kept flowing as our miming of the ingredients became more extravagant and funnier. We collapsed into futons late in the evening for a wonderful night's sleep, what a glorious day.

We bulleted our way west from Tsumago in the highlands to the near coastal town of Kanazawa – *the jewel of Japan. Extraordinary beauty and artistry at every turn.* The main turn is the Kenrokuen Garden the name of which refers to the six attributes that are vital in creating the very best Japanese gardens: spaciousness, tranquillity, artifice, antiquity, water and magnificent views. I reckon they missed one here, the gardens also attract dozens of young ladies in traditional dress, the beautifully designed and colourful kimono. They did look wonderful tottering around on their high wooden clogs barely able to step more than a few inches being restricted by the tight layers of cloth and broad sashes.

We visited some traditional houses in the Samurai quarter where the military nobility made their homes, including miniature versions of the Kenrokuen Garden and buildings that were similar to the ryokan we had so much fun at in the mountains. But it was a short stopover on our way to Kyoto travelling on the wonderfully named Thunderbird Limited Express. It was FAB.

Kyoto was the capital of Japan for over 1,000 years and remains the most culturally important city in the country with one thousand seven hundred Buddhist temples and three hundred Shinto shrines as well as palaces and castles. Our hotel the Granvia was, as it suggests, a grand building made of glass above the large modern station, quite an architectural feat and ideally placed to explore the city by its myriad of subway routes and buses.

There are a few wonderful Japanese idiosyncrasies with their transportation system that I really love. The city taxis seem to be automotive extras from an old TV show called Z-Cars and bizarrely their rear doors spring open to welcome you and then close automatically once you're seated. Helene had the audacity to close one herself and was given an awful look by the driver as he auto opened it again and closed it from his secret lever hidden somewhere in the front.

The underground subway system also has its peculiarity, everyone entering a platform from the staircases triggers a birdsong broadcast over the station tannoy. It may be a simple hoot of a cuckoo, the tweet of a robin or the rather pleasant chorus of a nightingale, on busy days it sounds like the dawn chorus in an aviary.

One eccentricity they all share, whether they are driving a bus, taxi, train or underground, is the white gloves. The Japanese love a uniform, even the guys working on the building sites or roads are in matching boiler suits and helmets, but all drivers wear a polished peaked cap and gleaming white gloves. Nice touch I think.

Kyoto has more Michelin star restaurants than any other city in the world, with some quoting a waiting list of over a year. We were booked in for dinner at Another C, an establishment owned, managed and run by one man, Dan Tominaga, who trained in New York but came back to his home town to provide a limited number of guests the best Kyoto can offer.

His hidden away fourth floor restaurant caters for only eight guests and provides a fixed menu entirely dependent on what Dan has found in the local market that day. There are no tables; each guest sits at the bar behind which Dan performs his culinary magic in the galley style kitchen talking us through his ingredients and techniques as he cooks. Not an easy thing to pull off with eight pairs of eyes scrutinising his every move and interrogating his methods. It was a splendid meal, which Dan celebrated by popping a bottle of Ruinart Rose Champagne for the four guests remaining after midnight.

We met our guide for the day, Mari a delightful local with long black bouncy hair and a personality to match. She promised us a visit that would challenge the Terracotta Army and a tour around the back streets of the Gion district where we might catch sight of a geisha girl making her way to the first visit of the night.

'I'd like to see a geisha,' I said.

'I bet you would, David,' Helene remarked.

'It's all part of the culture; I think we should really make an effort to understand this part of the Japanese way of life.'

'Well, I can't promise anything,' said Mari, 'they are very secretive and quite elusive.'

'Maybe we should spend a bit more time in Gion than the temple?' I suggested.

'I'm not spending the afternoon searching the back streets of Kyoto looking for a painted lady.' Helene dug her heels in.

'It's okay,' Mari said, finding some middle ground, 'their first appointment is not until six in the evening so they won't be out until then.'

This seemed to settle the matter so we headed to Sanjusangendo, a Buddhist temple founded in 1164 and the longest wooden structure in Japan. On the face of it this may seem a bit of a dull accolade but inside was the awe inspiring sight of one thousand and one life-sized gold warriors known as the Thousand Armed Kannon standing in ten rows theatre style.

There were five hundred either side of a 3 metre tall seated gold statue of a one thousand armed Senju Kannon. It was a spectacular sight and clearly had similarities with the Terracotta Army, far more colourful and almost to the same scale yet somehow missing the magnificence, perhaps because the Army predates the Kannon by well over a 1000 years. You may be thinking why one thousand and one; the odd one covers the Senju Kannon's back.

Mari explained that Kyoto is both Buddhist and Shinto, two religions that seem to sit comfortably with each other, so boasts over 1,600 temples and they are all popular with the locals who visit not only to worship but to ask for good fortune. There was a lot of wishing going on at those that we visited; bell ringing, stone lifting, box rattling, hand washing, hanging notes on trees, and burning bamboo tags written by monks, in fact a myriad of ways to encourage those looking for good luck to part with 50 Yen or so.

We arrived in the geisha district of Gion a little early.

'So, David, what are we going to do for the next hour or so before they start work?' Helene asked.

'Let's visit one of their party houses,' I suggested.

'That will not be possible,' Mari advised. 'It's by invitation only and even then you have to pay to meet a geisha.'

'Fine, I think that would be a great way to really understand the culture, how much is it?'

'Two hours in the company of an apprentice geisha serving you a drink and her dumplings, would start at 50,000 Yen.'

'Good grief, she must have pretty impressive…'

'David!' interrupted Helene.

'They are very talented girls,' said Mari, perhaps a little over protectively.

She told us that geisha have a diverse set of skills taught over the 5 years it takes for an apprentice or Maiko as they are called, meaning Woman of Dance, to become fully qualified. These include classical music, traditional dance, party games and witty conversation, and presumably how to make damn good dumplings.

The training can start as young as 15 years of age although in the past they may have started as young as 6 years old, apparently the training is so tough half drop out in the first year. Today they live in groups of up to six in boarding houses identified by the small wooden white tablets above the door, each featuring the girls Maiko name.

'So, why is this tablet black?' I asked Mari.

'That indicates a party house,' she replied, 'and it's getting close to six o'clock.'

Intending to continue my geisha watch I turned from the door to find myself staring into the pale white face of a tall lady with dark black hair swept off her face, piled high on her head and held in place with a garland of pink blossom. She wore a light blue kimono with a wide deep red waistband or obi, that was clearly far too tight and she was perched on what looked like a pair of flip flops with 1970's style platform heels.

She raised an inscrutable thick black eyebrow as she glowered down at me and pursed her bright red bow-shaped lips. This, I believe, meant "get out of my way".

'Hi, busy night?' Sometimes the wrong words never fail me.

Her minder, a smaller man in an intense pink shirt, who Mari later advised me was the dresser, they are always male oddly enough, moved me gently aside, and my geisha girl had gone.

'You were very lucky, David,' said Mari, 'very few people get to meet a geisha, without paying for it, of course.'

'Yes, I think we had a moment together there.'

'Oh! Good grief,' said Helene.

It was while we were visiting one of the most popular and no doubt the shiniest building in Japan, the Kinkakuji or Golden Pavilion due to its covering in gold leaf, that Helene sprang the surprise.

'Great news, I've worked with Audley to book us two nights in a monastery.'

'Good heavens, really?'

'A vegetarian monastery,' she continued.

'Why on earth would you do that?'

'A vegetarian monastery without a bar,' she added.

'It's not getting any better, is it?' I said.

'It'll be fun, up early to watch the monks in their fire ritual followed by a healthy...

'How early?'

'Six'ish, but it's okay we'll be in bed early because I think the village may have, well, it may have a curfew.'

'A curfew?' I spluttered. 'What are they, monks with ASBOs?'

'Don't be ridiculous. There are no bars or restaurants in the village anyway, everybody eats in the monastery.'

'Well, I'm not sure about this,' I said, 'this needs a lot more discussion before we agree to go.'

We arrived at the monastery by cable car.

The village of Koyasan on Mount Koya is the most sacred place in Japan. It is also remote, so after 4 hours of travel by subway, local trains, a bullet, the Nankai Electric Railway, a bus and the aforementioned cable car we arrived at our temple lodgings known as a Shukubo. The shaven-headed monks greeted us warmly with lots of bowing and, new footwear allocated, showed us to a surprisingly comfortable and spacious ryokan room.

One of the monks, Obu, a thickset young man – do monks work out? – invited us on a night walk around Okunoin Cemetery. He offered to take us to the cemetery's mausoleum of Kobo Daishi the monument that makes this area the most sacred part of the most sacred place in Japan and the reason there are forty-eight temples and monasteries in the small village.

Kobo Daishi studied Shingon Buddhism in China and brought it back to Japan when his master died. He was granted use of Koyasan by Emperor Saga in 816AD. Obu narrated the story as we walked through the forest of the extensive cemetery towards the mausoleum. Kobo Daishi was led to the area by two dogs, one black, one white, representing the gods. He identified Koyasan as the centre to preach Esoteric Buddhism and started to erect temples.

One day he went to meditate as he always did, but for no apparent reason he didn't stop. Some years later a monk found him still meditating. The monk cut his hair and beard and left him to continue meditating, never to be visited or seen again.

'We believe,' said Obu, 'that he entered eternal meditation and is still there meditating today, over a 1000 years later.'

The cemetery was an extraordinary place, over two hundred thousand ornate and often huge tombstones littered the landscape amongst towering cedar trees several hundred years old. As we walked the 2 kilometre path through the cemetery to the still meditating Kobo Daishi, Helene asked what lay beneath the tombstones.

'Perhaps another two or three hundred thousand graves,' said Obu. 'People of all classes and all religions have been buried here, providing they believe, they can have a place.'

'That must make it awfully busy below ground,' I said.

'Not really,' replied Obu, 'we only bury the throat.' Now, that was a startling piece of news and clearly prompted the next question.

'The rest of the bones are with the family of the deceased,' explained Obu.

The Adams Apple, that apparently looks like a sitting Buddha, is removed and is the only body part buried under the tombstone. Helene, who knows about these things, explained that it is the air from the chest going through the hyoid that gives each person their unique sound, so perhaps the hyoid is removed to allow the soul to communicate in the afterlife. Could well be, we all agreed.

We returned the following morning, after an early start for meditation, attendance at the monks' daily fire ceremony and a vegetarian breakfast. It was even more spectacular in the brightness of the morning and despite a busier path through the cemetery it was as peaceful and serene as the night before. Any sound seemed to be absorbed by the giant ancient trees creating the most tranquil and calm atmosphere as we strolled to visit the meditating Kobo again. The thousands of tombstones, some covered in hundreds of years of lichen and others gleaming in their newness, were an awe inspiring sight.

In the daylight, the entrance to his resting place was remarkable, beautifully embellished with flickering candles and red paper lanterns waving in the cool breeze, and tall gold sculptured lotus flowers shining brightly in the sun either side of the ornate entrance to his tomb.

We spent all morning in the calmness of the forest cemetery but that was okay, it is a spiritual place where time stands still somehow. We strolled around some of the temples Kobo Daishi had built a 1000 years ago and picnicked under a blossom tree in an ornamental garden with a classic Japanese arched red bridge.

Helene was right of course, although I would clearly never make it as a monk, it was a special visit and a privilege to share such an exceptional experience.

We were getting close to the end of our trip to wonderful Japan and close to the end of our whole adventure, but no visit to Japan would be complete without seeing Mount Fuji – *a mountain of religion and art*. We had been teased with high-speed distant glimpses of it from the bullet train but our last day included a few more highly efficient trains to the town of Kawaguchi-ko for an ascent to the viewing platform on the wonderfully named Kachi Kachi Yama Ropeway. Or cable car as we may know it.

We checked into our hotel, the Konansou, overlooking the calm lake with glorious views of the mountain. This ryokan provided the added comfort of our own onsen open air bath on our balcony, what a lovely indulgence for later; I put the Sauvignon on ice.

Rather bizarrely the queuing system for the Kachi Kachi required the use of a QR scanner on your mobile, whatever that is; Japanese efficiency taken a little too far perhaps. But once we had alighted from the Ropeway, been bowed to by the staff and made our way to the high viewing platform, my goodness what a treat. The scene was crystal clear, the sky the brightest blue and there stood Mount Fuji with the sun glistening on its snow covered top and its slopes a verdant forest green.

We stood and hugged as the Magic Kingdom Moment inevitably overcame Helene and I swallowed hard. We'd seen some impressive sights during our 10 months away but this had to be one of the best. The mountain is a perfectly formed cone with no other hills or mountains in front, behind or around it. It sits alone in its own formidable solitary magnificence, and it **is** magnificent. This may make it look a little out of place, like a backdrop created on a blue screen, but it is absolutely breathtaking in its beauty.

We said a final farewell to the mountain that seemed to encapsulate all that is wonderful about Japan. It is a sedate and dignified society with people who are proud yet respectful. The culture is built on thousands of years of tradition and custom creating some memorable sights and experiences. We loved it.

That evening we soaked in the hot bubbling onsen on our seventh floor terrace with a couple of glasses of wine and looked out over the beautiful lake with the sun going down over snowcapped Mount Fuji.

'What a wonderful way to finish our adventure,' said Helene.

'Yes, it's been everything we hoped for, and more.'

'It certainly was, what a great idea to celebrate your retirement,' she said.

'I'm not entirely sure it was my idea.'

'Of course it was; where are you planning to take us next?' she asked.

'Next? I thought this was a-once-in-a-lifetime adventure?'

'I know you did, darling. I know you did.'

My beautiful tea partner at the Quing Shan Ju Tea House in Beijing, China that set me back £120 in assorted teas.

One of the colourful Chinese Dragons we met on our way up to the Great Wall of China.

Helene close to a "Magic Kingdom Moment" on the Great Wall of China, who can blame her.

Making Bang Bang Noodles on our food tour of X'ian, China. They taste better than they sound.

The astonishing Terracotta Army protecting the 2,200 year old tomb of Qin Shi Huang – "the emperor of two miracles".

Punting on the lazy river at Yangshuo, China with the dramatic pitons behind.

65 year old Pin, from the Yao people in Huangluo, China demonstrating her two metre hair - and not a single strand of grey.

Not sure Shanghai was ready for our version of Wallace and Gromit, a great way to see the city though.

On the Bund in Shanghai, doing its best to imitate major cities around the world.

No disguising this robot at the Miraikan, the Museum of Emerging Science and Technology in Tokyo.

The hike on the Nakasendo Highway in Japan required us to "Ring the bell hard against bears".

Dinner in our yukatas at the Tsumago Ryokan after a rather careful onsen bath.

On the way to the Kenrokuen Garden in Kanazawa, these beautiful ladies in traditional kimono turned a few heads.

Another rare sighting of the illusive geisha girls after my brief encounter in the Gion district of Kyoto.

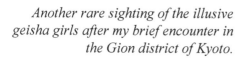

The beautiful Kinkakuji or Golden Pavilion The Zen Buddhist temple in Kyoto, is one of the most visited buildings in Japan.

The Okunoin Cemetery in Koyasan on Mount Koya, the most sacred place in Japan. Home to 200,000 tombs including Kobo Daishi in eternal meditation.

Helene loving the view over the gloriously impressive Mount Fuji.

TURNING LEFT AROUND THE WORLD

Mount Fuji, Japan

I hope you enjoyed reading the book as much as I enjoyed writing it. If you did perhaps you would be kind enough to post a review online as it may help other readers to discover it, many thanks.

Happy travels